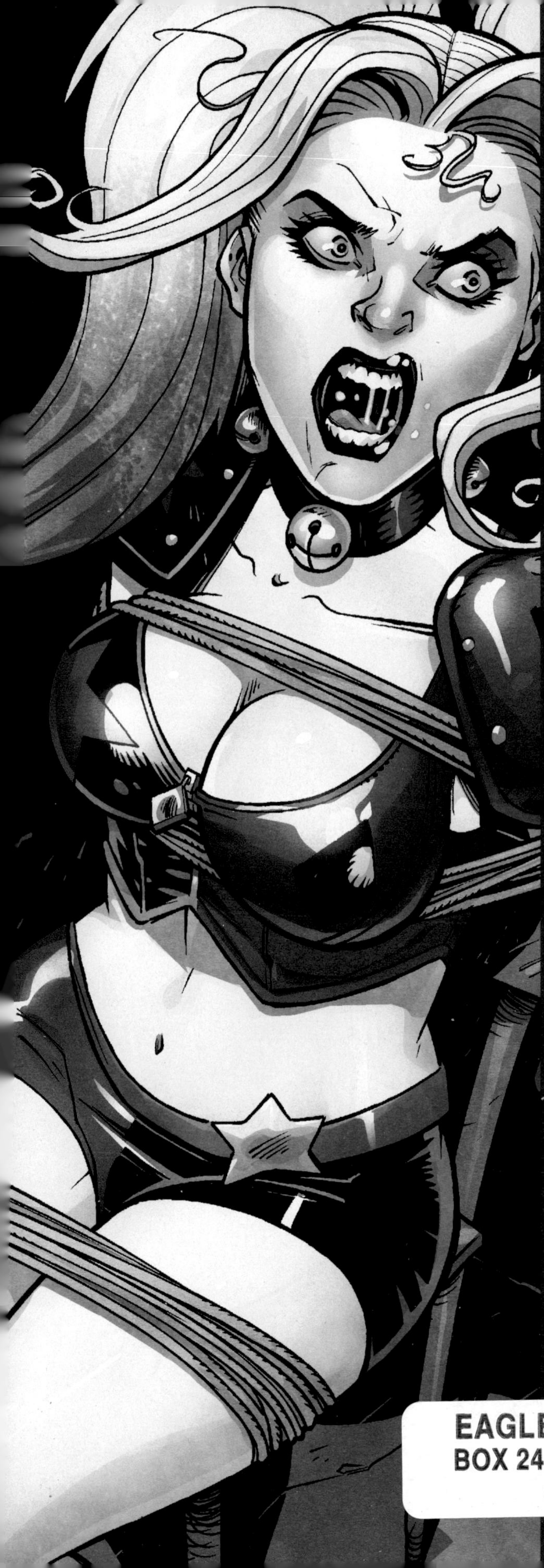

HARLEY QUINN AND HER GANG OF HARLEYS

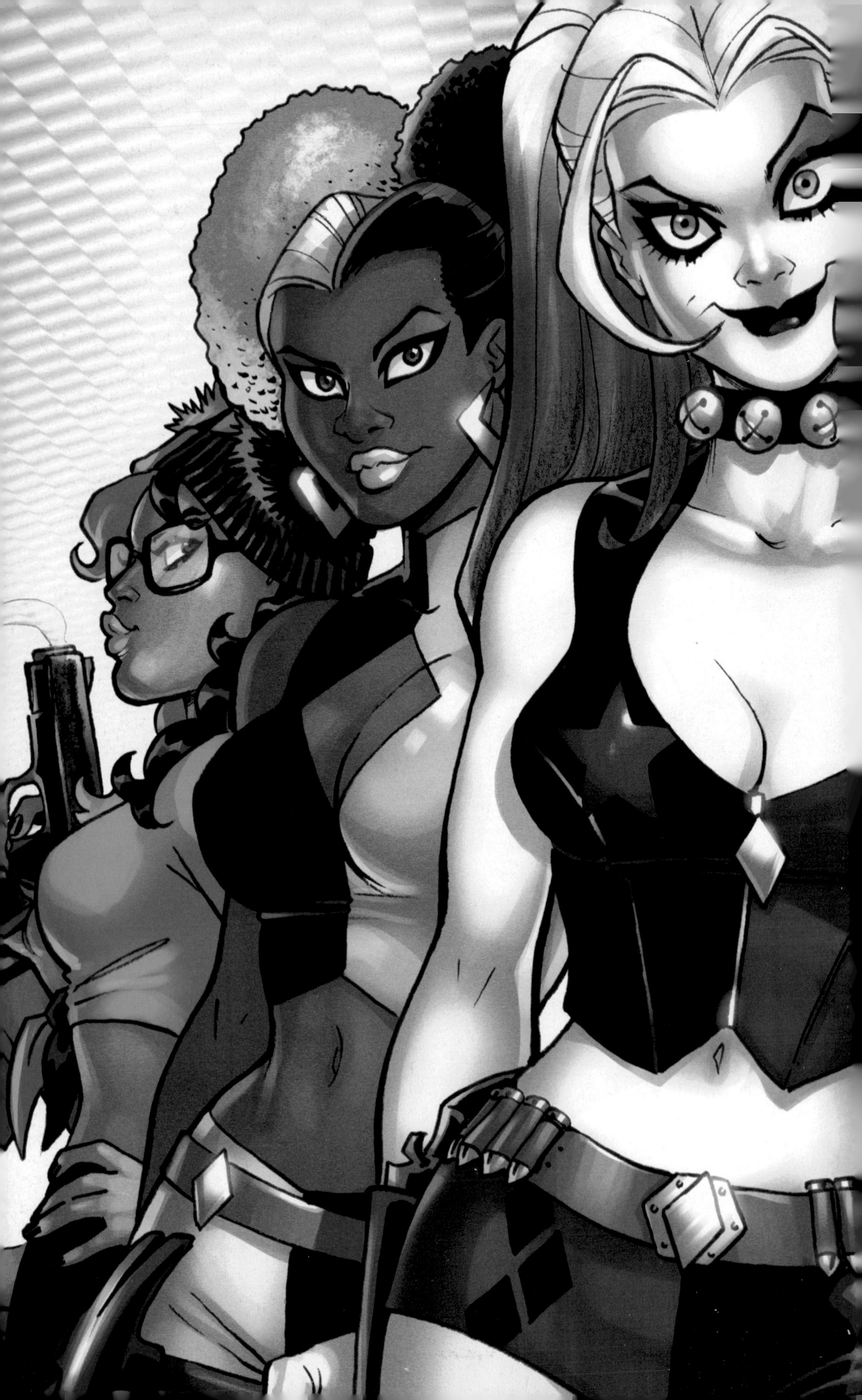

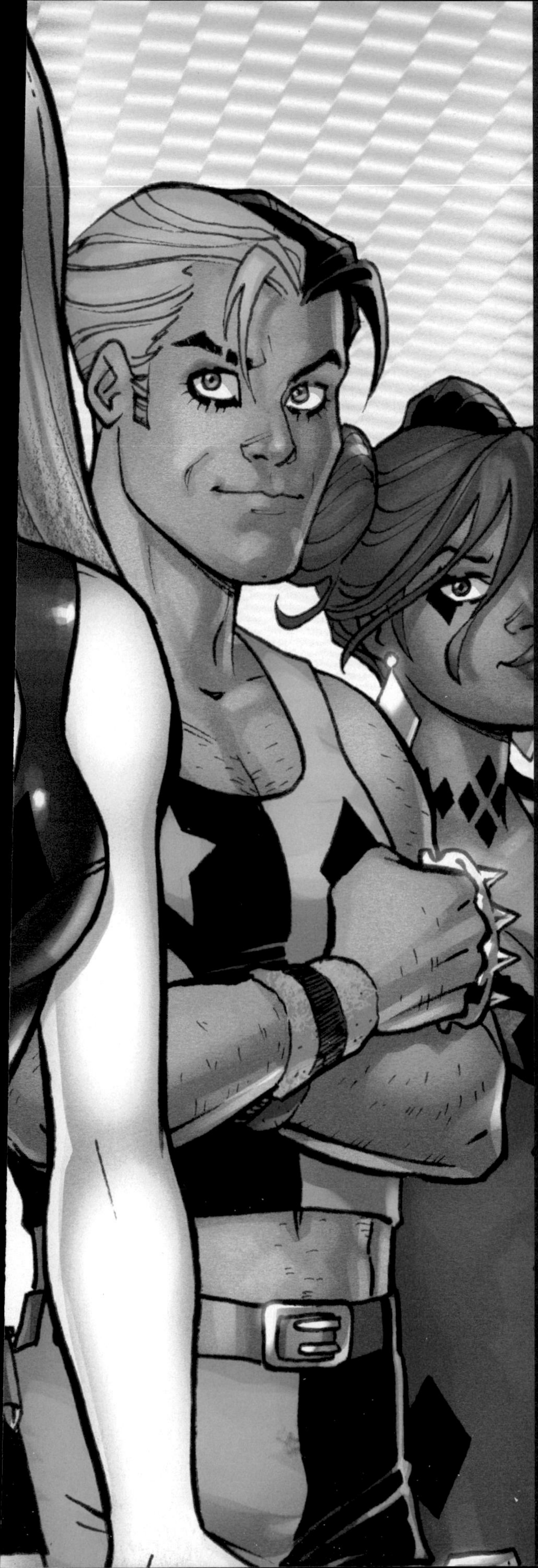

HARLEY QUINN AND HER GANG OF HARLEYS

WRITTEN BY
FRANK TIERI
JIMMY PALMIOTTI

ART BY
MAURICET
ALEX TEFENKGI
INAKI MIRANDA
DAWN McTEIGUE
RAY McCARTHY
MARK ROSLAN

COLOR BY
HI-FI

LETTERS BY
DAVE SHARPE
JOSH REED

COLLECTION COVER ART BY
AMANDA CONNER
& ALEX SINCLAIR

HARLEY QUINN CREATED BY
PAUL DINI & BRUCE TIMM

DAVID WOHL   CHRIS CONROY Editors – Original Series
JEB WOODARD Group Editor – Collected Editions
ROBIN WILDMAN Editor – Collected Edition
STEVE COOK Design Director – Books
LOUIS PRANDI Publication Design

BOB HARRAS Senior VP – Editor-in-Chief, DC Comics

DIANE NELSON President
DAN DiDIO Publisher
JIM LEE Publisher
GEOFF JOHNS President & Chief Creative Officer
AMIT DESAI Executive VP – Business & Marketing Strategy, Direct to Consumer & Global Franchise Management
SAM ADES Senior VP – Direct to Consumer
BOBBIE CHASE VP – Talent Development
MARK CHIARELLO Senior VP – Art, Design & Collected Editions
JOHN CUNNINGHAM Senior VP – Sales & Trade Marketing
ANNE DePIES Senior VP – Business Strategy, Finance & Administration
DON FALLETTI VP – Manufacturing Operations
LAWRENCE GANEM VP – Editorial Administration & Talent Relations
ALISON GILL Senior VP – Manufacturing & Operations
HANK KANALZ Senior VP – Editorial Strategy & Administration
JAY KOGAN VP – Legal Affairs
THOMAS LOFTUS VP – Business Affairs
JACK MAHAN VP – Business Affairs
NICK J. NAPOLITANO VP – Manufacturing Administration
EDDIE SCANNELL VP – Consumer Marketing
COURTNEY SIMMONS Senior VP – Publicity & Communications
JIM (SKI) SOKOLOWSKI VP – Comic Book Specialty Sales & Trade Marketing
NANCY SPEARS VP – Mass, Book, Digital Sales & Trade Marketing

HARLEY QUINN AND HER GANG OF HARLEYS

DC Comics, 2900 West Alameda Ave., Burbank, CA 91505
Printed by LSC Communications, Salem, VA, USA. 12/30/16. First Printing.
ISBN: 978-1-4012-6785-8

Library of Congress Cataloging-in-Publication Data is available.

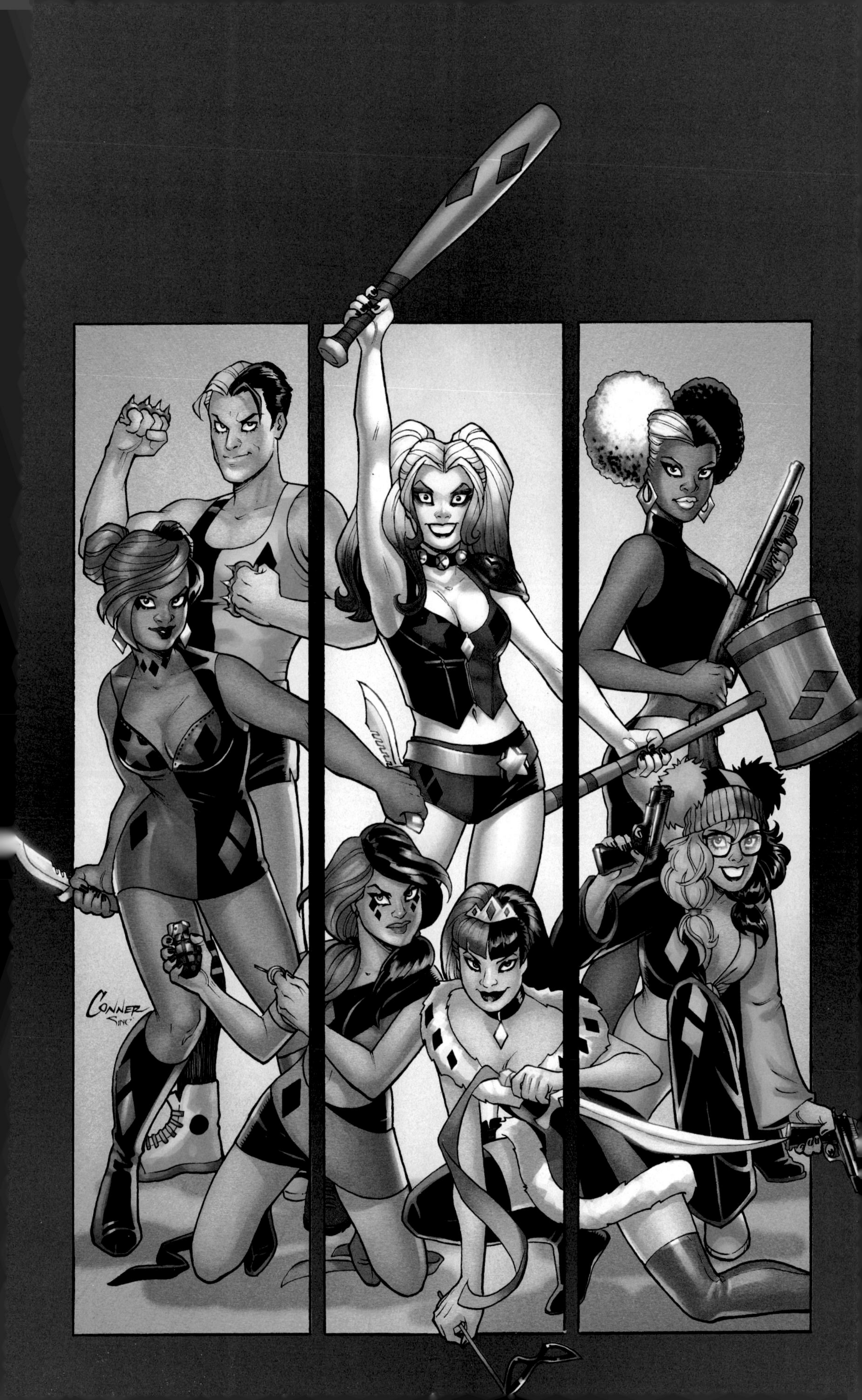
CONNER

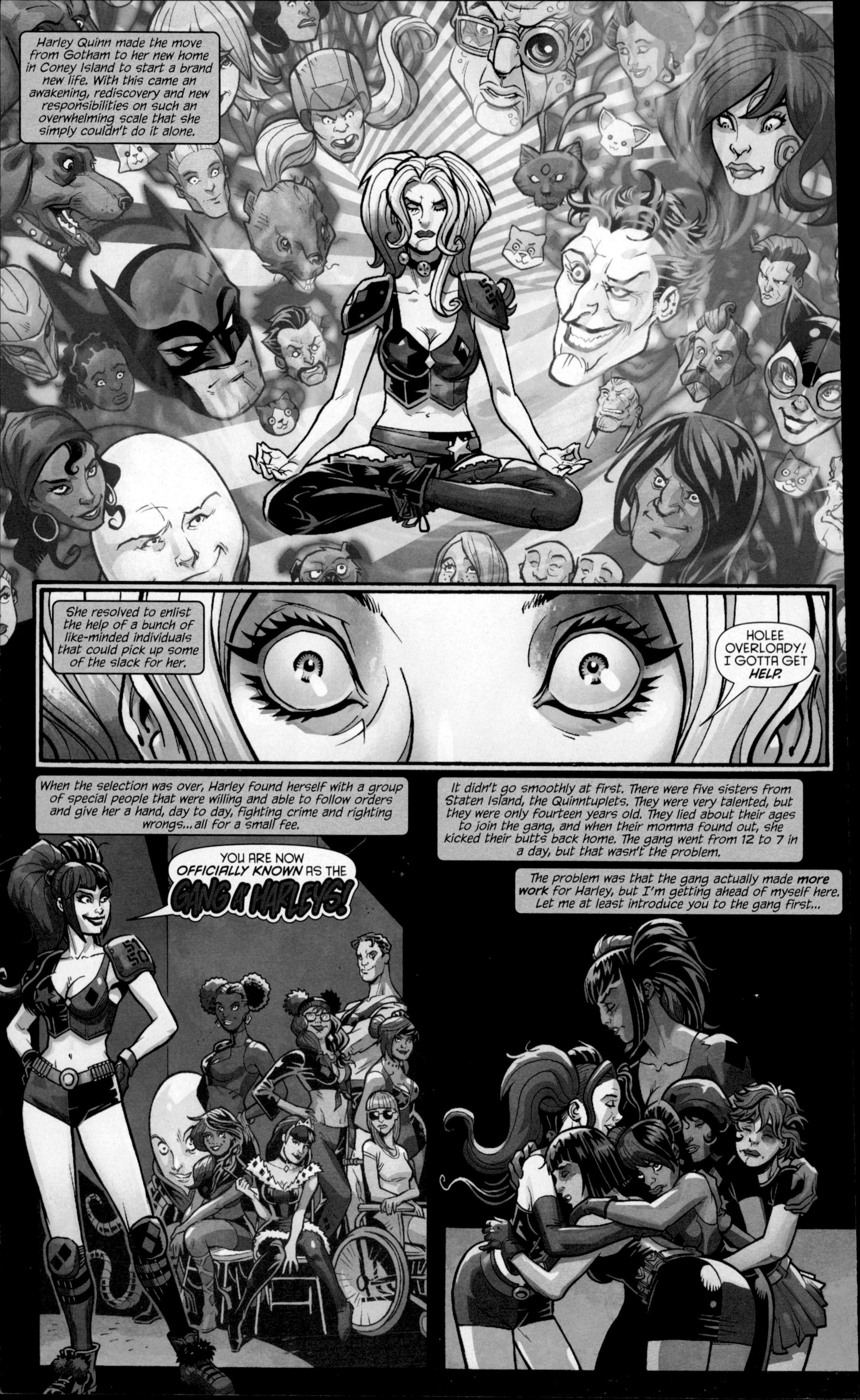

Harley Quinn made the move from Gotham to her new home in Coney Island to start a brand new life. With this came an awakening, rediscovery and new responsibilities on such an overwhelming scale that she simply couldn't do it alone.
She resolved to enlist the help of a bunch of like-minded individuals that could pick up some of the slack for her.
HOLEE OVERLOADY! I GOTTA GET HELP.
When the selection was over, Harley found herself with a group of special people that were willing and able to follow orders and give her a hand, day to day, fighting crime and righting wrongs... all for a small fee.
YOU ARE NOW OFFICIALLY KNOWN AS THE GANG A' HARLEYS!
It didn't go smoothly at first. There were five sisters from Staten Island, the Quinntuplets. They were very talented, but they were only fourteen years old. They lied about their ages to join the gang, and when their momma found out, she kicked their butts back home. The gang went from 12 to 7 in a day, but that wasn't the problem.
The problem was that the gang actually made more work for Harley, but I'm getting ahead of myself here. Let me at least introduce you to the gang first...

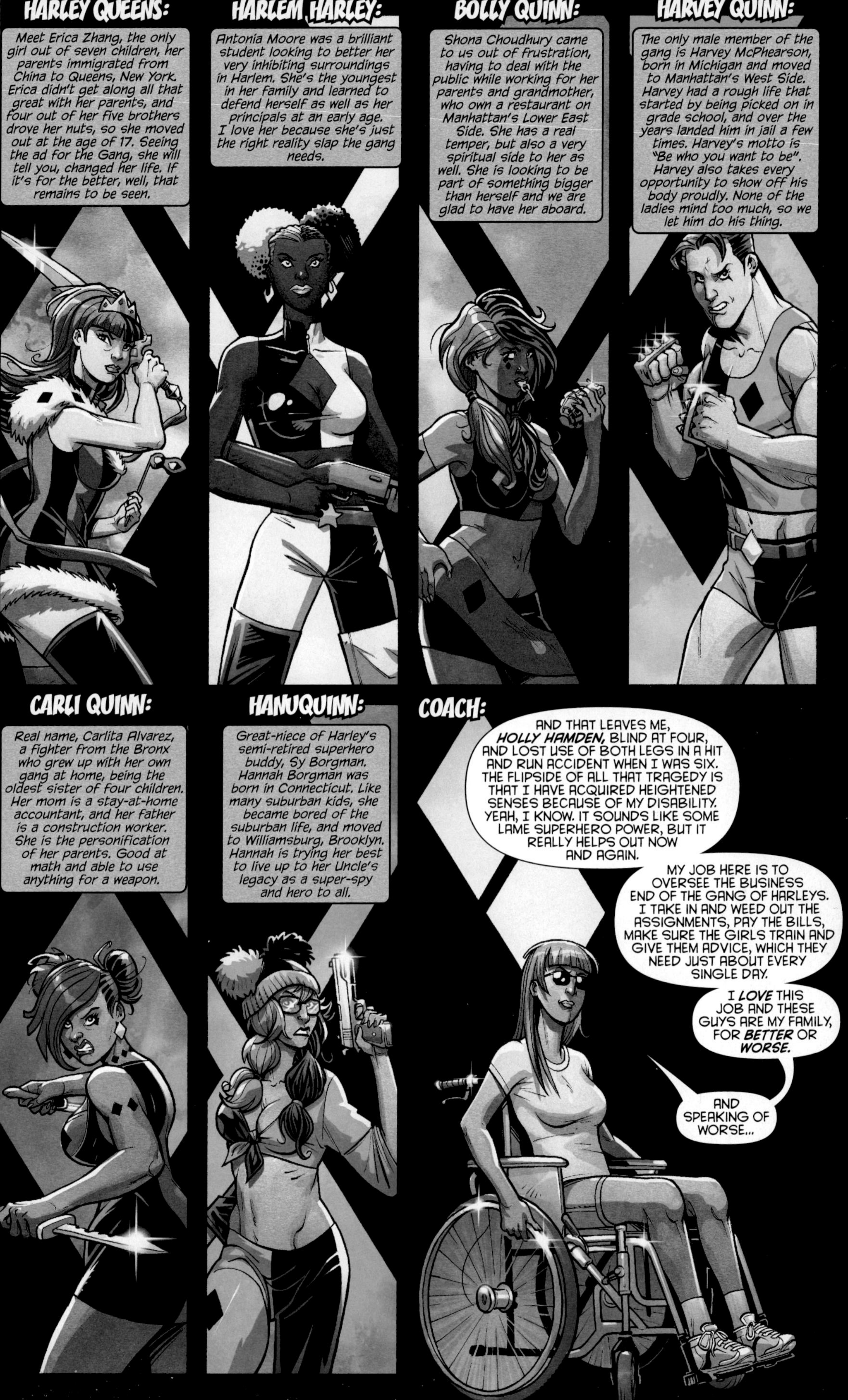
HARLEY QUEENS:
Meet Erica Zhang, the only girl out of seven children, her parents immigrated from China to Queens, New York. Erica didn't get along all that great with her parents, and four out of her five brothers drove her nuts, so she moved out at the age of 17. Seeing the ad for the Gang, she will tell you, changed her life. If it's for the better, well, that remains to be seen.
HARLEM HARLEY:
Antonia Moore was a brilliant student looking to better her very inhibiting surroundings in Harlem. She's the youngest in her family and learned to defend herself as well as her principals at an early age. I love her because she's just the right reality slap the gang needs.
BOLLY QUINN:
Shona Choudhury came to us out of frustration, having to deal with the public while working for her parents and grandmother, who own a restaurant on Manhattan's Lower East Side. She has a real temper, but also a very spiritual side to her as well. She is looking to be part of something bigger than herself and we are glad to have her aboard.
HARVEY QUINN:
The only male member of the gang is Harvey McPhearson, born in Michigan and moved to Manhattan's West Side. Harvey had a rough life that started by being picked on in grade school, and over the years landed him in jail a few times. Harvey's motto is "Be who you want to be". Harvey also takes every opportunity to show off his body proudly. None of the ladies mind too much, so we let him do his thing.
CARLI QUINN:
Real name, Carlita Alvarez, a fighter from the Bronx who grew up with her own gang at home, being the oldest sister of four children. Her mom is a stay-at-home accountant, and her father is a construction worker. She is the personification of her parents. Good at math and able to use anything for a weapon.
HANUQUINN:
Great-niece of Harley's semi-retired superhero buddy, Sy Borgman. Hannah Borgman was born in Connecticut. Like many suburban kids, she became bored of the suburban life, and moved to Williamsburg, Brooklyn. Hannah is trying her best to live up to her Uncle's legacy as a super-spy and hero to all.
COACH:
AND THAT LEAVES ME, *HOLLY HAMDEN,* BLIND AT FOUR, AND LOST USE OF BOTH LEGS IN A HIT AND RUN ACCIDENT WHEN I WAS SIX. THE FLIPSIDE OF ALL THAT TRAGEDY IS THAT I HAVE ACQUIRED HEIGHTENED SENSES BECAUSE OF MY DISABILITY. YEAH, I KNOW. IT SOUNDS LIKE SOME LAME SUPERHERO POWER, BUT IT REALLY HELPS OUT NOW AND AGAIN.
MY JOB HERE IS TO OVERSEE THE BUSINESS END OF THE GANG OF HARLEYS. I TAKE IN AND WEED OUT THE ASSIGNMENTS, PAY THE BILLS, MAKE SURE THE GIRLS TRAIN AND GIVE THEM ADVICE, WHICH THEY NEED JUST ABOUT EVERY SINGLE DAY.
I *LOVE* THIS JOB AND THESE GUYS ARE MY FAMILY, FOR *BETTER* OR *WORSE.*
AND SPEAKING OF WORSE...

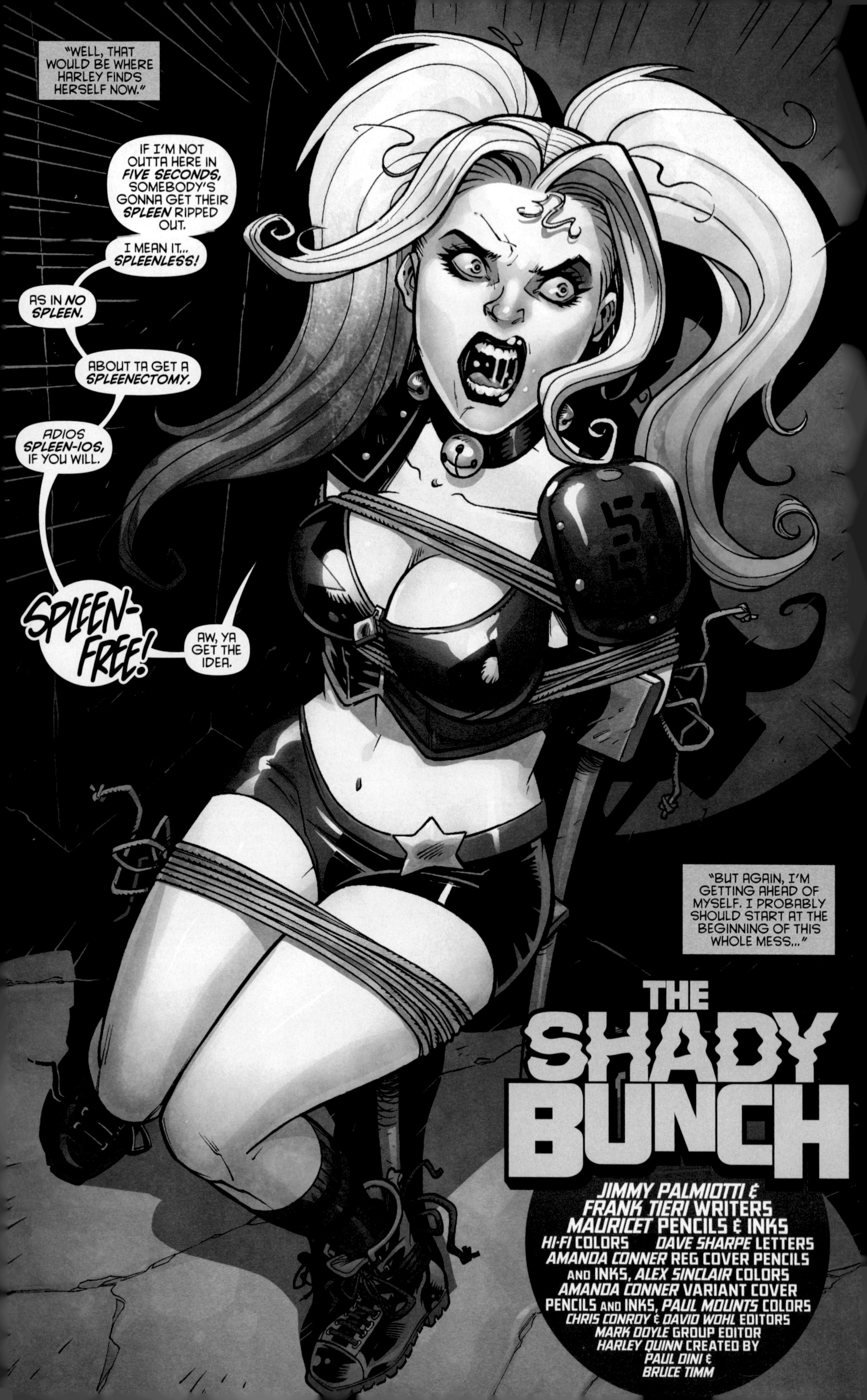
"WELL, THAT WOULD BE WHERE HARLEY FINDS HERSELF NOW."
IF I'M NOT OUTTA HERE IN FIVE SECONDS, SOMEBODY'S GONNA GET THEIR SPLEEN RIPPED OUT.
I MEAN IT... SPLEENLESS!
AS IN NO SPLEEN.
ABOUT TA GET A SPLEENECTOMY.
ADIOS SPLEEN-IOS, IF YOU WILL.
SPLEEN-FREE!
AW, YA GET THE IDEA.
"BUT AGAIN, I'M GETTING AHEAD OF MYSELF. I PROBABLY SHOULD START AT THE BEGINNING OF THIS WHOLE MESS..."
THE SHADY BUNCH
JIMMY PALMIOTTI & FRANK TIERI WRITERS
MAURICET PENCILS & INKS
HI-FI COLORS DAVE SHARPE LETTERS
AMANDA CONNER REG COVER PENCILS AND INKS, ALEX SINCLAIR COLORS
AMANDA CONNER VARIANT COVER PENCILS AND INKS, PAUL MOUNTS COLORS
CHRIS CONROY & DAVID WOHL EDITORS
MARK DOYLE GROUP EDITOR
HARLEY QUINN CREATED BY PAUL DINI & BRUCE TIMM

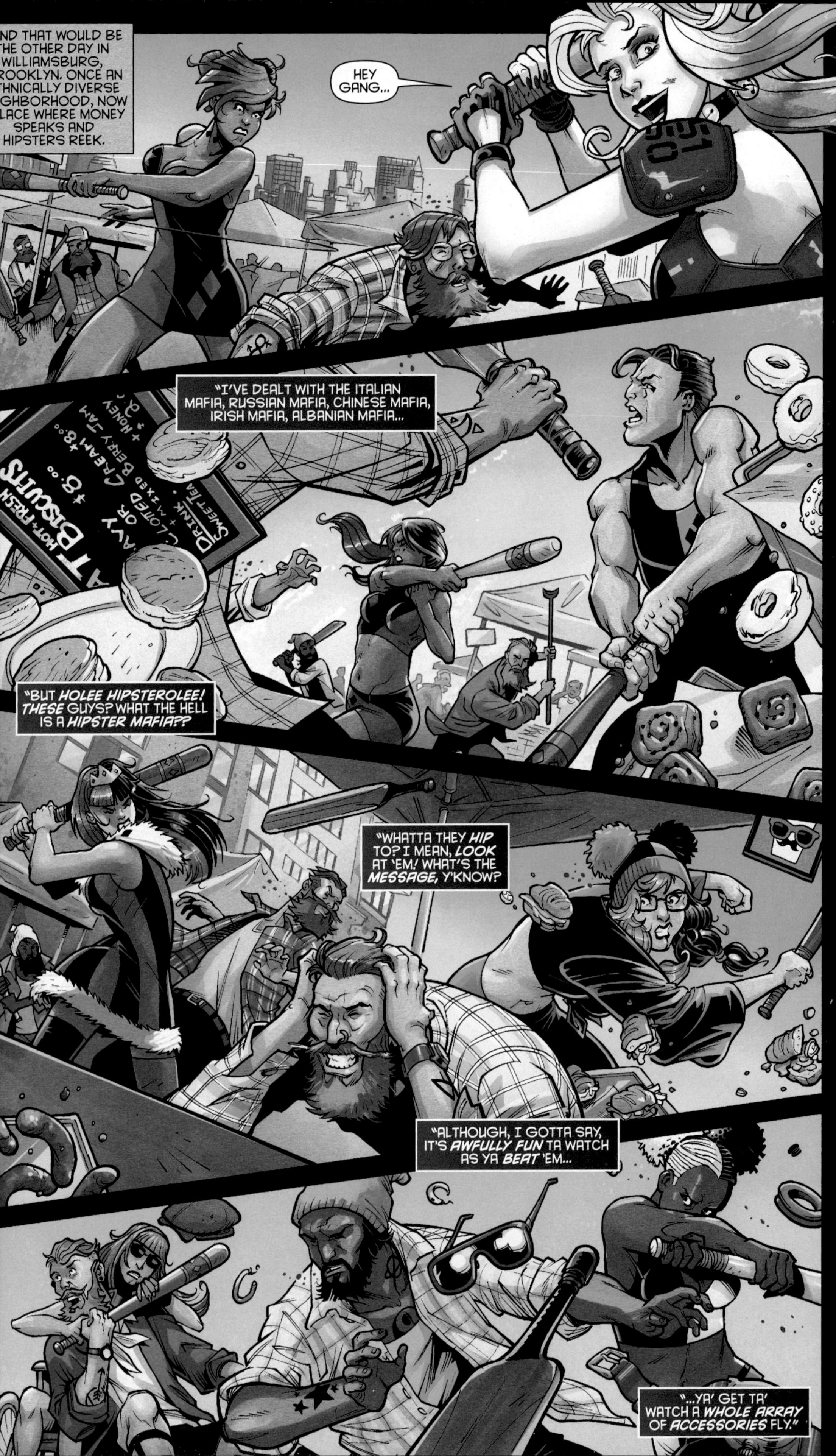

ND THAT WOULD BE THE OTHER DAY IN WILLIAMSBURG, ROOKLYN. ONCE AN THNICALLY DIVERSE GHBORHOOD, NOW LACE WHERE MONEY SPEAKS AND HIPSTERS REEK.
HEY GANG...
"I'VE DEALT WITH THE ITALIAN MAFIA, RUSSIAN MAFIA, CHINESE MAFIA, IRISH MAFIA, ALBANIAN MAFIA...
"BUT HOLEE HIPSTEROLEE! THESE GUYS? WHAT THE HELL IS A HIPSTER MAFIA??
"WHATTA THEY HIP TO? I MEAN, LOOK AT 'EM! WHAT'S THE MESSAGE, Y'KNOW?
"ALTHOUGH, I GOTTA SAY, IT'S AWFULLY FUN TA WATCH AS YA BEAT 'EM...
"...YA' GET TA' WATCH A WHOLE ARRAY OF ACCESSORIES FLY."

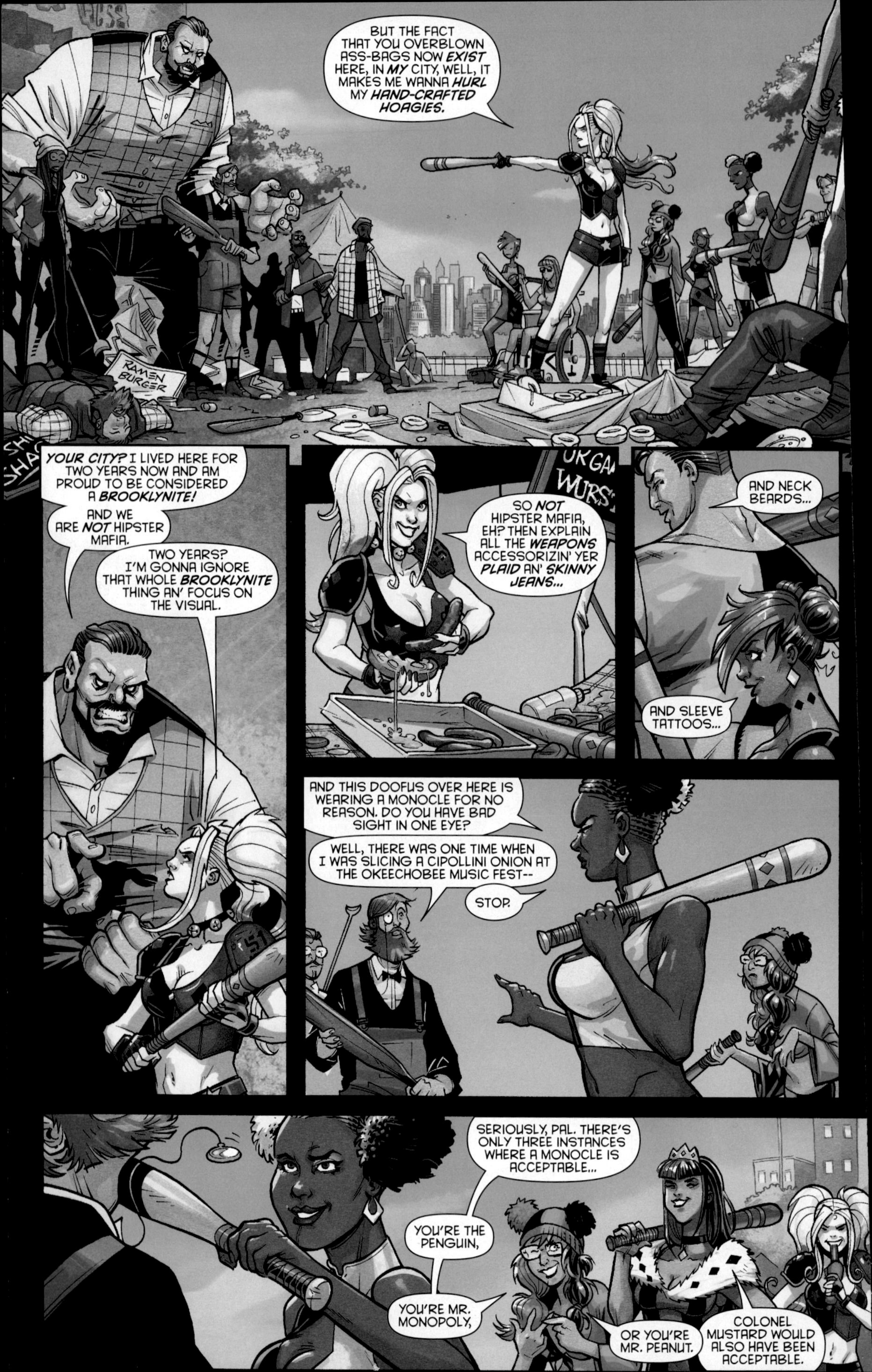
BUT THE FACT THAT YOU OVERBLOWN ASS-BAGS NOW EXIST HERE, IN MY CITY, WELL, IT MAKES ME WANNA HURL MY HAND-CRAFTED HOAGIES.
RAMEN BURGER
YOUR CITY? I LIVED HERE FOR TWO YEARS NOW AND AM PROUD TO BE CONSIDERED A BROOKLYNITE!
AND WE ARE NOT HIPSTER MAFIA.
TWO YEARS? I'M GONNA IGNORE THAT WHOLE BROOKLYNITE THING AN' FOCUS ON THE VISUAL.
SO NOT HIPSTER MAFIA, EH? THEN EXPLAIN ALL THE WEAPONS ACCESSORIZIN' YER PLAID AN' SKINNY JEANS...
AND NECK BEARDS...
AND SLEEVE TATTOOS...
AND THIS DOOFUS OVER HERE IS WEARING A MONOCLE FOR NO REASON. DO YOU HAVE BAD SIGHT IN ONE EYE?
WELL, THERE WAS ONE TIME WHEN I WAS SLICING A CIPOLLINI ONION AT THE OKEECHOBEE MUSIC FEST--
STOP.
SERIOUSLY, PAL. THERE'S ONLY THREE INSTANCES WHERE A MONOCLE IS ACCEPTABLE...
YOU'RE THE PENGUIN,
YOU'RE MR. MONOPOLY,
OR YOU'RE MR. PEANUT.
COLONEL MUSTARD WOULD ALSO HAVE BEEN ACCEPTABLE.

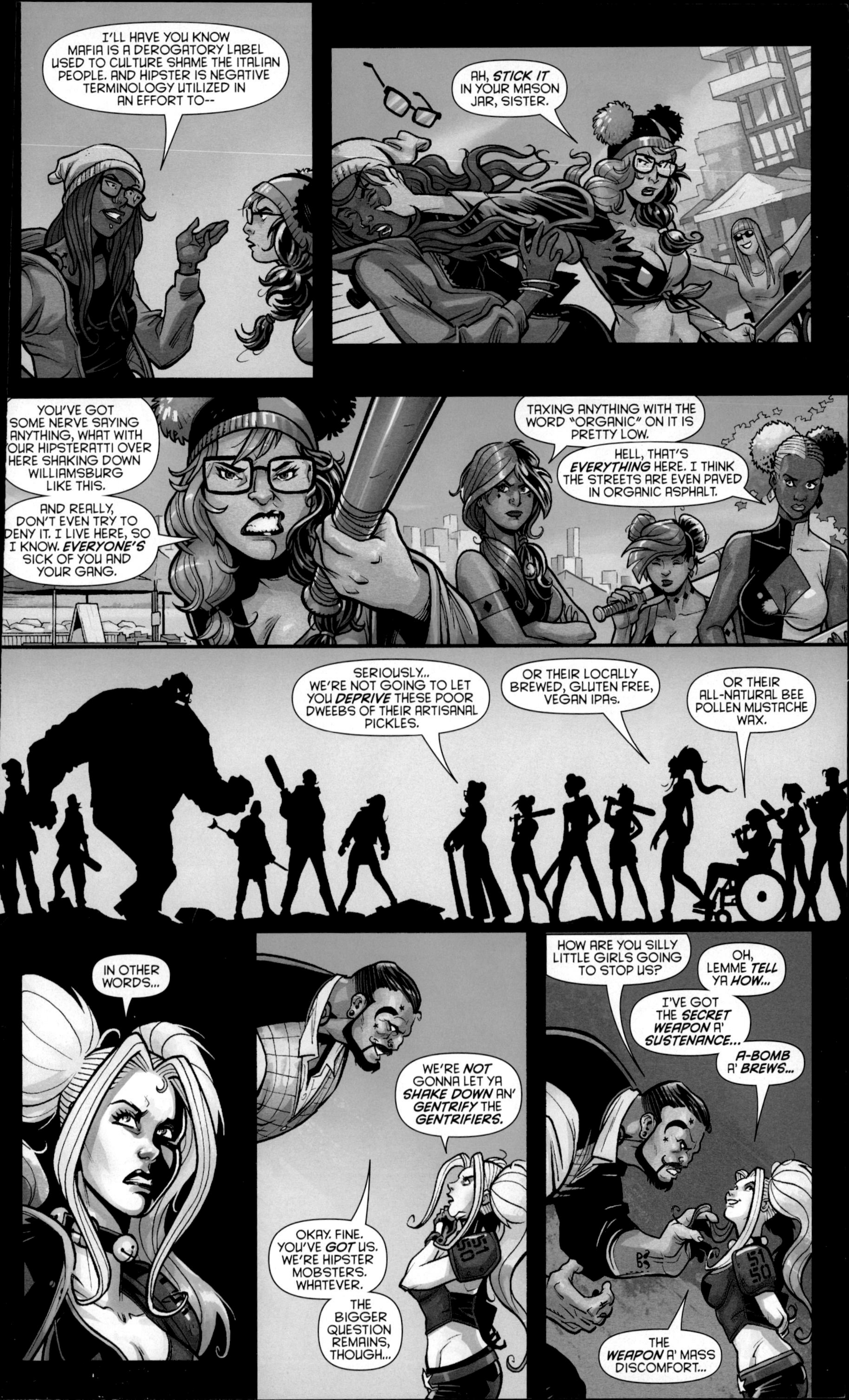
I'LL HAVE YOU KNOW MAFIA IS A DEROGATORY LABEL USED TO CULTURE SHAME THE ITALIAN PEOPLE. AND HIPSTER IS NEGATIVE TERMINOLOGY UTILIZED IN AN EFFORT TO--
AH, STICK IT IN YOUR MASON JAR, SISTER.
YOU'VE GOT SOME NERVE SAYING ANYTHING, WHAT WITH YOUR HIPSTERATTI OVER HERE SHAKING DOWN WILLIAMSBURG LIKE THIS.
AND REALLY, DON'T EVEN TRY TO DENY IT. I LIVE HERE, SO I KNOW. EVERYONE'S SICK OF YOU AND YOUR GANG.
TAXING ANYTHING WITH THE WORD "ORGANIC" ON IT IS PRETTY LOW.
HELL, THAT'S EVERYTHING HERE. I THINK THE STREETS ARE EVEN PAVED IN ORGANIC ASPHALT.
SERIOUSLY... WE'RE NOT GOING TO LET YOU DEPRIVE THESE POOR DWEEBS OF THEIR ARTISANAL PICKLES.
OR THEIR LOCALLY BREWED, GLUTEN FREE, VEGAN IPAs.
OR THEIR ALL-NATURAL BEE POLLEN MUSTACHE WAX.
IN OTHER WORDS...
WE'RE NOT GONNA LET YA SHAKE DOWN AN' GENTRIFY THE GENTRIFIERS.
OKAY. FINE. YOU'VE GOT US. WE'RE HIPSTER MOBSTERS. WHATEVER.
THE BIGGER QUESTION REMAINS, THOUGH...
HOW ARE YOU SILLY LITTLE GIRLS GOING TO STOP US?
OH, LEMME TELL YA HOW...
I'VE GOT THE SECRET WEAPON A' SUSTENANCE...
A-BOMB A' BREWS...
THE WEAPON A' MASS DISCOMFORT...

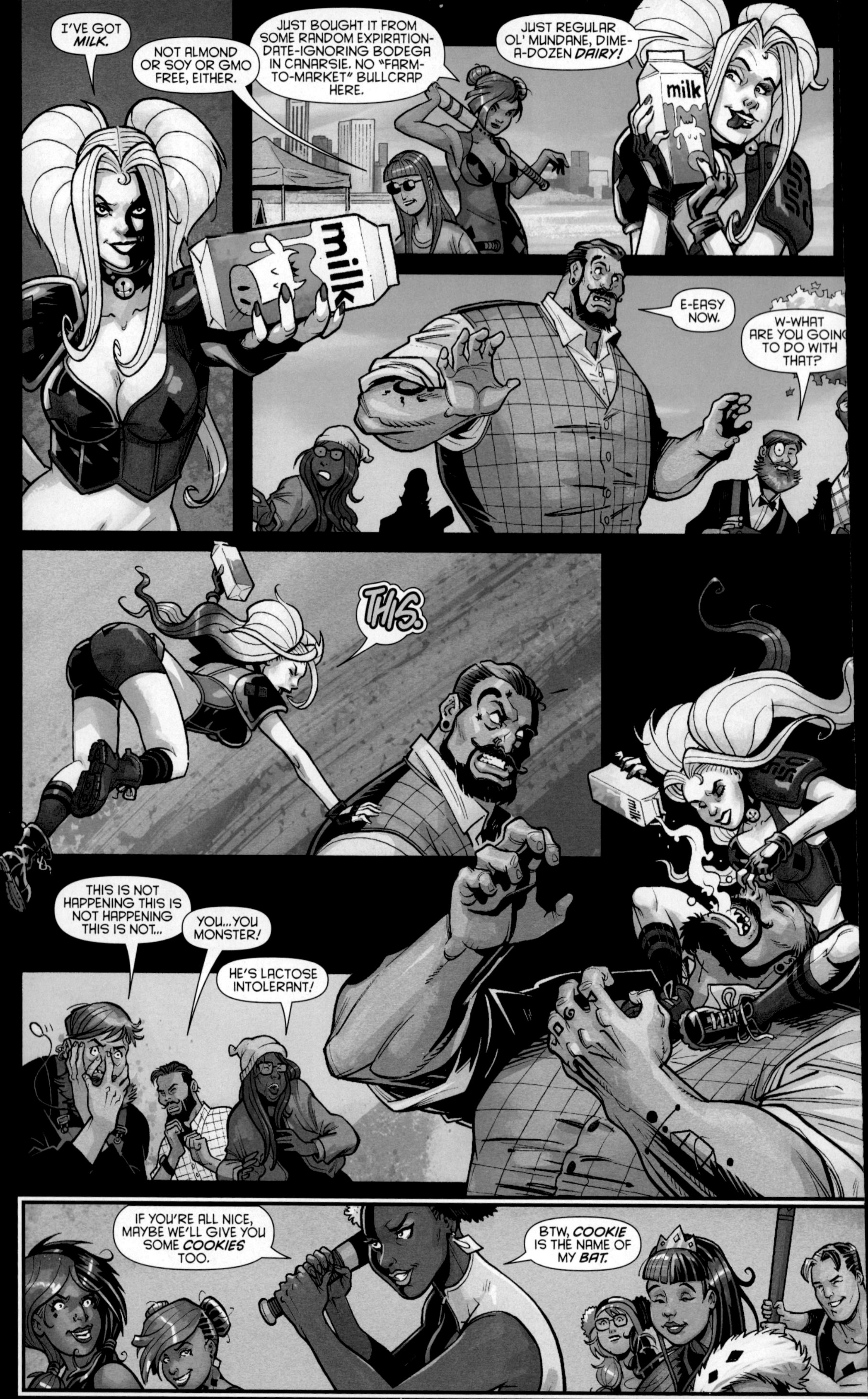
I'VE GOT MILK.
NOT ALMOND OR SOY OR GMO FREE, EITHER.
JUST BOUGHT IT FROM SOME RANDOM EXPIRATION-DATE-IGNORING BODEGA IN CANARSIE. NO "FARM-TO-MARKET" BULLCRAP HERE.
JUST REGULAR OL' MUNDANE, DIME-A-DOZEN DAIRY!
milk
milk
E-EASY NOW.
W-WHAT ARE YOU GOING TO DO WITH THAT?
THIS.
milk
THIS IS NOT HAPPENING THIS IS NOT HAPPENING THIS IS NOT...
YOU...YOU MONSTER!
HE'S LACTOSE INTOLERANT!
IF YOU'RE ALL NICE, MAYBE WE'LL GIVE YOU SOME COOKIES TOO.
BTW, COOKIE IS THE NAME OF MY BAT.

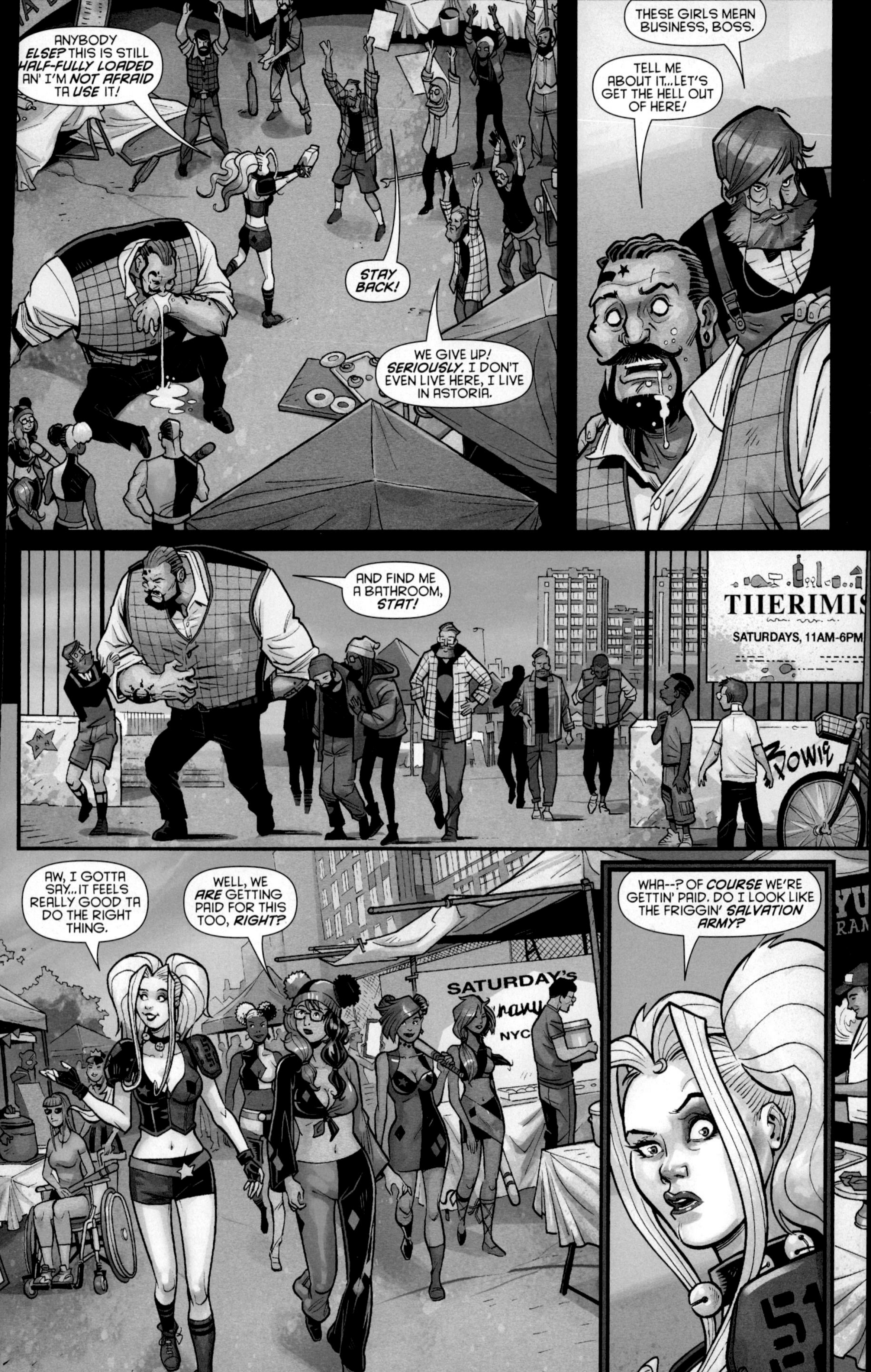
ANYBODY ELSE? THIS IS STILL HALF-FULLY LOADED AN' I'M NOT AFRAID TA USE IT!
STAY BACK!
WE GIVE UP! SERIOUSLY. I DON'T EVEN LIVE HERE, I LIVE IN ASTORIA.
THESE GIRLS MEAN BUSINESS, BOSS.
TELL ME ABOUT IT...LET'S GET THE HELL OUT OF HERE!
AND FIND ME A BATHROOM, STAT!
TIIERIMIS
SATURDAYS, 11AM-6PM
BOWIE
AW, I GOTTA SAY...IT FEELS REALLY GOOD TA DO THE RIGHT THING.
WELL, WE ARE GETTING PAID FOR THIS TOO, RIGHT?
SATURDAY'S
NYC
WHA--? OF COURSE WE'RE GETTIN' PAID. DO I LOOK LIKE THE FRIGGIN' SALVATION ARMY?

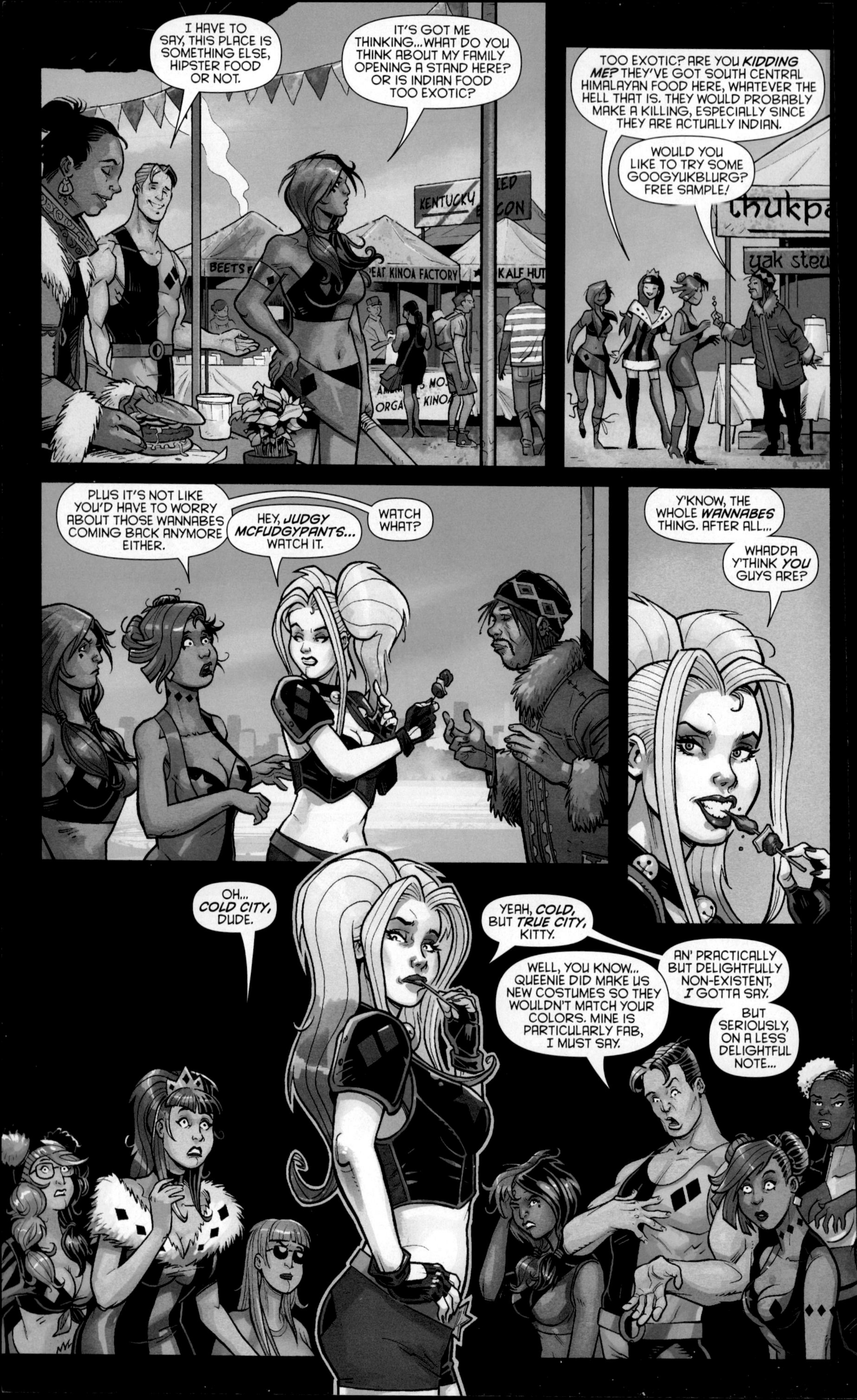
I HAVE TO SAY, THIS PLACE IS SOMETHING ELSE, HIPSTER FOOD OR NOT.
IT'S GOT ME THINKING... WHAT DO YOU THINK ABOUT MY FAMILY OPENING A STAND HERE? OR IS INDIAN FOOD TOO EXOTIC?
KENTUCKY FRIED BACON
BEETS
KINOA FACTORY
KALF HUT
TOO EXOTIC? ARE YOU KIDDING ME? THEY'VE GOT SOUTH CENTRAL HIMALAYAN FOOD HERE, WHATEVER THE HELL THAT IS. THEY WOULD PROBABLY MAKE A KILLING, ESPECIALLY SINCE THEY ARE ACTUALLY INDIAN.
WOULD YOU LIKE TO TRY SOME GOOGYUKBLURG? FREE SAMPLE!
yak stew
PLUS IT'S NOT LIKE YOU'D HAVE TO WORRY ABOUT THOSE WANNABES COMING BACK ANYMORE EITHER.
HEY, JUDGY MCFUDGYPANTS... WATCH IT.
WATCH WHAT?
Y'KNOW, THE WHOLE WANNABES THING. AFTER ALL...
WHADDA Y'THINK YOU GUYS ARE?
OH... COLD CITY, DUDE.
YEAH, COLD, BUT TRUE CITY, KITTY.
WELL, YOU KNOW... QUEENIE DID MAKE US NEW COSTUMES SO THEY WOULDN'T MATCH YOUR COLORS. MINE IS PARTICULARLY FAB, I MUST SAY.
AN' PRACTICALLY BUT DELIGHTFULLY NON-EXISTENT, I GOTTA SAY.
BUT SERIOUSLY, ON A LESS DELIGHTFUL NOTE...

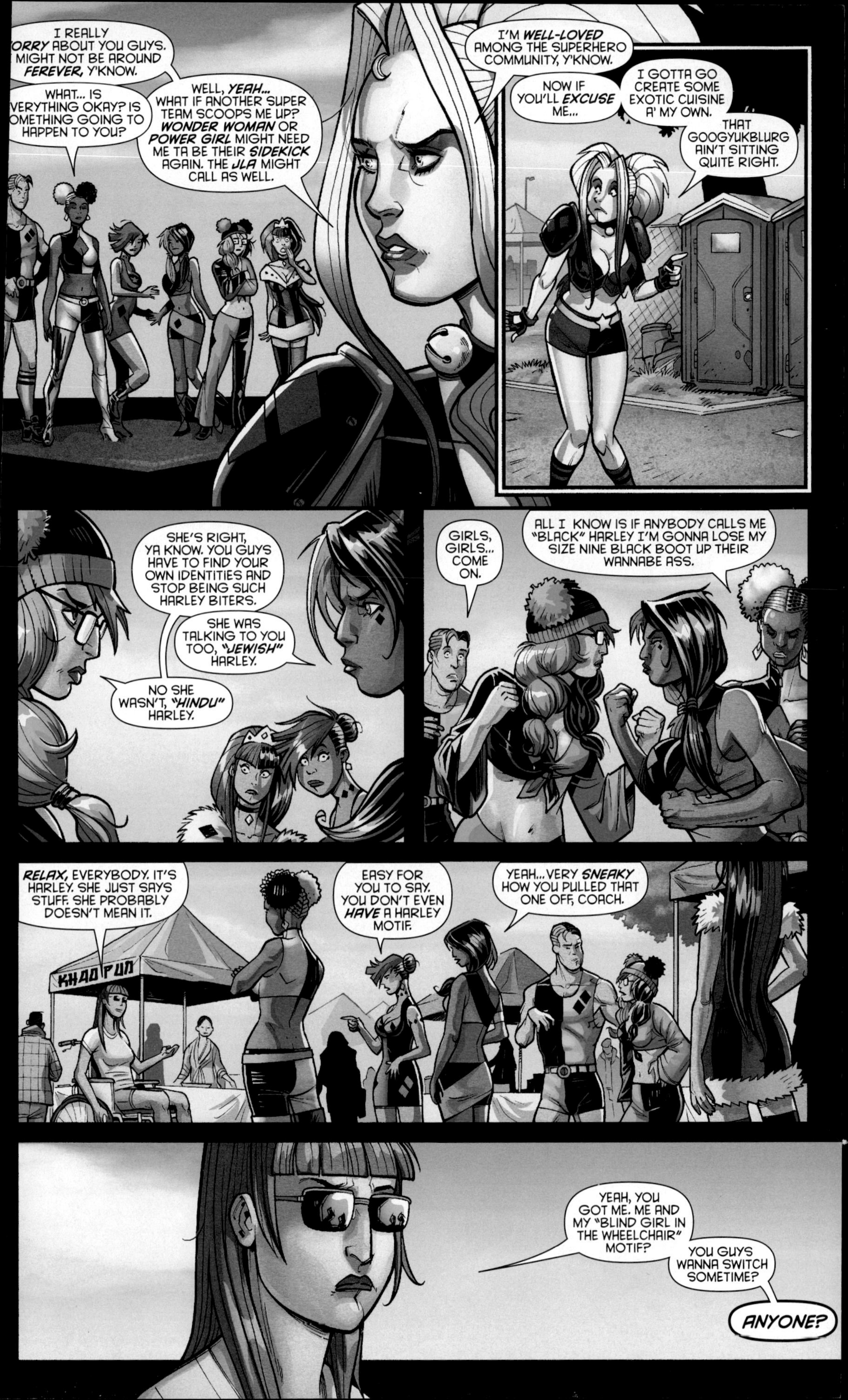
I REALLY WORRY ABOUT YOU GUYS. I MIGHT NOT BE AROUND FEREVER, Y'KNOW.
WHAT... IS EVERYTHING OKAY? IS SOMETHING GOING TO HAPPEN TO YOU?
WELL, YEAH... WHAT IF ANOTHER SUPER TEAM SCOOPS ME UP? WONDER WOMAN OR POWER GIRL MIGHT NEED ME TA BE THEIR SIDEKICK AGAIN. THE JLA MIGHT CALL AS WELL.
I'M WELL-LOVED AMONG THE SUPERHERO COMMUNITY, Y'KNOW.
NOW IF YOU'LL EXCUSE ME...
I GOTTA GO CREATE SOME EXOTIC CUISINE A' MY OWN.
THAT GOOGYUKBLURG AIN'T SITTING QUITE RIGHT.
SHE'S RIGHT, YA KNOW. YOU GUYS HAVE TO FIND YOUR OWN IDENTITIES AND STOP BEING SUCH HARLEY BITERS.
SHE WAS TALKING TO YOU TOO, "JEWISH" HARLEY.
NO SHE WASN'T, "HINDU" HARLEY.
GIRLS, GIRLS... COME ON.
ALL I KNOW IS IF ANYBODY CALLS ME "BLACK" HARLEY I'M GONNA LOSE MY SIZE NINE BLACK BOOT UP THEIR WANNABE ASS.
RELAX, EVERYBODY. IT'S HARLEY. SHE JUST SAYS STUFF. SHE PROBABLY DOESN'T MEAN IT.
KHAO PUN
EASY FOR YOU TO SAY. YOU DON'T EVEN HAVE A HARLEY MOTIF.
YEAH... VERY SNEAKY HOW YOU PULLED THAT ONE OFF, COACH.
YEAH, YOU GOT ME. ME AND MY "BLIND GIRL IN THE WHEELCHAIR" MOTIF?
YOU GUYS WANNA SWITCH SOMETIME?
ANYONE?

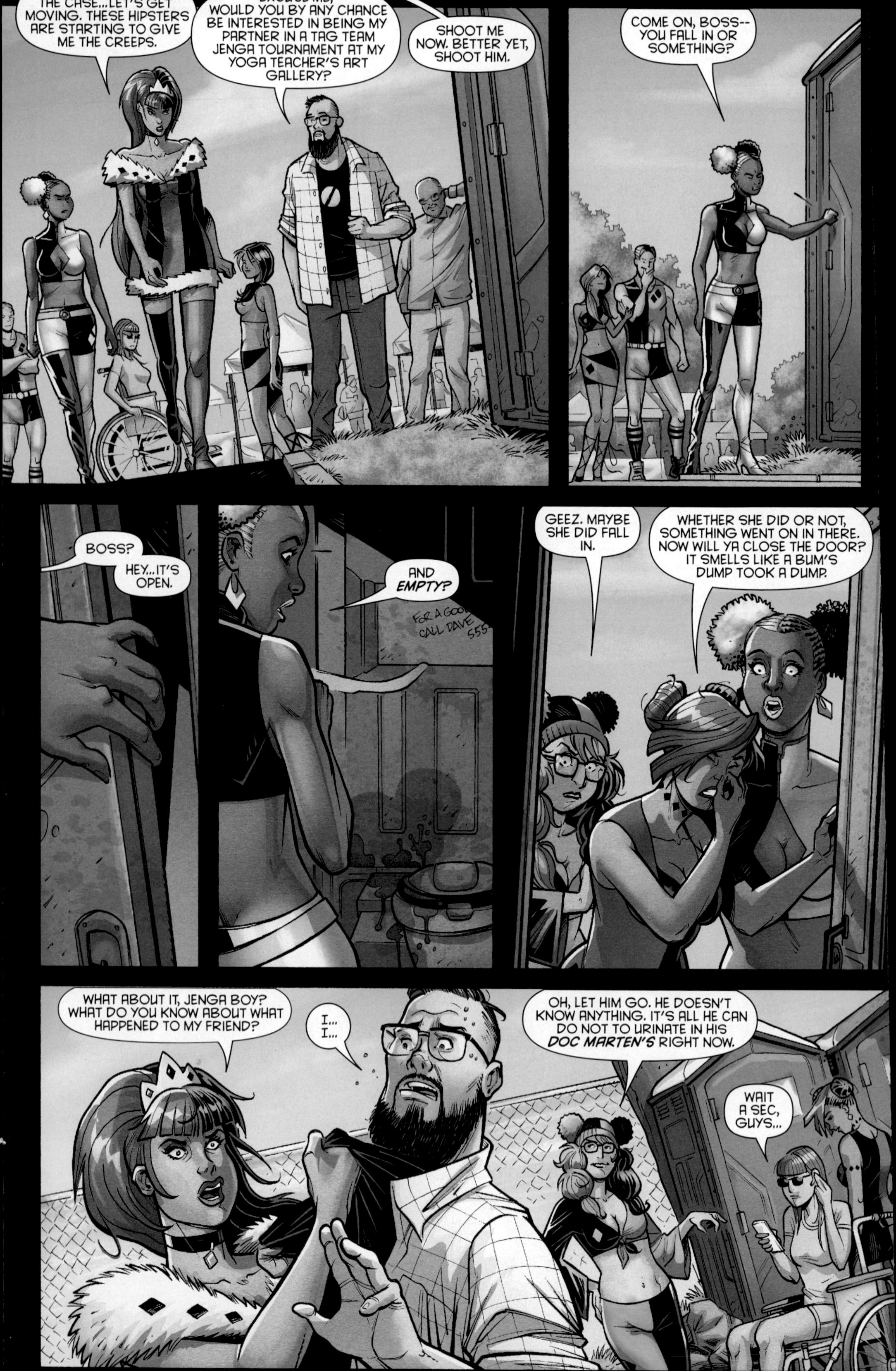
WELL, WHATEVER, THE CASE...LET'S GET MOVING. THESE HIPSTERS ARE STARTING TO GIVE ME THE CREEPS.
EXCUSE ME, WOULD YOU BY ANY CHANCE BE INTERESTED IN BEING MY PARTNER IN A TAG TEAM JENGA TOURNAMENT AT MY YOGA TEACHER'S ART GALLERY?
SHOOT ME NOW. BETTER YET, SHOOT HIM.
COME ON, BOSS-- YOU FALL IN OR SOMETHING?
BOSS?
HEY...IT'S OPEN.
AND *EMPTY?*
FOR A GOO
CALL DAVE 555
GEEZ. MAYBE SHE DID FALL IN.
WHETHER SHE DID OR NOT, SOMETHING WENT ON IN THERE. NOW WILL YA CLOSE THE DOOR? IT SMELLS LIKE A BUM'S DUMP TOOK A DUMP.
WHAT ABOUT IT, JENGA BOY? WHAT DO YOU KNOW ABOUT WHAT HAPPENED TO MY FRIEND?
I... I...
OH, LET HIM GO. HE DOESN'T KNOW ANYTHING. IT'S ALL HE CAN DO NOT TO URINATE IN HIS *DOC MARTEN'S* RIGHT NOW.
WAIT A SEC, GUYS...

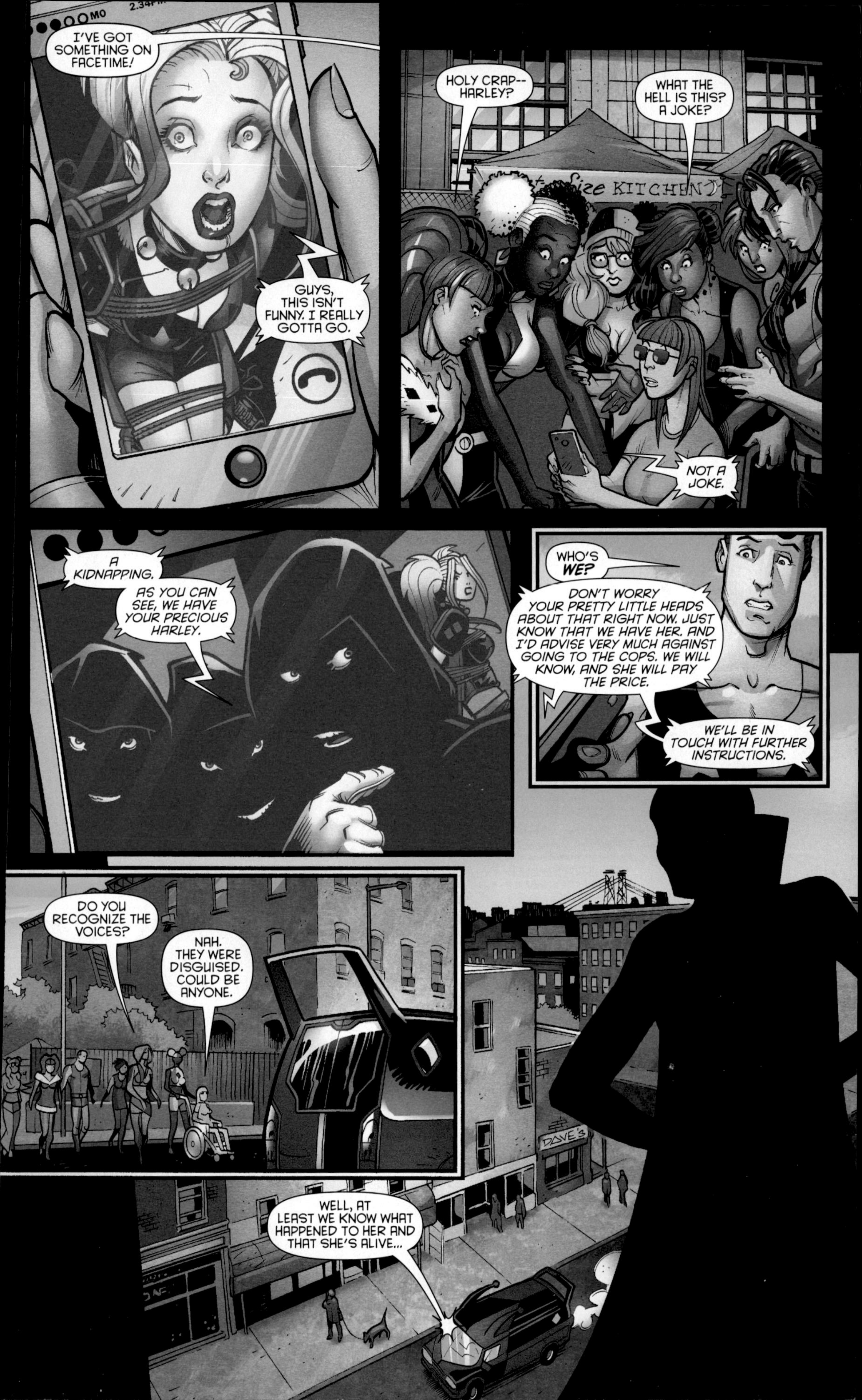

I'VE GOT SOMETHING ON FACETIME!
GUYS, THIS ISN'T FUNNY. I REALLY GOTTA GO.
HOLY CRAP-- HARLEY?
WHAT THE HELL IS THIS? A JOKE?
NOT A JOKE.
A KIDNAPPING.
AS YOU CAN SEE, WE HAVE YOUR PRECIOUS HARLEY.
WHO'S WE?
DON'T WORRY YOUR PRETTY LITTLE HEADS ABOUT THAT RIGHT NOW. JUST KNOW THAT WE HAVE HER. AND I'D ADVISE VERY MUCH AGAINST GOING TO THE COPS. WE WILL KNOW, AND SHE WILL PAY THE PRICE.
WE'LL BE IN TOUCH WITH FURTHER INSTRUCTIONS.
DO YOU RECOGNIZE THE VOICES?
NAH. THEY WERE DISGUISED. COULD BE ANYONE.
DAVE'S
WELL, AT LEAST WE KNOW WHAT HAPPENED TO HER AND THAT SHE'S ALIVE...

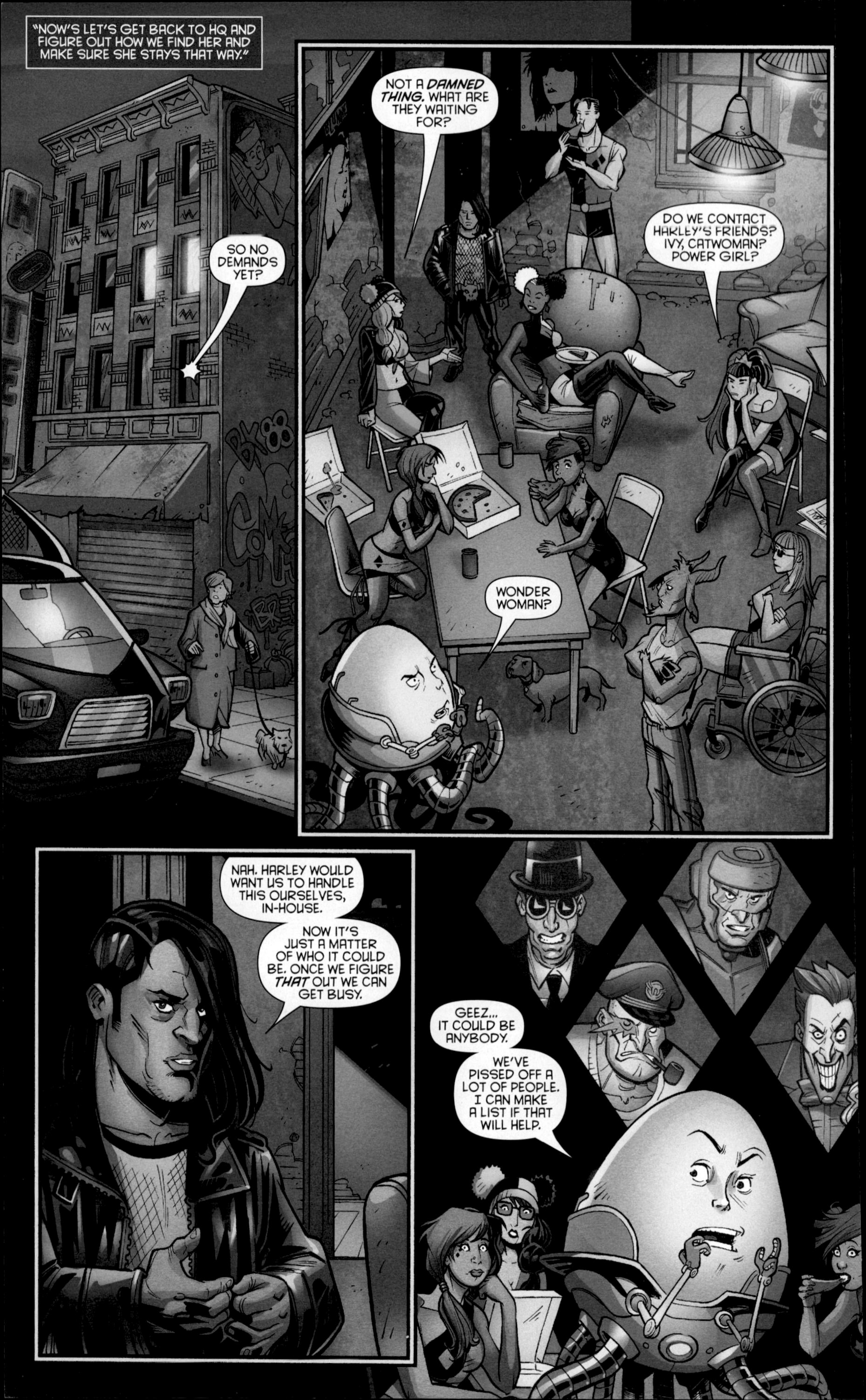
"NOW'S LET'S GET BACK TO HQ AND FIGURE OUT HOW WE FIND HER AND MAKE SURE SHE STAYS THAT WAY."
SO NO DEMANDS YET?
NOT A *DAMNED THING.* WHAT ARE THEY WAITING FOR?
DO WE CONTACT HARLEY'S FRIENDS? IVY, CATWOMAN? POWER GIRL?
WONDER WOMAN?
NAH. HARLEY WOULD WANT US TO HANDLE THIS OURSELVES, IN-HOUSE.
NOW IT'S JUST A MATTER OF WHO IT COULD BE. ONCE WE FIGURE *THAT* OUT WE CAN GET BUSY.
GEEZ... IT COULD BE ANYBODY.
WE'VE PISSED OFF A LOT OF PEOPLE. I CAN MAKE A LIST IF THAT WILL HELP.

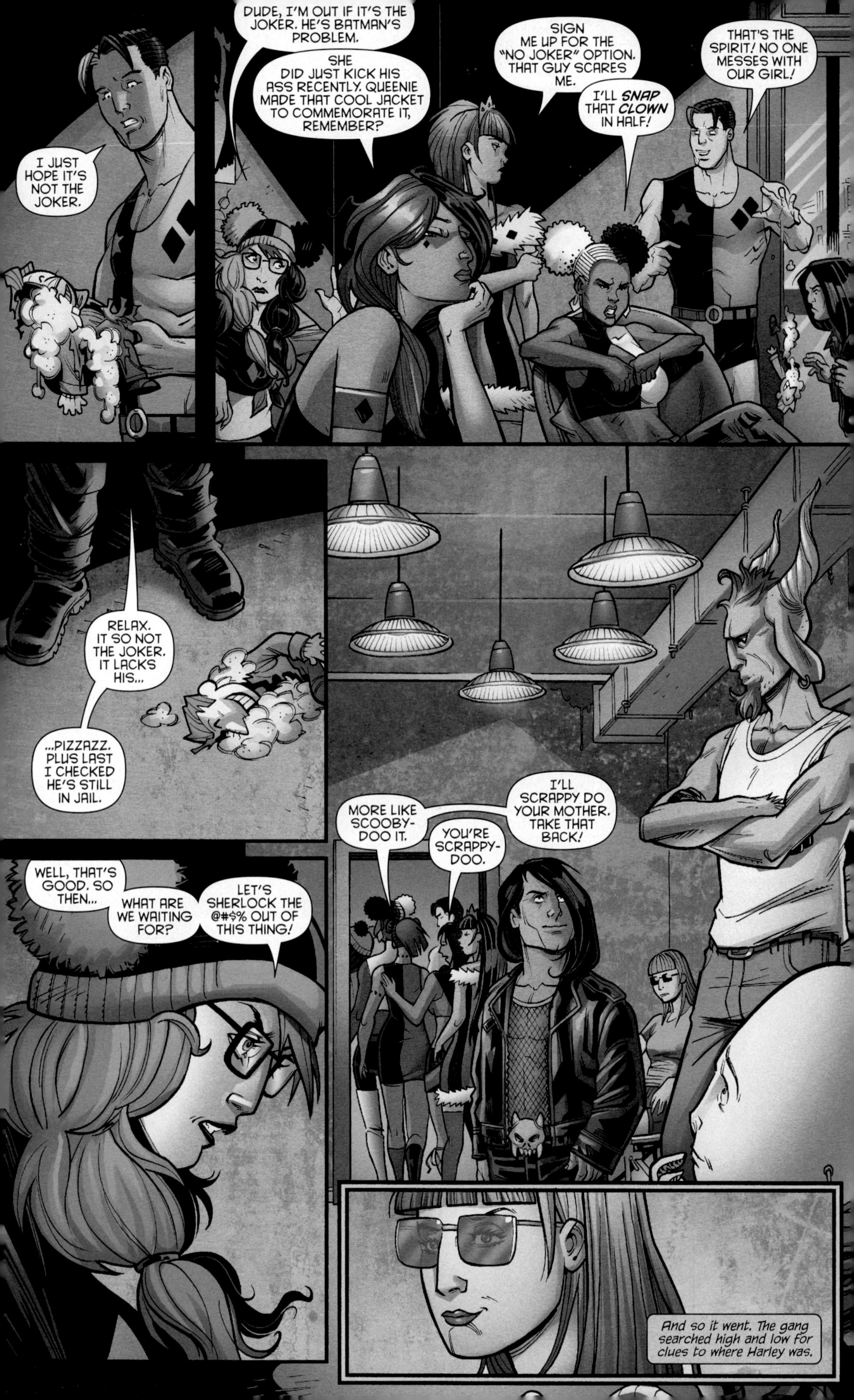
I JUST HOPE IT'S NOT THE JOKER.
DUDE, I'M OUT IF IT'S THE JOKER. HE'S BATMAN'S PROBLEM.
SHE DID JUST KICK HIS ASS RECENTLY. QUEENIE MADE THAT COOL JACKET TO COMMEMORATE IT, REMEMBER?
SIGN ME UP FOR THE "NO JOKER" OPTION. THAT GUY SCARES ME.
I'LL SNAP THAT CLOWN IN HALF!
THAT'S THE SPIRIT! NO ONE MESSES WITH OUR GIRL!
RELAX. IT SO NOT THE JOKER. IT LACKS HIS...
...PIZZAZZ. PLUS LAST I CHECKED HE'S STILL IN JAIL.
WELL, THAT'S GOOD. SO THEN...
WHAT ARE WE WAITING FOR?
LET'S SHERLOCK THE @#$% OUT OF THIS THING!
MORE LIKE SCOOBY-DOO IT.
YOU'RE SCRAPPY-DOO.
I'LL SCRAPPY DO YOUR MOTHER. TAKE THAT BACK!
And so it went. The gang searched high and low for clues to where Harley was.

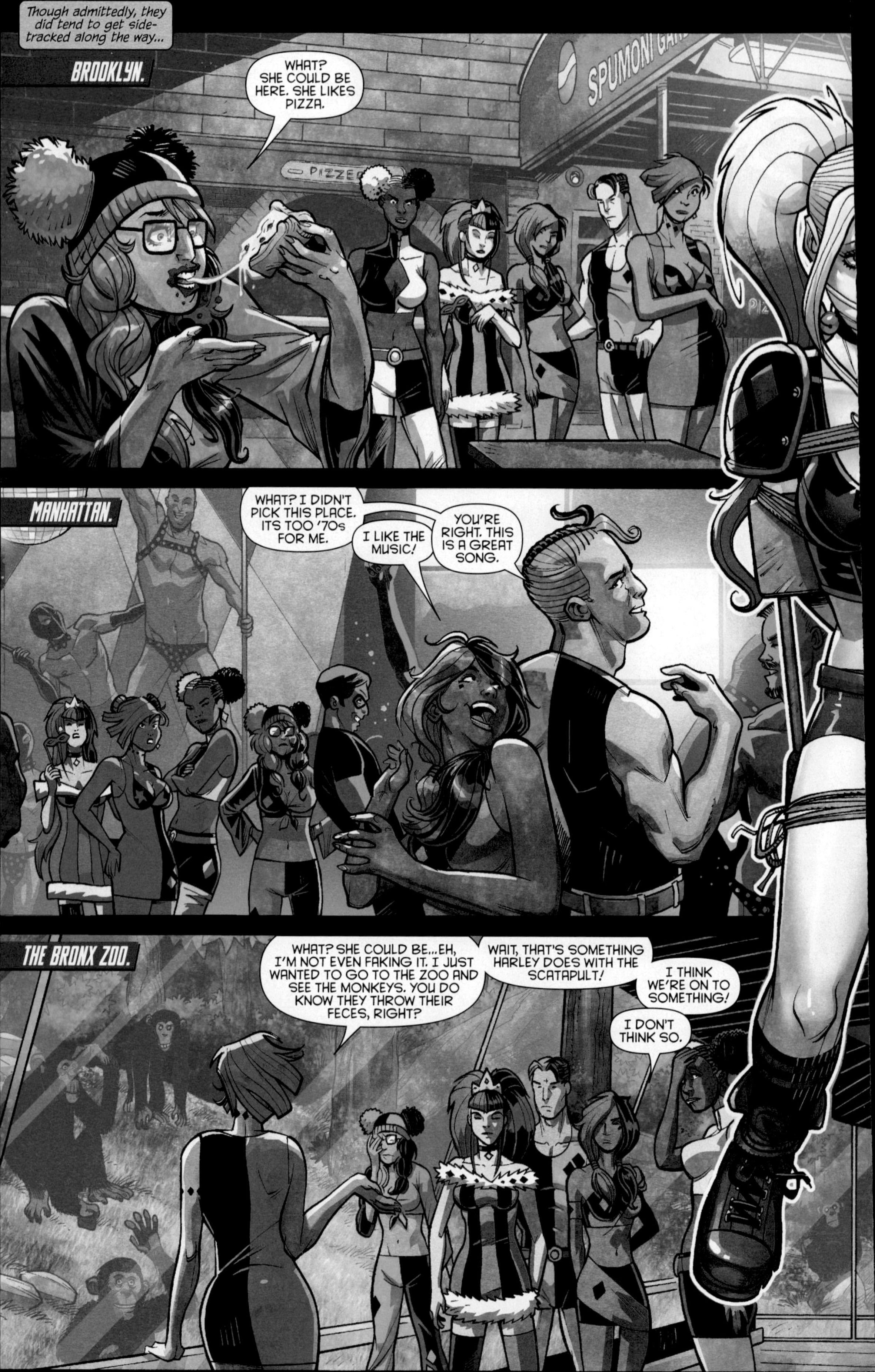

Though admittedly, they did tend to get side-tracked along the way...
BROOKLYN.
SPUMONI GAR
PIZZE
WHAT? SHE COULD BE HERE. SHE LIKES PIZZA.
MANHATTAN.
WHAT? I DIDN'T PICK THIS PLACE. ITS TOO '70s FOR ME.
I LIKE THE MUSIC!
YOU'RE RIGHT. THIS IS A GREAT SONG.
THE BRONX ZOO.
WHAT? SHE COULD BE...EH, I'M NOT EVEN FAKING IT. I JUST WANTED TO GO TO THE ZOO AND SEE THE MONKEYS. YOU DO KNOW THEY THROW THEIR FECES, RIGHT?
WAIT, THAT'S SOMETHING HARLEY DOES WITH THE SCATAPULT!
I THINK WE'RE ON TO SOMETHING!
I DON'T THINK SO.

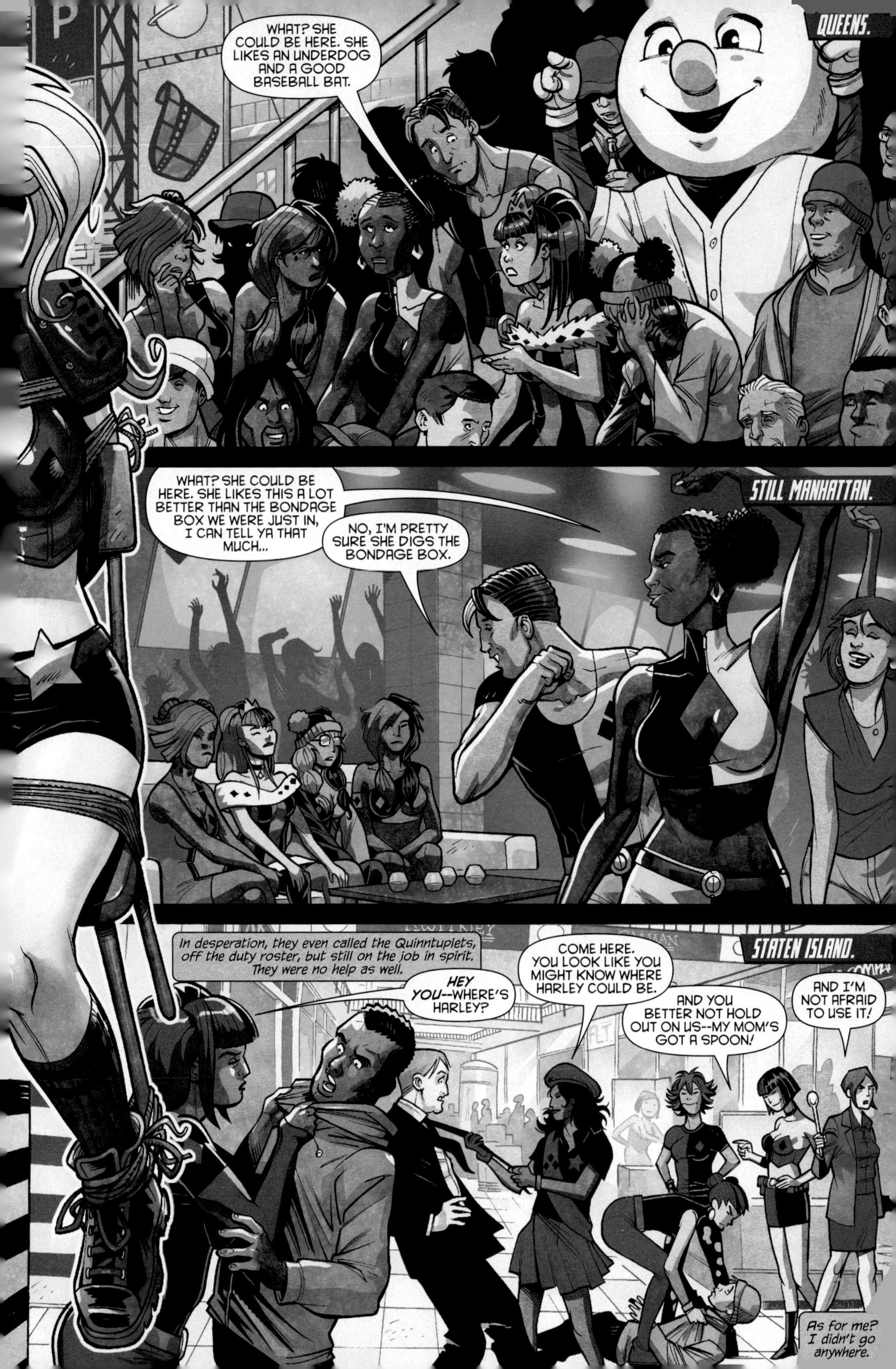
QUEENS.
WHAT? SHE COULD BE HERE. SHE LIKES AN UNDERDOG AND A GOOD BASEBALL BAT.
STILL MANHATTAN.
WHAT? SHE COULD BE HERE. SHE LIKES THIS A LOT BETTER THAN THE BONDAGE BOX WE WERE JUST IN, I CAN TELL YA THAT MUCH...
NO, I'M PRETTY SURE SHE DIGS THE BONDAGE BOX.
STATEN ISLAND.
In desperation, they even called the Quinntuplets, off the duty roster, but still on the job in spirit. They were no help as well.
HEY YOU--WHERE'S HARLEY?
COME HERE. YOU LOOK LIKE YOU MIGHT KNOW WHERE HARLEY COULD BE.
AND YOU BETTER NOT HOLD OUT ON US--MY MOM'S GOT A SPOON!
AND I'M NOT AFRAID TO USE IT!
As for me? I didn't go anywhere.

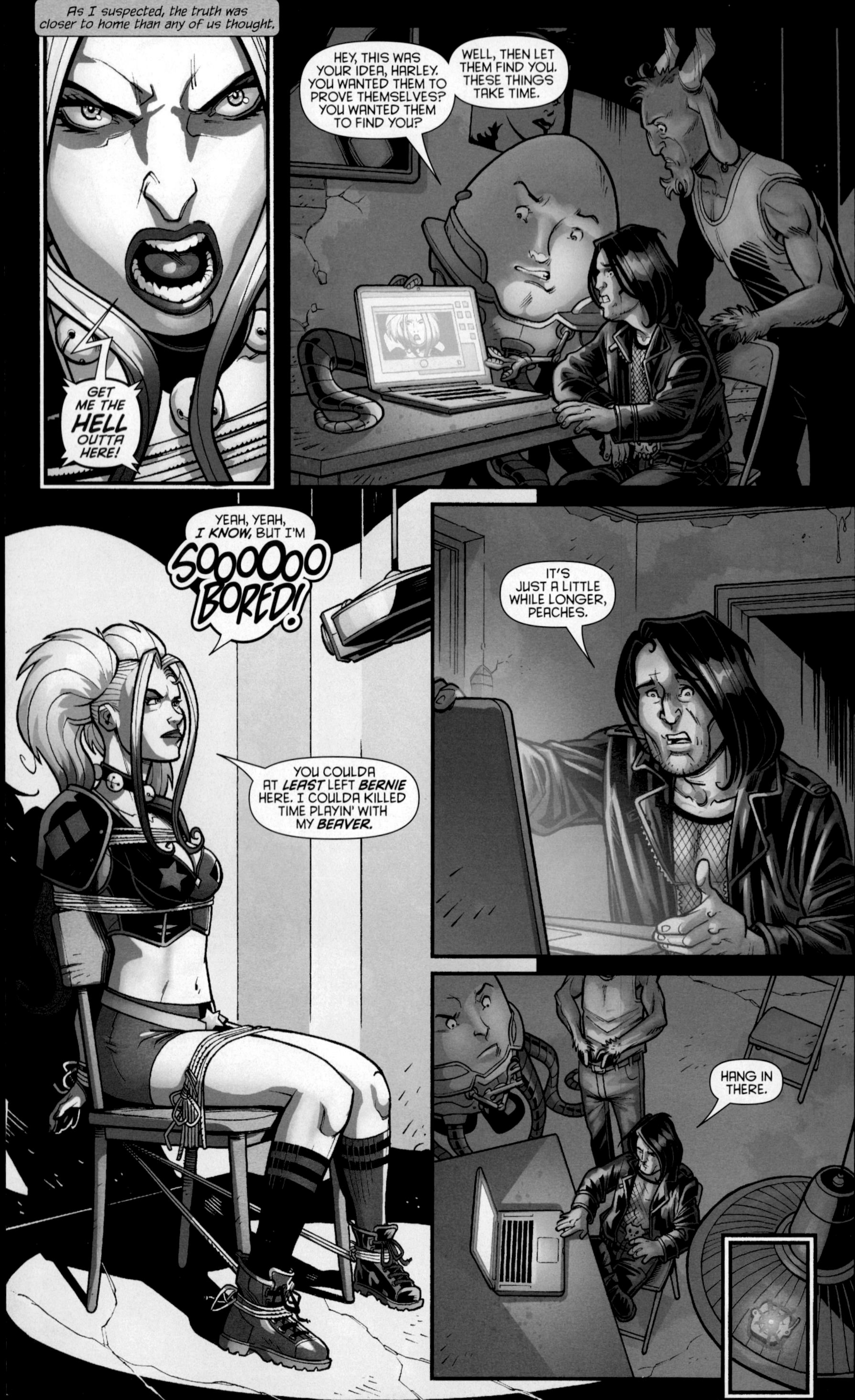
As I suspected, the truth was closer to home than any of us thought.
GET ME THE HELL OUTTA HERE!
HEY, THIS WAS YOUR IDEA, HARLEY. YOU WANTED THEM TO PROVE THEMSELVES? YOU WANTED THEM TO FIND YOU?
WELL, THEN LET THEM FIND YOU. THESE THINGS TAKE TIME.
YEAH, YEAH, I KNOW, BUT I'M SOOOOOO BORED!
YOU COULDA AT LEAST LEFT BERNIE HERE. I COULDA KILLED TIME PLAYIN' WITH MY BEAVER.
IT'S JUST A LITTLE WHILE LONGER, PEACHES.
HANG IN THERE.

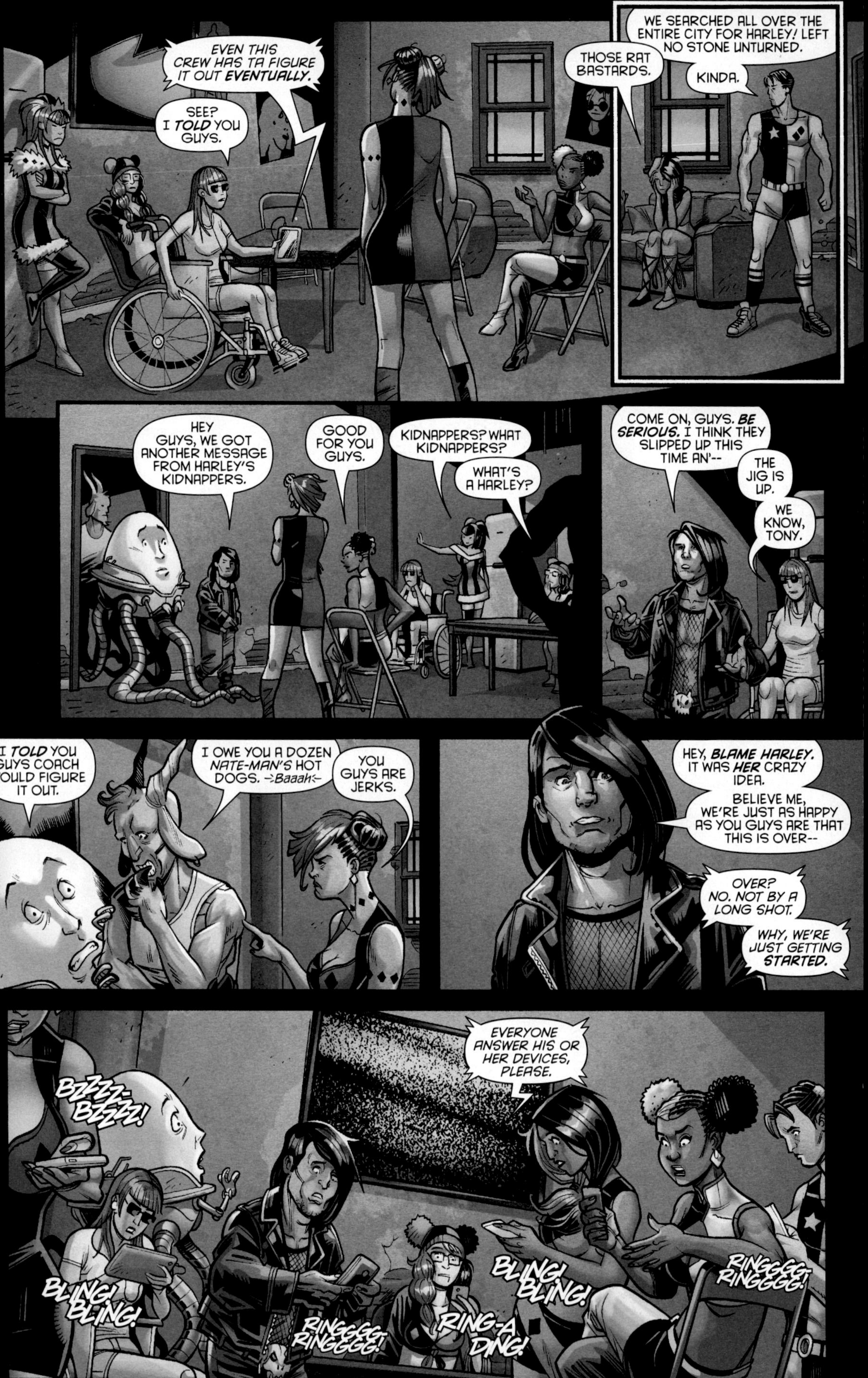

EVEN THIS CREW HAS TA FIGURE IT OUT EVENTUALLY.
SEE? I TOLD YOU GUYS.
THOSE RAT BASTARDS.
WE SEARCHED ALL OVER THE ENTIRE CITY FOR HARLEY! LEFT NO STONE UNTURNED.
KINDA.
HEY GUYS, WE GOT ANOTHER MESSAGE FROM HARLEY'S KIDNAPPERS.
GOOD FOR YOU GUYS.
KIDNAPPERS? WHAT KIDNAPPERS?
WHAT'S A HARLEY?
COME ON, GUYS. BE SERIOUS. I THINK THEY SLIPPED UP THIS TIME AN'--
THE JIG IS UP.
WE KNOW, TONY.
I TOLD YOU GUYS COACH WOULD FIGURE IT OUT.
I OWE YOU A DOZEN NATE-MAN'S HOT DOGS. -Baaah-
YOU GUYS ARE JERKS.
HEY, BLAME HARLEY. IT WAS HER CRAZY IDEA.
BELIEVE ME, WE'RE JUST AS HAPPY AS YOU GUYS ARE THAT THIS IS OVER--
OVER? NO. NOT BY A LONG SHOT.
WHY, WE'RE JUST GETTING STARTED.
EVERYONE ANSWER HIS OR HER DEVICES, PLEASE.
BZZZZ-BZZZZ!
BLING! BLING!
RINGGGG! RINGGGG!
RING-A DING!
BLING! BLING!
RINGGGG! RINGGGG!

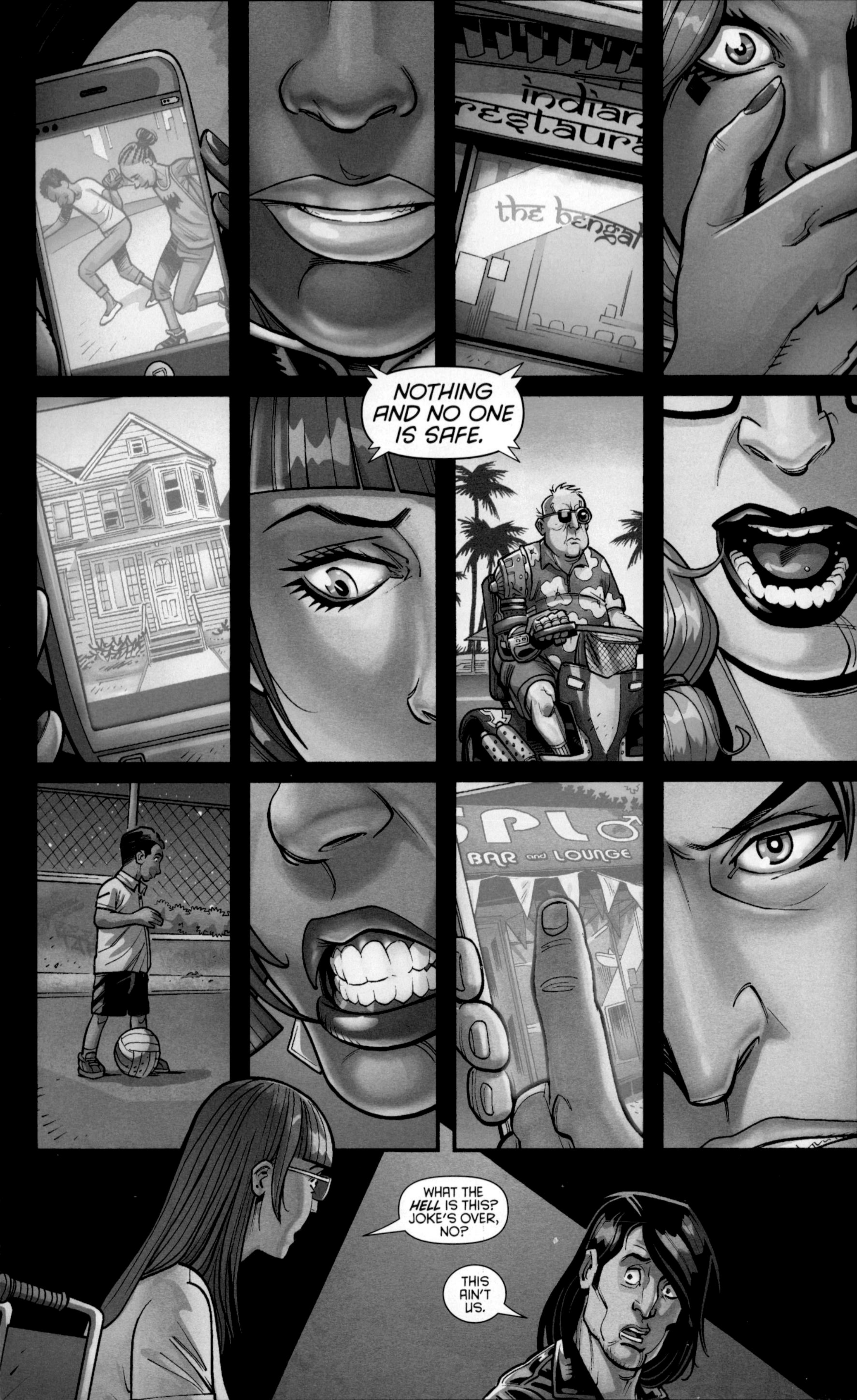
indian restaur
the bengal
NOTHING AND NO ONE IS SAFE.
BAR and LOUNGE
WHAT THE HELL IS THIS? JOKE'S OVER, NO?
THIS AIN'T US.

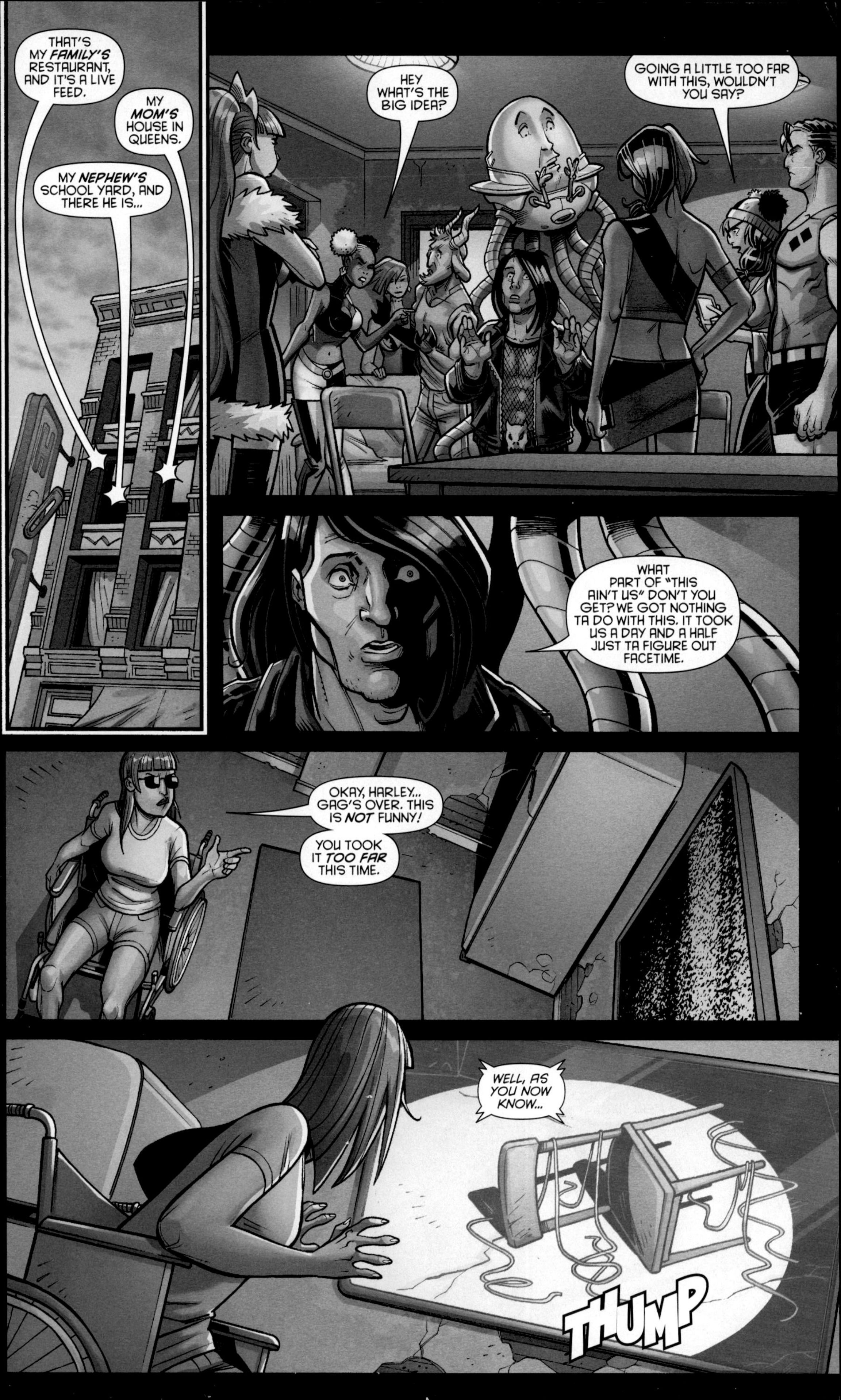
THAT'S MY *FAMILY'S* RESTAURANT, AND IT'S A LIVE FEED.
MY *MOM'S* HOUSE IN QUEENS.
MY *NEPHEW'S* SCHOOL YARD, AND THERE HE IS...
HEY WHAT'S THE BIG IDEA?
GOING A LITTLE TOO FAR WITH THIS, WOULDN'T YOU SAY?
WHAT PART OF "THIS AIN'T US" DON'T YOU GET? WE GOT NOTHING TA DO WITH THIS. IT TOOK US A DAY AND A HALF JUST TA FIGURE OUT FACETIME.
OKAY, HARLEY... GAG'S OVER. THIS IS *NOT* FUNNY!
YOU TOOK IT *TOO FAR* THIS TIME.
WELL, AS YOU NOW KNOW...
THUMP

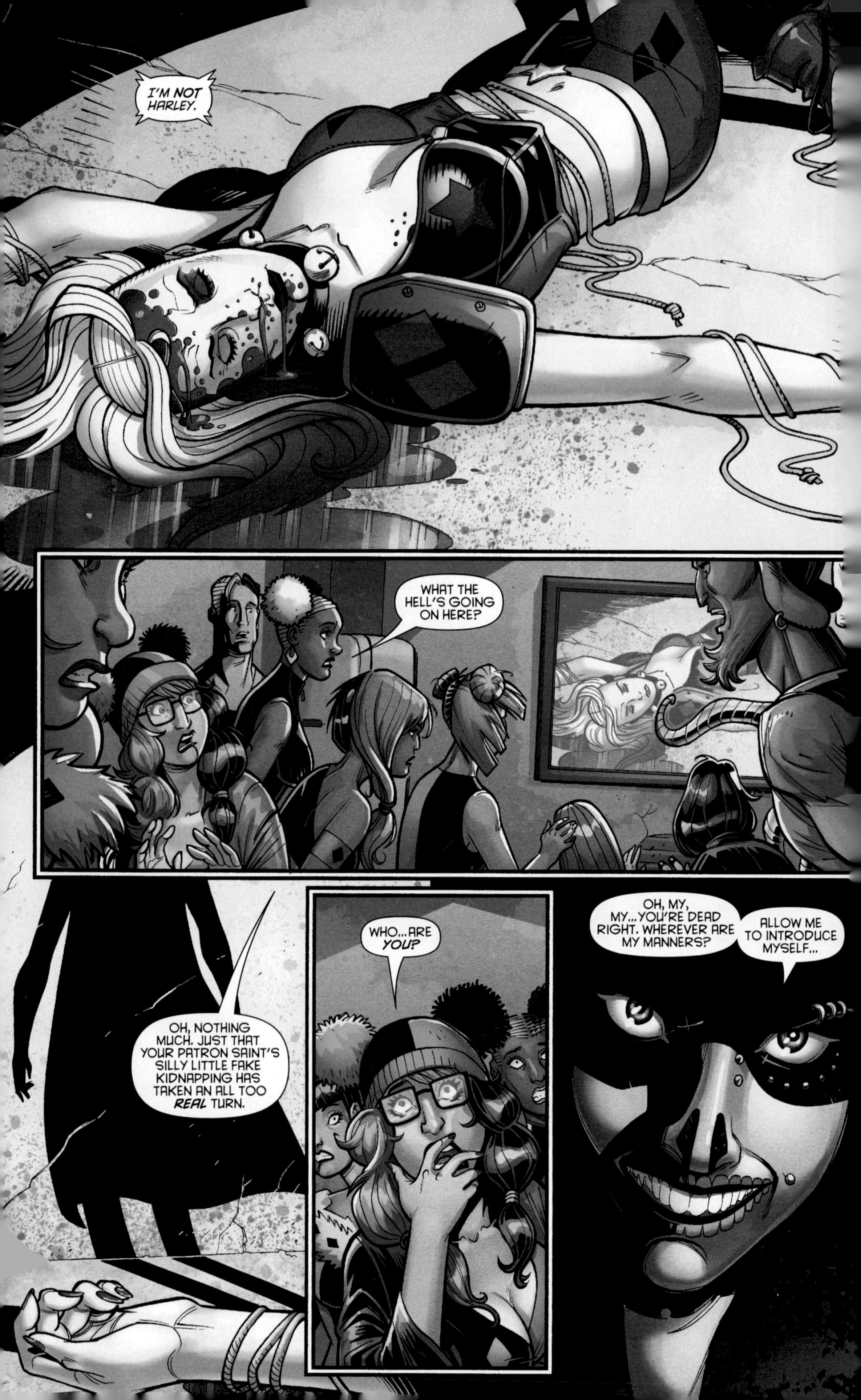
I'M NOT HARLEY.
WHAT THE HELL'S GOING ON HERE?
OH, NOTHING MUCH. JUST THAT YOUR PATRON SAINT'S SILLY LITTLE FAKE KIDNAPPING HAS TAKEN AN ALL TOO REAL TURN.
WHO...ARE YOU?
OH, MY, MY...YOU'RE DEAD RIGHT. WHEREVER ARE MY MANNERS?
ALLOW ME TO INTRODUCE MYSELF...

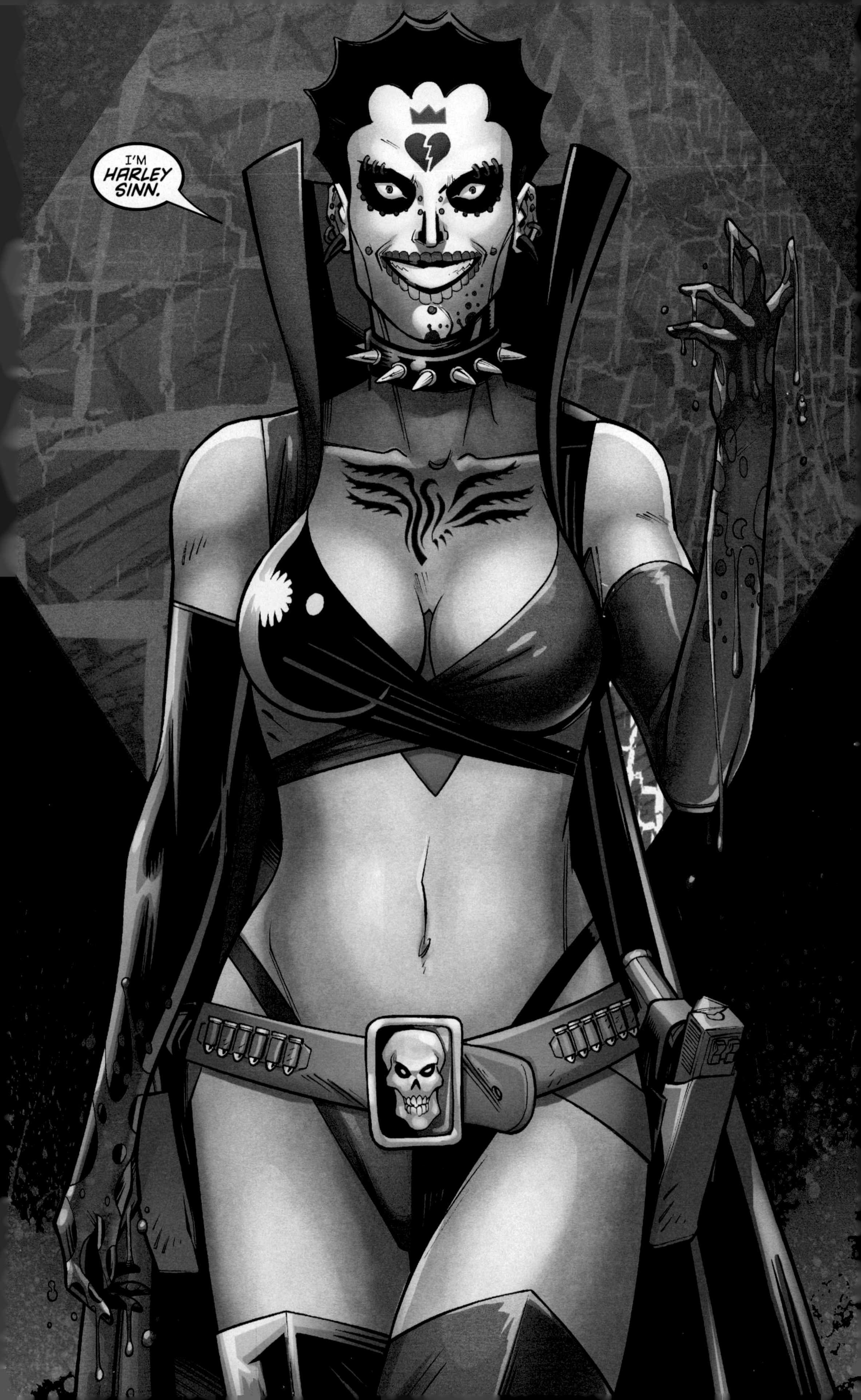
I'M HARLEY SINN.

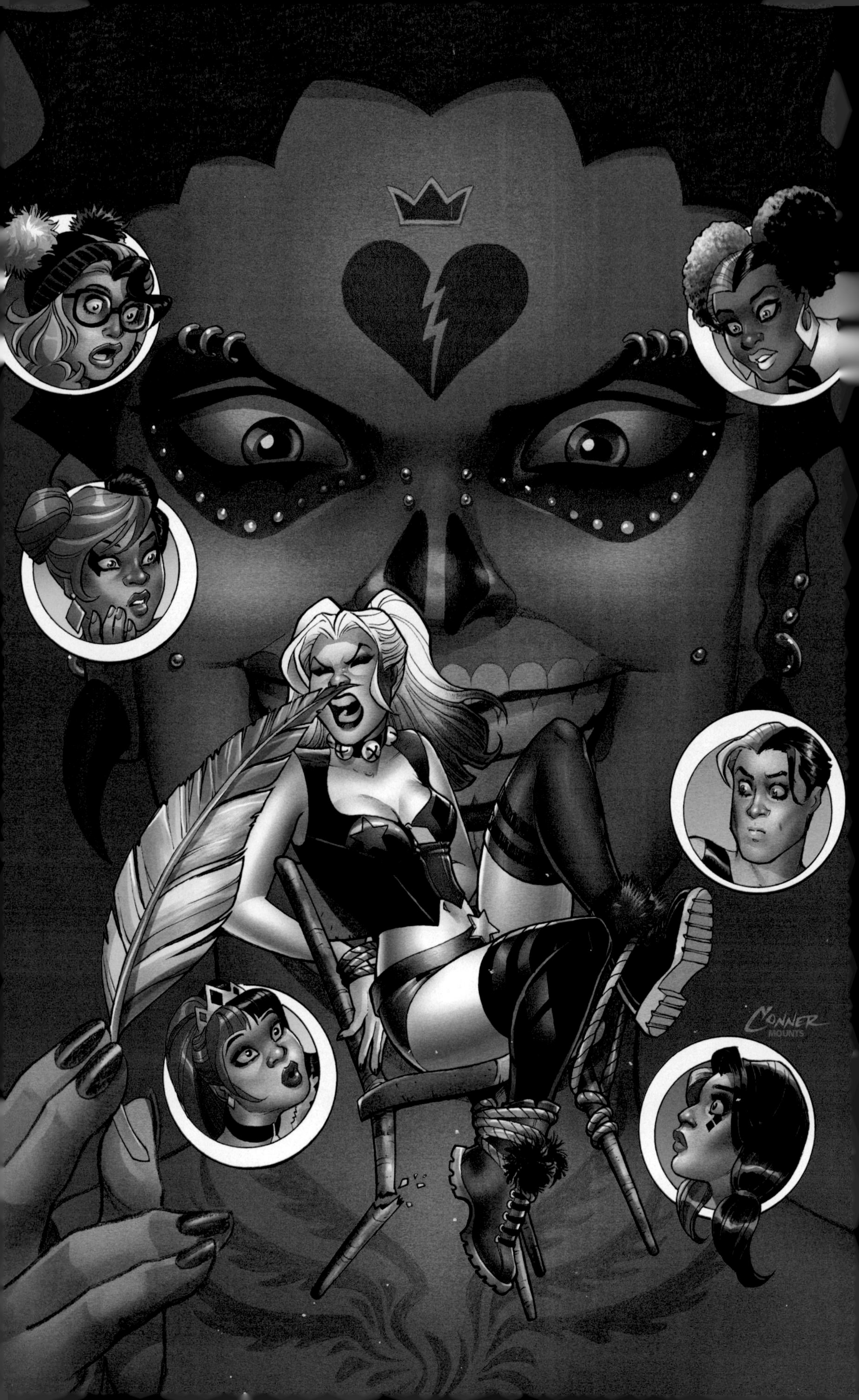
CONNER
MOUNTS

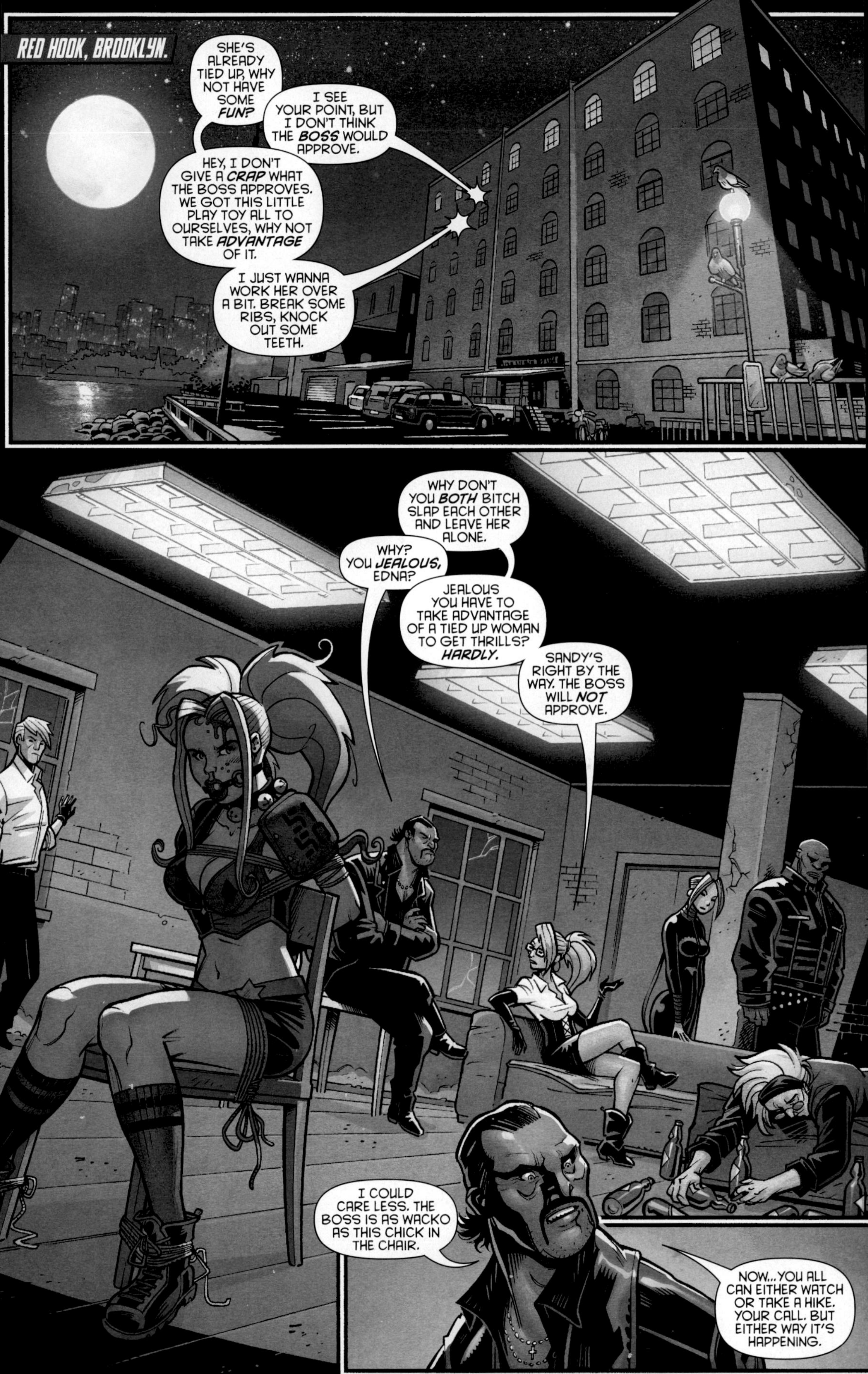
RED HOOK, BROOKLYN.
SHE'S ALREADY TIED UP, WHY NOT HAVE SOME FUN?
I SEE YOUR POINT, BUT I DON'T THINK THE BOSS WOULD APPROVE.
HEY, I DON'T GIVE A CRAP WHAT THE BOSS APPROVES. WE GOT THIS LITTLE PLAY TOY ALL TO OURSELVES, WHY NOT TAKE ADVANTAGE OF IT.
I JUST WANNA WORK HER OVER A BIT. BREAK SOME RIBS, KNOCK OUT SOME TEETH.
WHY DON'T YOU BOTH BITCH SLAP EACH OTHER AND LEAVE HER ALONE.
WHY? YOU JEALOUS, EDNA?
JEALOUS YOU HAVE TO TAKE ADVANTAGE OF A TIED UP WOMAN TO GET THRILLS? HARDLY.
SANDY'S RIGHT BY THE WAY. THE BOSS WILL NOT APPROVE.
I COULD CARE LESS. THE BOSS IS AS WACKO AS THIS CHICK IN THE CHAIR.
NOW... YOU ALL CAN EITHER WATCH OR TAKE A HIKE. YOUR CALL. BUT EITHER WAY IT'S HAPPENING.

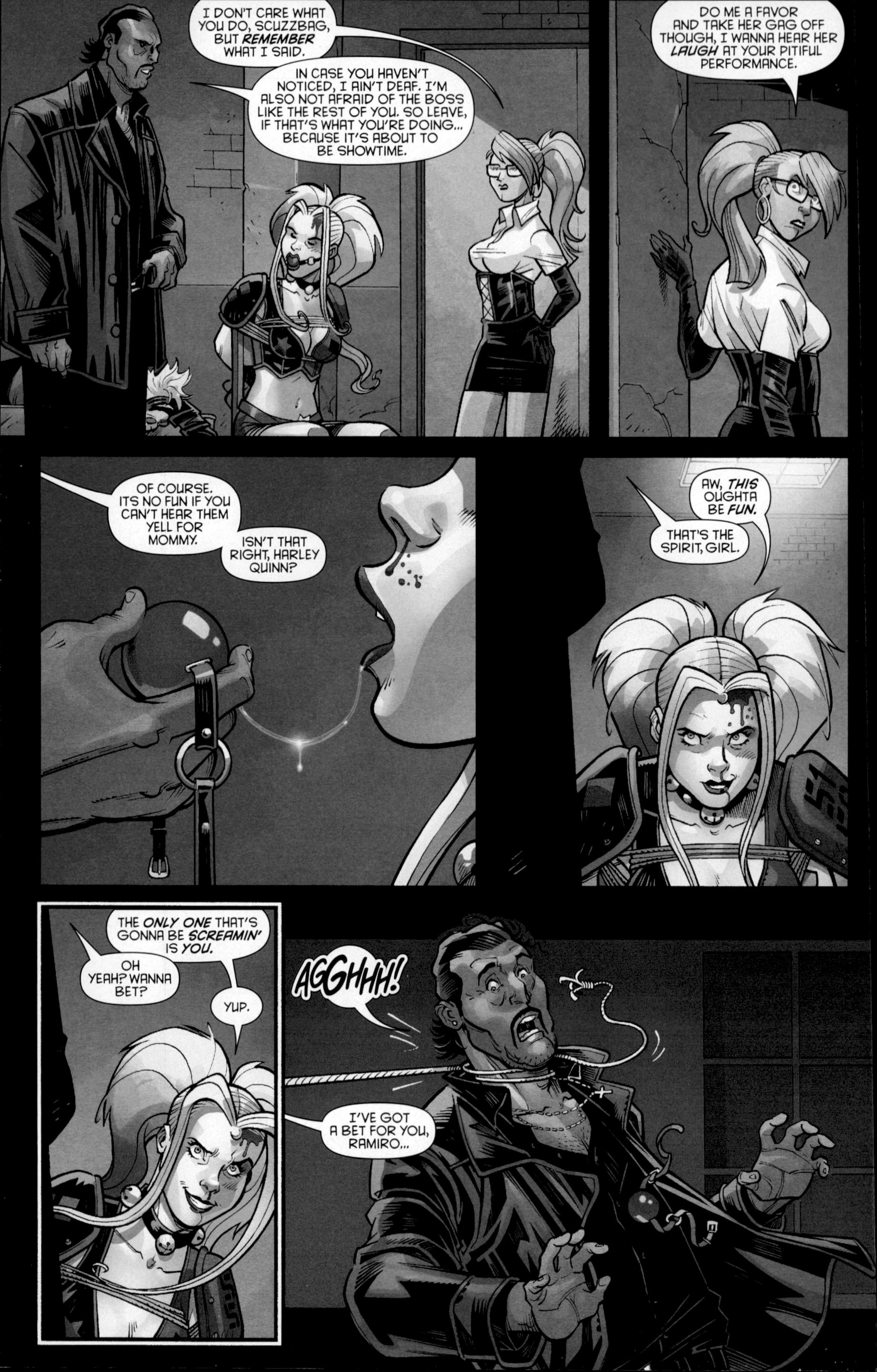

I DON'T CARE WHAT YOU DO, SCUZZBAG, BUT REMEMBER WHAT I SAID.
IN CASE YOU HAVEN'T NOTICED, I AIN'T DEAF. I'M ALSO NOT AFRAID OF THE BOSS LIKE THE REST OF YOU. SO LEAVE, IF THAT'S WHAT YOU'RE DOING... BECAUSE IT'S ABOUT TO BE SHOWTIME.
DO ME A FAVOR AND TAKE HER GAG OFF THOUGH, I WANNA HEAR HER LAUGH AT YOUR PITIFUL PERFORMANCE.
OF COURSE. ITS NO FUN IF YOU CAN'T HEAR THEM YELL FOR MOMMY.
ISN'T THAT RIGHT, HARLEY QUINN?
AW, THIS OUGHTA BE FUN.
THAT'S THE SPIRIT, GIRL.
THE ONLY ONE THAT'S GONNA BE SCREAMIN' IS YOU.
OH YEAH? WANNA BET?
YUP.
I'VE GOT A BET FOR YOU, RAMIRO...
AGGHHH!

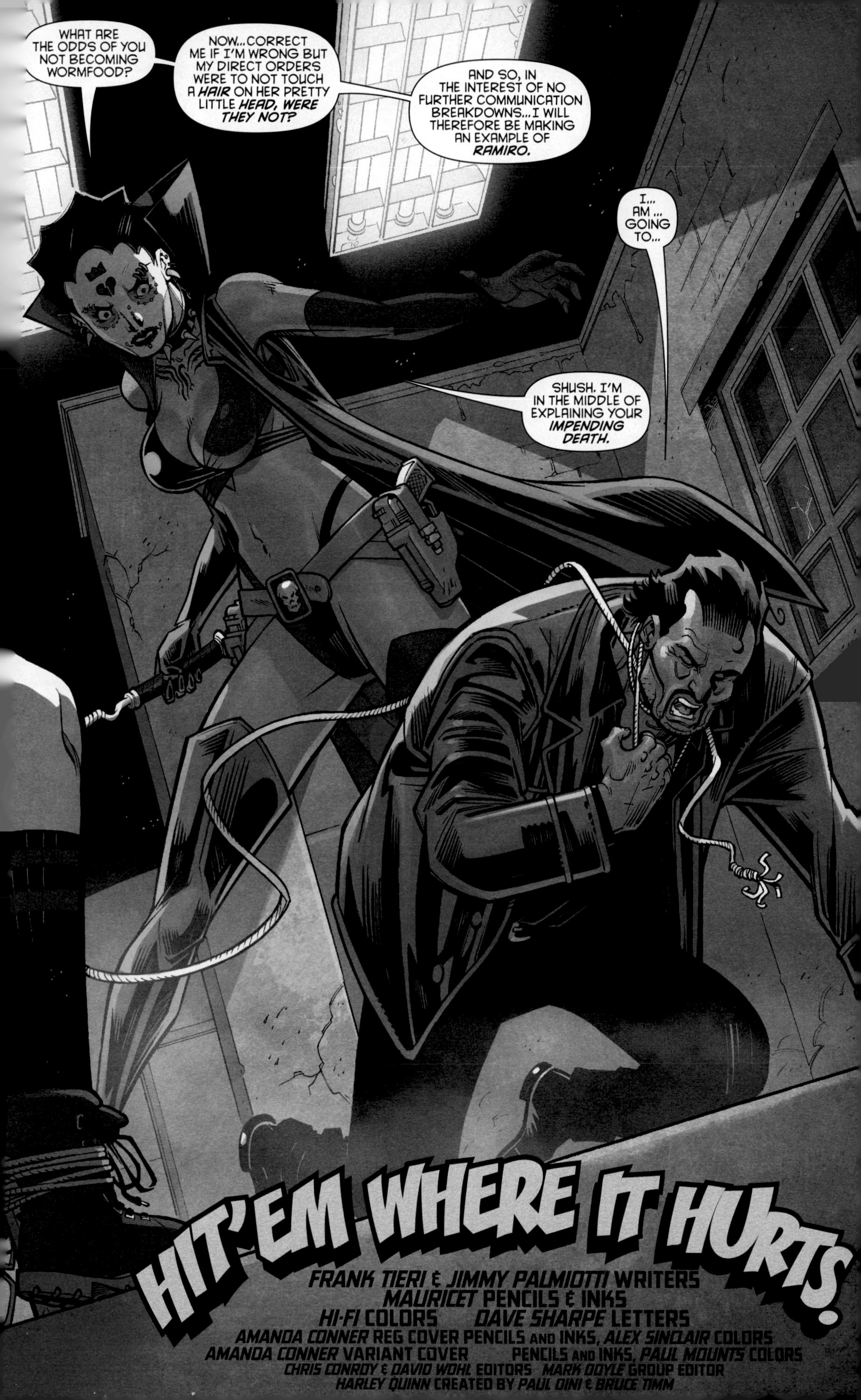
WHAT ARE THE ODDS OF YOU NOT BECOMING WORMFOOD?
NOW...CORRECT ME IF I'M WRONG BUT MY DIRECT ORDERS WERE TO NOT TOUCH A HAIR ON HER PRETTY LITTLE HEAD, WERE THEY NOT?
AND SO, IN THE INTEREST OF NO FURTHER COMMUNICATION BREAKDOWNS...I WILL THEREFORE BE MAKING AN EXAMPLE OF RAMIRO.
I... AM... GOING TO...
SHUSH. I'M IN THE MIDDLE OF EXPLAINING YOUR IMPENDING DEATH.
HIT'EM WHERE IT HURTS!
FRANK TIERI & JIMMY PALMIOTTI WRITERS
MAURICET PENCILS & INKS
HI-FI COLORS DAVE SHARPE LETTERS
AMANDA CONNER REG COVER PENCILS AND INKS, ALEX SINCLAIR COLORS
AMANDA CONNER VARIANT COVER PENCILS AND INKS, PAUL MOUNTS COLORS
CHRIS CONROY & DAVID WOHL EDITORS MARK DOYLE GROUP EDITOR
HARLEY QUINN CREATED BY PAUL DINI & BRUCE TIMM

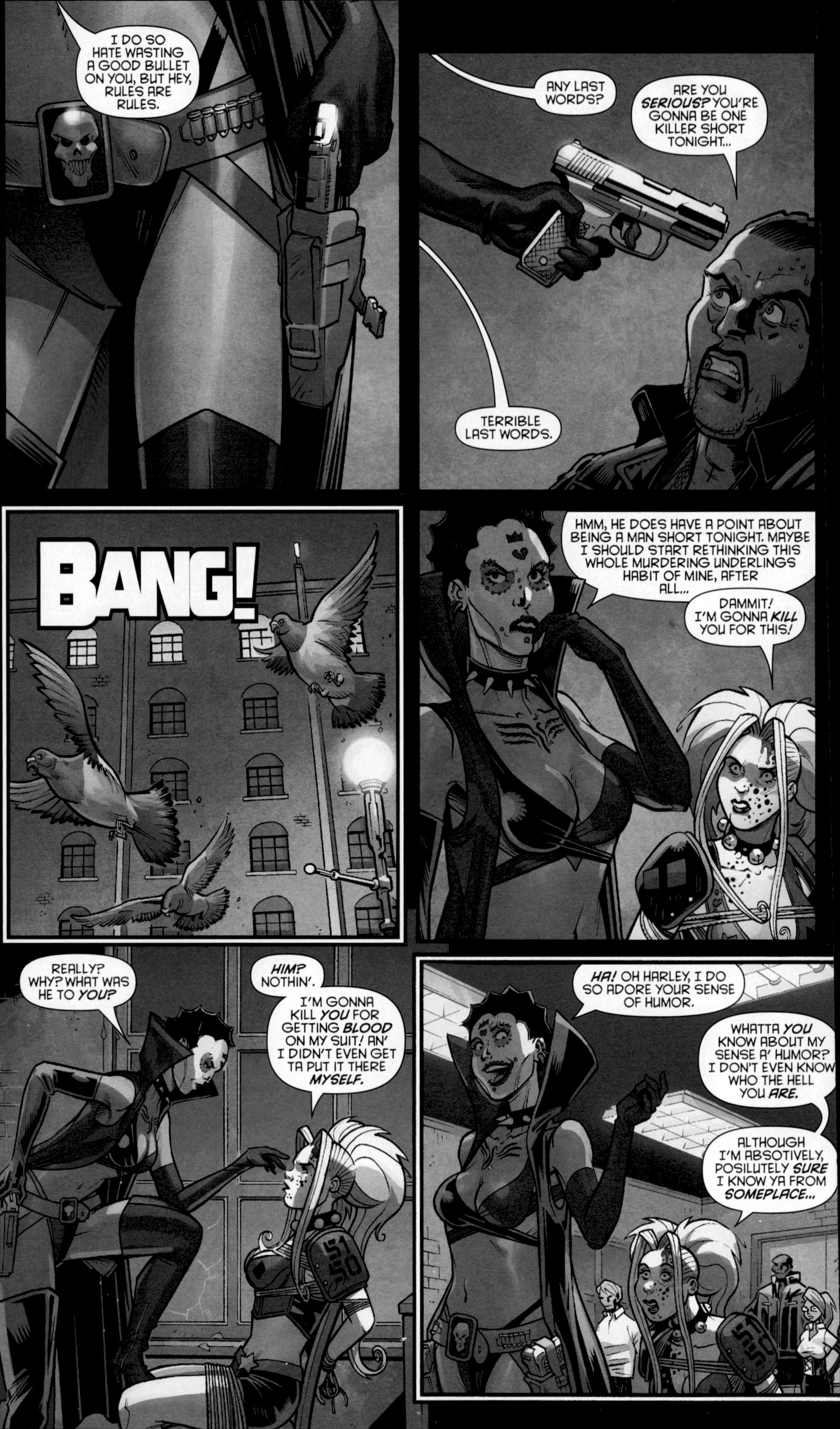
I DO SO HATE WASTING A GOOD BULLET ON YOU, BUT HEY, RULES ARE RULES.
ANY LAST WORDS?
ARE YOU SERIOUS? YOU'RE GONNA BE ONE KILLER SHORT TONIGHT...
TERRIBLE LAST WORDS.
BANG!
HMM, HE DOES HAVE A POINT ABOUT BEING A MAN SHORT TONIGHT. MAYBE I SHOULD START RETHINKING THIS WHOLE MURDERING UNDERLINGS HABIT OF MINE, AFTER ALL...
DAMMIT! I'M GONNA KILL YOU FOR THIS!
REALLY? WHY? WHAT WAS HE TO YOU?
HIM? NOTHIN'.
I'M GONNA KILL YOU FOR GETTING BLOOD ON MY SUIT! AN' I DIDN'T EVEN GET TA PUT IT THERE MYSELF.
HA! OH HARLEY, I DO SO ADORE YOUR SENSE OF HUMOR.
WHATTA YOU KNOW ABOUT MY SENSE A' HUMOR? I DON'T EVEN KNOW WHO THE HELL YOU ARE.
ALTHOUGH I'M ABSOTIVELY, POSILUTELY SURE I KNOW YA FROM SOMEPLACE...

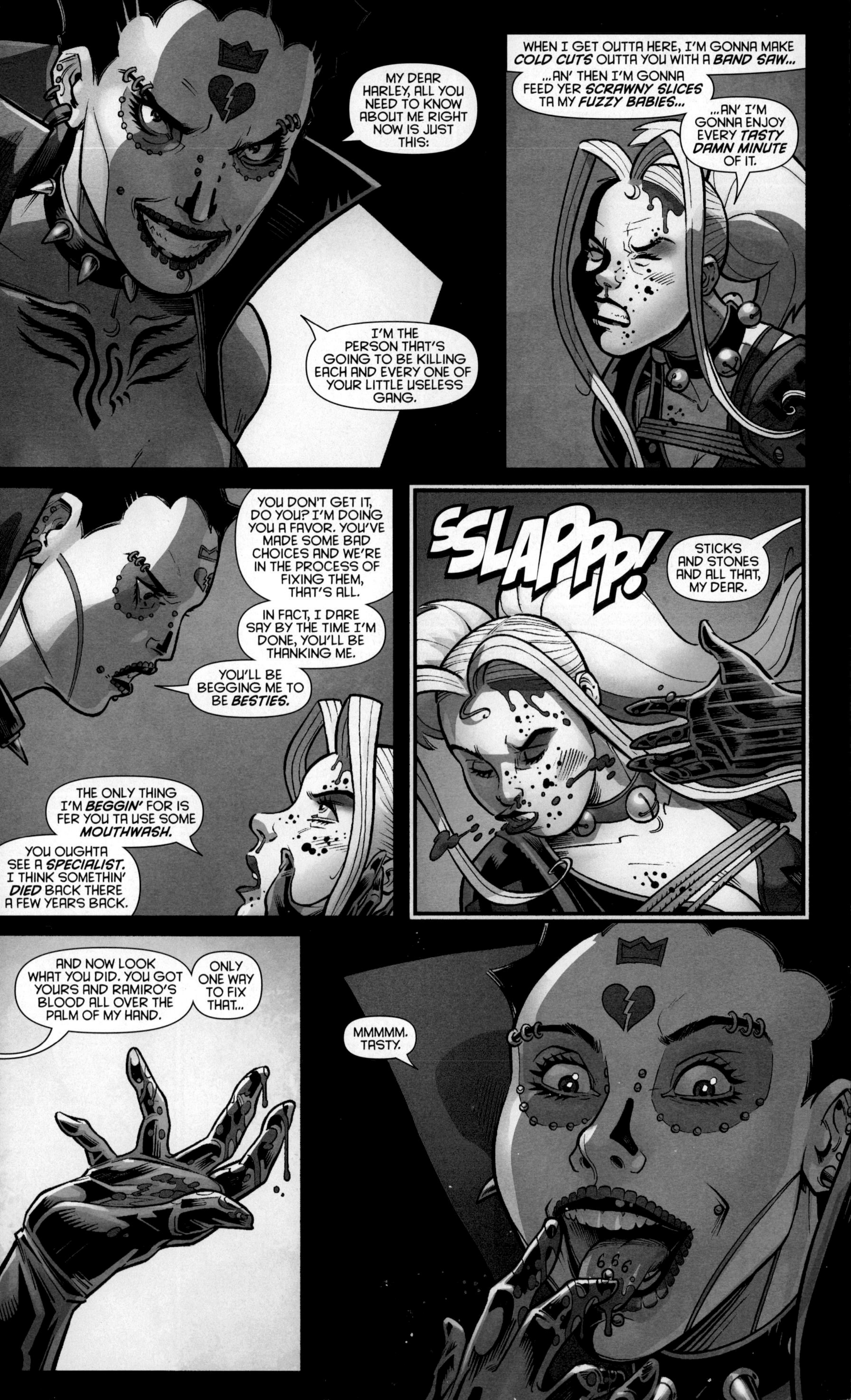
MY DEAR HARLEY, ALL YOU NEED TO KNOW ABOUT ME RIGHT NOW IS JUST THIS:
I'M THE PERSON THAT'S GOING TO BE KILLING EACH AND EVERY ONE OF YOUR LITTLE USELESS GANG.
WHEN I GET OUTTA HERE, I'M GONNA MAKE *COLD CUTS* OUTTA YOU WITH A *BAND SAW*...
...AN' THEN I'M GONNA FEED YER *SCRAWNY SLICES* TA MY *FUZZY BABIES*...
...AN' I'M GONNA ENJOY EVERY *TASTY DAMN MINUTE* OF IT.
YOU DON'T GET IT, DO YOU? I'M DOING YOU A FAVOR. YOU'VE MADE SOME BAD CHOICES AND WE'RE IN THE PROCESS OF FIXING THEM, THAT'S ALL.
IN FACT, I DARE SAY BY THE TIME I'M DONE, YOU'LL BE THANKING ME.
YOU'LL BE BEGGING ME TO BE *BESTIES.*
THE ONLY THING I'M *BEGGIN'* FOR IS FER YOU TA USE SOME *MOUTHWASH.*
YOU OUGHTA SEE A *SPECIALIST.* I THINK SOMETHIN' *DIED* BACK THERE A FEW YEARS BACK.
SSLAPPP!
STICKS AND STONES AND ALL THAT, MY DEAR.
AND NOW LOOK WHAT YOU DID. YOU GOT YOURS AND RAMIRO'S BLOOD ALL OVER THE PALM OF MY HAND.
ONLY ONE WAY TO FIX THAT...
MMMMM. TASTY.
666

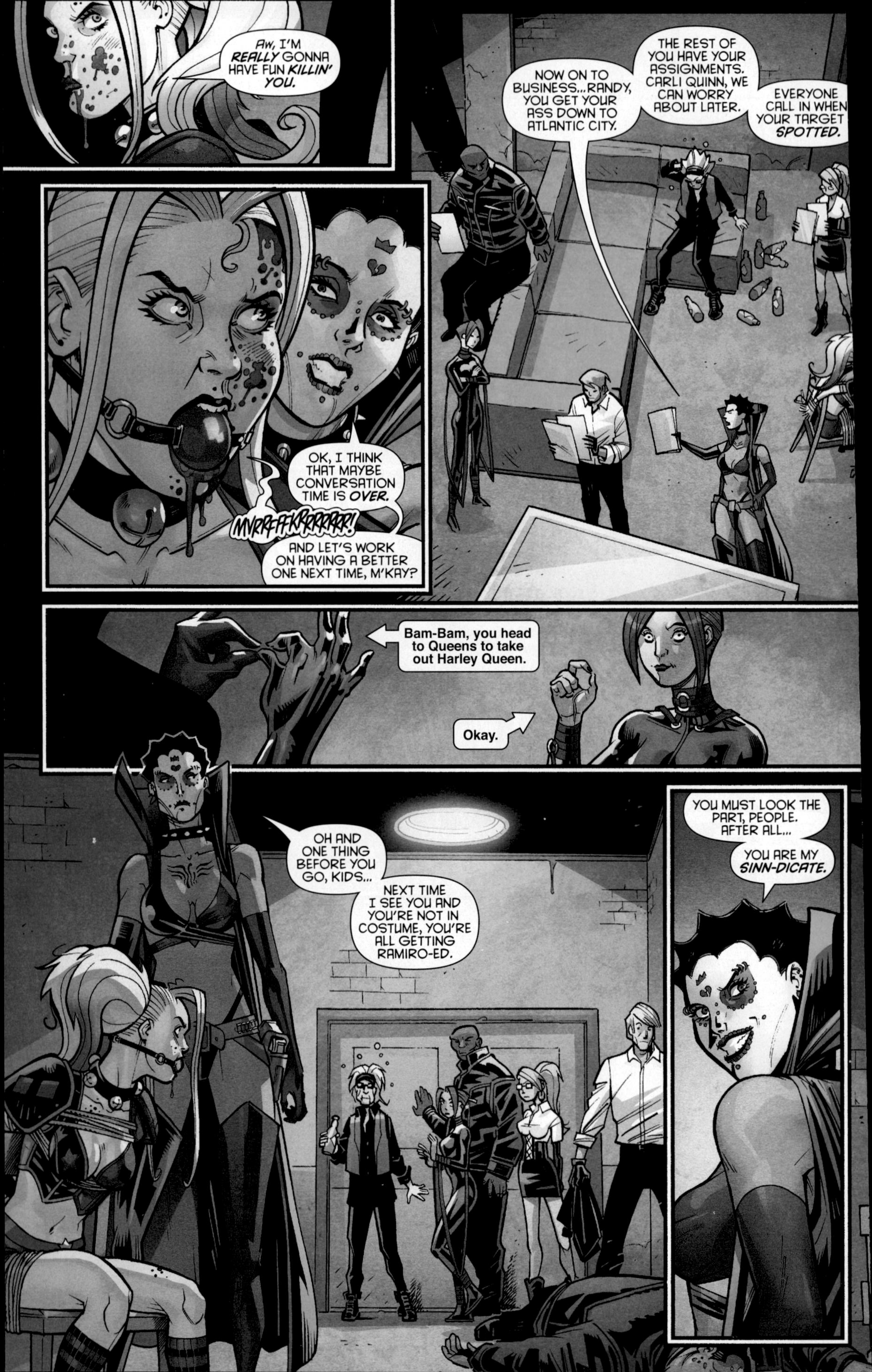
AW, I'M REALLY GONNA HAVE FUN KILLIN' YOU.
NOW ON TO BUSINESS... RANDY, YOU GET YOUR ASS DOWN TO ATLANTIC CITY.
THE REST OF YOU HAVE YOUR ASSIGNMENTS. CARLI QUINN, WE CAN WORRY ABOUT LATER.
EVERYONE CALL IN WHEN YOUR TARGET SPOTTED.
OK, I THINK THAT MAYBE CONVERSATION TIME IS OVER.
MVRRFFFKRRRRRR!
AND LET'S WORK ON HAVING A BETTER ONE NEXT TIME, M'KAY?
Bam-Bam, you head to Queens to take out Harley Queen.
Okay.
OH AND ONE THING BEFORE YOU GO, KIDS...
NEXT TIME I SEE YOU AND YOU'RE NOT IN COSTUME, YOU'RE ALL GETTING RAMIRO-ED.
YOU MUST LOOK THE PART, PEOPLE. AFTER ALL...
YOU ARE MY SINN-DICATE.

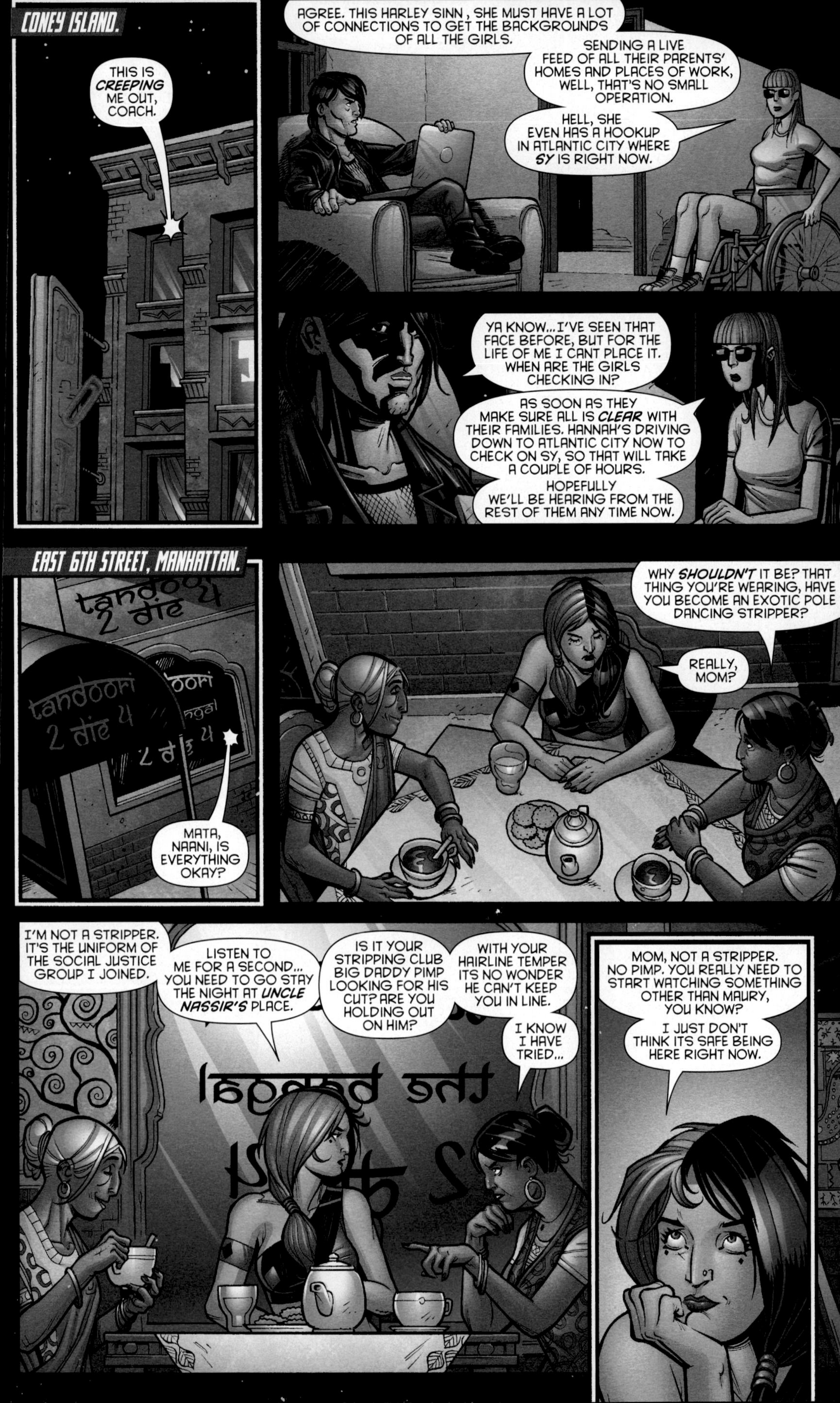

CONEY ISLAND.
THIS IS CREEPING ME OUT, COACH.
AGREE. THIS HARLEY SINN , SHE MUST HAVE A LOT OF CONNECTIONS TO GET THE BACKGROUNDS OF ALL THE GIRLS.
SENDING A LIVE FEED OF ALL THEIR PARENTS' HOMES AND PLACES OF WORK, WELL, THAT'S NO SMALL OPERATION.
HELL, SHE EVEN HAS A HOOKUP IN ATLANTIC CITY WHERE SY IS RIGHT NOW.
YA KNOW...I'VE SEEN THAT FACE BEFORE, BUT FOR THE LIFE OF ME I CANT PLACE IT. WHEN ARE THE GIRLS CHECKING IN?
AS SOON AS THEY MAKE SURE ALL IS CLEAR WITH THEIR FAMILIES. HANNAH'S DRIVING DOWN TO ATLANTIC CITY NOW TO CHECK ON SY, SO THAT WILL TAKE A COUPLE OF HOURS.
HOPEFULLY WE'LL BE HEARING FROM THE REST OF THEM ANY TIME NOW.
EAST 6TH STREET, MANHATTAN.
tandoori 2 die 4
MATA, NAANI, IS EVERYTHING OKAY?
WHY SHOULDN'T IT BE? THAT THING YOU'RE WEARING, HAVE YOU BECOME AN EXOTIC POLE DANCING STRIPPER?
REALLY, MOM?
I'M NOT A STRIPPER. IT'S THE UNIFORM OF THE SOCIAL JUSTICE GROUP I JOINED.
LISTEN TO ME FOR A SECOND... YOU NEED TO GO STAY THE NIGHT AT UNCLE NASSIR'S PLACE.
IS IT YOUR STRIPPING CLUB BIG DADDY PIMP LOOKING FOR HIS CUT? ARE YOU HOLDING OUT ON HIM?
WITH YOUR HAIRLINE TEMPER ITS NO WONDER HE CAN'T KEEP YOU IN LINE.
I KNOW I HAVE TRIED...
MOM, NOT A STRIPPER. NO PIMP. YOU REALLY NEED TO START WATCHING SOMETHING OTHER THAN MAURY, YOU KNOW?
I JUST DON'T THINK ITS SAFE BEING HERE RIGHT NOW.

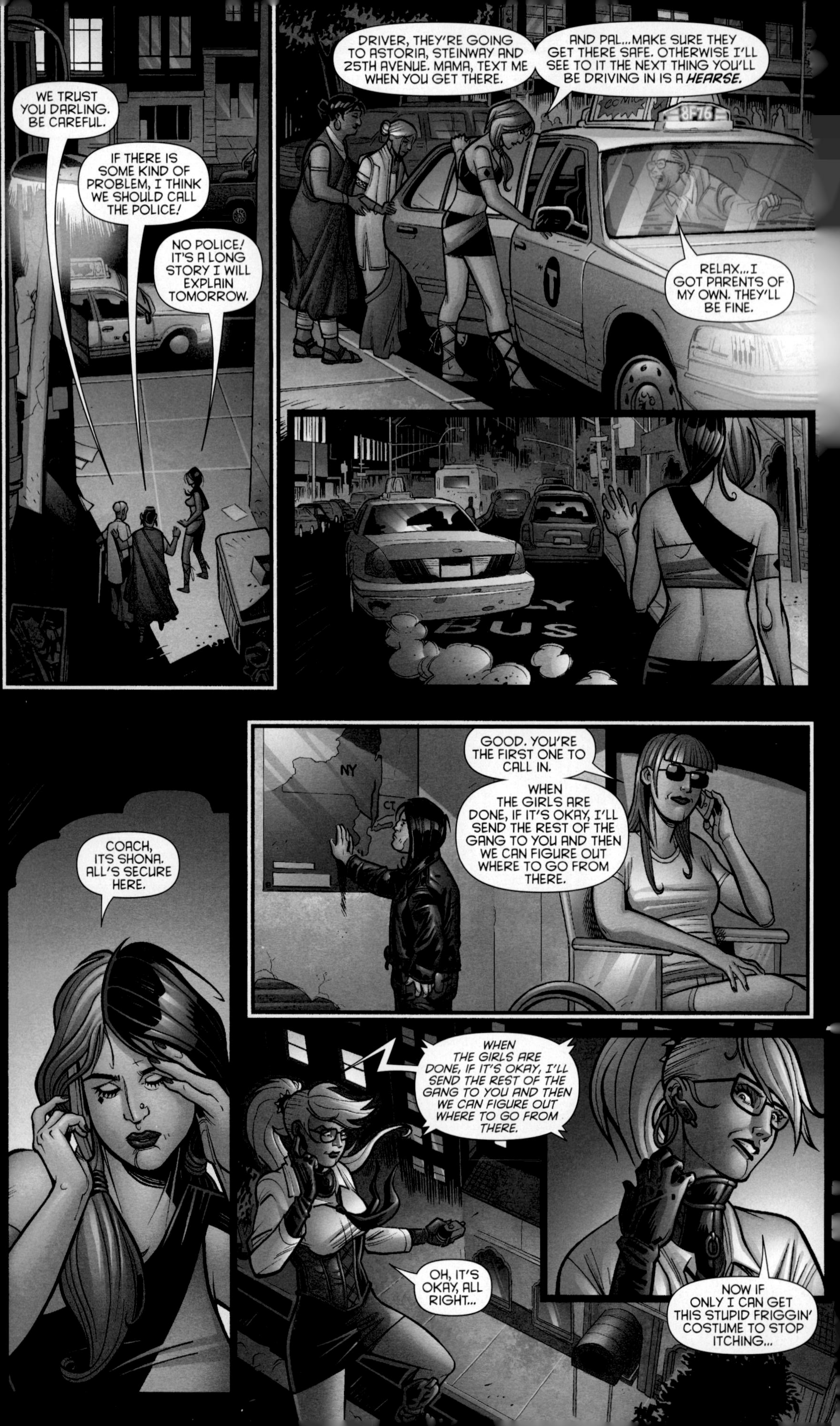
WE TRUST YOU DARLING. BE CAREFUL.
IF THERE IS SOME KIND OF PROBLEM, I THINK WE SHOULD CALL THE POLICE!
NO POLICE! IT'S A LONG STORY I WILL EXPLAIN TOMORROW.
DRIVER, THEY'RE GOING TO ASTORIA, STEINWAY AND 25TH AVENUE. MAMA, TEXT ME WHEN YOU GET THERE.
AND PAL...MAKE SURE THEY GET THERE SAFE. OTHERWISE I'LL SEE TO IT THE NEXT THING YOU'LL BE DRIVING IN IS A *HEARSE.*
RELAX...I GOT PARENTS OF MY OWN. THEY'LL BE FINE.
8F76
BUS
COACH, ITS SHONA. ALL'S SECURE HERE.
NY
CT
GOOD. YOU'RE THE FIRST ONE TO CALL IN.
WHEN THE GIRLS ARE DONE, IF IT'S OKAY, I'LL SEND THE REST OF THE GANG TO YOU AND THEN WE CAN FIGURE OUT WHERE TO GO FROM THERE.
WHEN THE GIRLS ARE DONE, IF IT'S OKAY, I'LL SEND THE REST OF THE GANG TO YOU AND THEN WE CAN FIGURE OUT WHERE TO GO FROM THERE.
OH, IT'S OKAY, ALL RIGHT...
NOW IF ONLY I CAN GET THIS STUPID FRIGGIN' COSTUME TO STOP ITCHING...

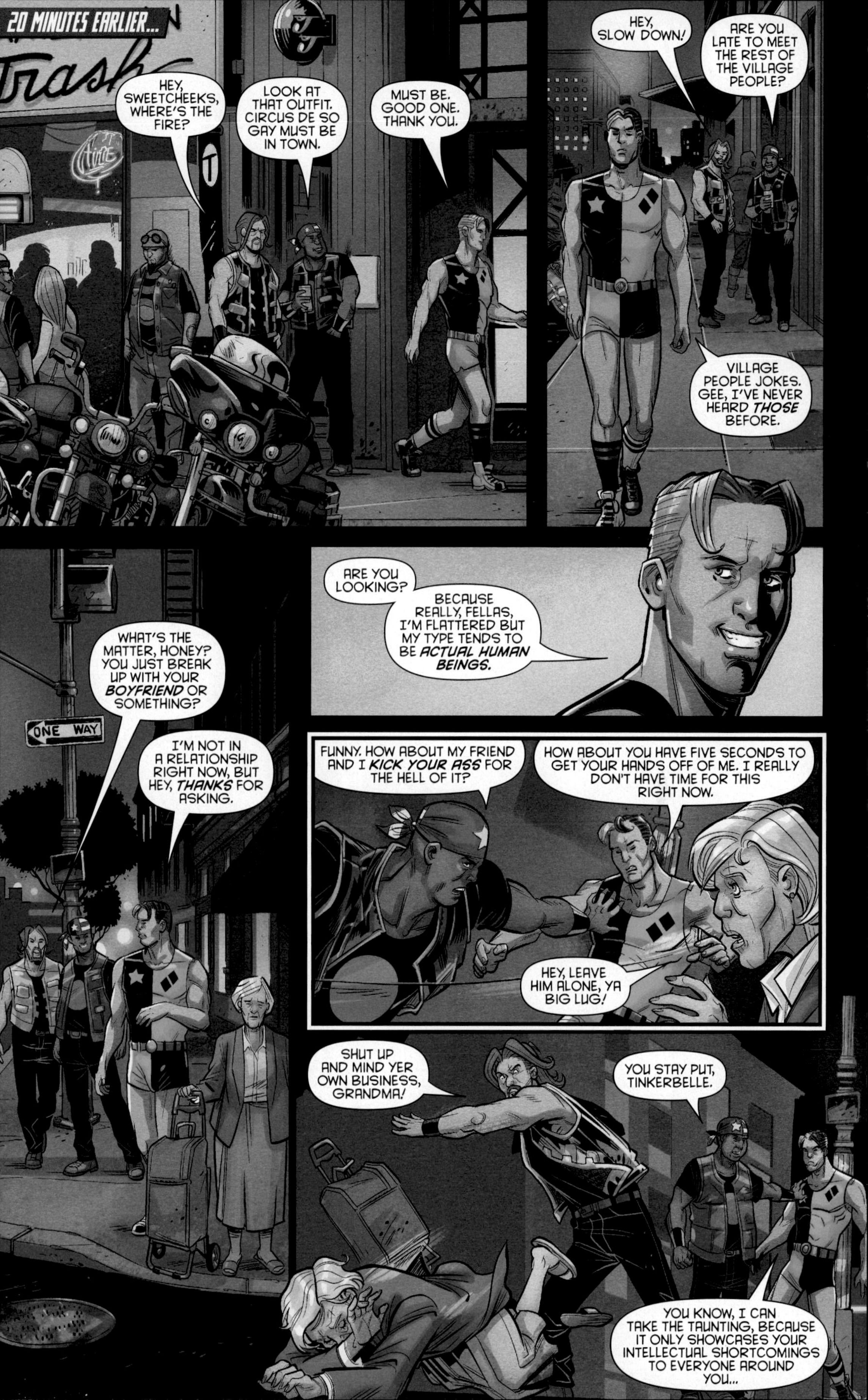
20 MINUTES EARLIER...
HEY, SWEETCHEEKS, WHERE'S THE FIRE?
LOOK AT THAT OUTFIT. CIRCUS DE SO GAY MUST BE IN TOWN.
MUST BE. GOOD ONE. THANK YOU.
HEY, SLOW DOWN!
ARE YOU LATE TO MEET THE REST OF THE VILLAGE PEOPLE?
VILLAGE PEOPLE JOKES. GEE, I'VE NEVER HEARD THOSE BEFORE.
WHAT'S THE MATTER, HONEY? YOU JUST BREAK UP WITH YOUR BOYFRIEND OR SOMETHING?
ONE WAY
I'M NOT IN A RELATIONSHIP RIGHT NOW, BUT HEY, THANKS FOR ASKING.
ARE YOU LOOKING?
BECAUSE REALLY, FELLAS, I'M FLATTERED BUT MY TYPE TENDS TO BE ACTUAL HUMAN BEINGS.
FUNNY. HOW ABOUT MY FRIEND AND I KICK YOUR ASS FOR THE HELL OF IT?
HOW ABOUT YOU HAVE FIVE SECONDS TO GET YOUR HANDS OFF OF ME. I REALLY DON'T HAVE TIME FOR THIS RIGHT NOW.
HEY, LEAVE HIM ALONE, YA BIG LUG!
SHUT UP AND MIND YER OWN BUSINESS, GRANDMA!
YOU STAY PUT, TINKERBELLE.
YOU KNOW, I CAN TAKE THE TAUNTING, BECAUSE IT ONLY SHOWCASES YOUR INTELLECTUAL SHORTCOMINGS TO EVERYONE AROUND YOU...

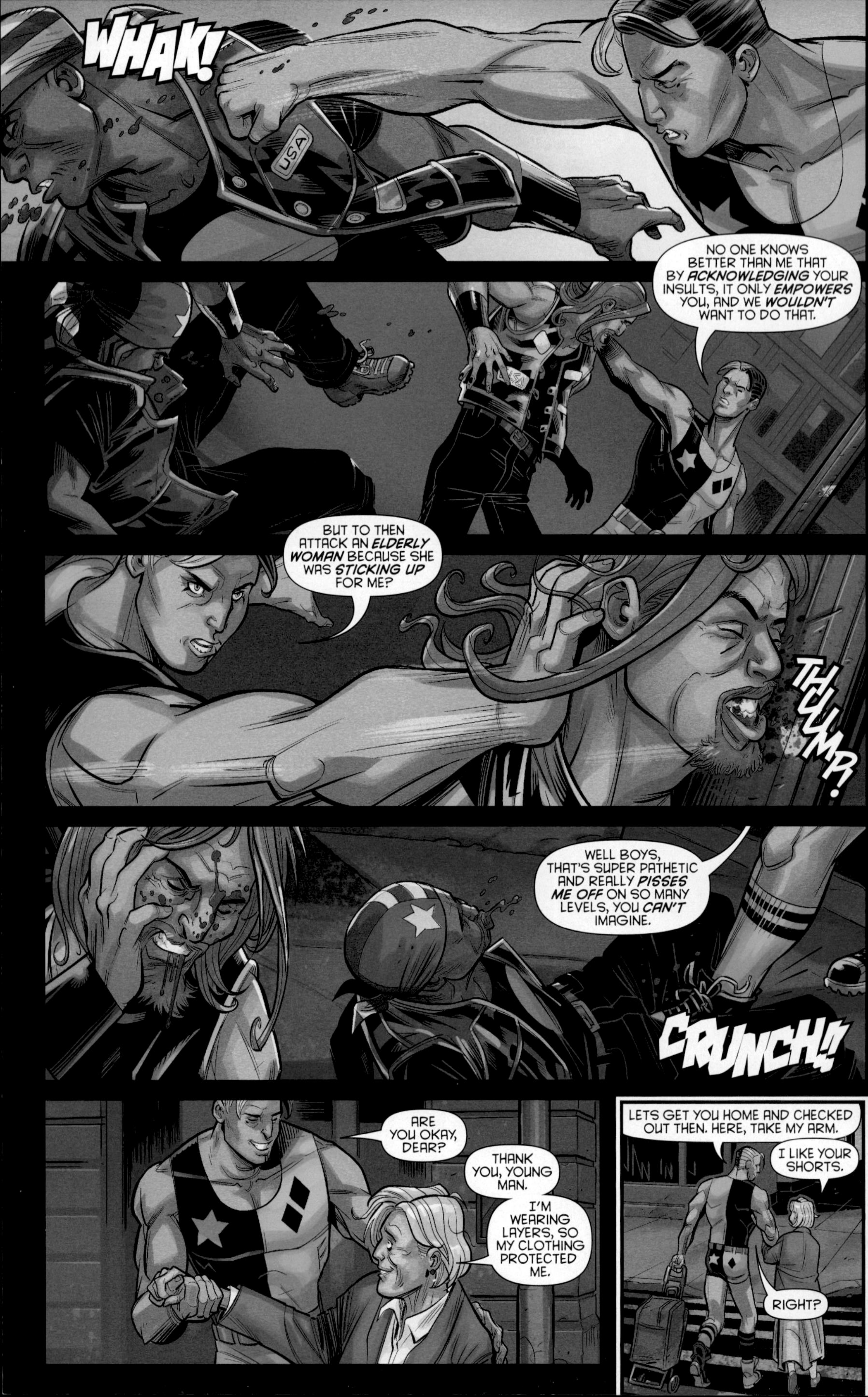
WHAK!
NO ONE KNOWS BETTER THAN ME THAT BY ACKNOWLEDGING YOUR INSULTS, IT ONLY EMPOWERS YOU, AND WE WOULDN'T WANT TO DO THAT.
BUT TO THEN ATTACK AN ELDERLY WOMAN BECAUSE SHE WAS STICKING UP FOR ME?
THUMP!
WELL BOYS, THAT'S SUPER PATHETIC AND REALLY PISSES ME OFF ON SO MANY LEVELS, YOU CAN'T IMAGINE.
CRUNCH!!
ARE YOU OKAY, DEAR?
THANK YOU, YOUNG MAN.
I'M WEARING LAYERS, SO MY CLOTHING PROTECTED ME.
LETS GET YOU HOME AND CHECKED OUT THEN. HERE, TAKE MY ARM.
I LIKE YOUR SHORTS.
RIGHT?

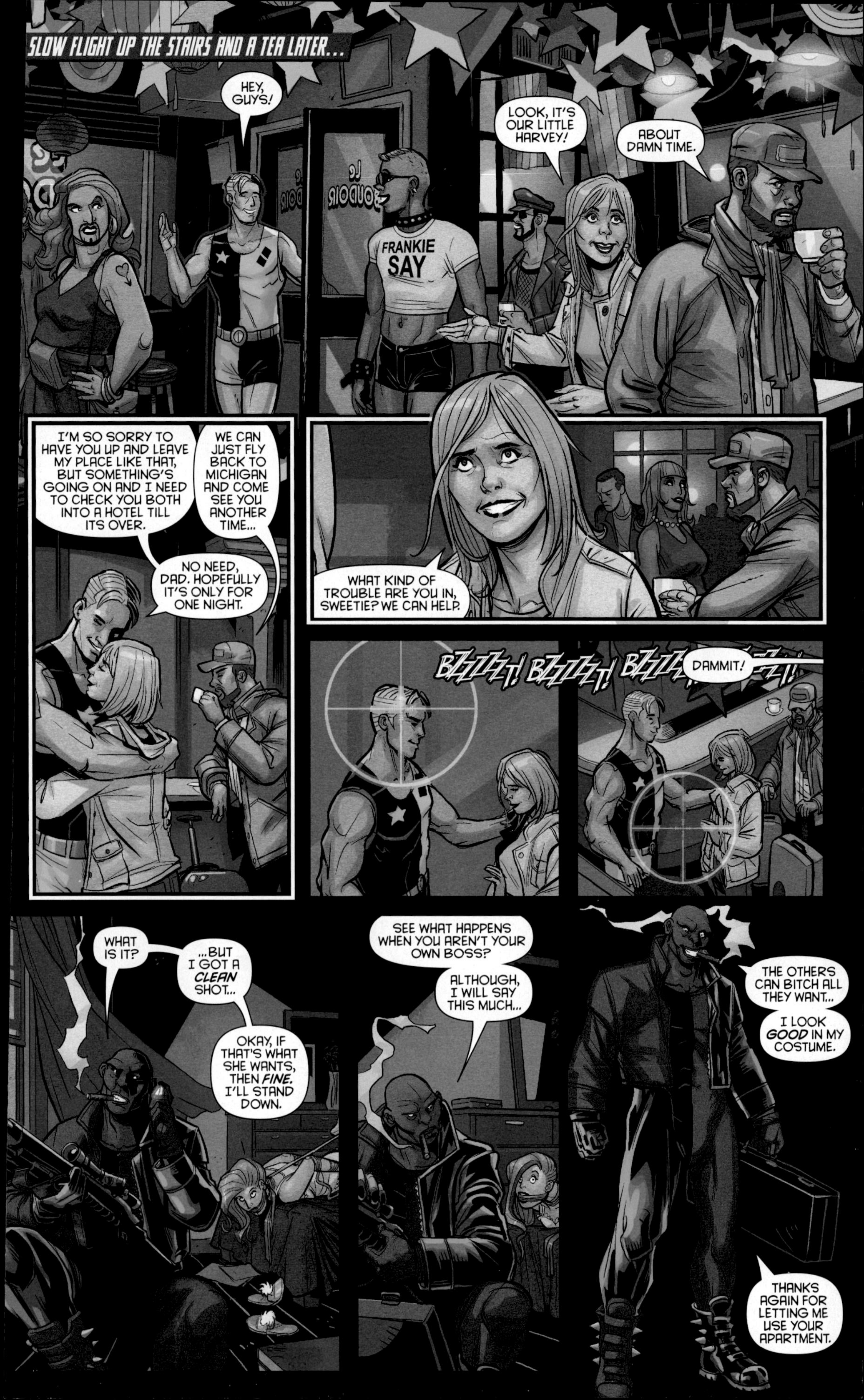
SLOW FLIGHT UP THE STAIRS AND A TEA LATER...
HEY, GUYS!
FRANKIE SAY
LOOK, IT'S OUR LITTLE HARVEY!
ABOUT DAMN TIME.
I'M SO SORRY TO HAVE YOU UP AND LEAVE MY PLACE LIKE THAT, BUT SOMETHING'S GOING ON AND I NEED TO CHECK YOU BOTH INTO A HOTEL TILL ITS OVER.
WE CAN JUST FLY BACK TO MICHIGAN AND COME SEE YOU ANOTHER TIME...
NO NEED, DAD. HOPEFULLY IT'S ONLY FOR ONE NIGHT.
WHAT KIND OF TROUBLE ARE YOU IN, SWEETIE? WE CAN HELP.
BZZZZT! BZZZZT!
DAMMIT!
WHAT IS IT?
...BUT I GOT A CLEAN SHOT...
OKAY, IF THAT'S WHAT SHE WANTS, THEN FINE. I'LL STAND DOWN.
SEE WHAT HAPPENS WHEN YOU AREN'T YOUR OWN BOSS?
ALTHOUGH, I WILL SAY THIS MUCH...
THE OTHERS CAN BITCH ALL THEY WANT...
I LOOK GOOD IN MY COSTUME.
THANKS AGAIN FOR LETTING ME USE YOUR APARTMENT.

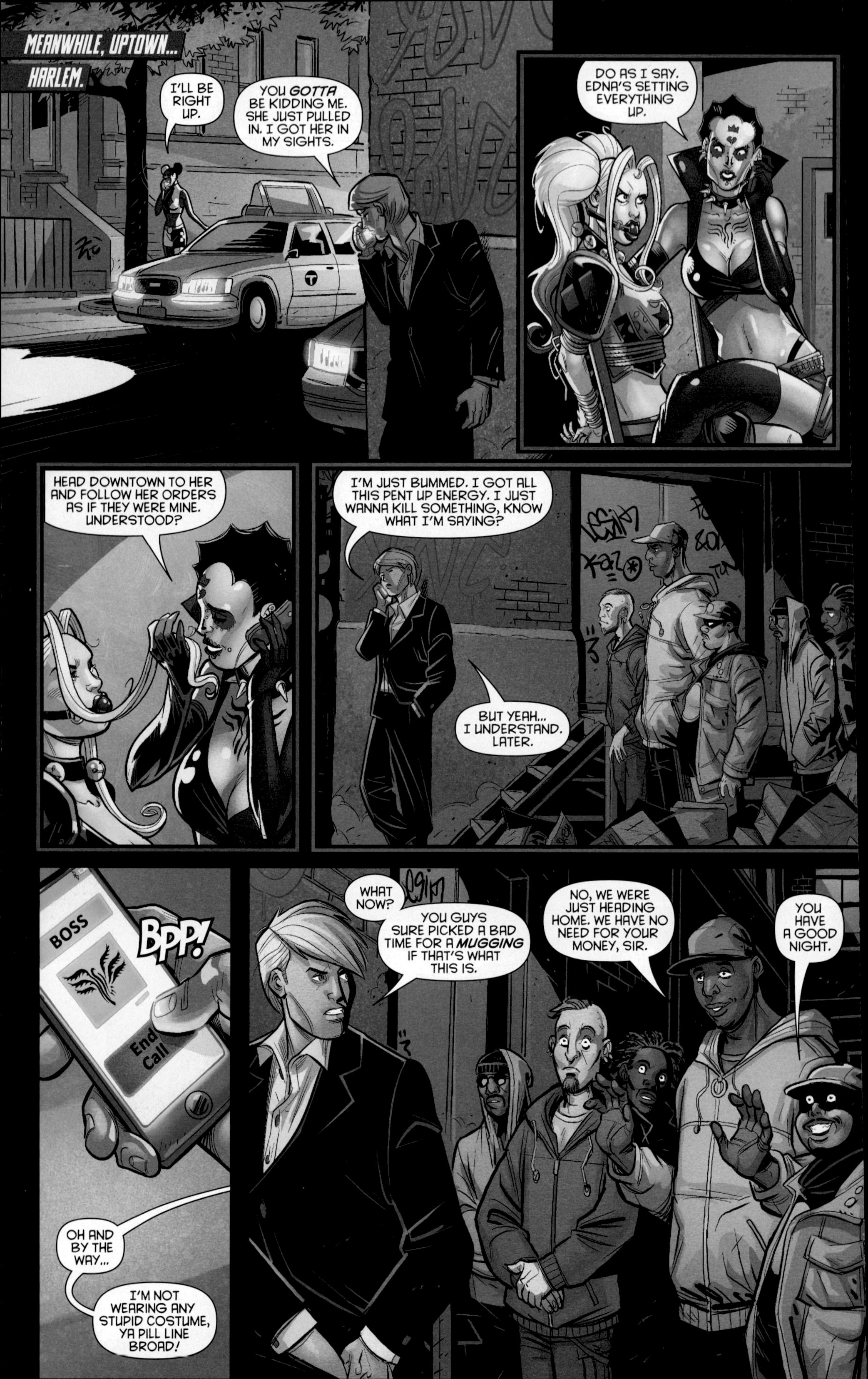
MEANWHILE, UPTOWN...
HARLEM.
I'LL BE RIGHT UP.
YOU GOTTA BE KIDDING ME. SHE JUST PULLED IN. I GOT HER IN MY SIGHTS.
DO AS I SAY. EDNA'S SETTING EVERYTHING UP.
HEAD DOWNTOWN TO HER AND FOLLOW HER ORDERS AS IF THEY WERE MINE. UNDERSTOOD?
I'M JUST BUMMED. I GOT ALL THIS PENT UP ENERGY. I JUST WANNA KILL SOMETHING, KNOW WHAT I'M SAYING?
BUT YEAH... I UNDERSTAND. LATER.
BOSS
End Call
BPP!
OH AND BY THE WAY...
I'M NOT WEARING ANY STUPID COSTUME, YA PILL LINE BROAD!
WHAT NOW?
YOU GUYS SURE PICKED A BAD TIME FOR A MUGGING IF THAT'S WHAT THIS IS.
NO, WE WERE JUST HEADING HOME. WE HAVE NO NEED FOR YOUR MONEY, SIR.
YOU HAVE A GOOD NIGHT.

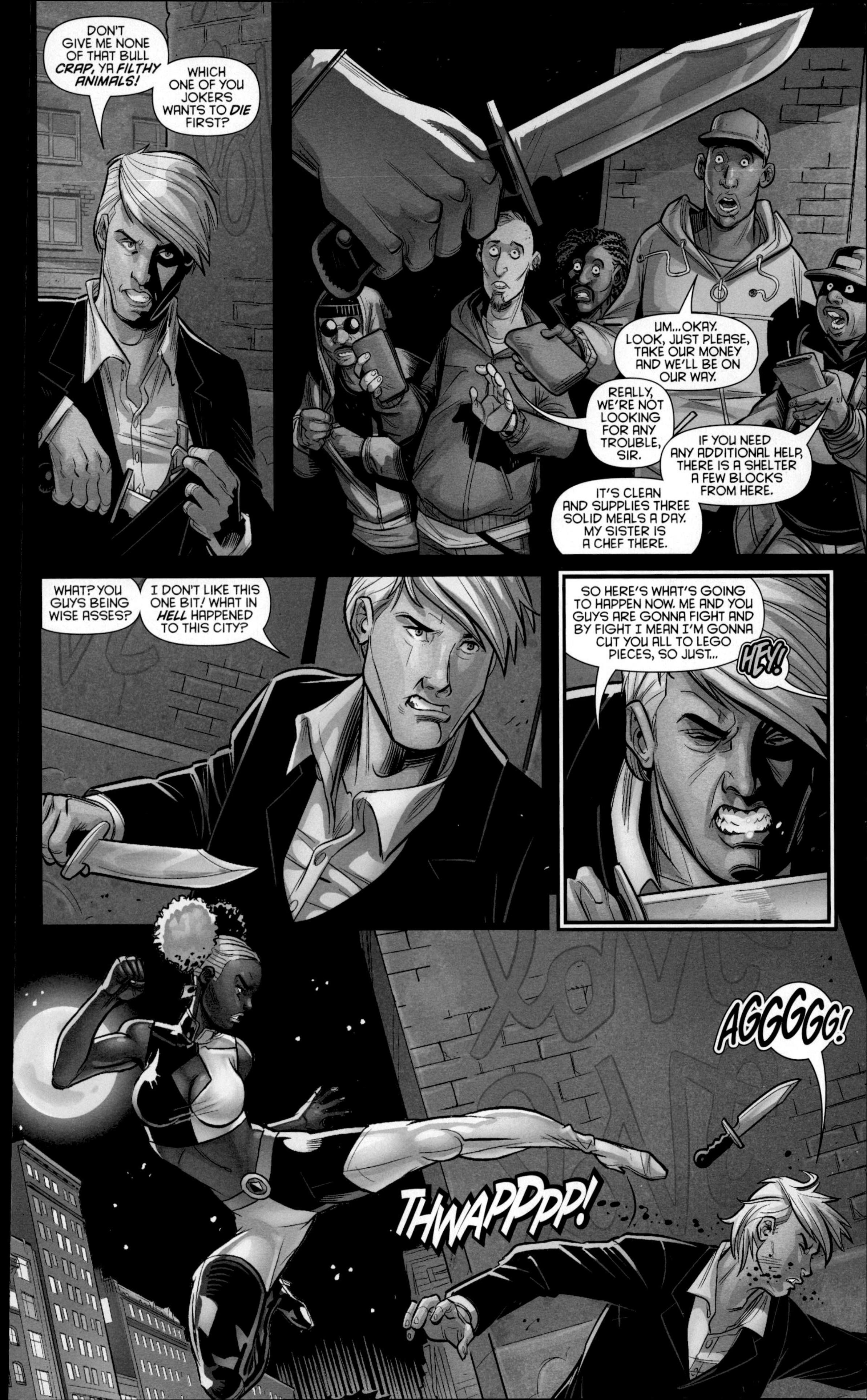
DON'T GIVE ME NONE OF THAT BULL CRAP, YA FILTHY ANIMALS!
WHICH ONE OF YOU JOKERS WANTS TO DIE FIRST?
UM...OKAY. LOOK, JUST PLEASE, TAKE OUR MONEY AND WE'LL BE ON OUR WAY.
REALLY, WE'RE NOT LOOKING FOR ANY TROUBLE, SIR.
IF YOU NEED ANY ADDITIONAL HELP, THERE IS A SHELTER A FEW BLOCKS FROM HERE.
IT'S CLEAN AND SUPPLIES THREE SOLID MEALS A DAY. MY SISTER IS A CHEF THERE.
WHAT? YOU GUYS BEING WISE ASSES?
I DON'T LIKE THIS ONE BIT! WHAT IN HELL HAPPENED TO THIS CITY?
SO HERE'S WHAT'S GOING TO HAPPEN NOW. ME AND YOU GUYS ARE GONNA FIGHT AND BY FIGHT I MEAN I'M GONNA CUT YOU ALL TO LEGO PIECES, SO JUST...
HEY!!
AGGGGG!
THWAPPPP!

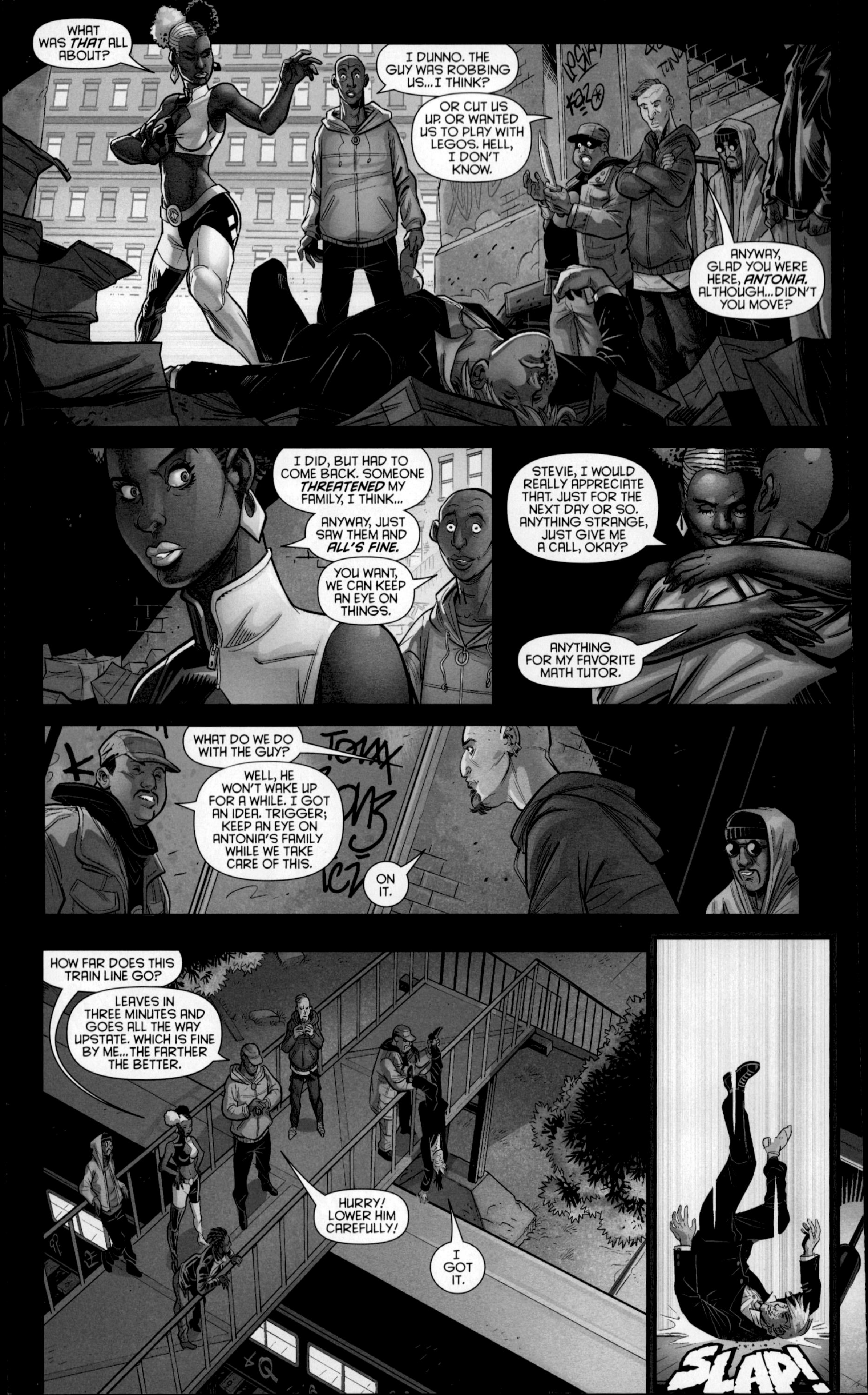
WHAT WAS THAT ALL ABOUT?
I DUNNO. THE GUY WAS ROBBING US...I THINK?
OR CUT US UP. OR WANTED US TO PLAY WITH LEGOS. HELL, I DON'T KNOW.
ANYWAY, GLAD YOU WERE HERE, ANTONIA. ALTHOUGH...DIDN'T YOU MOVE?
I DID, BUT HAD TO COME BACK. SOMEONE THREATENED MY FAMILY, I THINK...
ANYWAY, JUST SAW THEM AND ALL'S FINE.
YOU WANT, WE CAN KEEP AN EYE ON THINGS.
STEVIE, I WOULD REALLY APPRECIATE THAT. JUST FOR THE NEXT DAY OR SO. ANYTHING STRANGE, JUST GIVE ME A CALL, OKAY?
ANYTHING FOR MY FAVORITE MATH TUTOR.
WHAT DO WE DO WITH THE GUY?
WELL, HE WON'T WAKE UP FOR A WHILE. I GOT AN IDEA. TRIGGER; KEEP AN EYE ON ANTONIA'S FAMILY WHILE WE TAKE CARE OF THIS.
ON IT.
HOW FAR DOES THIS TRAIN LINE GO?
LEAVES IN THREE MINUTES AND GOES ALL THE WAY UPSTATE. WHICH IS FINE BY ME...THE FARTHER THE BETTER.
HURRY! LOWER HIM CAREFULLY!
I GOT IT.
SLAP!

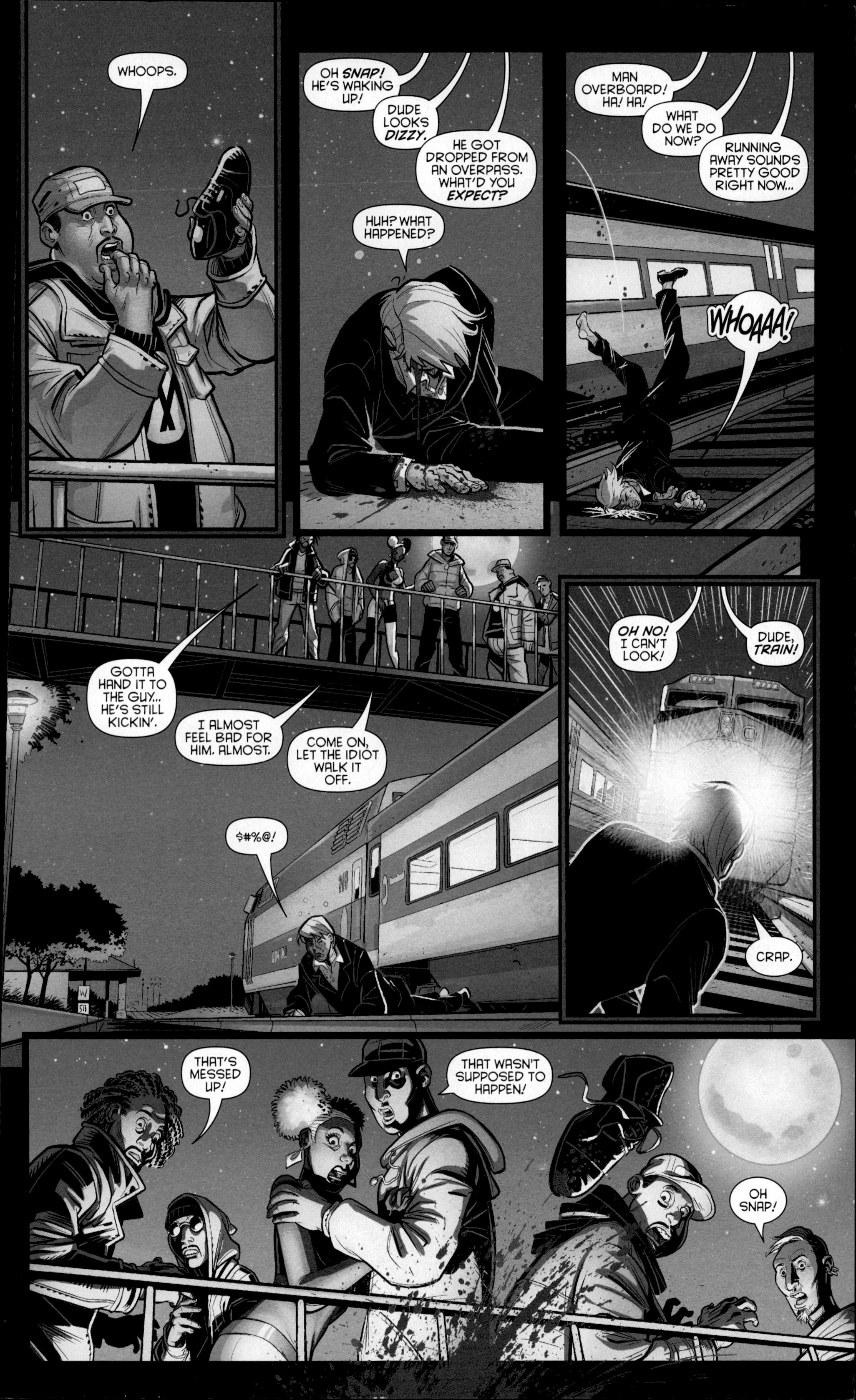
WHOOPS.
OH SNAP! HE'S WAKING UP!
DUDE LOOKS DIZZY.
HE GOT DROPPED FROM AN OVERPASS. WHAT'D YOU EXPECT?
HUH? WHAT HAPPENED?
MAN OVERBOARD! HA! HA!
WHAT DO WE DO NOW?
RUNNING AWAY SOUNDS PRETTY GOOD RIGHT NOW...
WHOAAA!
GOTTA HAND IT TO THE GUY... HE'S STILL KICKIN'.
I ALMOST FEEL BAD FOR HIM. ALMOST.
COME ON, LET THE IDIOT WALK IT OFF.
$#%@!
OH NO! I CAN'T LOOK!
DUDE, TRAIN!
CRAP.
THAT'S MESSED UP!
THAT WASN'T SUPPOSED TO HAPPEN!
OH SNAP!

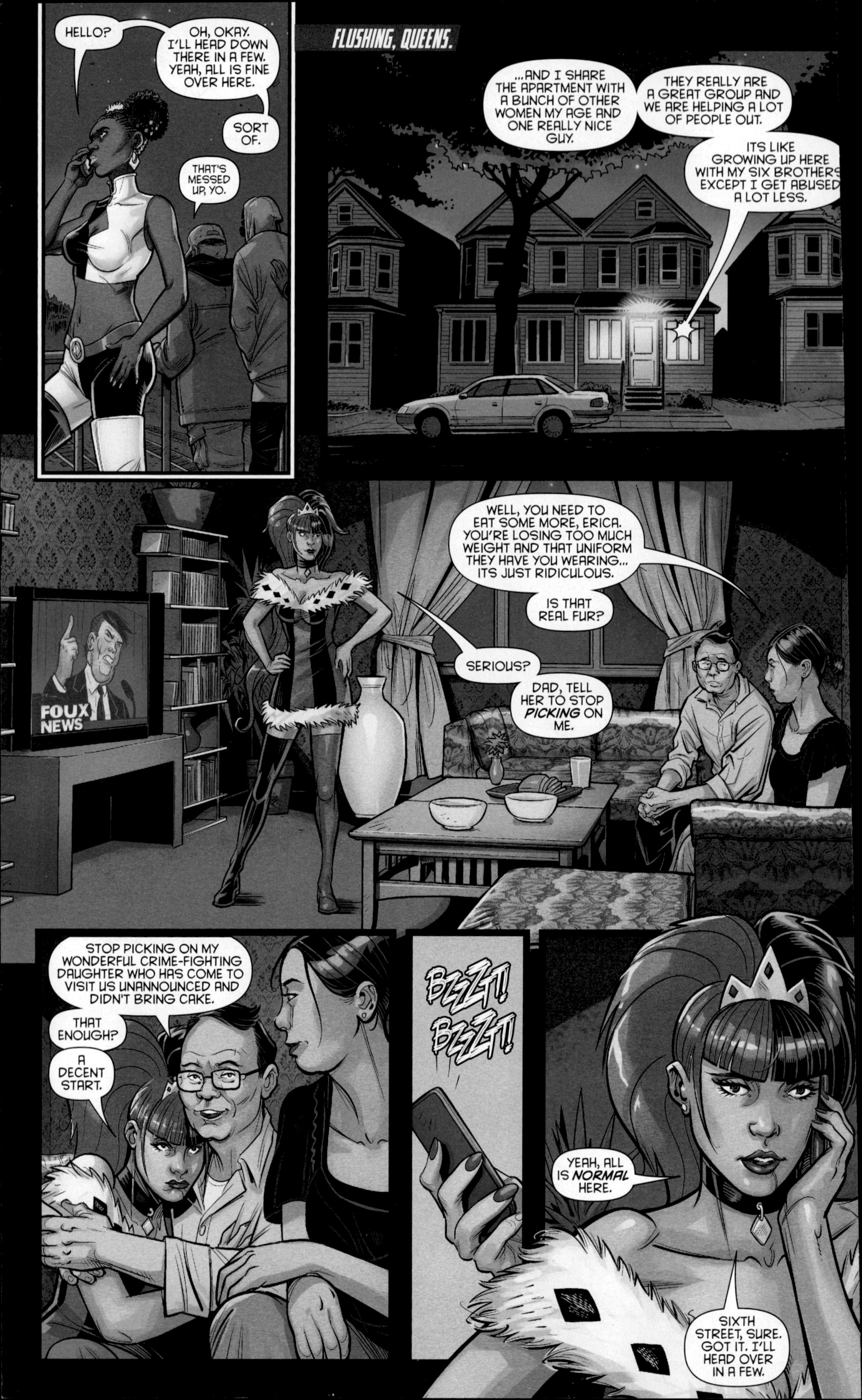
HELLO?
OH, OKAY. I'LL HEAD DOWN THERE IN A FEW. YEAH, ALL IS FINE OVER HERE.
SORT OF.
THAT'S MESSED UP, YO.
FLUSHING, QUEENS.
...AND I SHARE THE APARTMENT WITH A BUNCH OF OTHER WOMEN MY AGE AND ONE REALLY NICE GUY.
THEY REALLY ARE A GREAT GROUP AND WE ARE HELPING A LOT OF PEOPLE OUT.
ITS LIKE GROWING UP HERE WITH MY SIX BROTHERS EXCEPT I GET ABUSED A LOT LESS.
WELL, YOU NEED TO EAT SOME MORE, ERICA. YOU'RE LOSING TOO MUCH WEIGHT AND THAT UNIFORM THEY HAVE YOU WEARING... ITS JUST RIDICULOUS.
IS THAT REAL FUR?
SERIOUS?
DAD, TELL HER TO STOP PICKING ON ME.
FOUX NEWS
STOP PICKING ON MY WONDERFUL CRIME-FIGHTING DAUGHTER WHO HAS COME TO VISIT US UNANNOUNCED AND DIDN'T BRING CAKE.
THAT ENOUGH?
A DECENT START.
BZZZT! BZZZT!
YEAH, ALL IS NORMAL HERE.
SIXTH STREET, SURE. GOT IT. I'LL HEAD OVER IN A FEW.

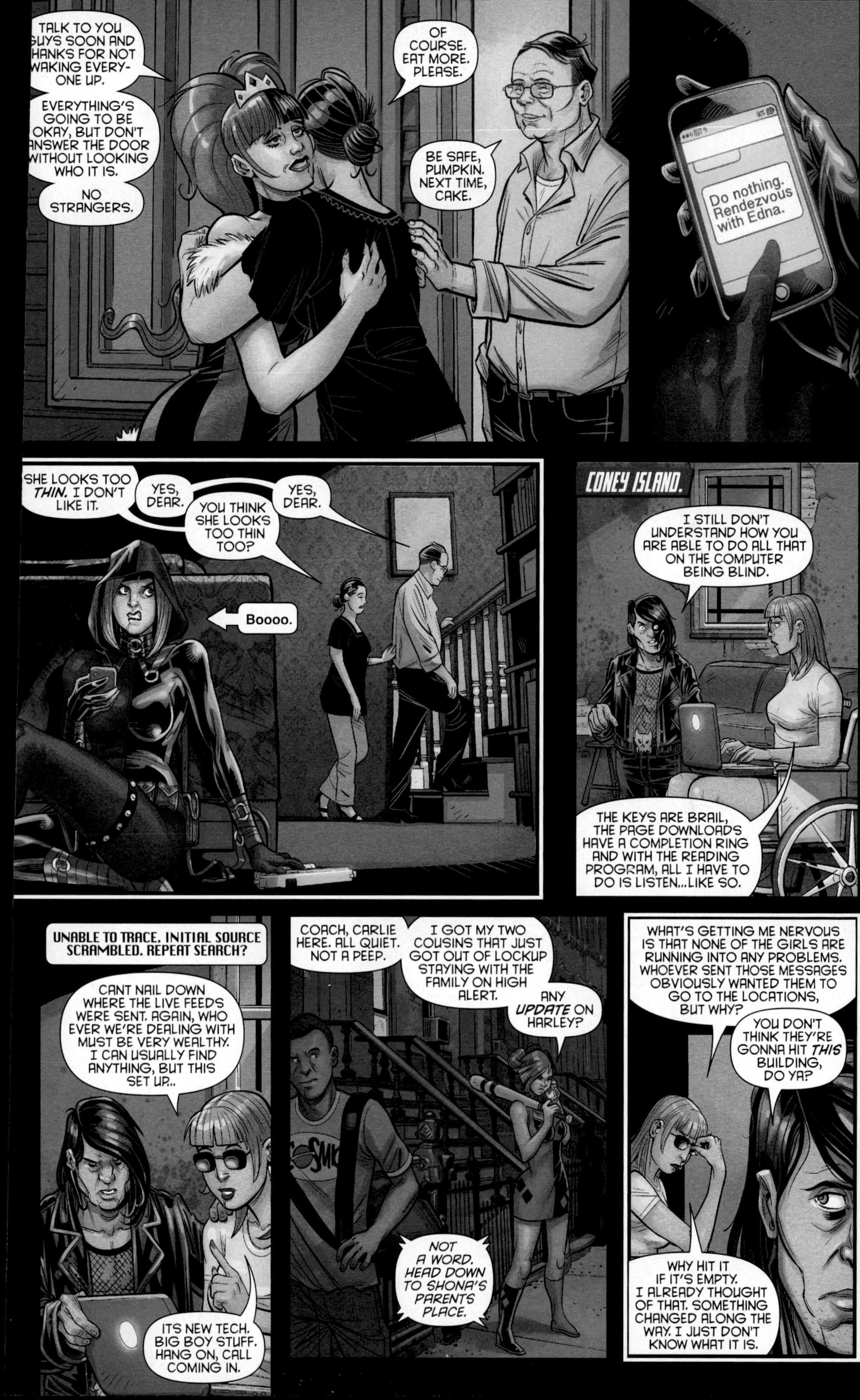
TALK TO YOU GUYS SOON AND THANKS FOR NOT WAKING EVERY-ONE UP.
EVERYTHING'S GOING TO BE OKAY, BUT DON'T ANSWER THE DOOR WITHOUT LOOKING WHO IT IS.
NO STRANGERS.
OF COURSE. EAT MORE. PLEASE.
BE SAFE, PUMPKIN. NEXT TIME, CAKE.
Do nothing. Rendezvous with Edna.
SHE LOOKS TOO THIN. I DON'T LIKE IT.
YES, DEAR.
YOU THINK SHE LOOKS TOO THIN TOO?
YES, DEAR.
Boooo.
CONEY ISLAND.
I STILL DON'T UNDERSTAND HOW YOU ARE ABLE TO DO ALL THAT ON THE COMPUTER BEING BLIND.
THE KEYS ARE BRAIL, THE PAGE DOWNLOADS HAVE A COMPLETION RING AND WITH THE READING PROGRAM, ALL I HAVE TO DO IS LISTEN...LIKE SO.
UNABLE TO TRACE. INITIAL SOURCE SCRAMBLED. REPEAT SEARCH?
CANT NAIL DOWN WHERE THE LIVE FEEDS WERE SENT. AGAIN, WHO EVER WE'RE DEALING WITH MUST BE VERY WEALTHY. I CAN USUALLY FIND ANYTHING, BUT THIS SET UP...
ITS NEW TECH. BIG BOY STUFF. HANG ON, CALL COMING IN.
COACH, CARLIE HERE. ALL QUIET. NOT A PEEP.
I GOT MY TWO COUSINS THAT JUST GOT OUT OF LOCKUP STAYING WITH THE FAMILY ON HIGH ALERT.
ANY UPDATE ON HARLEY?
NOT A WORD. HEAD DOWN TO SHONA'S PARENTS PLACE.
WHAT'S GETTING ME NERVOUS IS THAT NONE OF THE GIRLS ARE RUNNING INTO ANY PROBLEMS. WHOEVER SENT THOSE MESSAGES OBVIOUSLY WANTED THEM TO GO TO THE LOCATIONS, BUT WHY?
YOU DON'T THINK THEY'RE GONNA HIT THIS BUILDING, DO YA?
WHY HIT IT IF IT'S EMPTY. I ALREADY THOUGHT OF THAT. SOMETHING CHANGED ALONG THE WAY. I JUST DON'T KNOW WHAT IT IS.

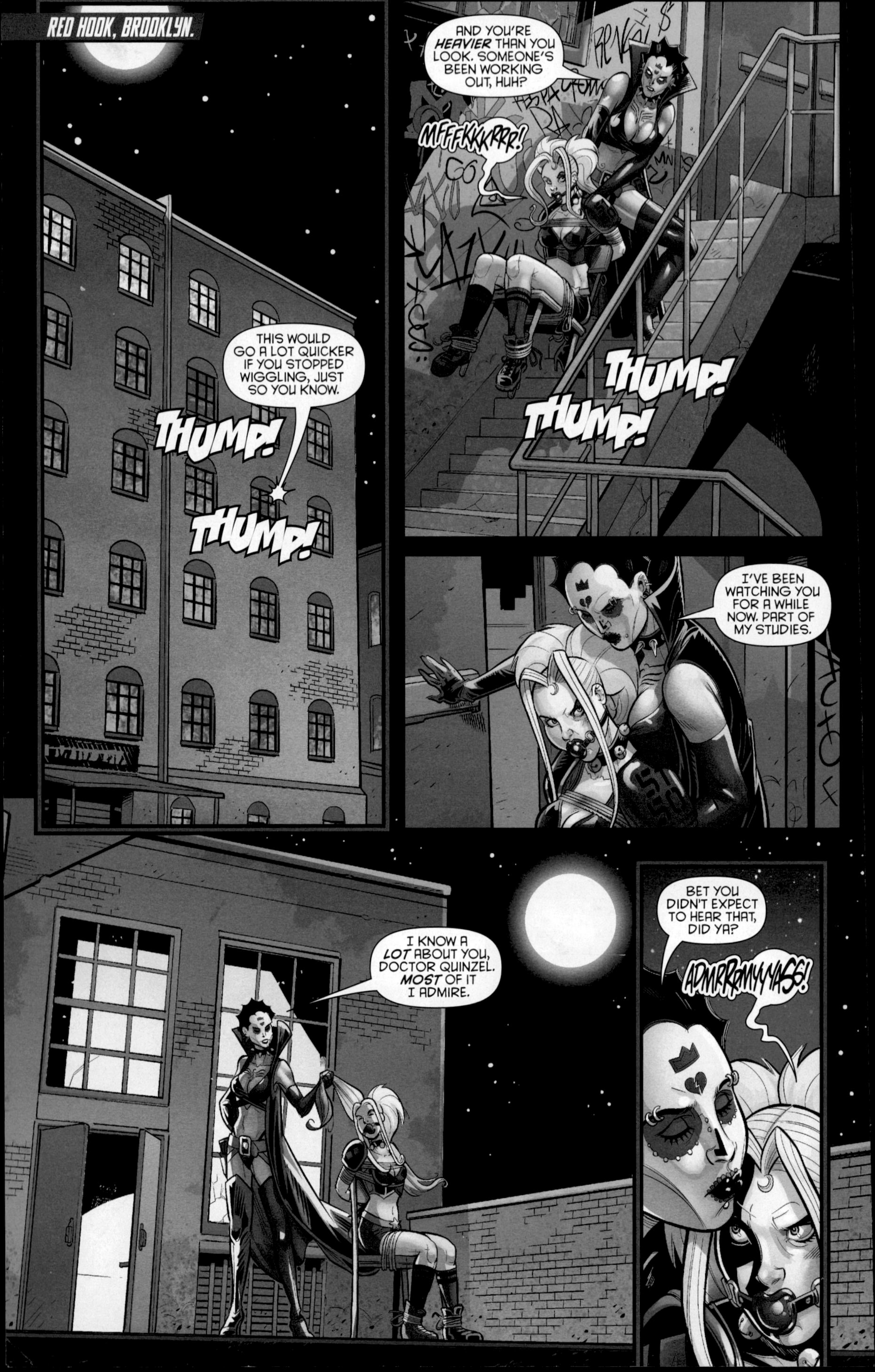
RED HOOK, BROOKLYN.
THIS WOULD GO A LOT QUICKER IF YOU STOPPED WIGGLING, JUST SO YOU KNOW.
THUMP!
THUMP!
AND YOU'RE HEAVIER THAN YOU LOOK. SOMEONE'S BEEN WORKING OUT, HUH?
MFFFKKKRRR!
THUMP!
THUMP!
I'VE BEEN WATCHING YOU FOR A WHILE NOW. PART OF MY STUDIES.
I KNOW A LOT ABOUT YOU, DOCTOR QUINZEL. MOST OF IT I ADMIRE.
BET YOU DIDN'T EXPECT TO HEAR THAT, DID YA?
ADMRRRMYYYASS!

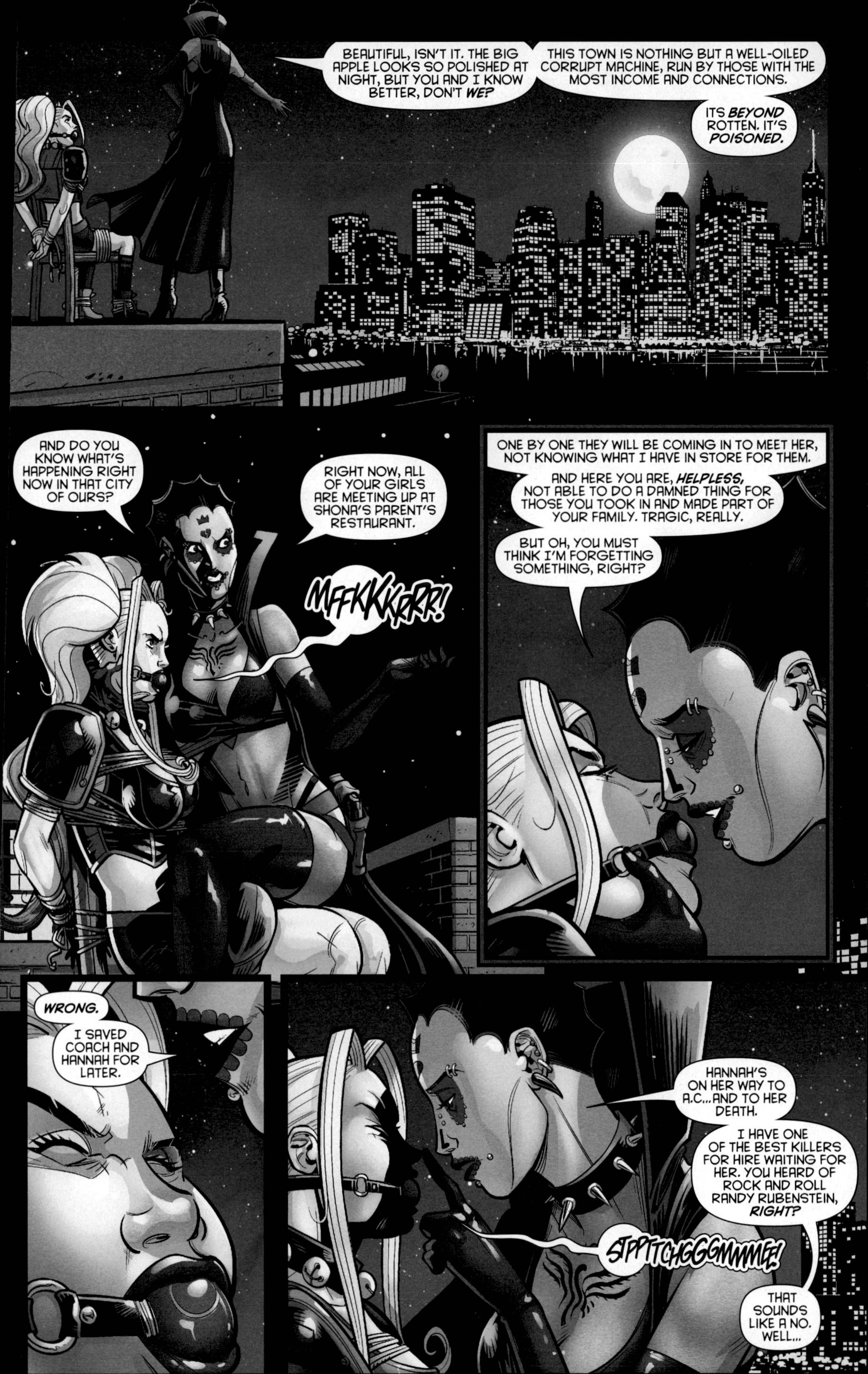

BEAUTIFUL, ISN'T IT. THE BIG APPLE LOOKS SO POLISHED AT NIGHT, BUT YOU AND I KNOW BETTER, DON'T *WE?*
THIS TOWN IS NOTHING BUT A WELL-OILED CORRUPT MACHINE, RUN BY THOSE WITH THE MOST INCOME AND CONNECTIONS.
ITS *BEYOND* ROTTEN. IT'S *POISONED.*
AND DO YOU KNOW WHAT'S HAPPENING RIGHT NOW IN THAT CITY OF OURS?
RIGHT NOW, ALL OF YOUR GIRLS ARE MEETING UP AT SHONA'S PARENT'S RESTAURANT.
MFFKKKRRR!
ONE BY ONE THEY WILL BE COMING IN TO MEET HER, NOT KNOWING WHAT I HAVE IN STORE FOR THEM.
AND HERE YOU ARE, *HELPLESS,* NOT ABLE TO DO A DAMNED THING FOR THOSE YOU TOOK IN AND MADE PART OF YOUR FAMILY. TRAGIC, REALLY.
BUT OH, YOU MUST THINK I'M FORGETTING SOMETHING, RIGHT?
WRONG.
I SAVED COACH AND HANNAH FOR LATER.
HANNAH'S ON HER WAY TO A.C... AND TO HER DEATH.
I HAVE ONE OF THE BEST KILLERS FOR HIRE WAITING FOR HER. YOU HEARD OF ROCK AND ROLL RANDY RUBENSTEIN, *RIGHT?*
STPPTCHGGGMMMEE!
THAT SOUNDS LIKE A NO. WELL...

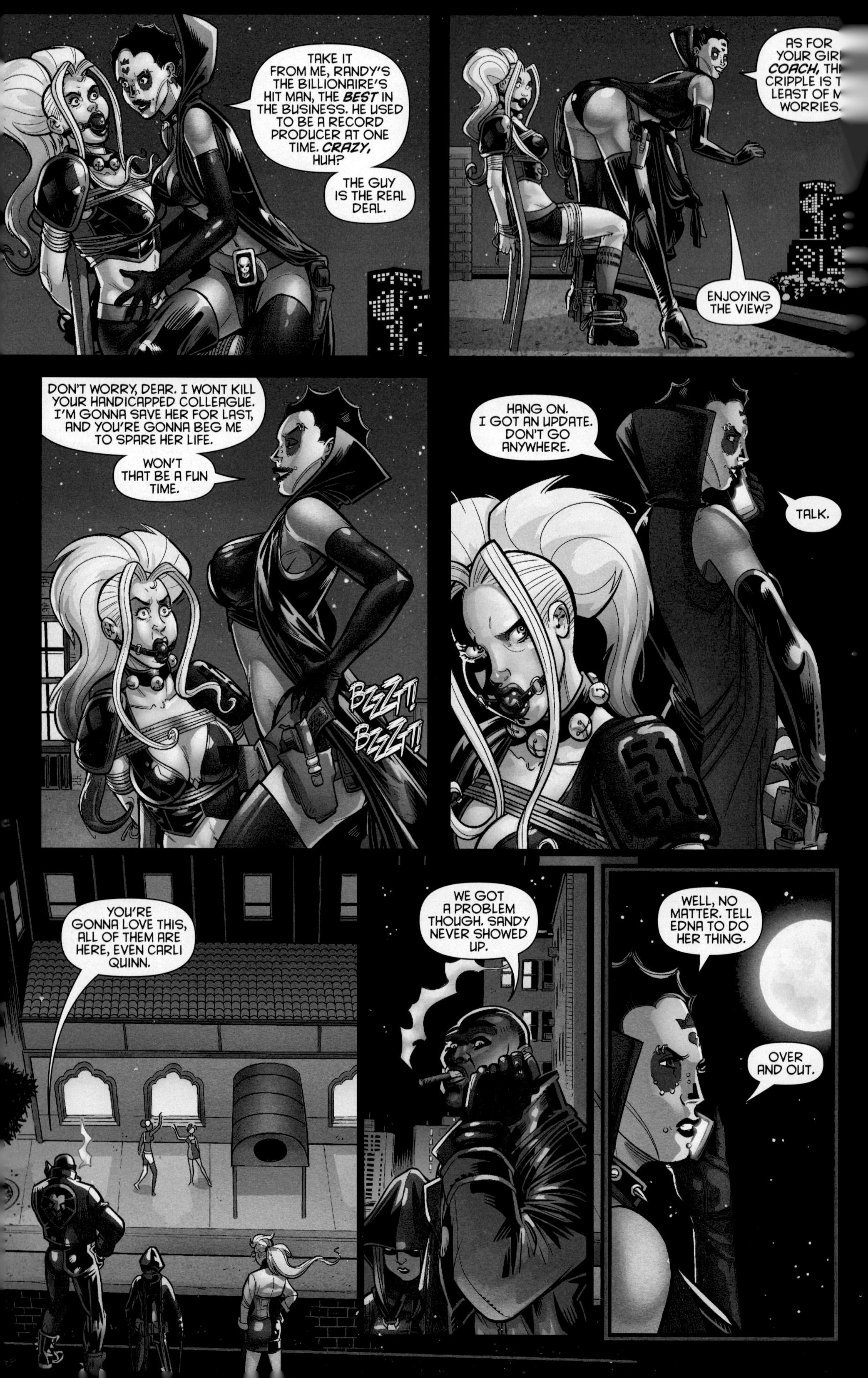
TAKE IT FROM ME, RANDY'S THE BILLIONAIRE'S HIT MAN, THE BEST IN THE BUSINESS. HE USED TO BE A RECORD PRODUCER AT ONE TIME. CRAZY, HUH?
THE GUY IS THE REAL DEAL.
AS FOR YOUR GIRL COACH, THE CRIPPLE IS THE LEAST OF MY WORRIES.
ENJOYING THE VIEW?
DON'T WORRY, DEAR. I WONT KILL YOUR HANDICAPPED COLLEAGUE. I'M GONNA SAVE HER FOR LAST, AND YOU'RE GONNA BEG ME TO SPARE HER LIFE.
WON'T THAT BE A FUN TIME.
BZZZT! BZZZT!
HANG ON. I GOT AN UPDATE. DON'T GO ANYWHERE.
TALK.
YOU'RE GONNA LOVE THIS, ALL OF THEM ARE HERE, EVEN CARLI QUINN.
WE GOT A PROBLEM THOUGH. SANDY NEVER SHOWED UP.
WELL, NO MATTER. TELL EDNA TO DO HER THING.
OVER AND OUT.

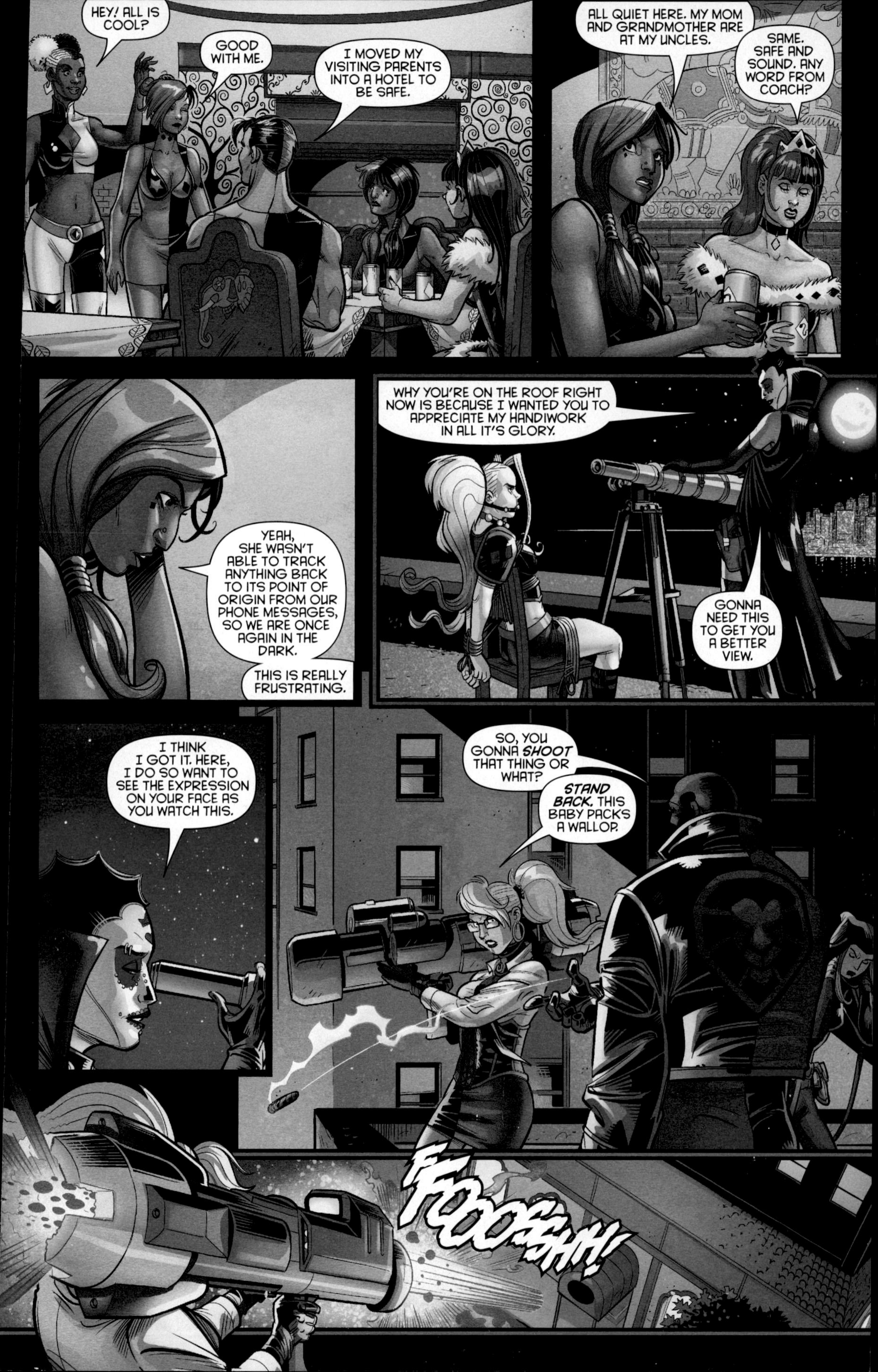
HEY! ALL IS COOL?
GOOD WITH ME.
I MOVED MY VISITING PARENTS INTO A HOTEL TO BE SAFE.
ALL QUIET HERE. MY MOM AND GRANDMOTHER ARE AT MY UNCLES.
SAME. SAFE AND SOUND. ANY WORD FROM COACH?
YEAH, SHE WASN'T ABLE TO TRACK ANYTHING BACK TO ITS POINT OF ORIGIN FROM OUR PHONE MESSAGES, SO WE ARE ONCE AGAIN IN THE DARK.
THIS IS REALLY FRUSTRATING.
WHY YOU'RE ON THE ROOF RIGHT NOW IS BECAUSE I WANTED YOU TO APPRECIATE MY HANDIWORK IN ALL IT'S GLORY.
GONNA NEED THIS TO GET YOU A BETTER VIEW.
I THINK I GOT IT. HERE, I DO SO WANT TO SEE THE EXPRESSION ON YOUR FACE AS YOU WATCH THIS.
SO, YOU GONNA SHOOT THAT THING OR WHAT?
STAND BACK. THIS BABY PACKS A WALLOP.
FFOOOSHH!

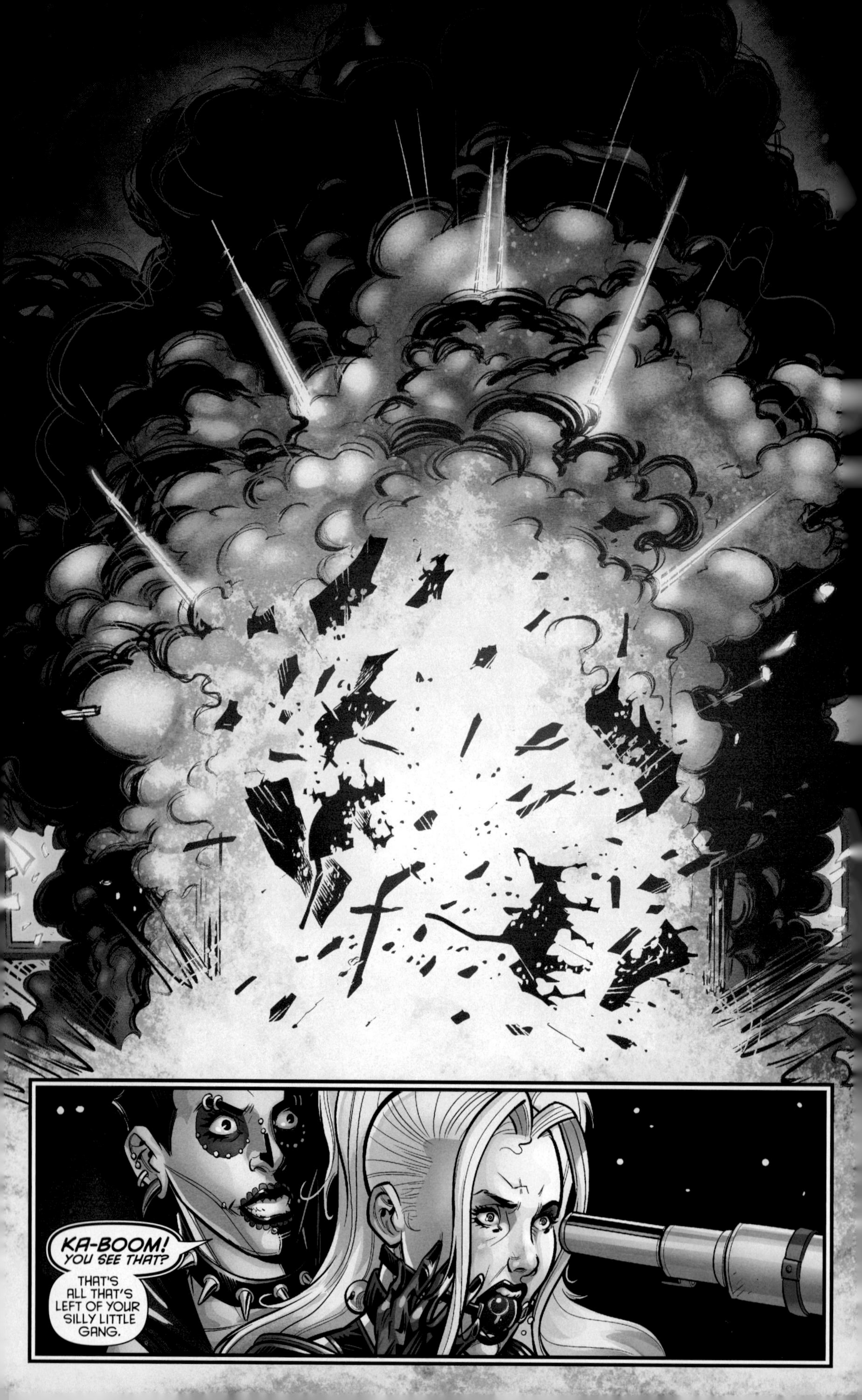
KA-BOOM! YOU SEE THAT?
THAT'S ALL THAT'S LEFT OF YOUR SILLY LITTLE GANG.

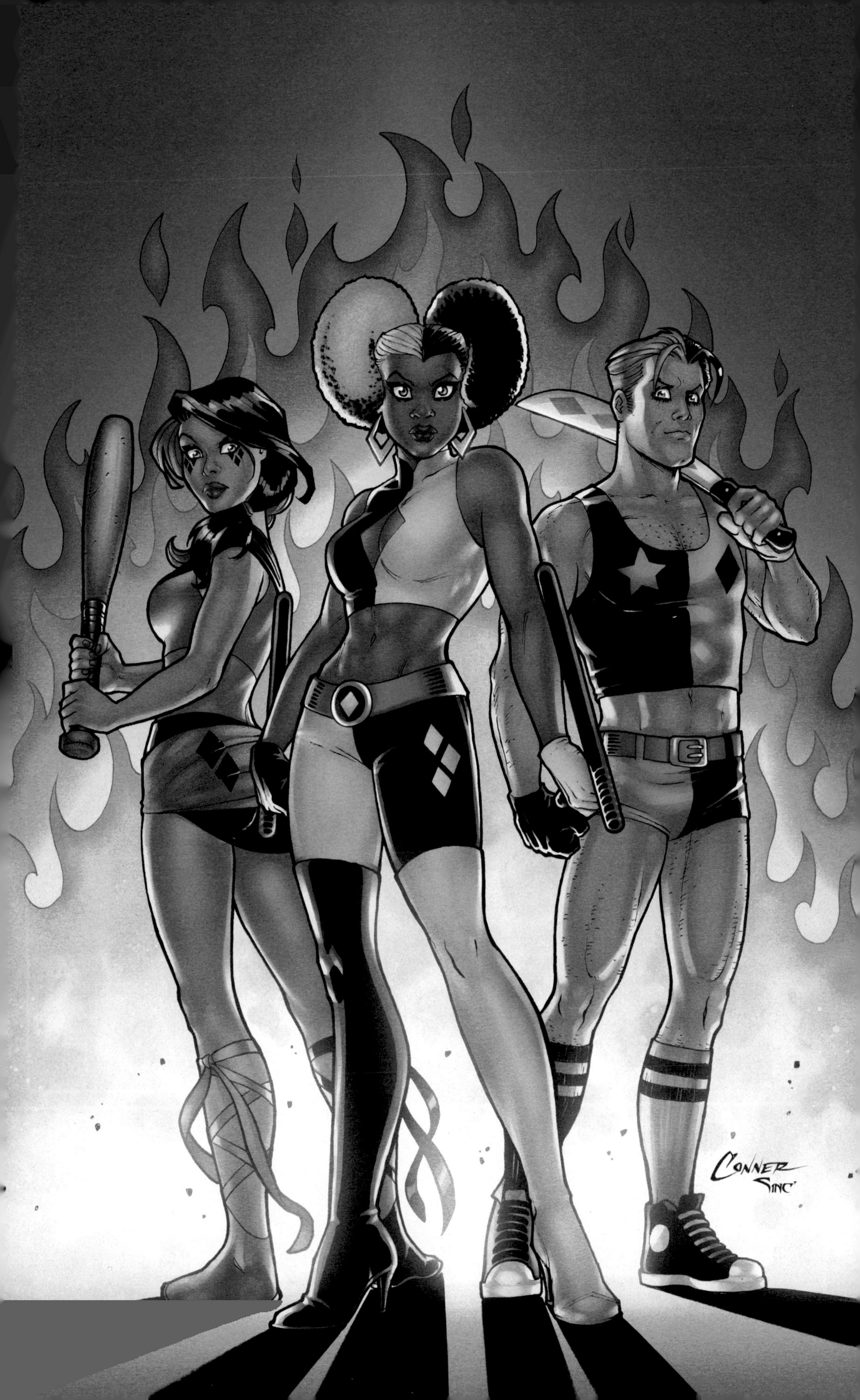
CONNER
SINC'

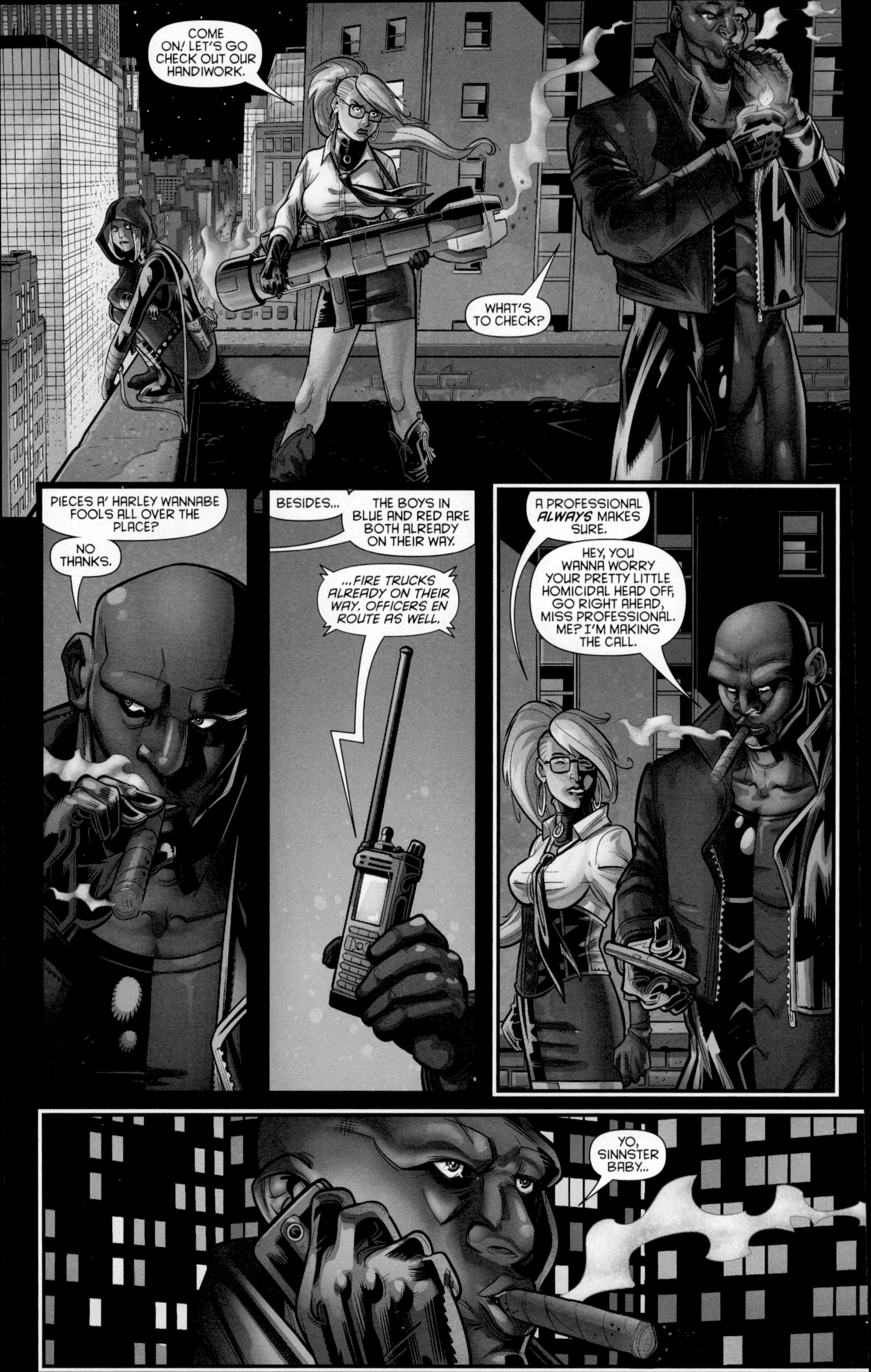
COME ON! LET'S GO CHECK OUT OUR HANDIWORK.
WHAT'S TO CHECK?
PIECES A' HARLEY WANNABE FOOLS ALL OVER THE PLACE?
NO THANKS.
BESIDES...
THE BOYS IN BLUE AND RED ARE BOTH ALREADY ON THEIR WAY.
...FIRE TRUCKS ALREADY ON THEIR WAY. OFFICERS EN ROUTE AS WELL.
A PROFESSIONAL ALWAYS MAKES SURE.
HEY, YOU WANNA WORRY YOUR PRETTY LITTLE HOMICIDAL HEAD OFF, GO RIGHT AHEAD, MISS PROFESSIONAL. ME? I'M MAKING THE CALL.
YO, SINNSTER BABY...

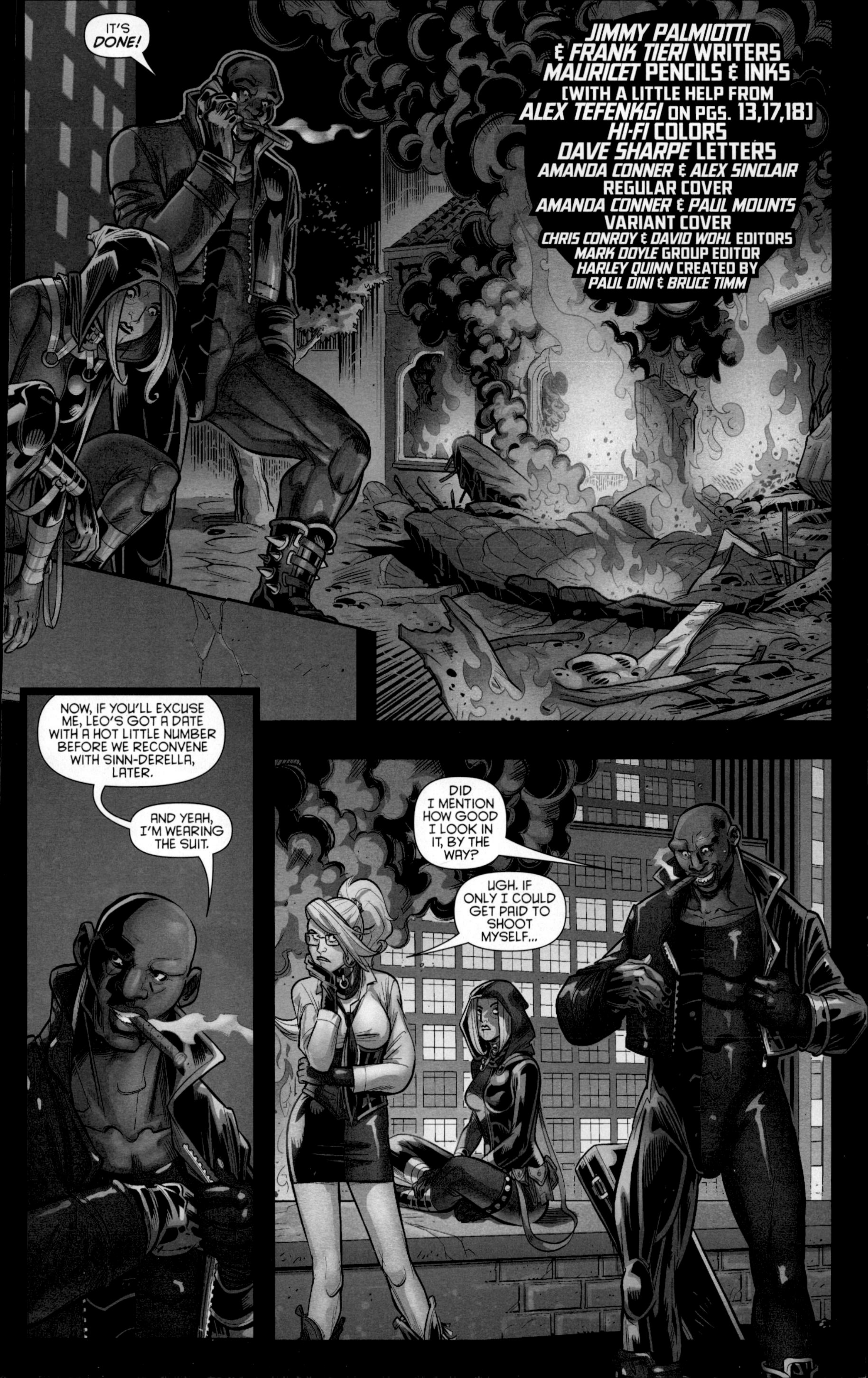
IT'S DONE!
JIMMY PALMIOTTI & FRANK TIERI WRITERS
MAURICET PENCILS & INKS
[WITH A LITTLE HELP FROM ALEX TEFENKGI ON PGS. 13,17,18]
HI-FI COLORS
DAVE SHARPE LETTERS
AMANDA CONNER & ALEX SINCLAIR REGULAR COVER
AMANDA CONNER & PAUL MOUNTS VARIANT COVER
CHRIS CONROY & DAVID WOHL EDITORS
MARK DOYLE GROUP EDITOR
HARLEY QUINN CREATED BY PAUL DINI & BRUCE TIMM
NOW, IF YOU'LL EXCUSE ME, LEO'S GOT A DATE WITH A HOT LITTLE NUMBER BEFORE WE RECONVENE WITH SINN-DERELLA, LATER.
AND YEAH, I'M WEARING THE SUIT.
DID I MENTION HOW GOOD I LOOK IN IT, BY THE WAY?
UGH. IF ONLY I COULD GET PAID TO SHOOT MYSELF...

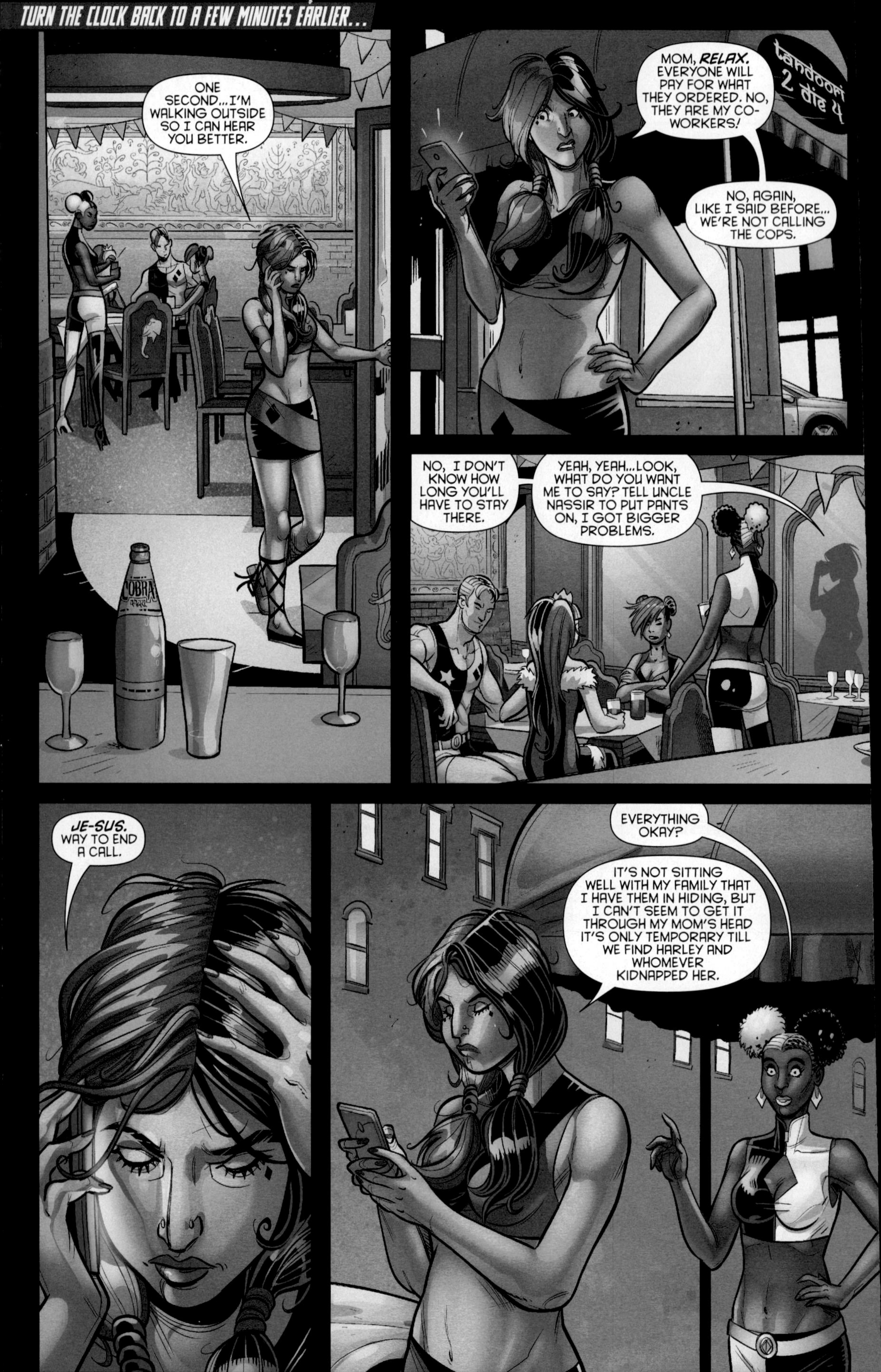
TURN THE CLOCK BACK TO A FEW MINUTES EARLIER...
ONE SECOND... I'M WALKING OUTSIDE SO I CAN HEAR YOU BETTER.
COBRA
MOM, **RELAX.** EVERYONE WILL PAY FOR WHAT THEY ORDERED. NO, THEY ARE MY CO-WORKERS!
tandoori 2 die 4
NO, AGAIN, LIKE I SAID BEFORE... WE'RE NOT CALLING THE COPS.
NO, I DON'T KNOW HOW LONG YOU'LL HAVE TO STAY THERE.
YEAH, YEAH... LOOK, WHAT DO YOU WANT ME TO SAY? TELL UNCLE NASSIR TO PUT PANTS ON, I GOT BIGGER PROBLEMS.
JE-SUS. WAY TO END A CALL.
EVERYTHING OKAY?
IT'S NOT SITTING WELL WITH MY FAMILY THAT I HAVE THEM IN HIDING, BUT I CAN'T SEEM TO GET IT THROUGH MY MOM'S HEAD IT'S ONLY TEMPORARY TILL WE FIND HARLEY AND WHOMEVER KIDNAPPED HER.

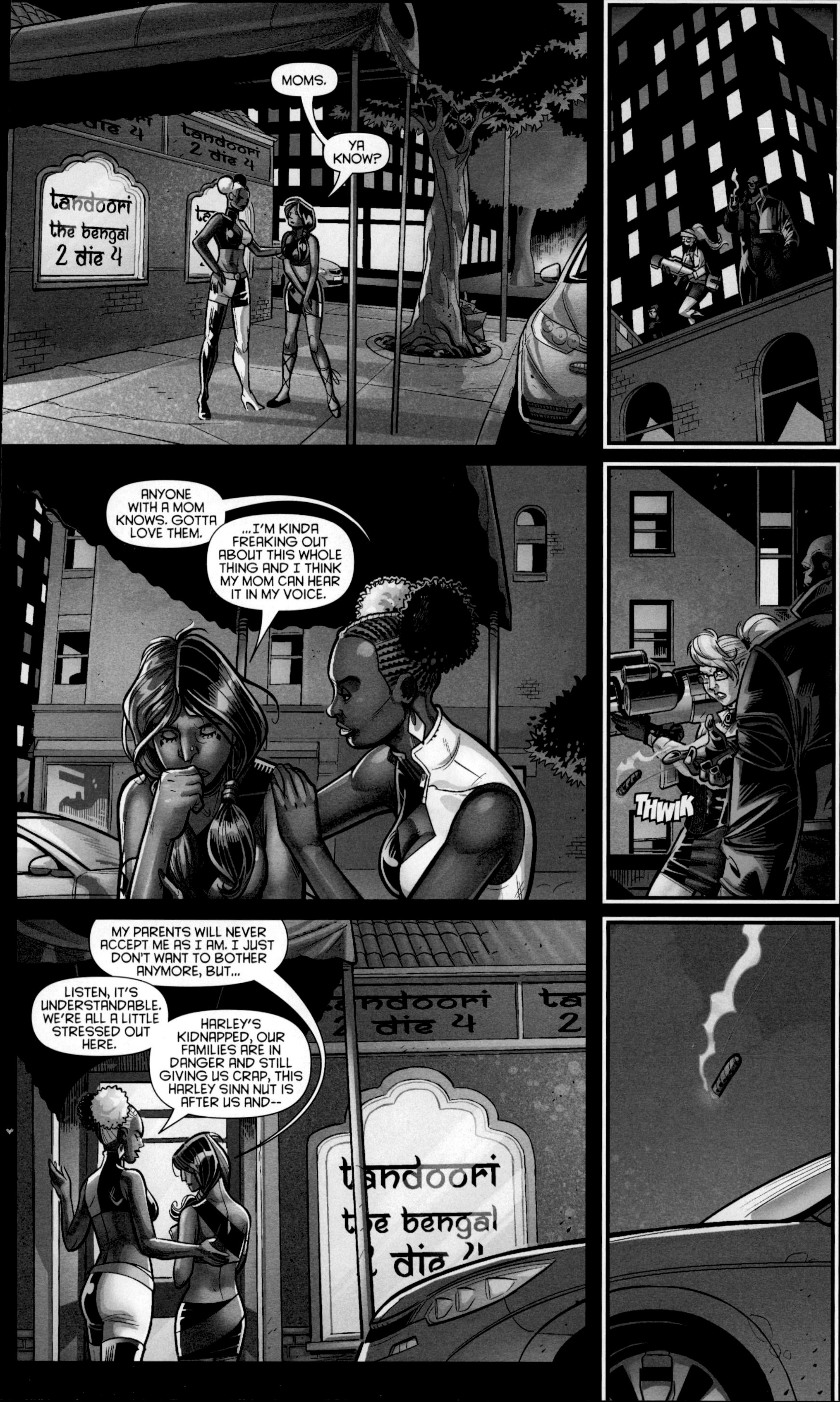
tandoori 2 die 4
tandoori the bengal 2 die 4
MOMS.
YA KNOW?
ANYONE WITH A MOM KNOWS. GOTTA LOVE THEM.
...I'M KINDA FREAKING OUT ABOUT THIS WHOLE THING AND I THINK MY MOM CAN HEAR IT IN MY VOICE.
THWIK
MY PARENTS WILL NEVER ACCEPT ME AS I AM. I JUST DON'T WANT TO BOTHER ANYMORE, BUT...
LISTEN, IT'S UNDERSTANDABLE. WE'RE ALL A LITTLE STRESSED OUT HERE.
HARLEY'S KIDNAPPED, OUR FAMILIES ARE IN DANGER AND STILL GIVING US CRAP, THIS HARLEY SINN NUT IS AFTER US AND--

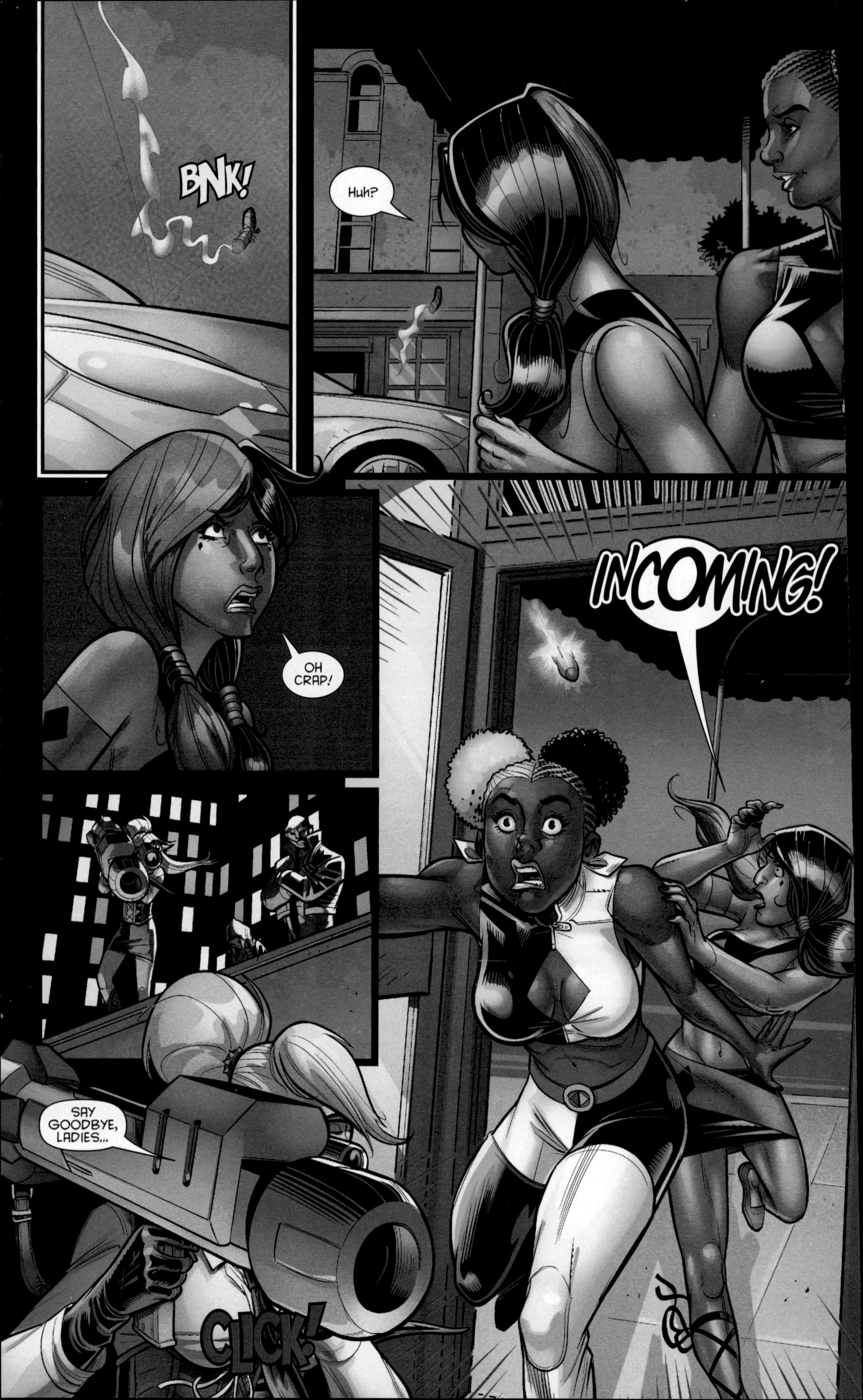
BNK!
Huh?
OH CRAP!
INCOMING!
SAY GOODBYE, LADIES...
CLICK!

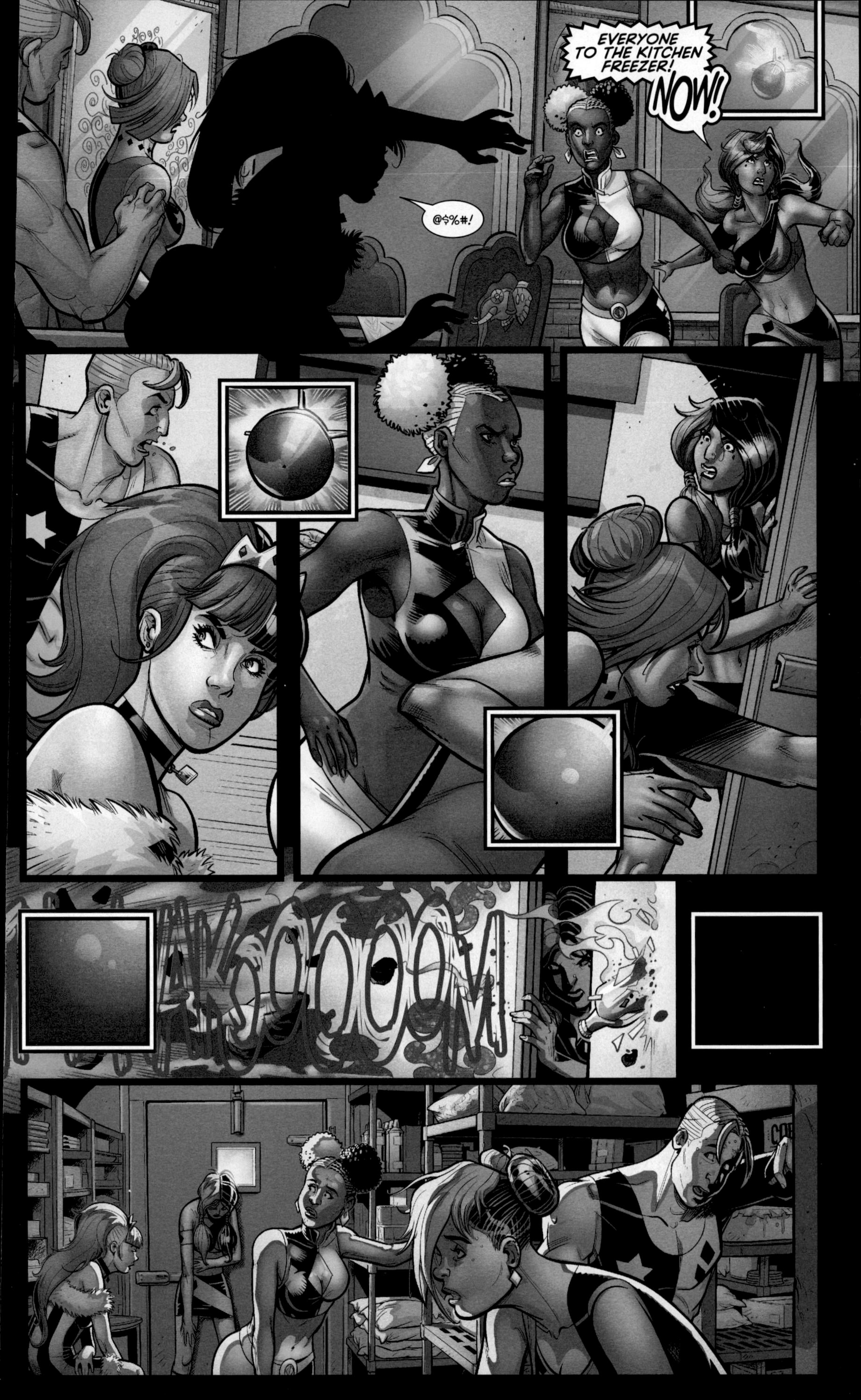
EVERYONE TO THE KITCHEN FREEZER! NOW!!
@$%#!
KAKOOOOOM

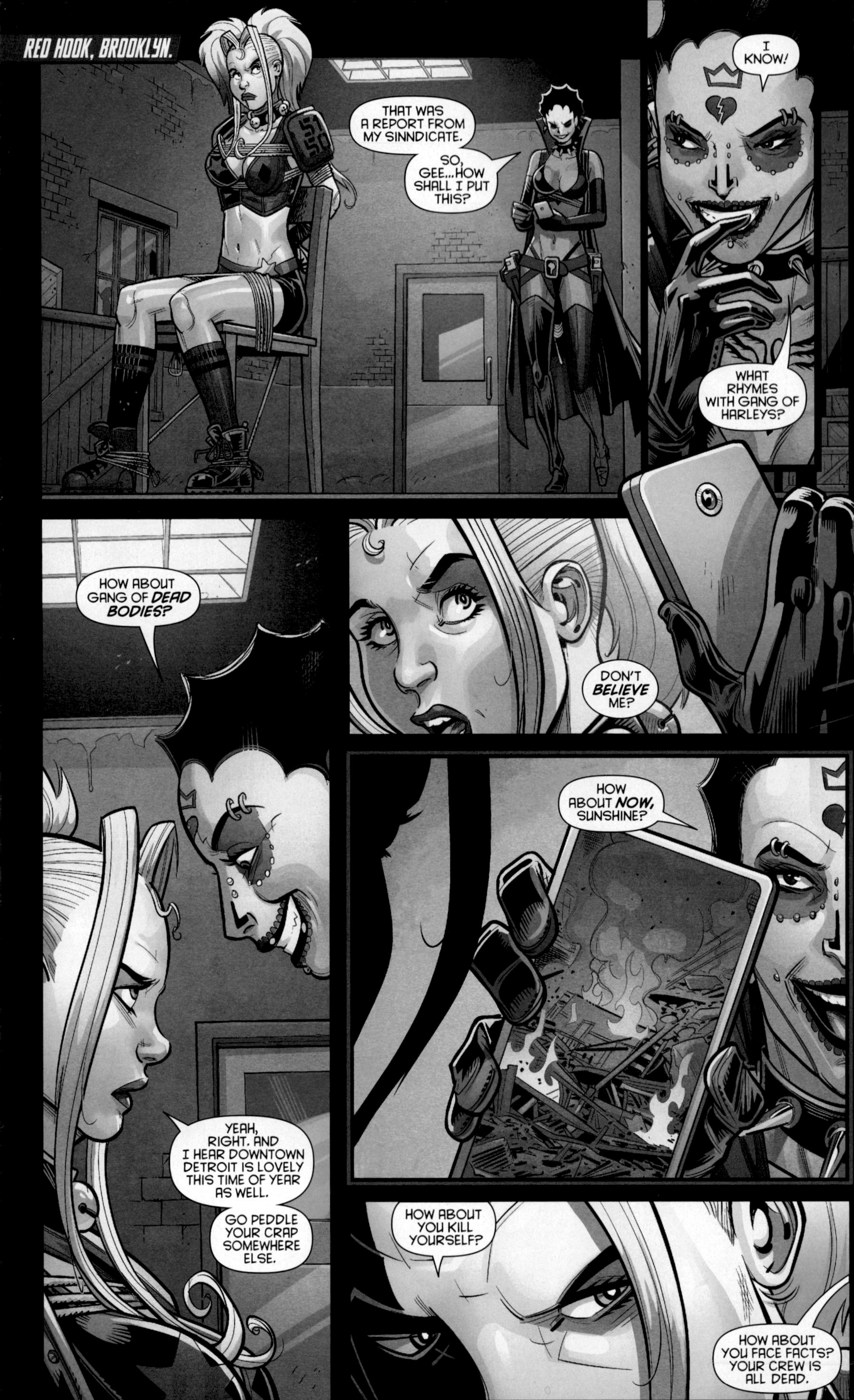
RED HOOK, BROOKLYN.
THAT WAS A REPORT FROM MY SINNDICATE.
SO, GEE...HOW SHALL I PUT THIS?
I KNOW!
WHAT RHYMES WITH GANG OF HARLEYS?
HOW ABOUT GANG OF DEAD BODIES?
DON'T BELIEVE ME?
YEAH, RIGHT. AND I HEAR DOWNTOWN DETROIT IS LOVELY THIS TIME OF YEAR AS WELL.
GO PEDDLE YOUR CRAP SOMEWHERE ELSE.
HOW ABOUT NOW, SUNSHINE?
HOW ABOUT YOU KILL YOURSELF?
HOW ABOUT YOU FACE FACTS? YOUR CREW IS ALL DEAD.

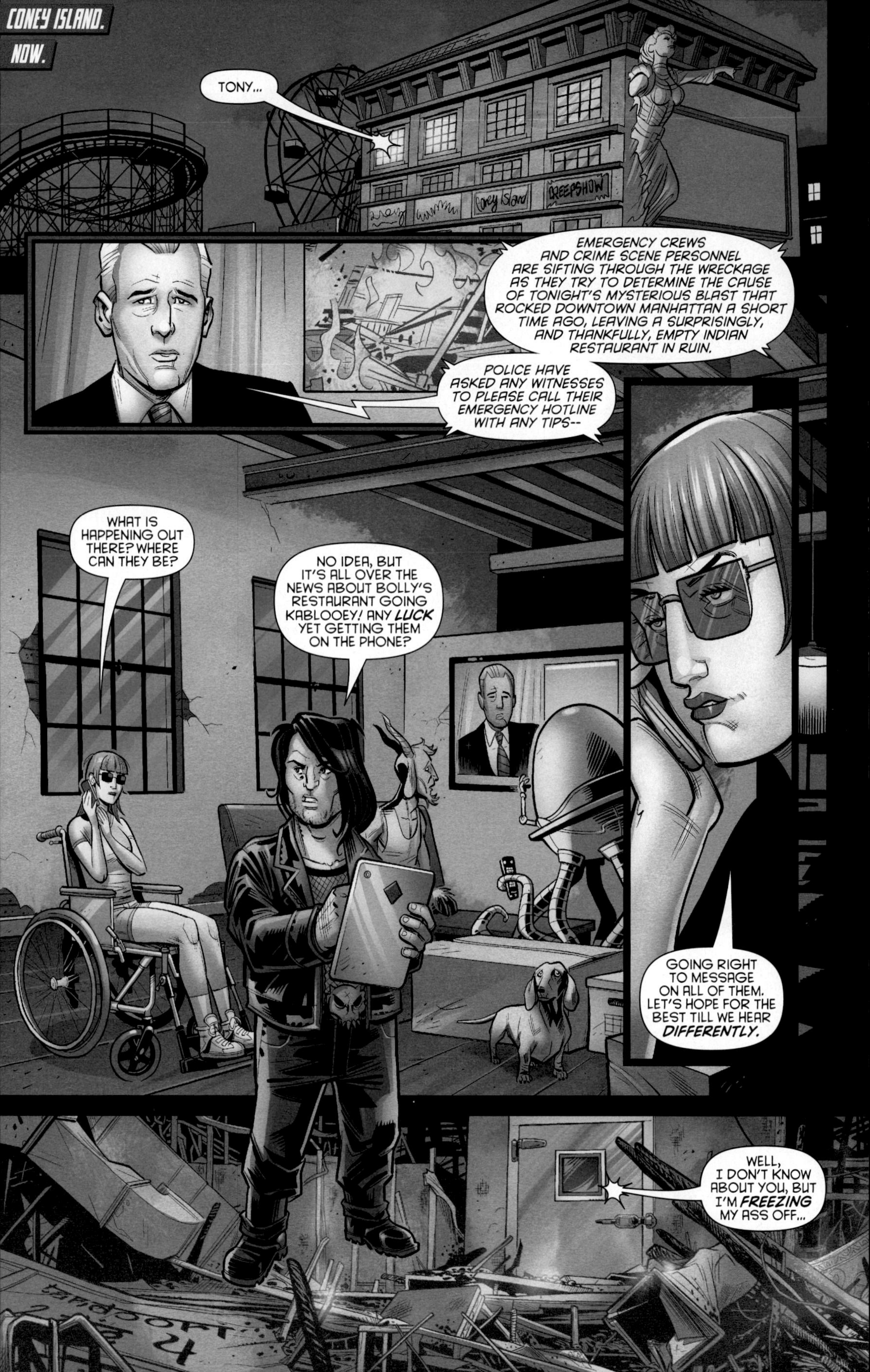
CONEY ISLAND.
NOW.
TONY...
Coney Island
CREEPSHOW
EMERGENCY CREWS AND CRIME SCENE PERSONNEL ARE SIFTING THROUGH THE WRECKAGE AS THEY TRY TO DETERMINE THE CAUSE OF TONIGHT'S MYSTERIOUS BLAST THAT ROCKED DOWNTOWN MANHATTAN A SHORT TIME AGO, LEAVING A SURPRISINGLY, AND THANKFULLY, EMPTY INDIAN RESTAURANT IN RUIN.
POLICE HAVE ASKED ANY WITNESSES TO PLEASE CALL THEIR EMERGENCY HOTLINE WITH ANY TIPS--
WHAT IS HAPPENING OUT THERE? WHERE CAN THEY BE?
NO IDEA, BUT IT'S ALL OVER THE NEWS ABOUT BOLLY'S RESTAURANT GOING KABLOOEY! ANY LUCK YET GETTING THEM ON THE PHONE?
GOING RIGHT TO MESSAGE ON ALL OF THEM. LET'S HOPE FOR THE BEST TILL WE HEAR DIFFERENTLY.
WELL, I DON'T KNOW ABOUT YOU, BUT I'M FREEZING MY ASS OFF...

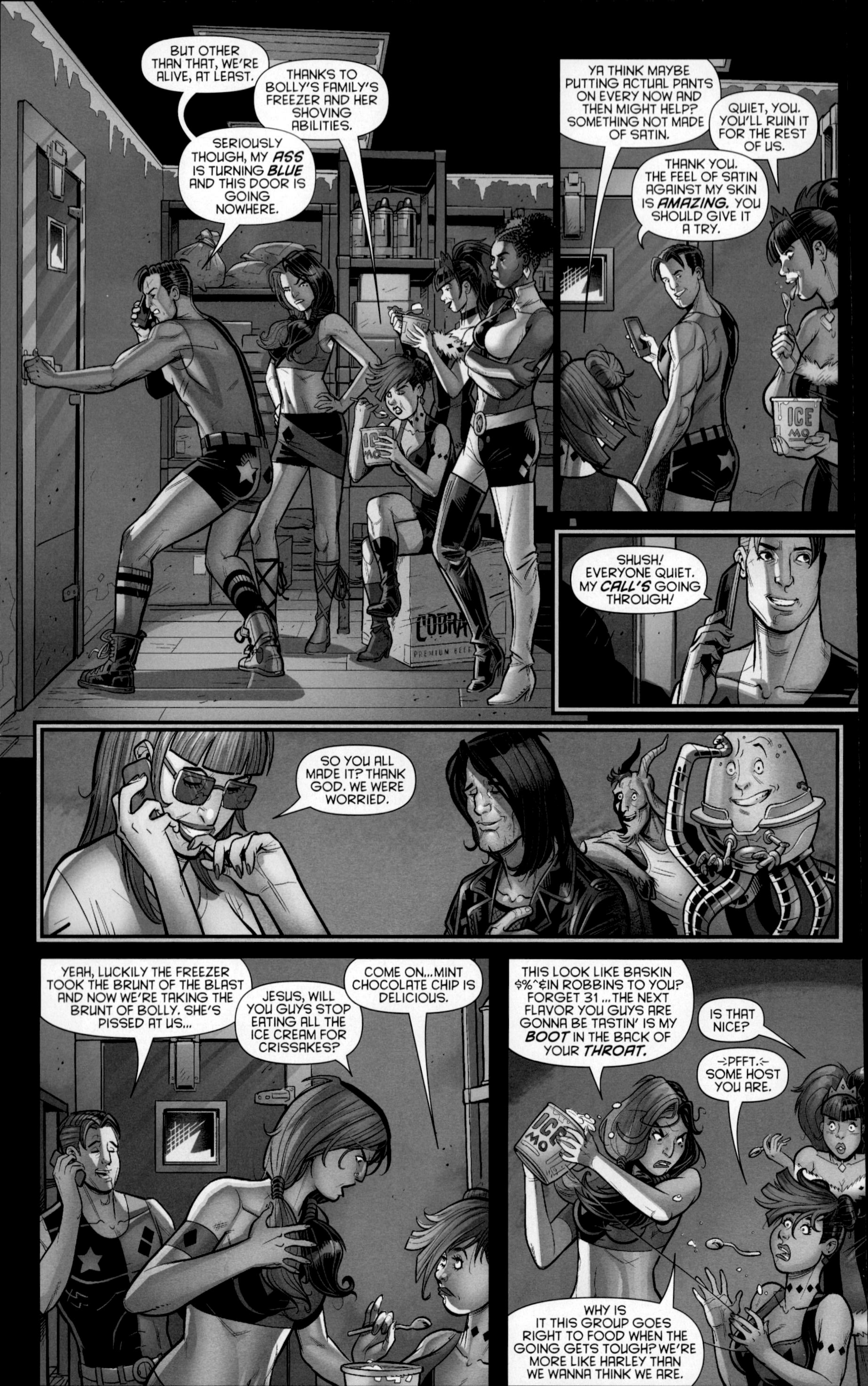
BUT OTHER THAN THAT, WE'RE ALIVE, AT LEAST.
THANKS TO BOLLY'S FAMILY'S FREEZER AND HER SHOVING ABILITIES.
SERIOUSLY THOUGH, MY **ASS** IS TURNING **BLUE** AND THIS DOOR IS GOING NOWHERE.
COBRA PREMIUM BEEF
ICE MO
YA THINK MAYBE PUTTING ACTUAL PANTS ON EVERY NOW AND THEN MIGHT HELP? SOMETHING NOT MADE OF SATIN.
QUIET, YOU. YOU'LL RUIN IT FOR THE REST OF US.
THANK YOU. THE FEEL OF SATIN AGAINST MY SKIN IS **AMAZING.** YOU SHOULD GIVE IT A TRY.
ICE MO
SHUSH! EVERYONE QUIET. MY **CALL'S** GOING THROUGH!
SO YOU ALL MADE IT? THANK GOD. WE WERE WORRIED.
YEAH, LUCKILY THE FREEZER TOOK THE BRUNT OF THE BLAST AND NOW WE'RE TAKING THE BRUNT OF BOLLY. SHE'S PISSED AT US...
JESUS, WILL YOU GUYS STOP EATING ALL THE ICE CREAM FOR CRISSAKES?
COME ON...MINT CHOCOLATE CHIP IS DELICIOUS.
THIS LOOK LIKE BASKIN $%^&IN ROBBINS TO YOU? FORGET 31...THE NEXT FLAVOR YOU GUYS ARE GONNA BE TASTIN' IS MY **BOOT** IN THE BACK OF YOUR **THROAT.**
IS THAT NICE?
-PFFT.- SOME HOST YOU ARE.
ICE MO
WHY IS IT THIS GROUP GOES RIGHT TO FOOD WHEN THE GOING GETS TOUGH? WE'RE MORE LIKE HARLEY THAN WE WANNA THINK WE ARE.

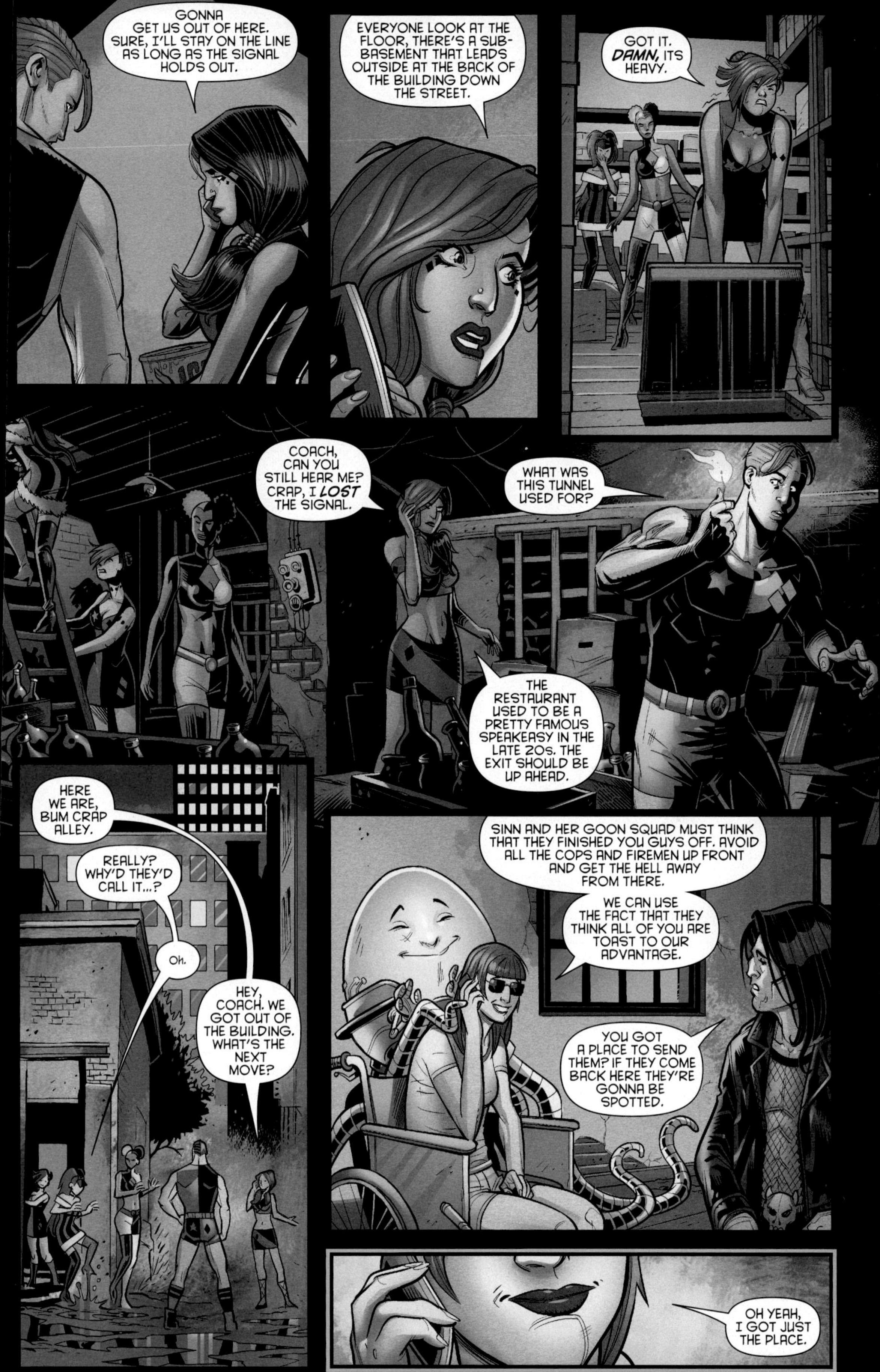
GONNA GET US OUT OF HERE. SURE, I'LL STAY ON THE LINE AS LONG AS THE SIGNAL HOLDS OUT.
EVERYONE LOOK AT THE FLOOR, THERE'S A SUB-BASEMENT THAT LEADS OUTSIDE AT THE BACK OF THE BUILDING DOWN THE STREET.
GOT IT. DAMN, ITS HEAVY.
COACH, CAN YOU STILL HEAR ME? CRAP, I LOST THE SIGNAL.
WHAT WAS THIS TUNNEL USED FOR?
THE RESTAURANT USED TO BE A PRETTY FAMOUS SPEAKEASY IN THE LATE 20s. THE EXIT SHOULD BE UP AHEAD.
HERE WE ARE, BUM CRAP ALLEY.
REALLY? WHY'D THEY'D CALL IT...?
Oh.
HEY, COACH. WE GOT OUT OF THE BUILDING. WHAT'S THE NEXT MOVE?
SINN AND HER GOON SQUAD MUST THINK THAT THEY FINISHED YOU GUYS OFF. AVOID ALL THE COPS AND FIREMEN UP FRONT AND GET THE HELL AWAY FROM THERE.
WE CAN USE THE FACT THAT THEY THINK ALL OF YOU ARE TOAST TO OUR ADVANTAGE.
YOU GOT A PLACE TO SEND THEM? IF THEY COME BACK HERE THEY'RE GONNA BE SPOTTED.
OH YEAH, I GOT JUST THE PLACE.

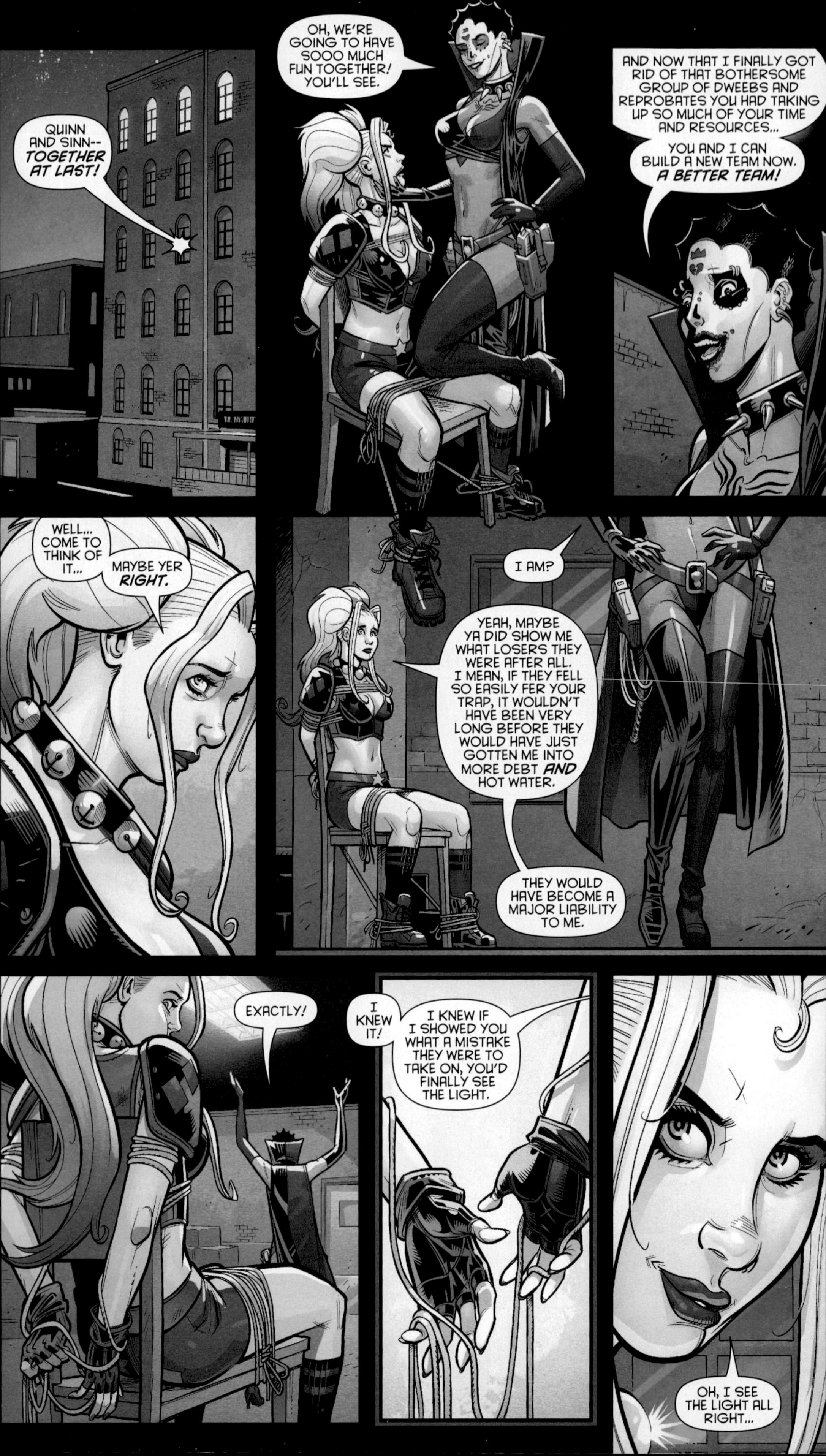
QUINN AND SINN-- *TOGETHER AT LAST!*
OH, WE'RE GOING TO HAVE SOOO MUCH FUN TOGETHER! YOU'LL SEE.
AND NOW THAT I FINALLY GOT RID OF THAT BOTHERSOME GROUP OF DWEEBS AND REPROBATES YOU HAD TAKING UP SO MUCH OF YOUR TIME AND RESOURCES...
YOU AND I CAN BUILD A NEW TEAM NOW. *A BETTER TEAM!*
WELL... COME TO THINK OF IT...
MAYBE YER *RIGHT.*
I AM?
YEAH, MAYBE YA *DID* SHOW ME WHAT LOSERS THEY WERE AFTER ALL. I MEAN, IF THEY FELL SO EASILY FER YOUR TRAP, IT WOULDN'T HAVE BEEN VERY LONG BEFORE THEY WOULD HAVE JUST GOTTEN ME INTO MORE DEBT *AND* HOT WATER.
THEY WOULD HAVE BECOME A MAJOR LIABILITY TO ME.
EXACTLY!
I KNEW IT!
I KNEW IF I SHOWED YOU WHAT A MISTAKE THEY WERE TO TAKE ON, YOU'D FINALLY SEE THE LIGHT.
OH, I SEE THE LIGHT ALL RIGHT...

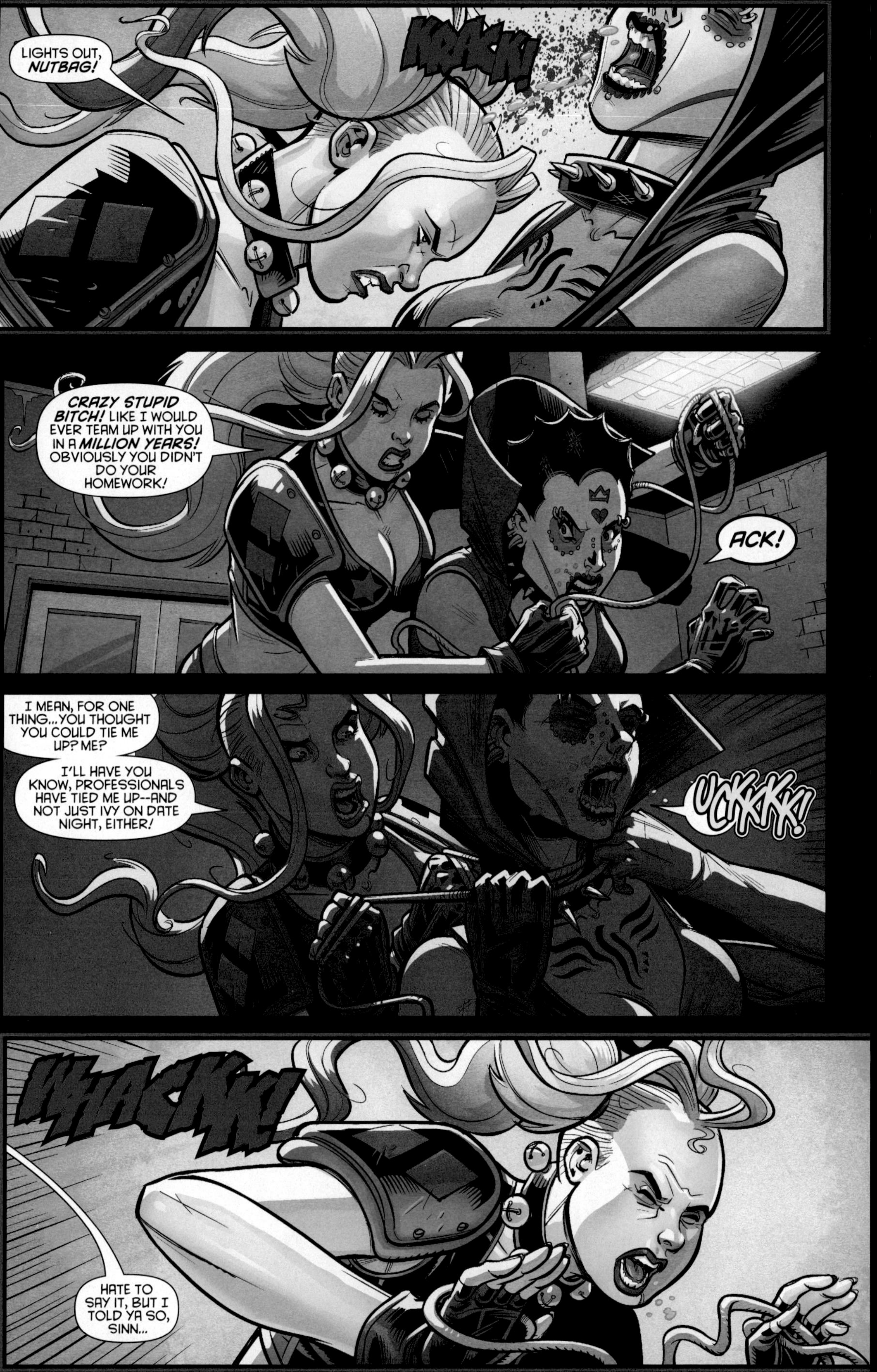
LIGHTS OUT, NUTBAG!
KRACK!
CRAZY STUPID BITCH! LIKE I WOULD EVER TEAM UP WITH YOU IN A MILLION YEARS! OBVIOUSLY YOU DIDN'T DO YOUR HOMEWORK!
ACK!
I MEAN, FOR ONE THING...YOU THOUGHT YOU COULD TIE ME UP? ME?
I'LL HAVE YOU KNOW, PROFESSIONALS HAVE TIED ME UP--AND NOT JUST IVY ON DATE NIGHT, EITHER!
UCKKKK!
WHACK!
HATE TO SAY IT, BUT I TOLD YA SO, SINN...

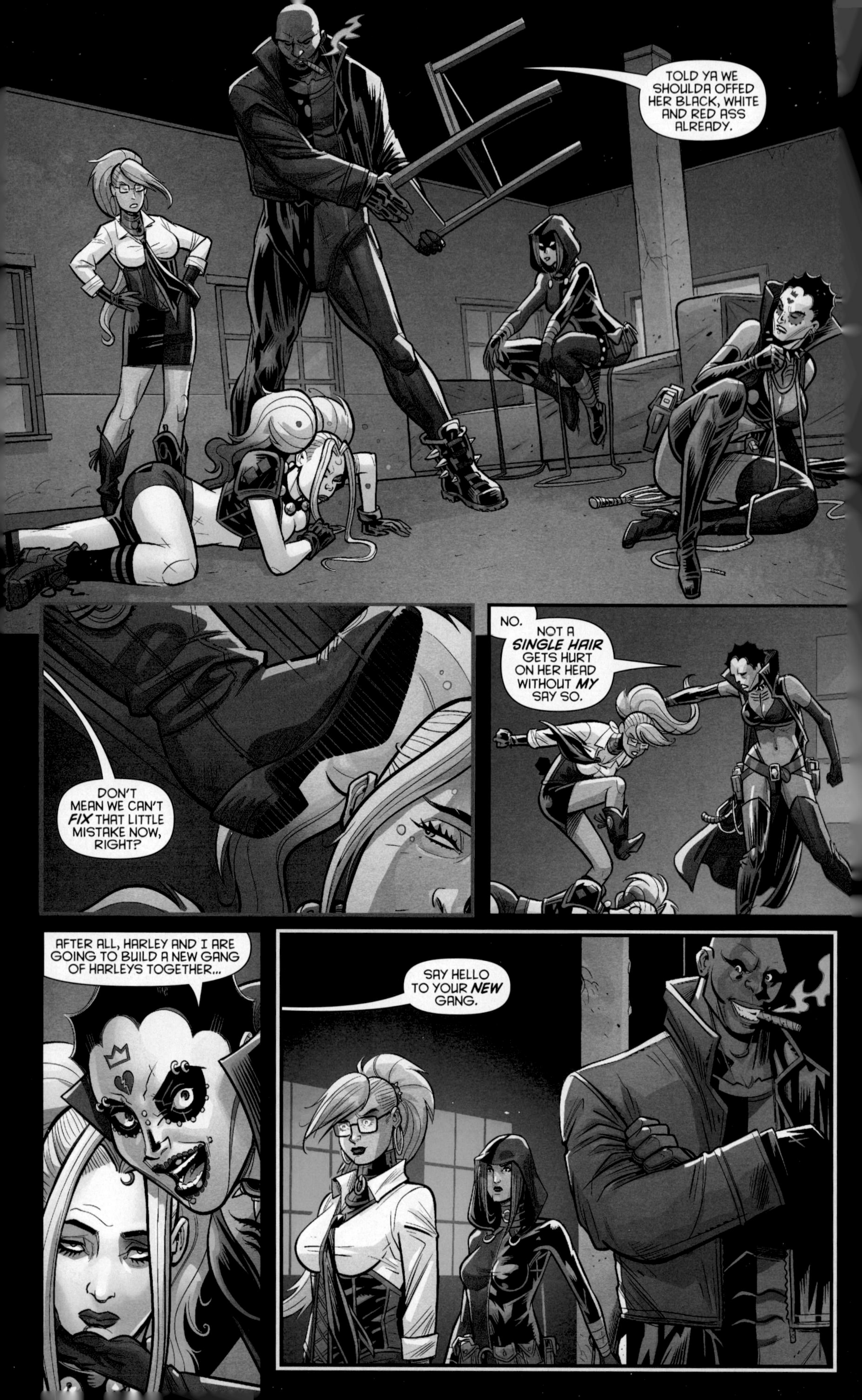
TOLD YA WE SHOULDA OFFED HER BLACK, WHITE AND RED ASS ALREADY.
DON'T MEAN WE CAN'T FIX THAT LITTLE MISTAKE NOW, RIGHT?
NO.
NOT A SINGLE HAIR GETS HURT ON HER HEAD WITHOUT MY SAY SO.
AFTER ALL, HARLEY AND I ARE GOING TO BUILD A NEW GANG OF HARLEYS TOGETHER...
SAY HELLO TO YOUR NEW GANG.

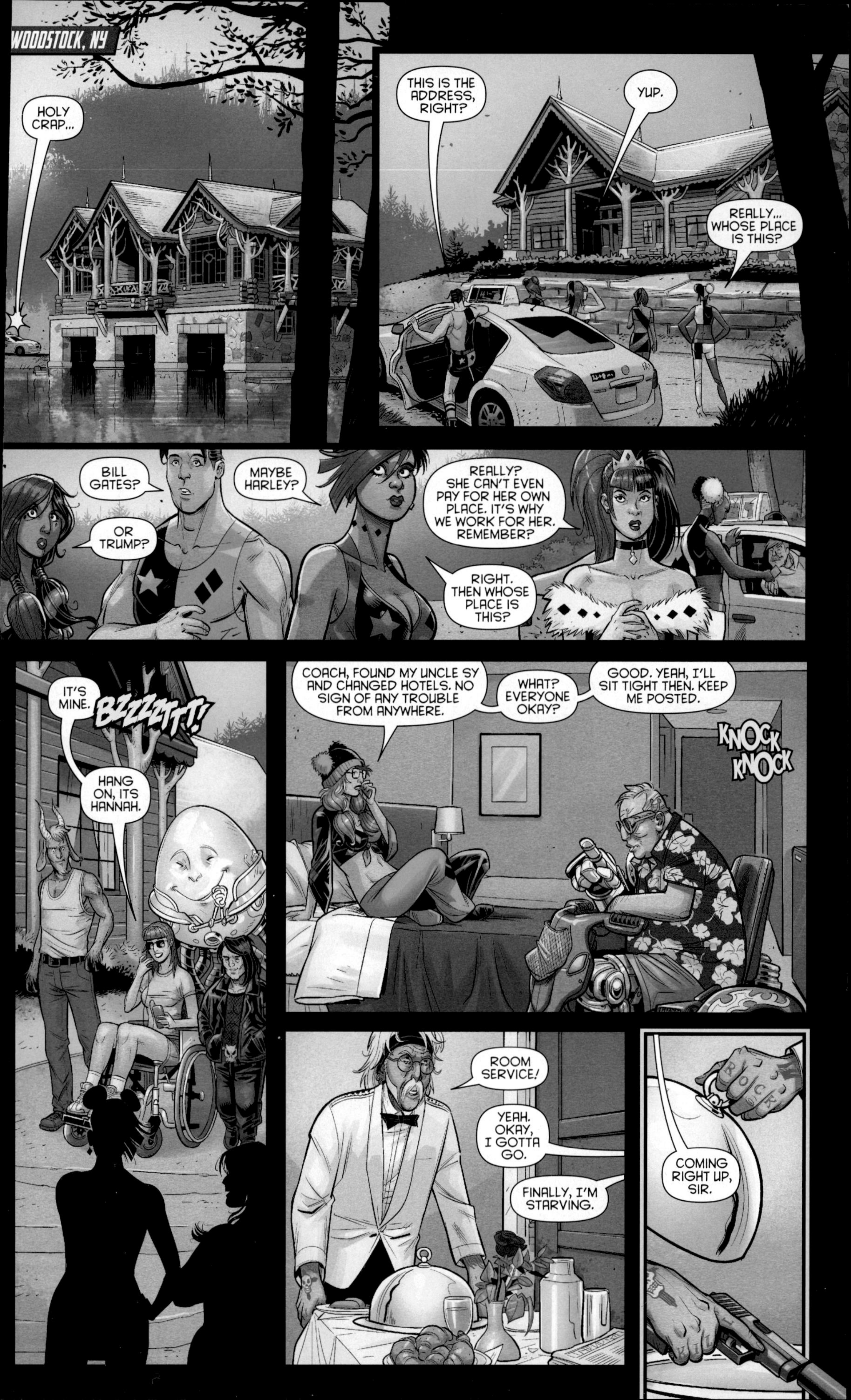
WOODSTOCK, NY
HOLY CRAP...
THIS IS THE ADDRESS, RIGHT?
YUP.
REALLY... WHOSE PLACE IS THIS?
BILL GATES?
OR TRUMP?
MAYBE HARLEY?
REALLY? SHE CAN'T EVEN PAY FOR HER OWN PLACE. IT'S WHY WE WORK FOR HER. REMEMBER?
RIGHT. THEN WHOSE PLACE IS THIS?
IT'S MINE.
BZZZZTTT!
HANG ON, ITS HANNAH.
COACH, FOUND MY UNCLE SY AND CHANGED HOTELS. NO SIGN OF ANY TROUBLE FROM ANYWHERE.
WHAT? EVERYONE OKAY?
GOOD. YEAH, I'LL SIT TIGHT THEN. KEEP ME POSTED.
KNOCK KNOCK
ROOM SERVICE!
YEAH. OKAY, I GOTTA GO.
FINALLY, I'M STARVING.
COMING RIGHT UP, SIR.

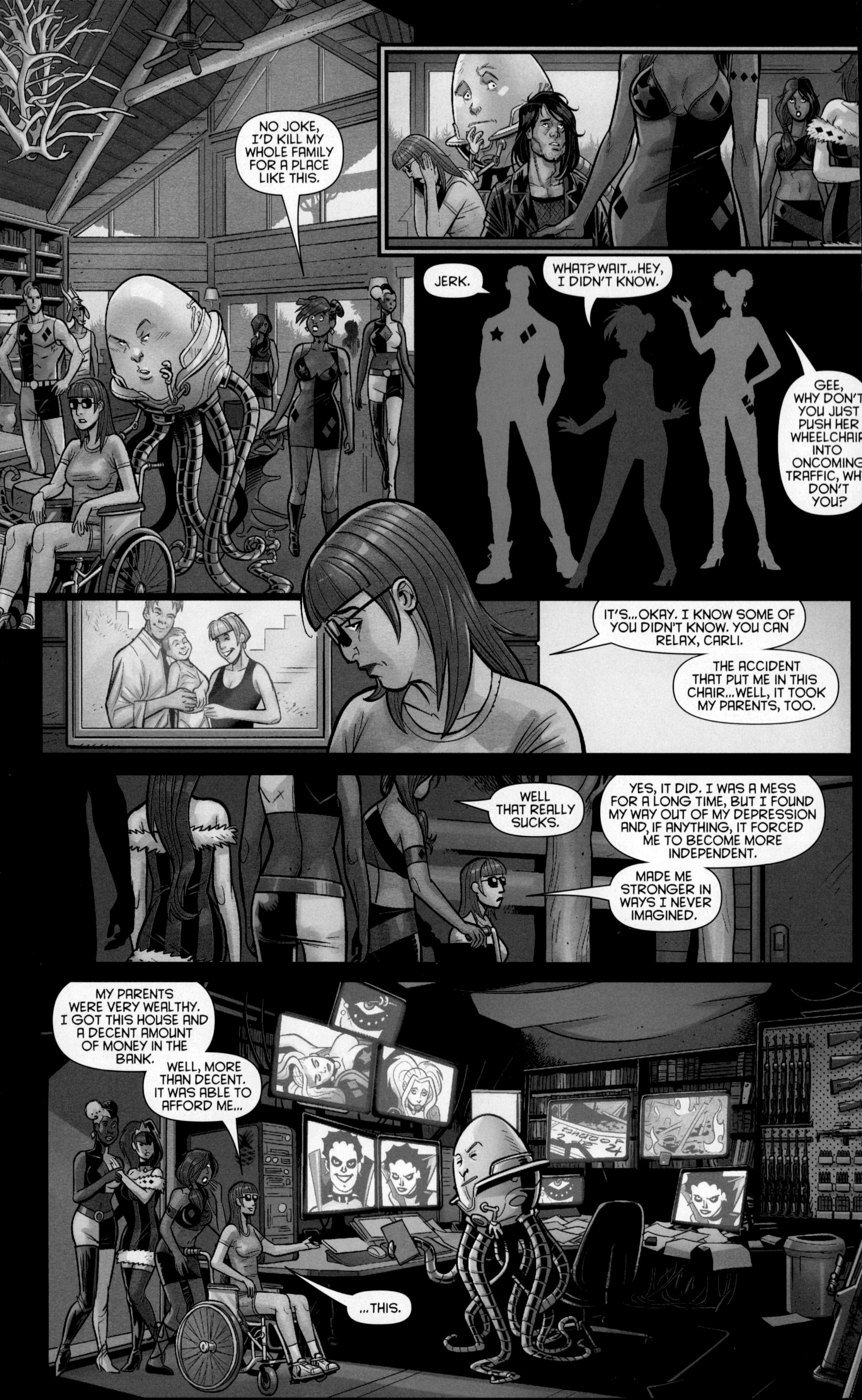
NO JOKE, I'D KILL MY WHOLE FAMILY FOR A PLACE LIKE THIS.
JERK.
WHAT? WAIT...HEY, I DIDN'T KNOW.
GEE, WHY DON'T YOU JUST PUSH HER WHEELCHAIR INTO ONCOMING TRAFFIC, WHY DON'T YOU?
IT'S...OKAY. I KNOW SOME OF YOU DIDN'T KNOW. YOU CAN RELAX, CARLI.
THE ACCIDENT THAT PUT ME IN THIS CHAIR...WELL, IT TOOK MY PARENTS, TOO.
WELL THAT REALLY SUCKS.
YES, IT DID. I WAS A MESS FOR A LONG TIME, BUT I FOUND MY WAY OUT OF MY DEPRESSION AND, IF ANYTHING, IT FORCED ME TO BECOME MORE INDEPENDENT.
MADE ME STRONGER IN WAYS I NEVER IMAGINED.
MY PARENTS WERE VERY WEALTHY. I GOT THIS HOUSE AND A DECENT AMOUNT OF MONEY IN THE BANK.
WELL, MORE THAN DECENT. IT WAS ABLE TO AFFORD ME...
...THIS.

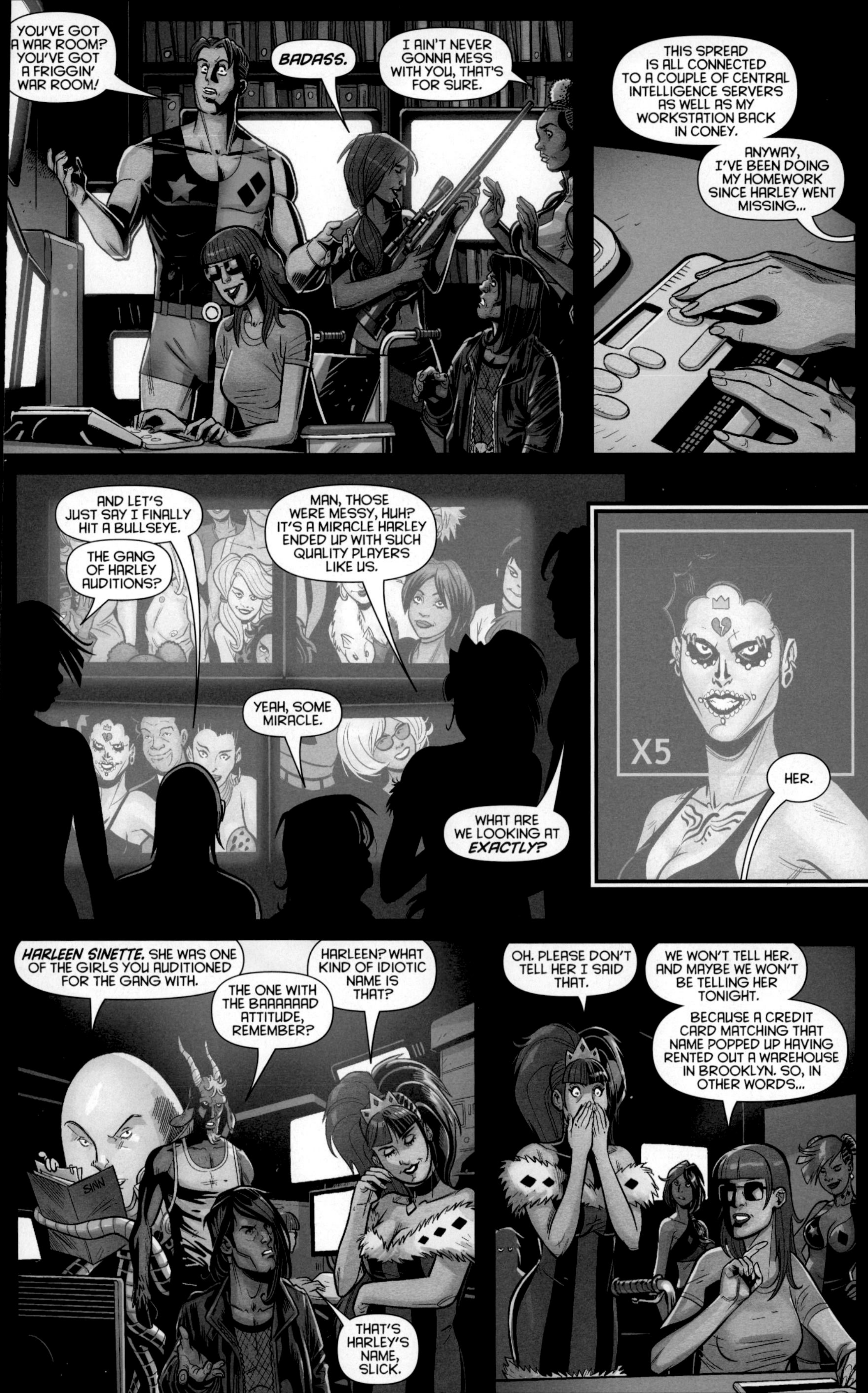

YOU'VE GOT A WAR ROOM? YOU'VE GOT A FRIGGIN' WAR ROOM!
BADASS.
I AIN'T NEVER GONNA MESS WITH YOU, THAT'S FOR SURE.
THIS SPREAD IS ALL CONNECTED TO A COUPLE OF CENTRAL INTELLIGENCE SERVERS AS WELL AS MY WORKSTATION BACK IN CONEY.
ANYWAY, I'VE BEEN DOING MY HOMEWORK SINCE HARLEY WENT MISSING...
AND LET'S JUST SAY I FINALLY HIT A BULLSEYE.
THE GANG OF HARLEY AUDITIONS?
MAN, THOSE WERE MESSY, HUH? IT'S A MIRACLE HARLEY ENDED UP WITH SUCH QUALITY PLAYERS LIKE US.
YEAH, SOME MIRACLE.
WHAT ARE WE LOOKING AT EXACTLY?
X5
HER.
HARLEEN SINETTE. SHE WAS ONE OF THE GIRLS YOU AUDITIONED FOR THE GANG WITH.
THE ONE WITH THE BAAAAAAD ATTITUDE, REMEMBER?
HARLEEN? WHAT KIND OF IDIOTIC NAME IS THAT?
SINN
THAT'S HARLEY'S NAME, SLICK.
OH. PLEASE DON'T TELL HER I SAID THAT.
WE WON'T TELL HER. AND MAYBE WE WON'T BE TELLING HER TONIGHT.
BECAUSE A CREDIT CARD MATCHING THAT NAME POPPED UP HAVING RENTED OUT A WAREHOUSE IN BROOKLYN. SO, IN OTHER WORDS...

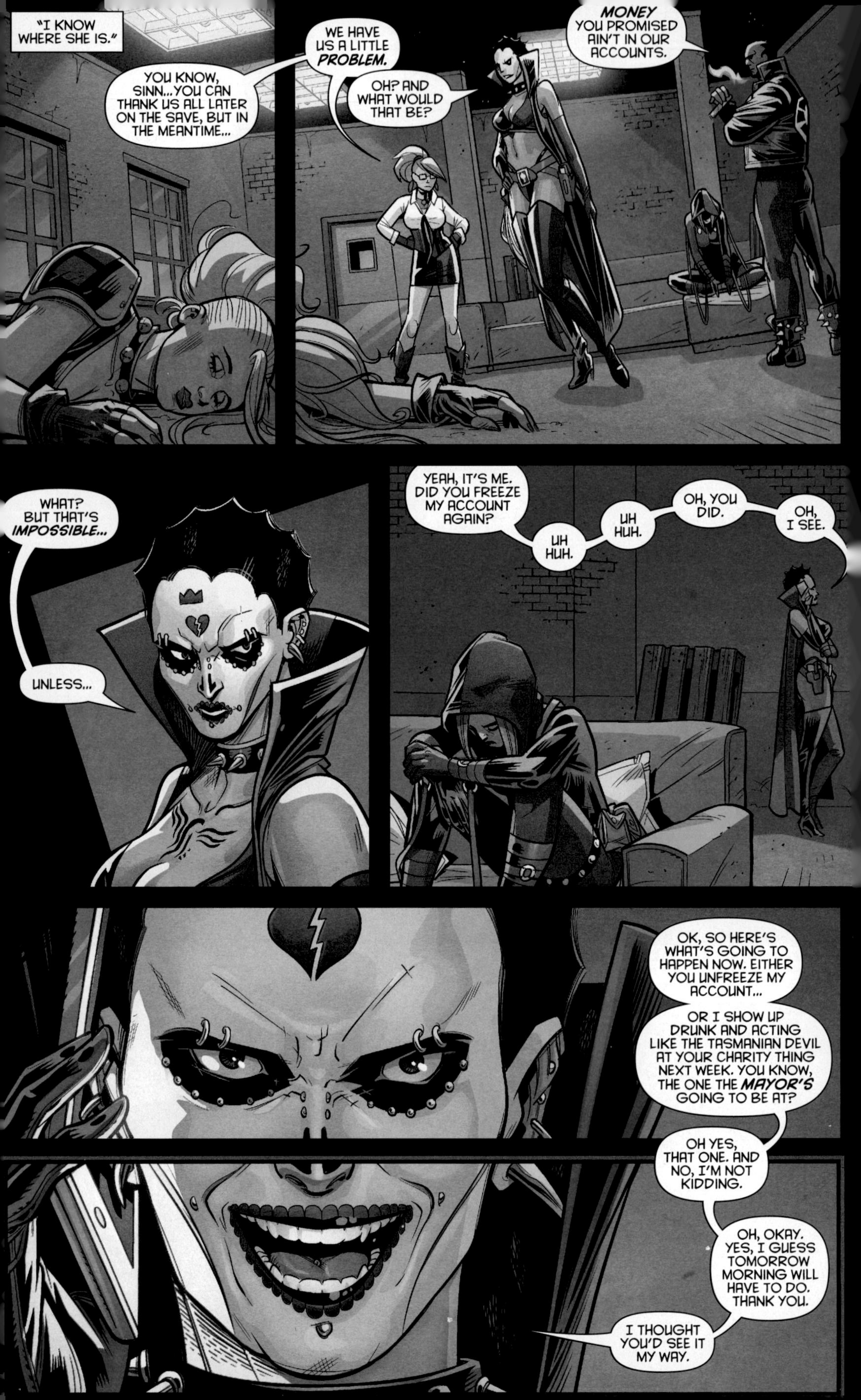
"I KNOW WHERE SHE IS."
YOU KNOW, SINN...YOU CAN THANK US ALL LATER ON THE SAVE, BUT IN THE MEANTIME...
WE HAVE US A LITTLE PROBLEM.
OH? AND WHAT WOULD THAT BE?
MONEY YOU PROMISED AIN'T IN OUR ACCOUNTS.
WHAT? BUT THAT'S IMPOSSIBLE...
UNLESS...
YEAH, IT'S ME. DID YOU FREEZE MY ACCOUNT AGAIN?
UH HUH.
UH HUH.
OH, YOU DID.
OH, I SEE.
OK, SO HERE'S WHAT'S GOING TO HAPPEN NOW. EITHER YOU UNFREEZE MY ACCOUNT...
OR I SHOW UP DRUNK AND ACTING LIKE THE TASMANIAN DEVIL AT YOUR CHARITY THING NEXT WEEK. YOU KNOW, THE ONE THE MAYOR'S GOING TO BE AT?
OH YES, THAT ONE. AND NO, I'M NOT KIDDING.
OH, OKAY. YES, I GUESS TOMORROW MORNING WILL HAVE TO DO. THANK YOU.
I THOUGHT YOU'D SEE IT MY WAY.

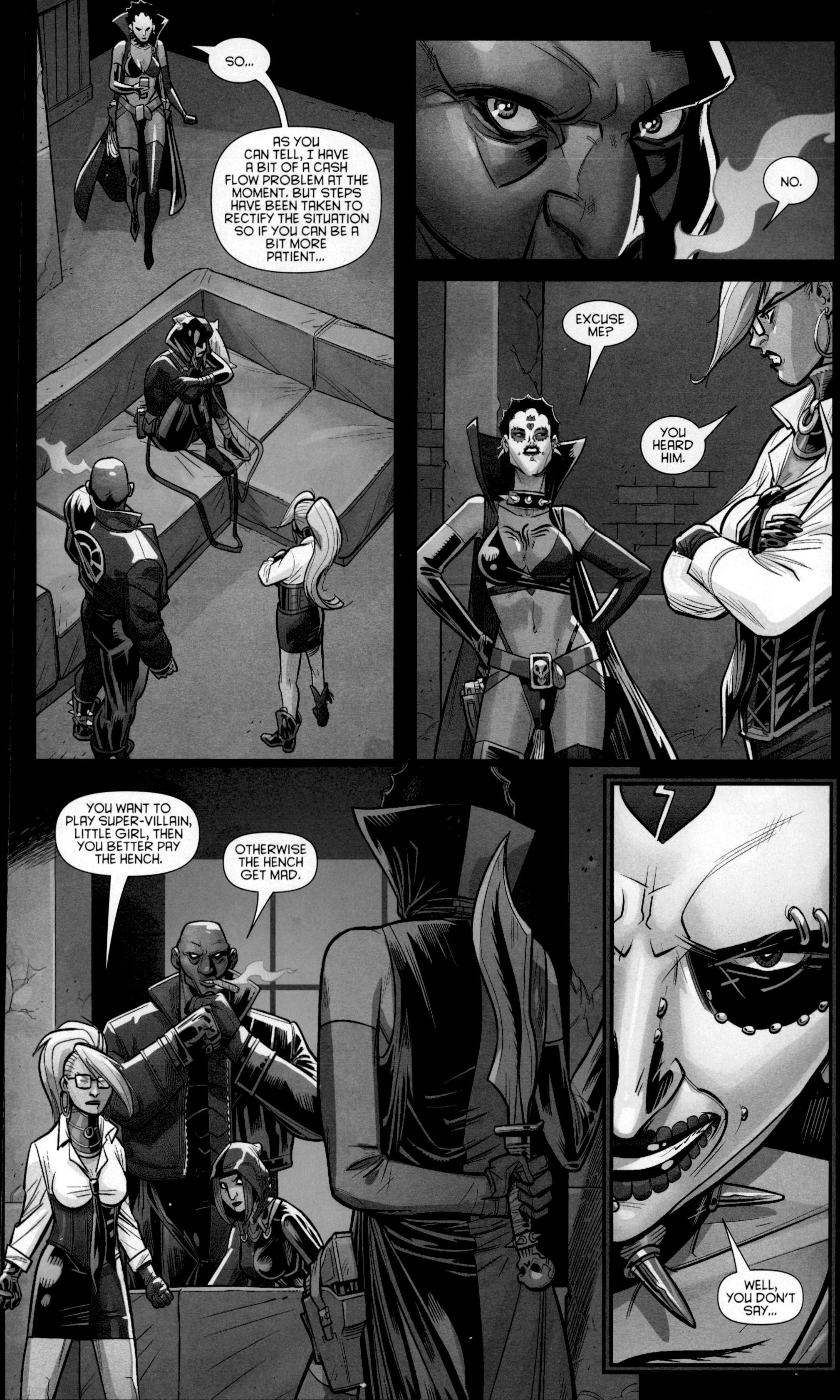

SO...
AS YOU CAN TELL, I HAVE A BIT OF A CASH FLOW PROBLEM AT THE MOMENT. BUT STEPS HAVE BEEN TAKEN TO RECTIFY THE SITUATION SO IF YOU CAN BE A BIT MORE PATIENT...
NO.
EXCUSE ME?
YOU HEARD HIM.
YOU WANT TO PLAY SUPER-VILLAIN, LITTLE GIRL, THEN YOU BETTER PAY THE HENCH.
OTHERWISE THE HENCH GET MAD.
WELL, YOU DON'T SAY...

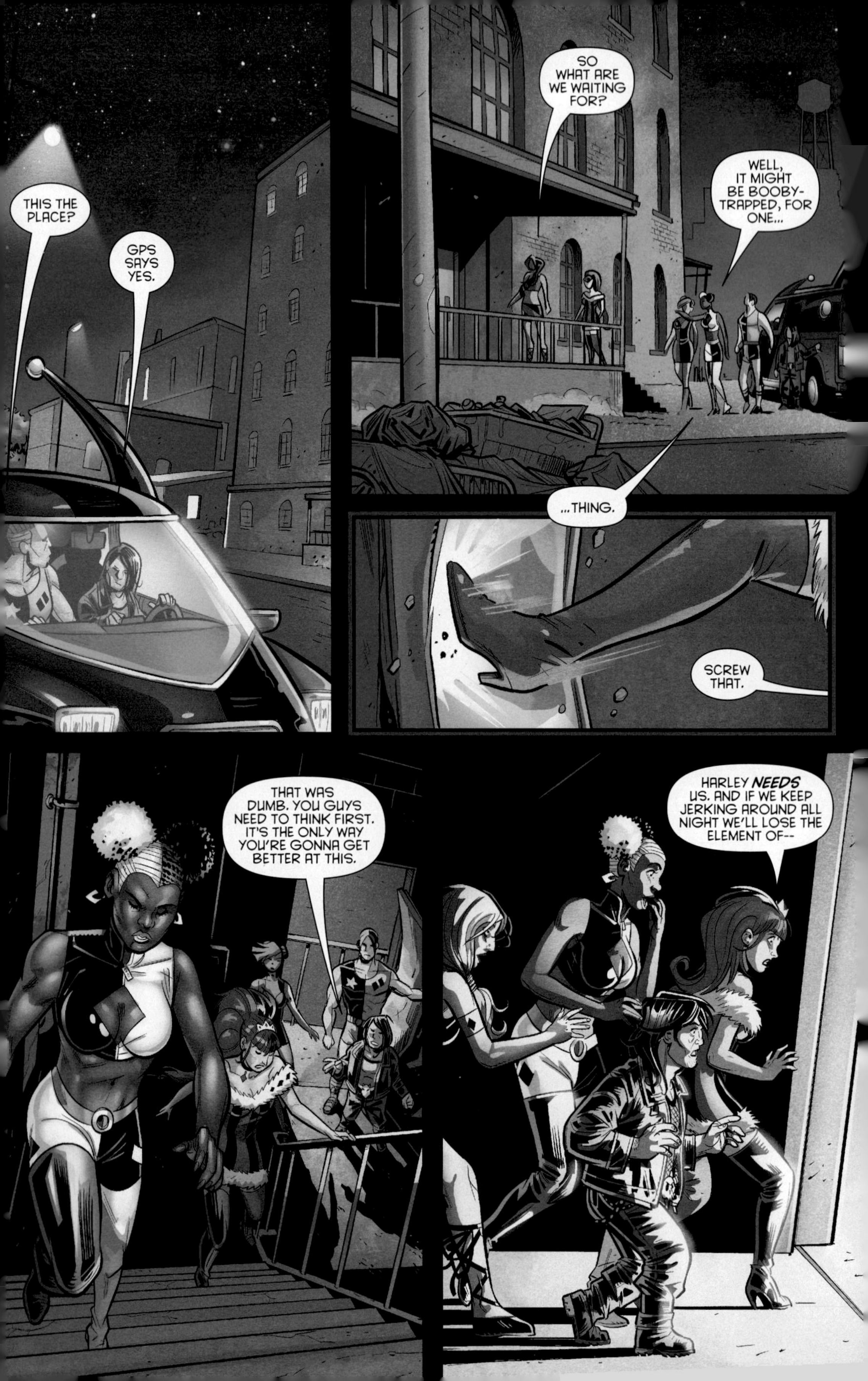
THIS THE PLACE?
GPS SAYS YES.
SO WHAT ARE WE WAITING FOR?
WELL, IT MIGHT BE BOOBY-TRAPPED, FOR ONE...
...THING.
SCREW THAT.
THAT WAS DUMB. YOU GUYS NEED TO THINK FIRST. IT'S THE ONLY WAY YOU'RE GONNA GET BETTER AT THIS.
HARLEY **NEEDS** US. AND IF WE KEEP JERKING AROUND ALL NIGHT WE'LL LOSE THE ELEMENT OF--

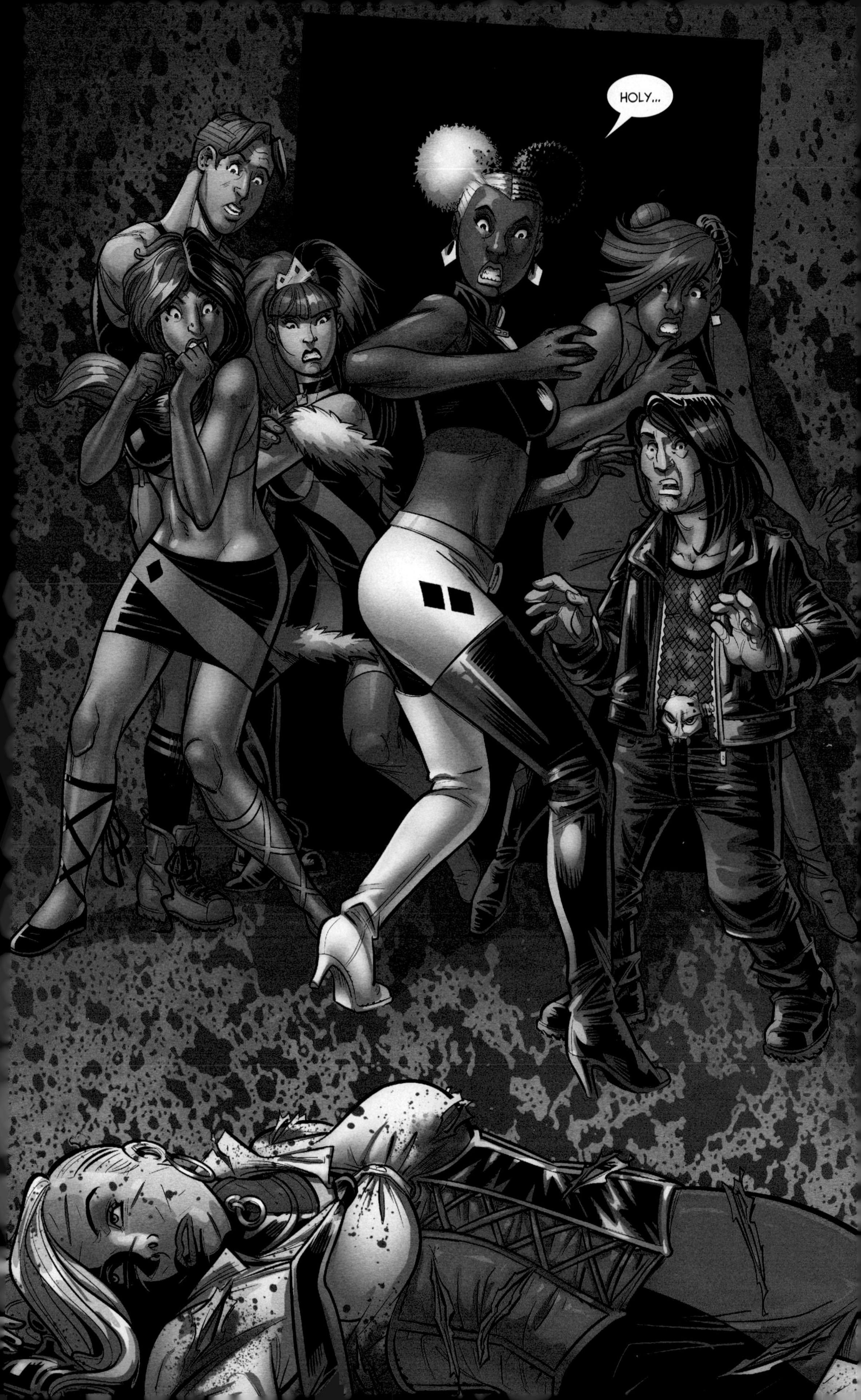
HOLY...

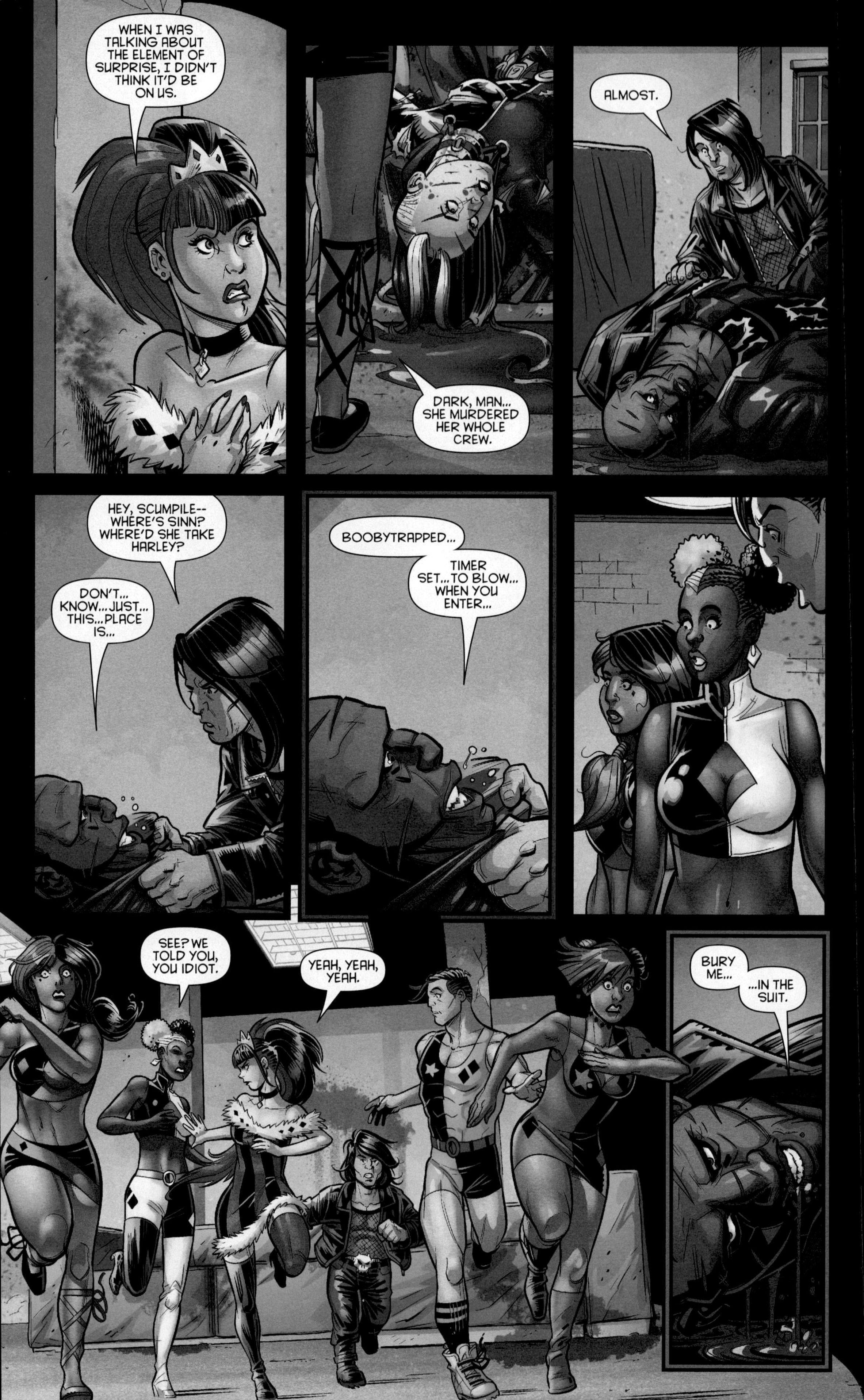
WHEN I WAS TALKING ABOUT THE ELEMENT OF SURPRISE, I DIDN'T THINK IT'D BE ON US.
DARK, MAN... SHE MURDERED HER WHOLE CREW.
ALMOST.
HEY, SCUMPILE-- WHERE'S SINN? WHERE'D SHE TAKE HARLEY?
DON'T... KNOW... JUST... THIS... PLACE IS...
BOOBYTRAPPED...
TIMER SET... TO BLOW... WHEN YOU ENTER...
SEE? WE TOLD YOU, YOU IDIOT.
YEAH, YEAH, YEAH.
BURY ME...
...IN THE SUIT.

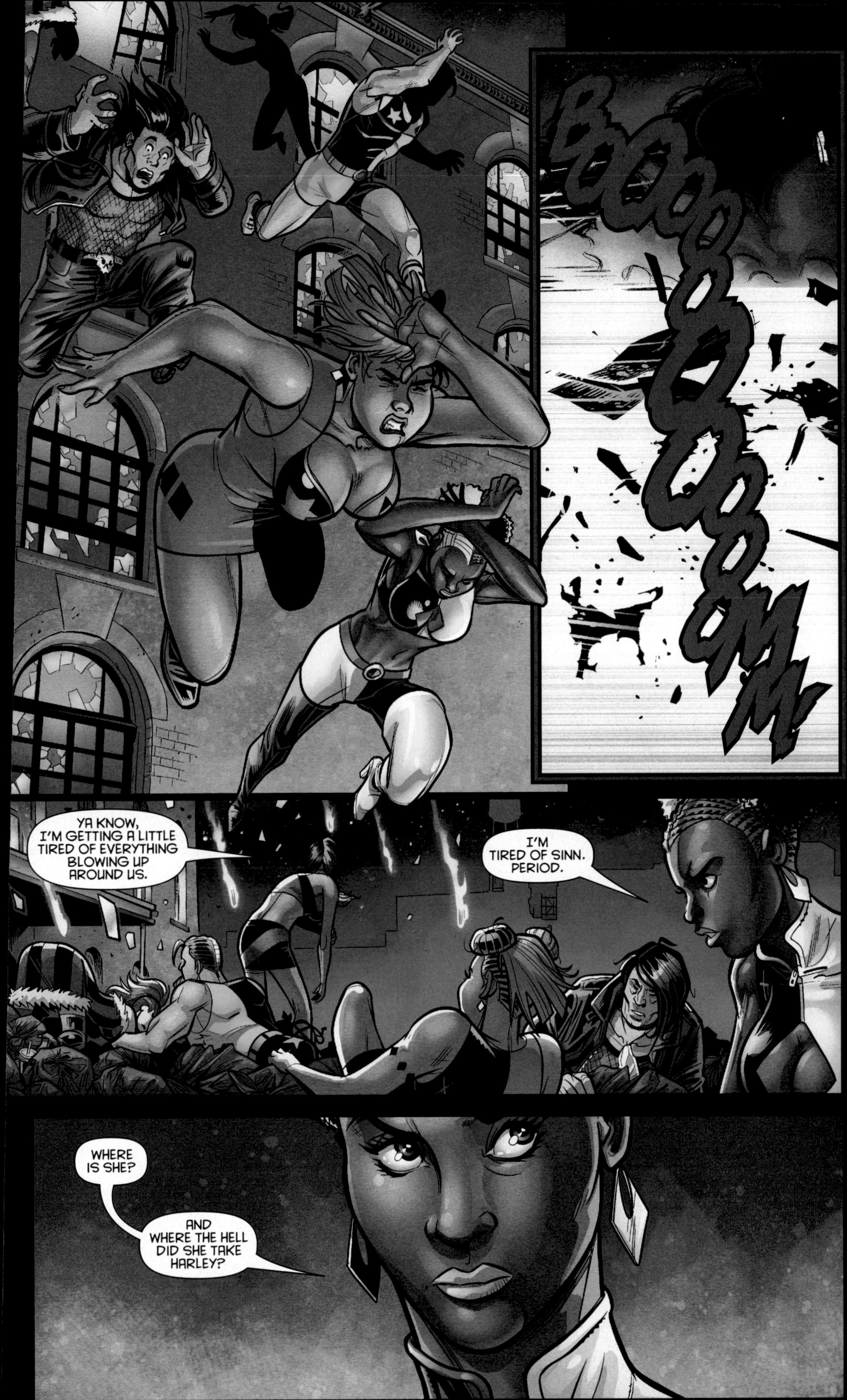
BOOOOOOOOOOOM!
YA KNOW, I'M GETTING A LITTLE TIRED OF EVERYTHING BLOWING UP AROUND US.
I'M TIRED OF SINN. PERIOD.
WHERE IS SHE?
AND WHERE THE HELL DID SHE TAKE HARLEY?

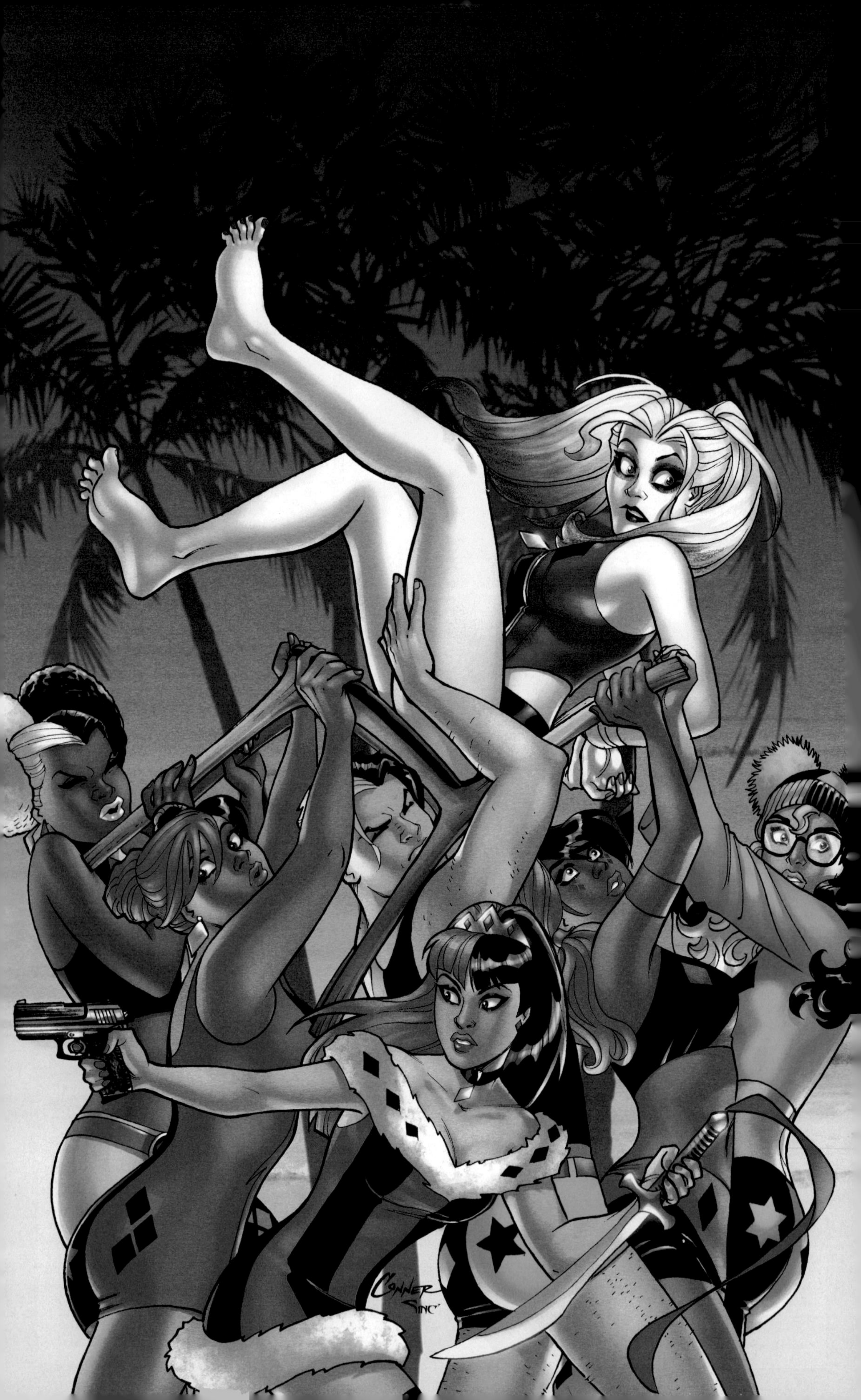

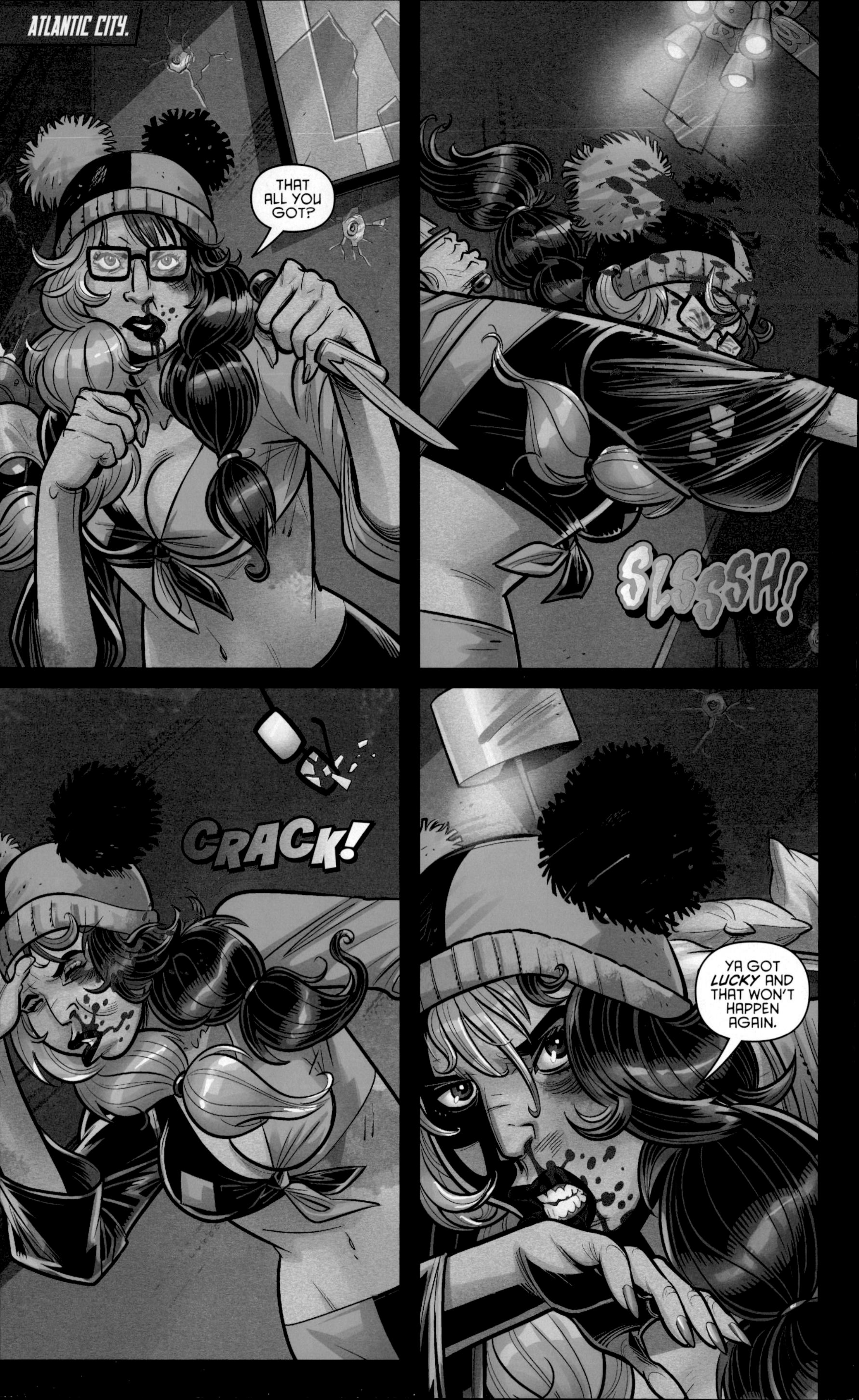
ATLANTIC CITY.
THAT ALL YOU GOT?
SLSSSH!
CRACK!
YA GOT *LUCKY* AND THAT WON'T HAPPEN AGAIN.

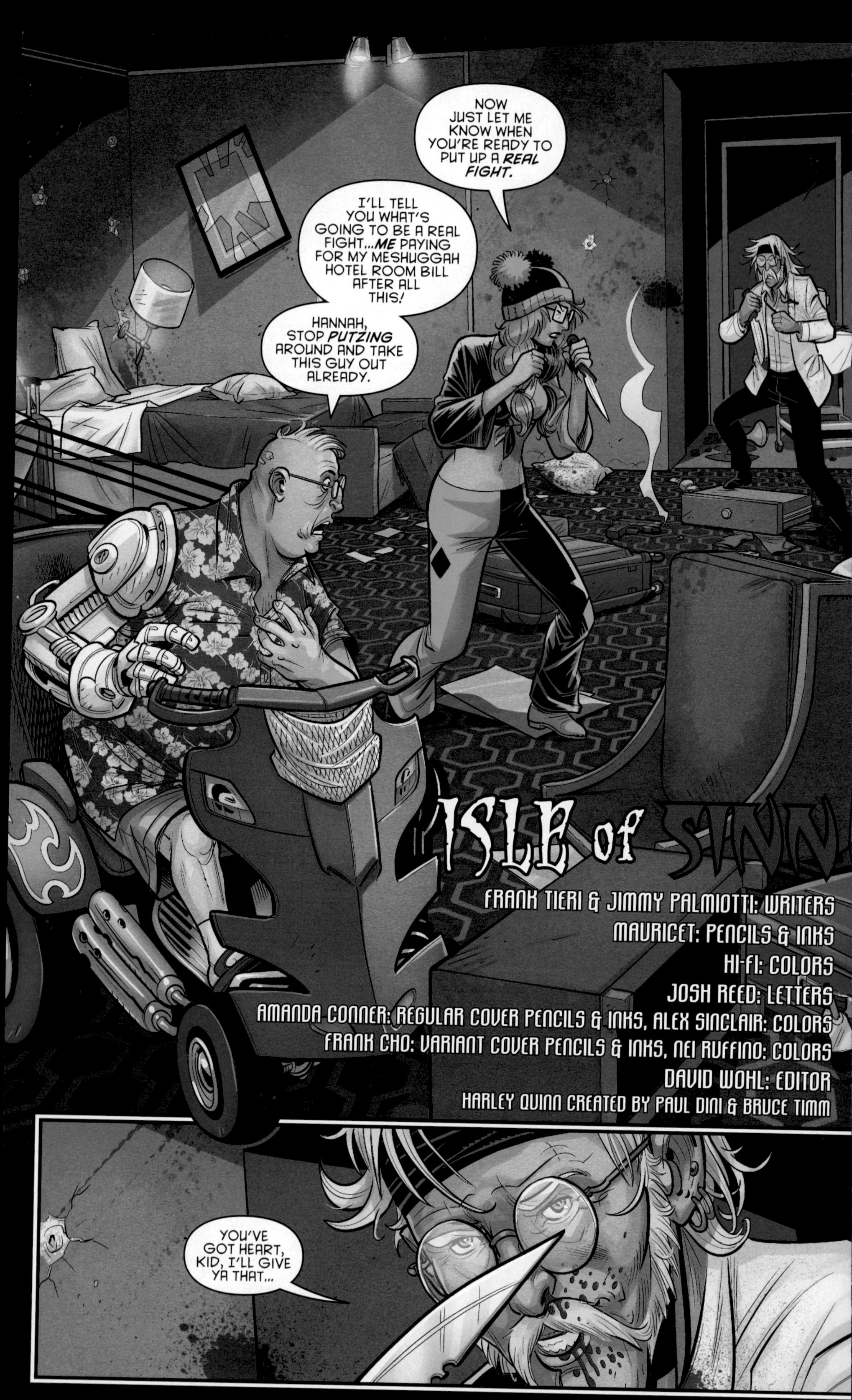
NOW JUST LET ME KNOW WHEN YOU'RE READY TO PUT UP A REAL FIGHT.
I'LL TELL YOU WHAT'S GOING TO BE A REAL FIGHT...ME PAYING FOR MY MESHUGGAH HOTEL ROOM BILL AFTER ALL THIS!
HANNAH, STOP PUTZING AROUND AND TAKE THIS GUY OUT ALREADY.
ISLE of
FRANK TIERI & JIMMY PALMIOTTI: WRITERS
MAURICET: PENCILS & INKS
HI-FI: COLORS
JOSH REED: LETTERS
AMANDA CONNER: REGULAR COVER PENCILS & INKS, ALEX SINCLAIR: COLORS
FRANK CHO: VARIANT COVER PENCILS & INKS, NEI RUFFINO: COLORS
DAVID WOHL: EDITOR
HARLEY QUINN CREATED BY PAUL DINI & BRUCE TIMM
YOU'VE GOT HEART, KID, I'LL GIVE YA THAT...

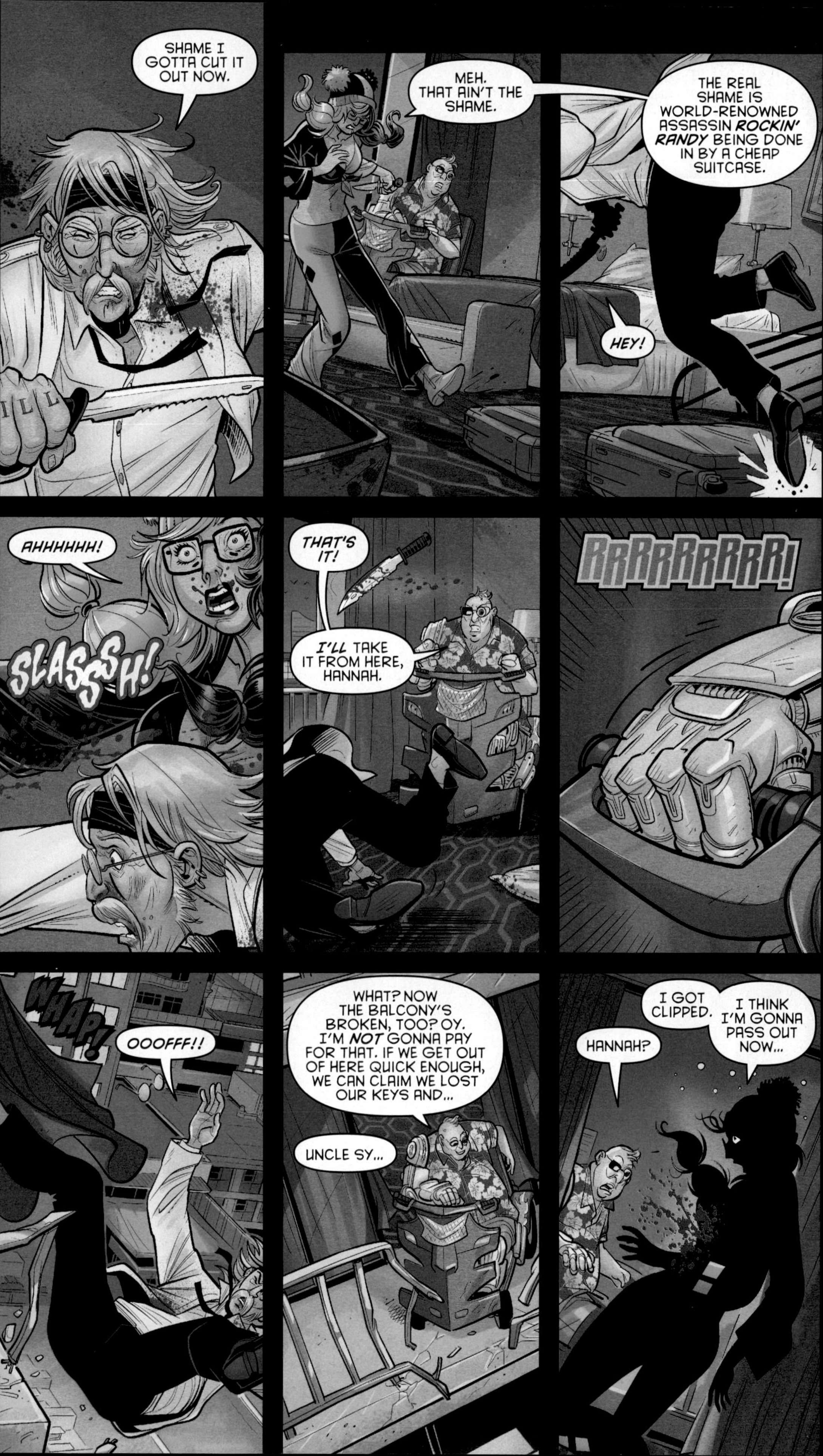

SHAME I GOTTA CUT IT OUT NOW.
MEH. THAT AIN'T THE SHAME.
THE REAL SHAME IS WORLD-RENOWNED ASSASSIN ROCKIN' RANDY BEING DONE IN BY A CHEAP SUITCASE.
HEY!
AHHHHHH!
SLASSSH!
THAT'S IT!
I'LL TAKE IT FROM HERE, HANNAH.
RRRRRRRRR!
WHAP!
OOOFFF!!
WHAT? NOW THE BALCONY'S BROKEN, TOO? OY. I'M NOT GONNA PAY FOR THAT. IF WE GET OUT OF HERE QUICK ENOUGH, WE CAN CLAIM WE LOST OUR KEYS AND...
UNCLE SY...
HANNAH?
I GOT CLIPPED.
I THINK I'M GONNA PASS OUT NOW...

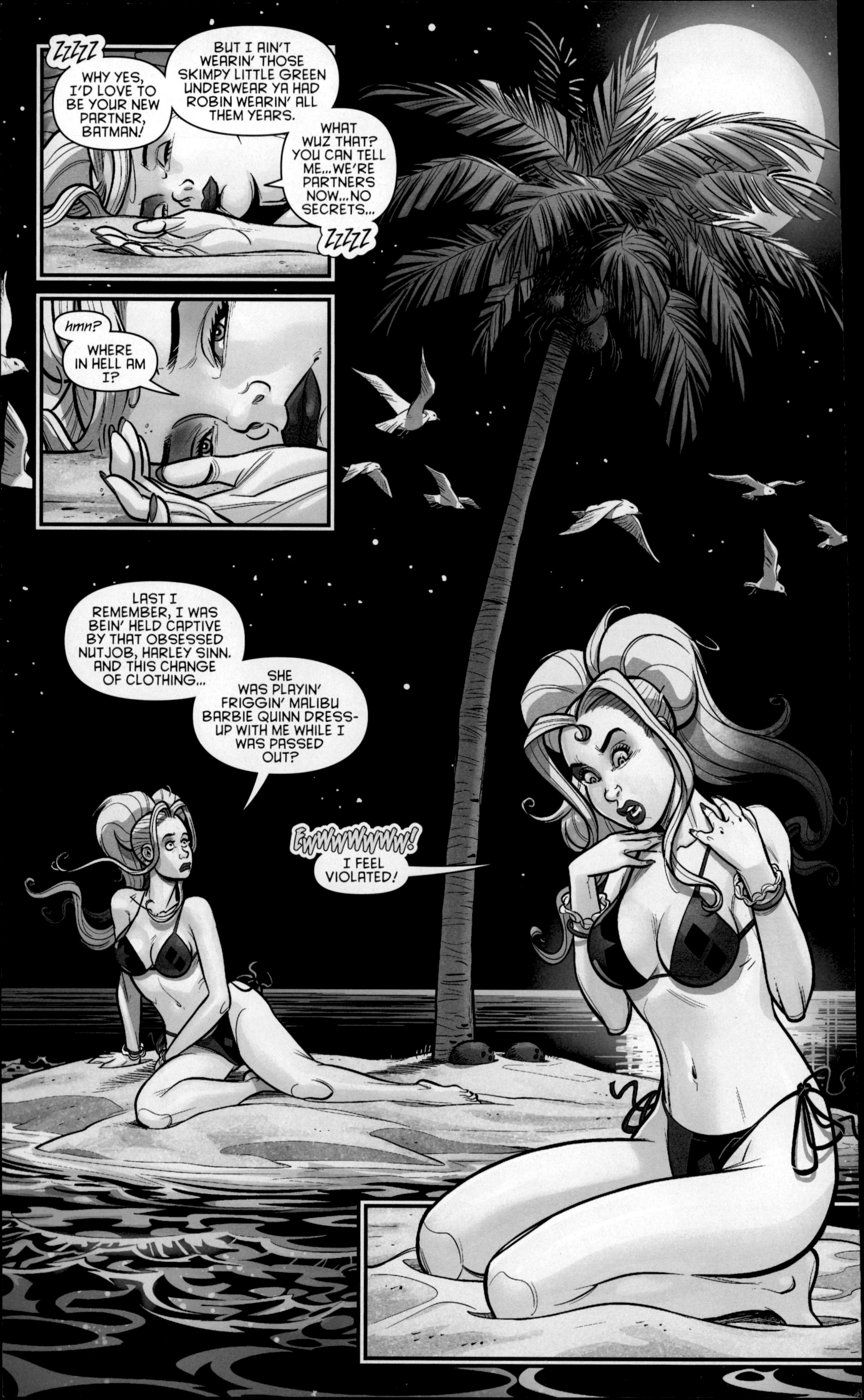

ZZZZZ
WHY YES, I'D LOVE TO BE YOUR NEW PARTNER, BATMAN!
BUT I AIN'T WEARIN' THOSE SKIMPY LITTLE GREEN UNDERWEAR YA HAD ROBIN WEARIN' ALL THEM YEARS.
WHAT WUZ THAT? YOU CAN TELL ME...WE'RE PARTNERS NOW...NO SECRETS...
ZZZZZ
hmn?
WHERE IN HELL AM I?
LAST I REMEMBER, I WAS BEIN' HELD CAPTIVE BY THAT OBSESSED NUTJOB, HARLEY SINN. AND THIS CHANGE OF CLOTHING...
SHE WAS PLAYIN' FRIGGIN' MALIBU BARBIE QUINN DRESS-UP WITH ME WHILE I WAS PASSED OUT?
EWWWWWWW! I FEEL VIOLATED!

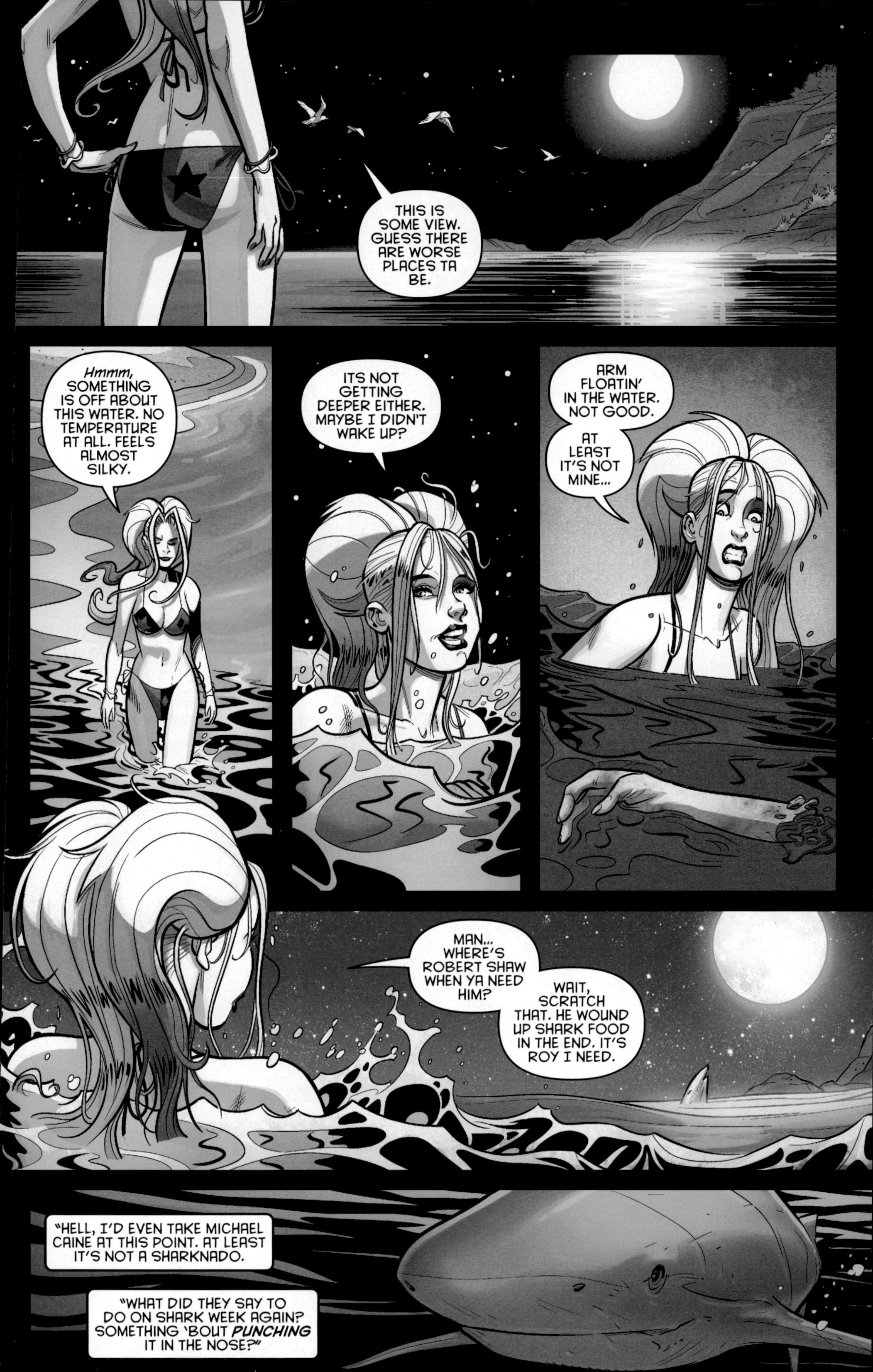
THIS IS SOME VIEW. GUESS THERE ARE WORSE PLACES TA BE.
Hmmm, SOMETHING IS OFF ABOUT THIS WATER. NO TEMPERATURE AT ALL. FEELS ALMOST SILKY.
ITS NOT GETTING DEEPER EITHER. MAYBE I DIDN'T WAKE UP?
ARM FLOATIN' IN THE WATER. NOT GOOD.
AT LEAST IT'S NOT MINE...
MAN... WHERE'S ROBERT SHAW WHEN YA NEED HIM?
WAIT, SCRATCH THAT. HE WOUND UP SHARK FOOD IN THE END. IT'S ROY I NEED.
"HELL, I'D EVEN TAKE MICHAEL CAINE AT THIS POINT. AT LEAST IT'S NOT A SHARKNADO.
"WHAT DID THEY SAY TO DO ON SHARK WEEK AGAIN? SOMETHING 'BOUT *PUNCHING* IT IN THE NOSE?"

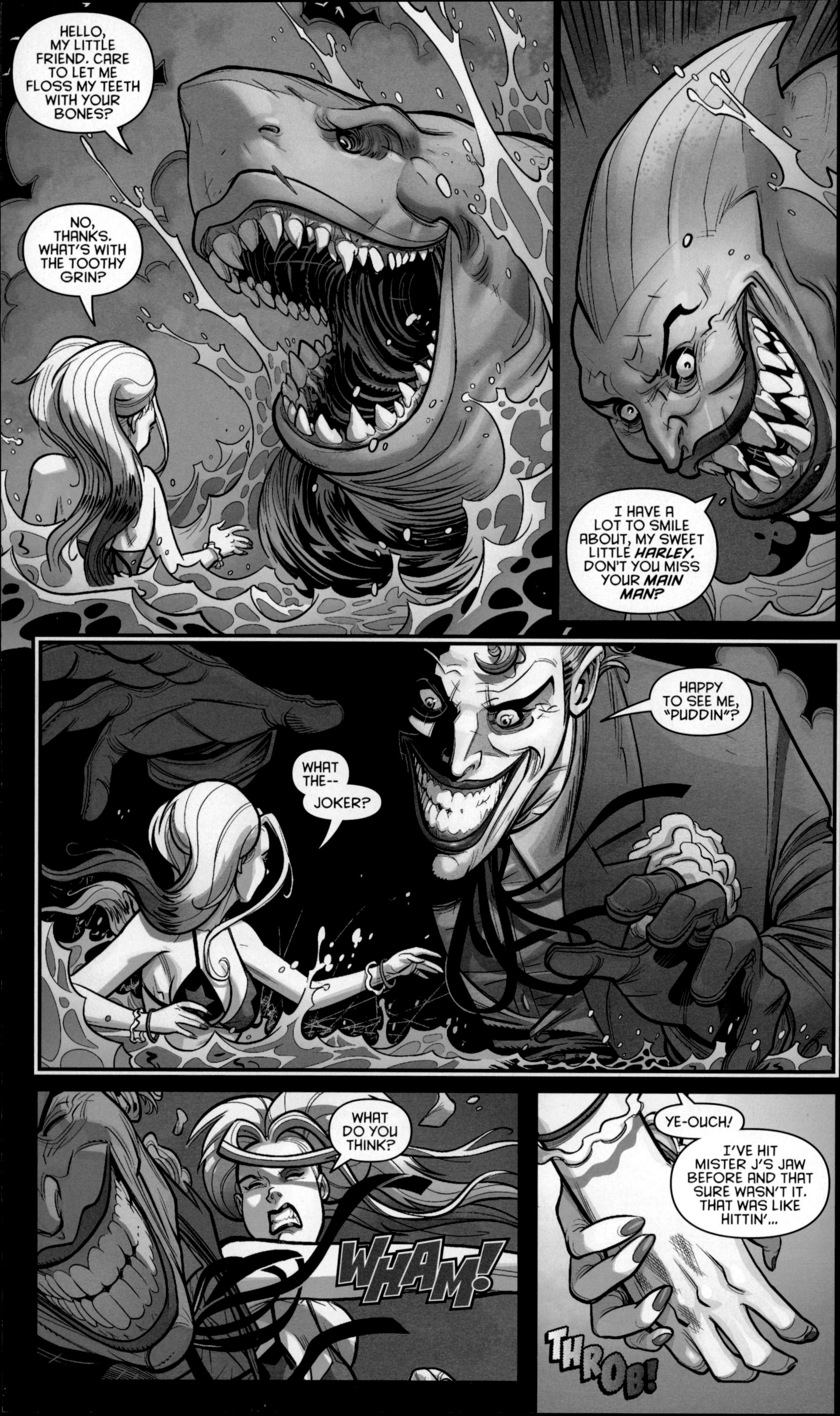
HELLO, MY LITTLE FRIEND. CARE TO LET ME FLOSS MY TEETH WITH YOUR BONES?
NO, THANKS. WHAT'S WITH THE TOOTHY GRIN?
I HAVE A LOT TO SMILE ABOUT, MY SWEET LITTLE *HARLEY*. DON'T YOU MISS YOUR *MAIN MAN?*
HAPPY TO SEE ME, "PUDDIN"?
WHAT THE-- JOKER?
WHAT DO YOU THINK?
WHAM!
YE-OUCH!
I'VE HIT MISTER J'S JAW BEFORE AND THAT SURE WASN'T IT. THAT WAS LIKE HITTIN'...
THROB!

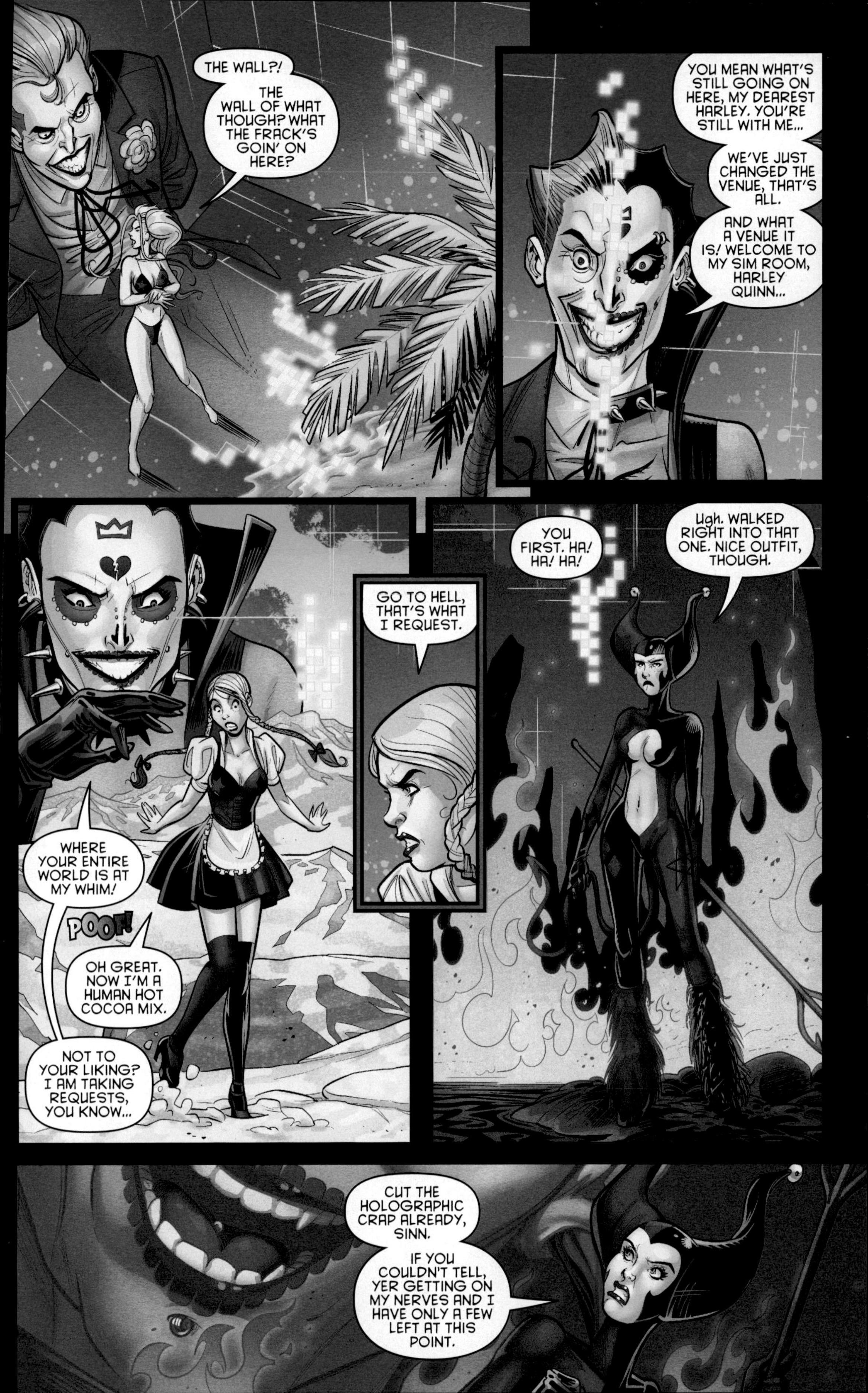
THE WALL?!
THE WALL OF WHAT THOUGH? WHAT THE FRACK'S GOIN' ON HERE?
YOU MEAN WHAT'S STILL GOING ON HERE, MY DEAREST HARLEY. YOU'RE STILL WITH ME...
WE'VE JUST CHANGED THE VENUE, THAT'S ALL.
AND WHAT A VENUE IT IS! WELCOME TO MY SIM ROOM, HARLEY QUINN...
WHERE YOUR ENTIRE WORLD IS AT MY WHIM!
POOF!
OH GREAT. NOW I'M A HUMAN HOT COCOA MIX.
NOT TO YOUR LIKING? I AM TAKING REQUESTS, YOU KNOW...
GO TO HELL, THAT'S WHAT I REQUEST.
YOU FIRST. HA! HA! HA!
Ugh. WALKED RIGHT INTO THAT ONE. NICE OUTFIT, THOUGH.
CUT THE HOLOGRAPHIC CRAP ALREADY, SINN.
IF YOU COULDN'T TELL, YER GETTING ON MY NERVES AND I HAVE ONLY A FEW LEFT AT THIS POINT.

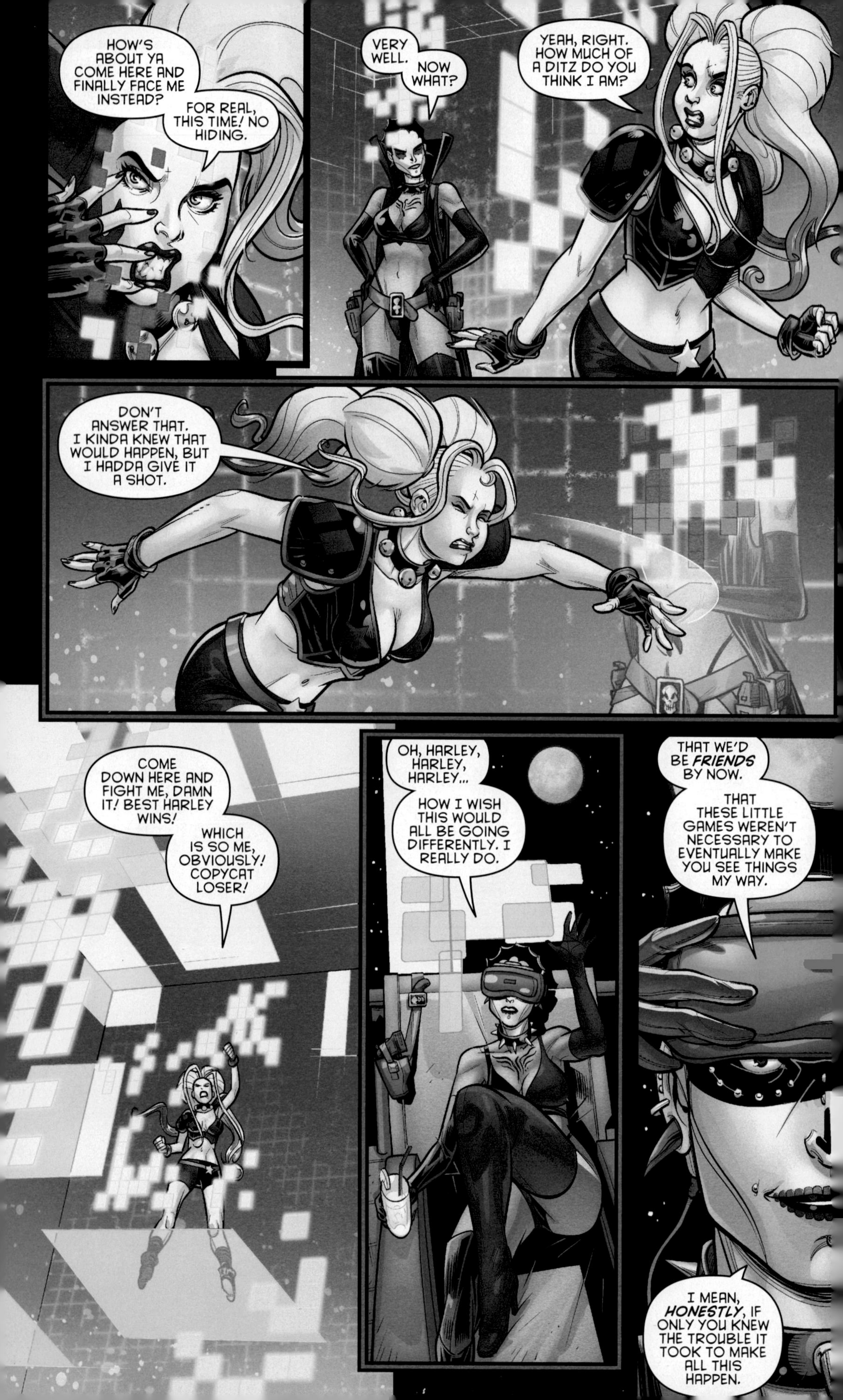
HOW'S ABOUT YA COME HERE AND FINALLY FACE ME INSTEAD?
FOR REAL, THIS TIME! NO HIDING.
VERY WELL.
NOW WHAT?
YEAH, RIGHT. HOW MUCH OF A DITZ DO YOU THINK I AM?
DON'T ANSWER THAT. I KINDA KNEW THAT WOULD HAPPEN, BUT I HADDA GIVE IT A SHOT.
COME DOWN HERE AND FIGHT ME, DAMN IT! BEST HARLEY WINS!
WHICH IS SO ME, OBVIOUSLY! COPYCAT LOSER!
OH, HARLEY, HARLEY, HARLEY...
HOW I WISH THIS WOULD ALL BE GOING DIFFERENTLY. I REALLY DO.
THAT WE'D BE *FRIENDS* BY NOW.
THAT THESE LITTLE GAMES WEREN'T NECESSARY TO EVENTUALLY MAKE YOU SEE THINGS MY WAY.
I MEAN, ***HONESTLY***, IF ONLY YOU KNEW THE TROUBLE IT TOOK TO MAKE ALL THIS HAPPEN.

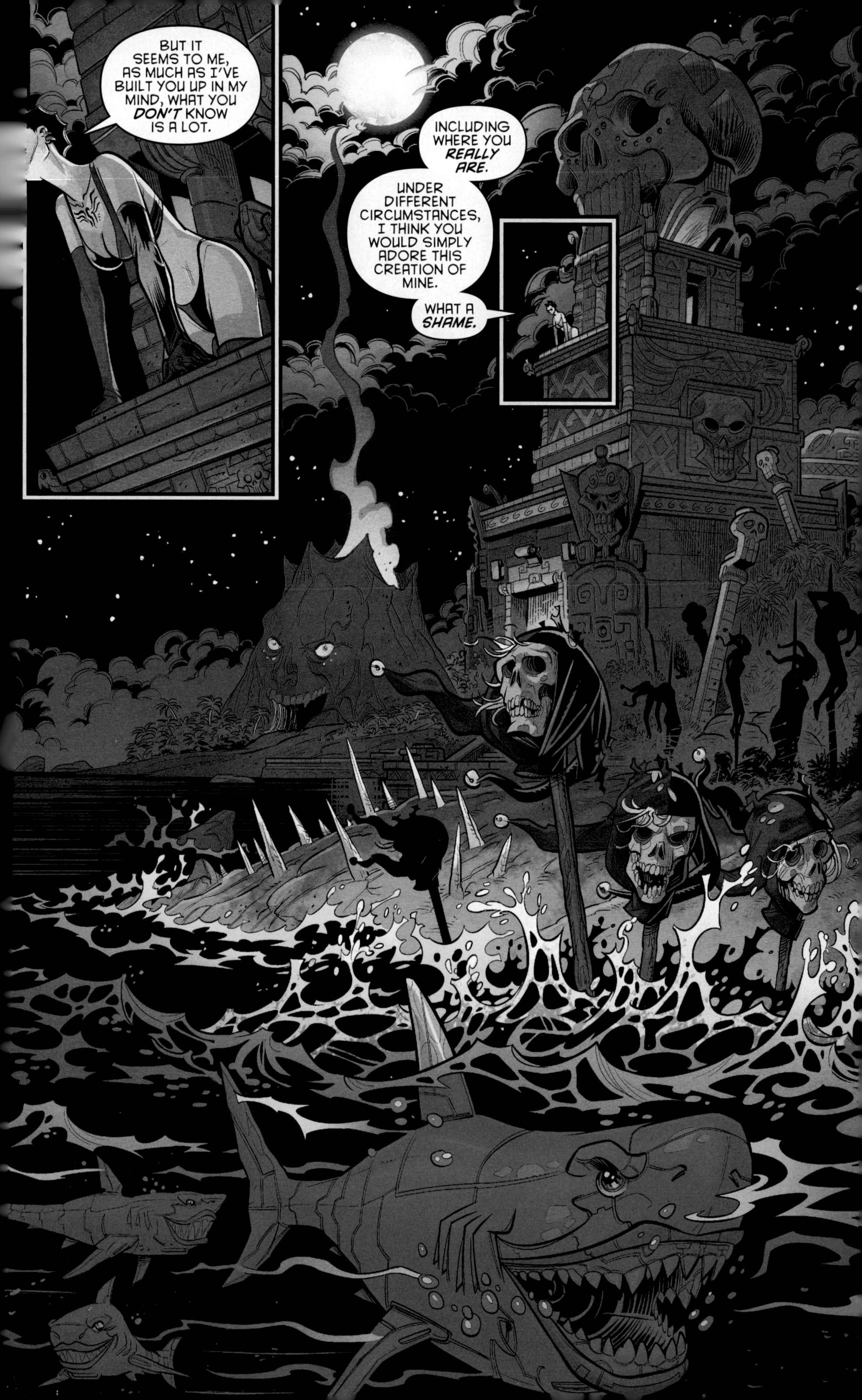
BUT IT SEEMS TO ME, AS MUCH AS I'VE BUILT YOU UP IN MY MIND, WHAT YOU *DON'T* KNOW IS A LOT.
INCLUDING WHERE YOU *REALLY ARE*.
UNDER DIFFERENT CIRCUMSTANCES, I THINK YOU WOULD SIMPLY ADORE THIS CREATION OF MINE.
WHAT A *SHAME*.

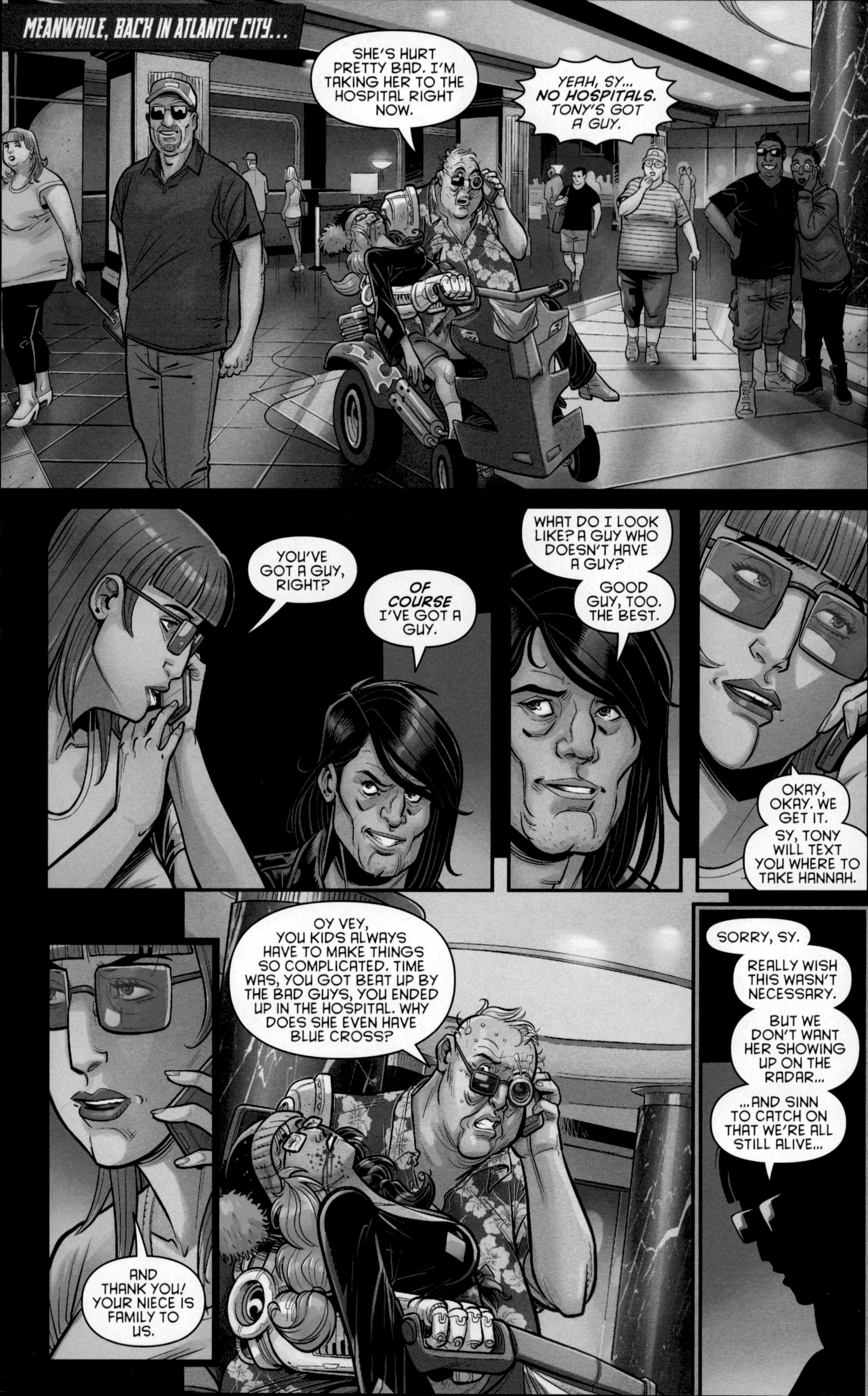
MEANWHILE, BACK IN ATLANTIC CITY...
SHE'S HURT PRETTY BAD. I'M TAKING HER TO THE HOSPITAL RIGHT NOW.
YEAH, SY... NO HOSPITALS. TONY'S GOT A GUY.
YOU'VE GOT A GUY, RIGHT?
OF COURSE I'VE GOT A GUY.
WHAT DO I LOOK LIKE? A GUY WHO DOESN'T HAVE A GUY?
GOOD GUY, TOO. THE BEST.
OKAY, OKAY. WE GET IT.
SY, TONY WILL TEXT YOU WHERE TO TAKE HANNAH.
OY VEY, YOU KIDS ALWAYS HAVE TO MAKE THINGS SO COMPLICATED. TIME WAS, YOU GOT BEAT UP BY THE BAD GUYS, YOU ENDED UP IN THE HOSPITAL. WHY DOES SHE EVEN HAVE BLUE CROSS?
AND THANK YOU! YOUR NIECE IS FAMILY TO US.
SORRY, SY.
REALLY WISH THIS WASN'T NECESSARY.
BUT WE DON'T WANT HER SHOWING UP ON THE RADAR...
...AND SINN TO CATCH ON THAT WE'RE ALL STILL ALIVE...

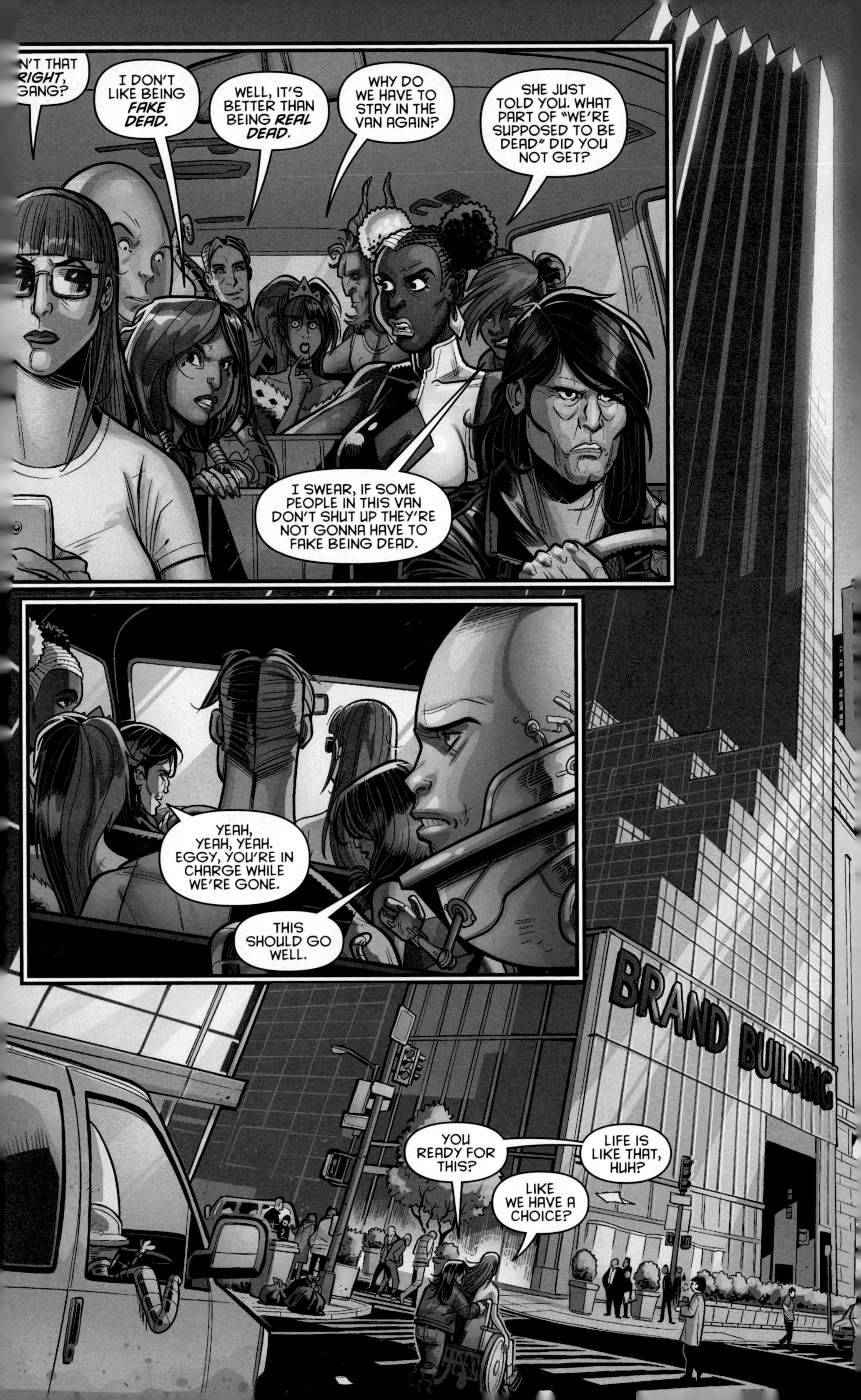
N'T THAT RIGHT, GANG?
I DON'T LIKE BEING *FAKE DEAD*.
WELL, IT'S BETTER THAN BEING *REAL DEAD*.
WHY DO WE HAVE TO STAY IN THE VAN AGAIN?
SHE JUST TOLD YOU. WHAT PART OF "WE'RE SUPPOSED TO BE DEAD" DID YOU NOT GET?
I SWEAR, IF SOME PEOPLE IN THIS VAN DON'T SHUT UP THEY'RE NOT GONNA HAVE TO FAKE BEING DEAD.
YEAH, YEAH, YEAH. EGGY, YOU'RE IN CHARGE WHILE WE'RE GONE.
THIS SHOULD GO WELL.
BRAND BUILDING
YOU READY FOR THIS?
LIFE IS LIKE THAT, HUH?
LIKE WE HAVE A CHOICE?

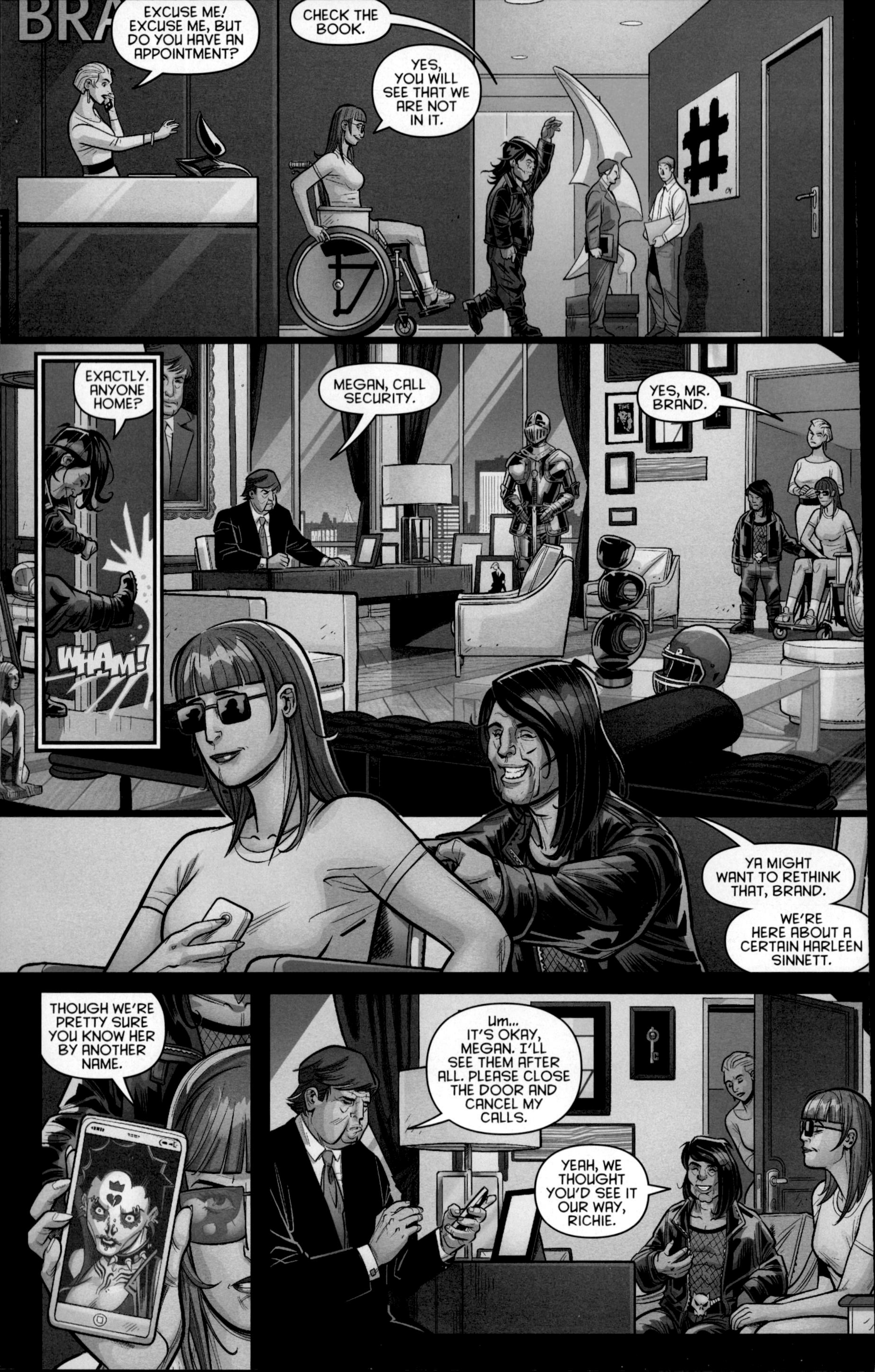
BRA
EXCUSE ME! EXCUSE ME, BUT DO YOU HAVE AN APPOINTMENT?
CHECK THE BOOK.
YES, YOU WILL SEE THAT WE ARE NOT IN IT.
EXACTLY. ANYONE HOME?
WHAM!
MEGAN, CALL SECURITY.
YES, MR. BRAND.
YA MIGHT WANT TO RETHINK THAT, BRAND.
WE'RE HERE ABOUT A CERTAIN HARLEEN SINNETT.
THOUGH WE'RE PRETTY SURE YOU KNOW HER BY ANOTHER NAME.
Um... IT'S OKAY, MEGAN. I'LL SEE THEM AFTER ALL. PLEASE CLOSE THE DOOR AND CANCEL MY CALLS.
YEAH, WE THOUGHT YOU'D SEE IT OUR WAY, RICHIE.

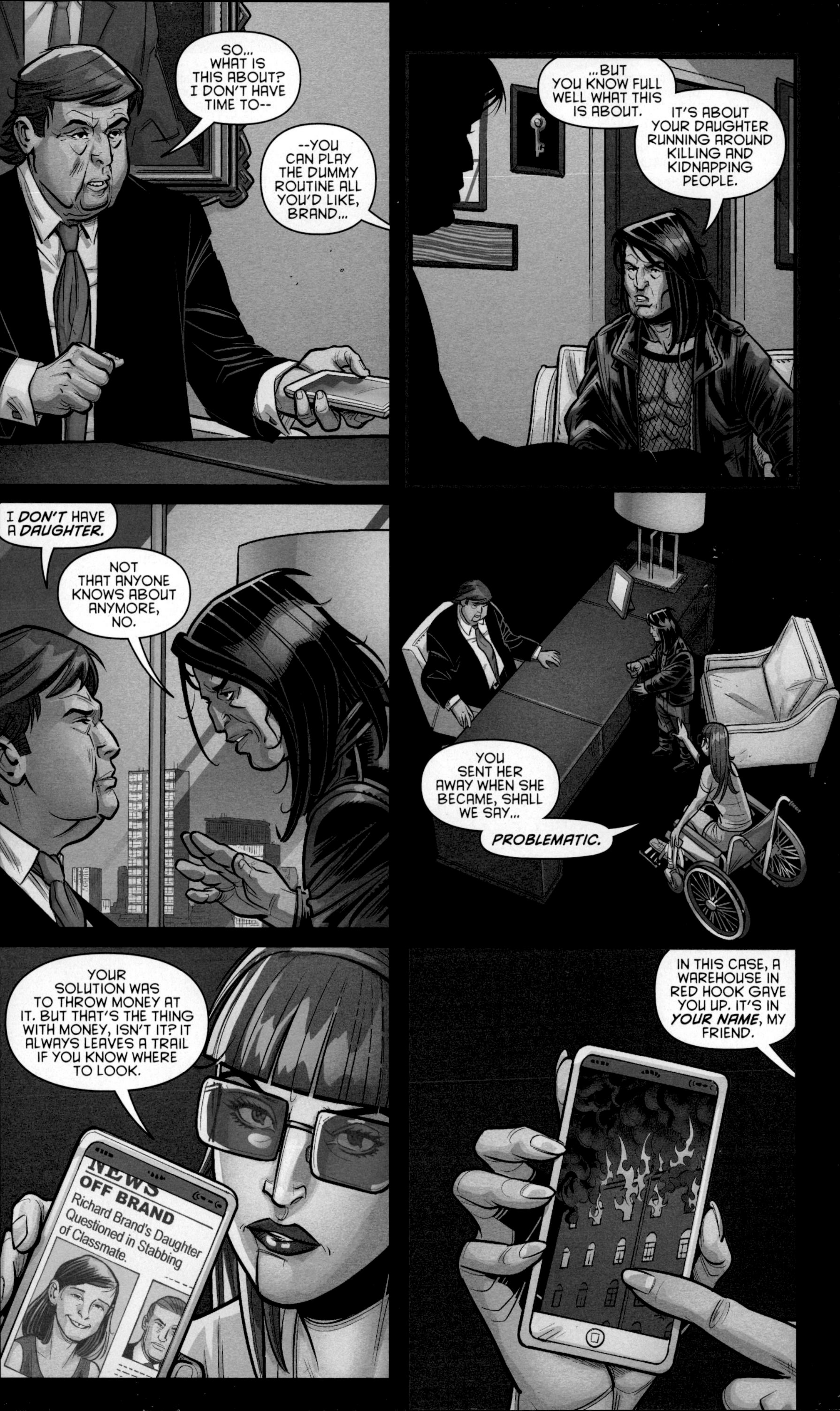

SO... WHAT IS THIS ABOUT? I DON'T HAVE TIME TO--
--YOU CAN PLAY THE DUMMY ROUTINE ALL YOU'D LIKE, BRAND...
...BUT YOU KNOW FULL WELL WHAT THIS IS ABOUT.
IT'S ABOUT YOUR DAUGHTER RUNNING AROUND KILLING AND KIDNAPPING PEOPLE.
I *DON'T* HAVE A *DAUGHTER.*
NOT THAT ANYONE KNOWS ABOUT ANYMORE, NO.
YOU SENT HER AWAY WHEN SHE BECAME, SHALL WE SAY...
PROBLEMATIC.
YOUR SOLUTION WAS TO THROW MONEY AT IT. BUT THAT'S THE THING WITH MONEY, ISN'T IT? IT ALWAYS LEAVES A TRAIL IF YOU KNOW WHERE TO LOOK.
OFF BRAND
Richard Brand's Daughter Questioned in Stabbing of Classmate.
IN THIS CASE, A WAREHOUSE IN RED HOOK GAVE YOU UP. IT'S IN *YOUR NAME*, MY FRIEND.

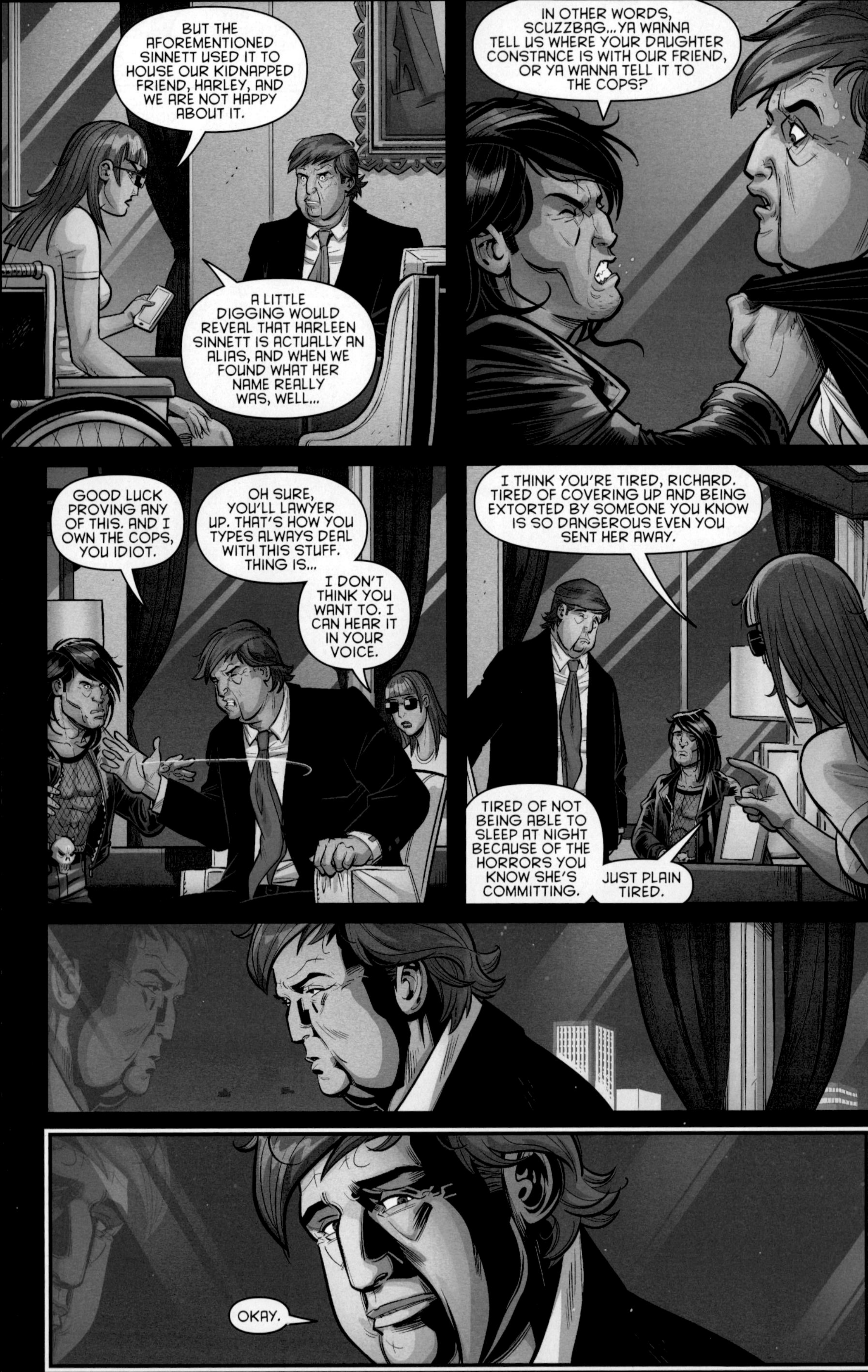
BUT THE AFOREMENTIONED SINNETT USED IT TO HOUSE OUR KIDNAPPED FRIEND, HARLEY, AND WE ARE NOT HAPPY ABOUT IT.
A LITTLE DIGGING WOULD REVEAL THAT HARLEEN SINNETT IS ACTUALLY AN ALIAS, AND WHEN WE FOUND WHAT HER NAME REALLY WAS, WELL...
IN OTHER WORDS, SCUZZBAG...YA WANNA TELL US WHERE YOUR DAUGHTER CONSTANCE IS WITH OUR FRIEND, OR YA WANNA TELL IT TO THE COPS?
GOOD LUCK PROVING ANY OF THIS. AND I OWN THE COPS, YOU IDIOT.
OH SURE, YOU'LL LAWYER UP. THAT'S HOW YOU TYPES ALWAYS DEAL WITH THIS STUFF. THING IS...
I DON'T THINK YOU WANT TO. I CAN HEAR IT IN YOUR VOICE.
I THINK YOU'RE TIRED, RICHARD. TIRED OF COVERING UP AND BEING EXTORTED BY SOMEONE YOU KNOW IS SO DANGEROUS EVEN YOU SENT HER AWAY.
TIRED OF NOT BEING ABLE TO SLEEP AT NIGHT BECAUSE OF THE HORRORS YOU KNOW SHE'S COMMITTING.
JUST PLAIN TIRED.
OKAY.

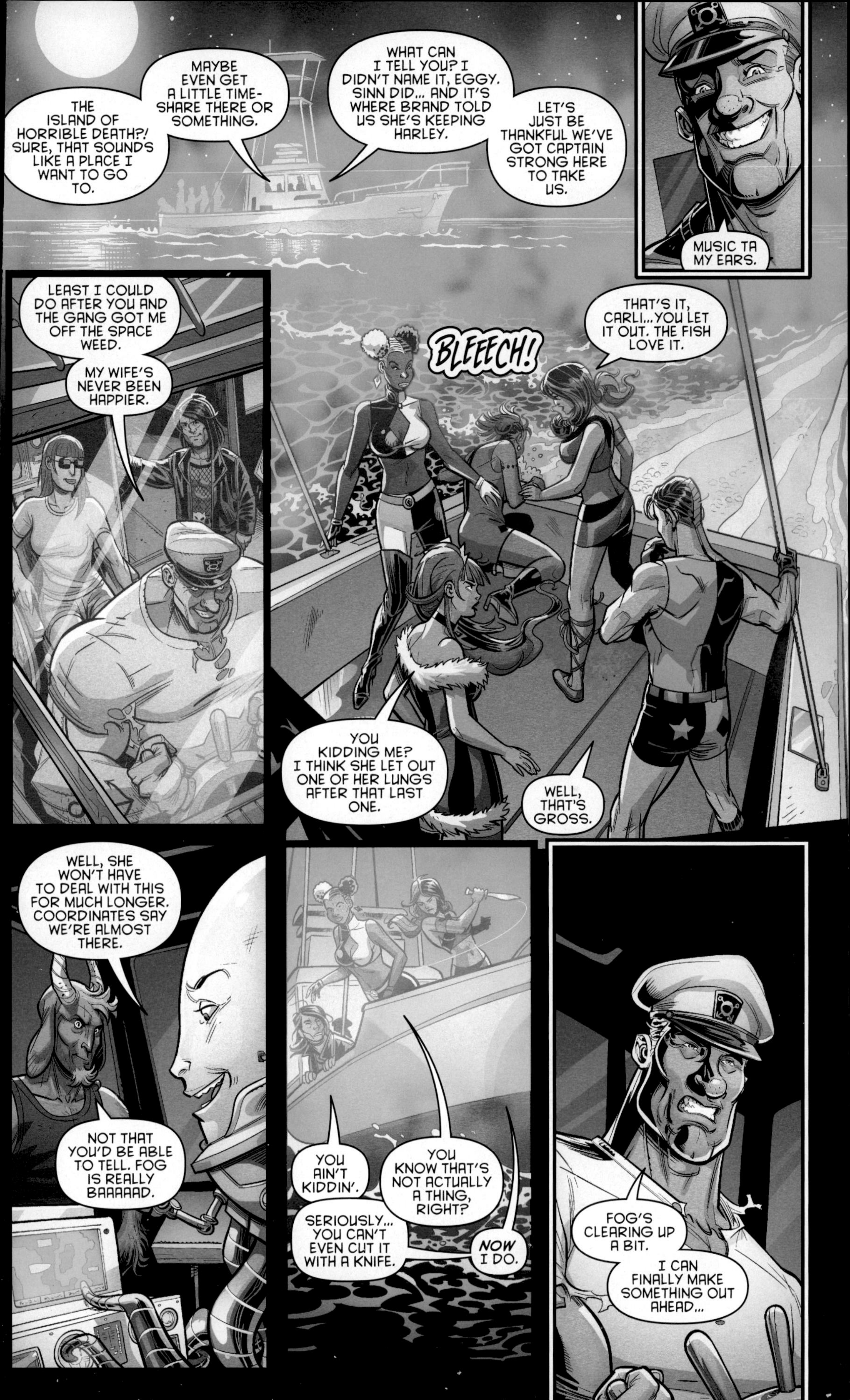

THE ISLAND OF HORRIBLE DEATH?! SURE, THAT SOUNDS LIKE A PLACE I WANT TO GO TO.
MAYBE EVEN GET A LITTLE TIME-SHARE THERE OR SOMETHING.
WHAT CAN I TELL YOU? I DIDN'T NAME IT, EGGY. SINN DID... AND IT'S WHERE BRAND TOLD US SHE'S KEEPING HARLEY.
LET'S JUST BE THANKFUL WE'VE GOT CAPTAIN STRONG HERE TO TAKE US.
MUSIC TA MY EARS.
LEAST I COULD DO AFTER YOU AND THE GANG GOT ME OFF THE SPACE WEED.
MY WIFE'S NEVER BEEN HAPPIER.
BLEEECH!
THAT'S IT, CARLI...YOU LET IT OUT. THE FISH LOVE IT.
YOU KIDDING ME? I THINK SHE LET OUT ONE OF HER LUNGS AFTER THAT LAST ONE.
WELL, THAT'S GROSS.
WELL, SHE WON'T HAVE TO DEAL WITH THIS FOR MUCH LONGER. COORDINATES SAY WE'RE ALMOST THERE.
NOT THAT YOU'D BE ABLE TO TELL. FOG IS REALLY BAAAAAD.
YOU AIN'T KIDDIN'.
YOU KNOW THAT'S NOT ACTUALLY A THING, RIGHT?
SERIOUSLY... YOU CAN'T EVEN CUT IT WITH A KNIFE.
NOW I DO.
FOG'S CLEARING UP A BIT.
I CAN FINALLY MAKE SOMETHING OUT AHEAD...

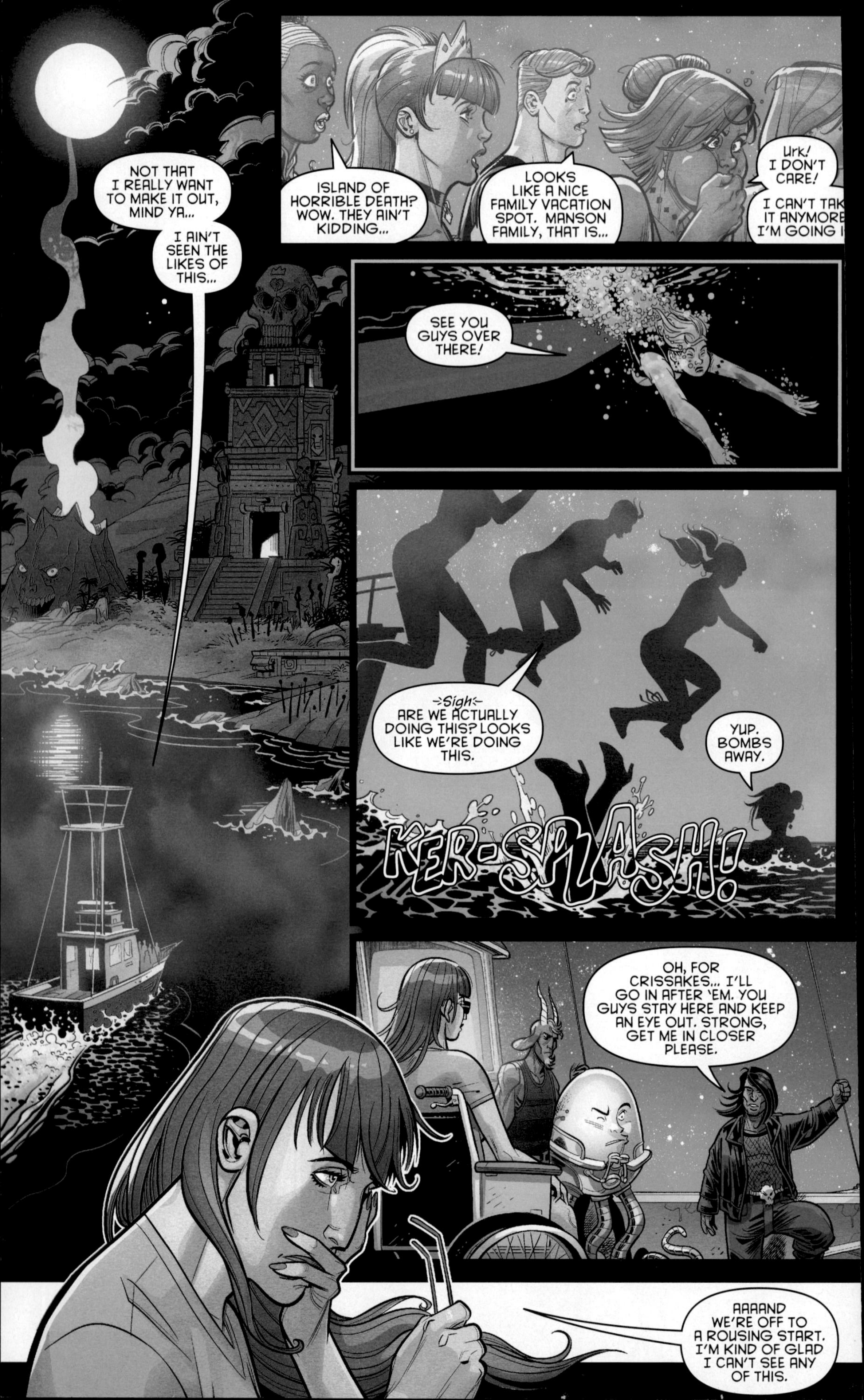
NOT THAT I REALLY WANT TO MAKE IT OUT, MIND YA...
I AIN'T SEEN THE LIKES OF THIS...
ISLAND OF HORRIBLE DEATH? WOW. THEY AIN'T KIDDING...
LOOKS LIKE A NICE FAMILY VACATION SPOT. MANSON FAMILY, THAT IS...
Urk! I DON'T CARE!
I CAN'T TAK IT ANYMORE I'M GOING I
SEE YOU GUYS OVER THERE!
Sigh
ARE WE ACTUALLY DOING THIS? LOOKS LIKE WE'RE DOING THIS.
YUP. BOMBS AWAY.
KER-SPLASH!
OH, FOR CRISSAKES... I'LL GO IN AFTER 'EM. YOU GUYS STAY HERE AND KEEP AN EYE OUT. STRONG, GET ME IN CLOSER PLEASE.
AAAAND WE'RE OFF TO A ROUSING START. I'M KIND OF GLAD I CAN'T SEE ANY OF THIS.

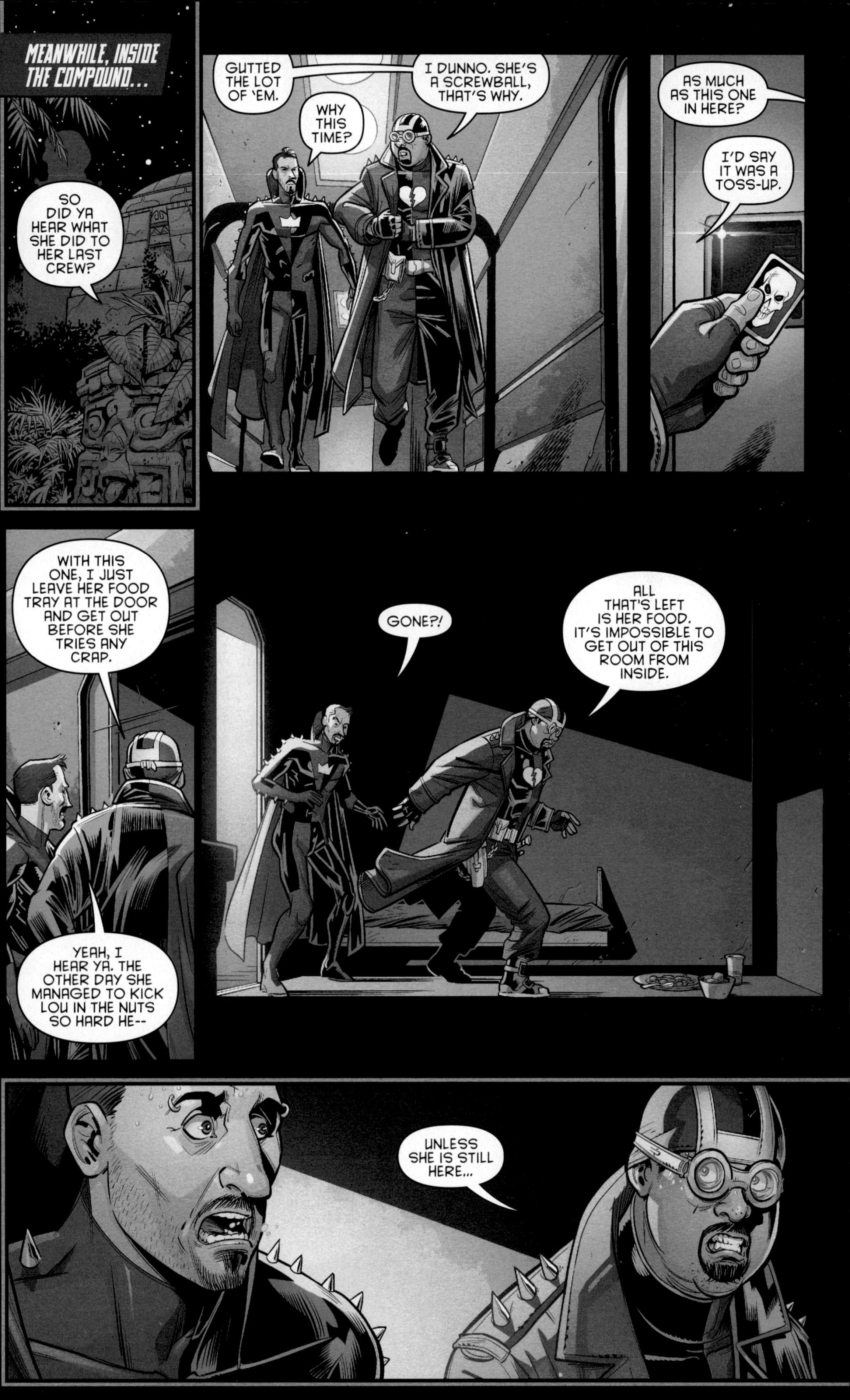
MEANWHILE, INSIDE THE COMPOUND...
SO DID YA HEAR WHAT SHE DID TO HER LAST CREW?
GUTTED THE LOT OF 'EM.
WHY THIS TIME?
I DUNNO. SHE'S A SCREWBALL, THAT'S WHY.
AS MUCH AS THIS ONE IN HERE?
I'D SAY IT WAS A TOSS-UP.
WITH THIS ONE, I JUST LEAVE HER FOOD TRAY AT THE DOOR AND GET OUT BEFORE SHE TRIES ANY CRAP.
YEAH, I HEAR YA. THE OTHER DAY SHE MANAGED TO KICK LOU IN THE NUTS SO HARD HE--
GONE?!
ALL THAT'S LEFT IS HER FOOD. IT'S IMPOSSIBLE TO GET OUT OF THIS ROOM FROM INSIDE.
UNLESS SHE IS STILL HERE...

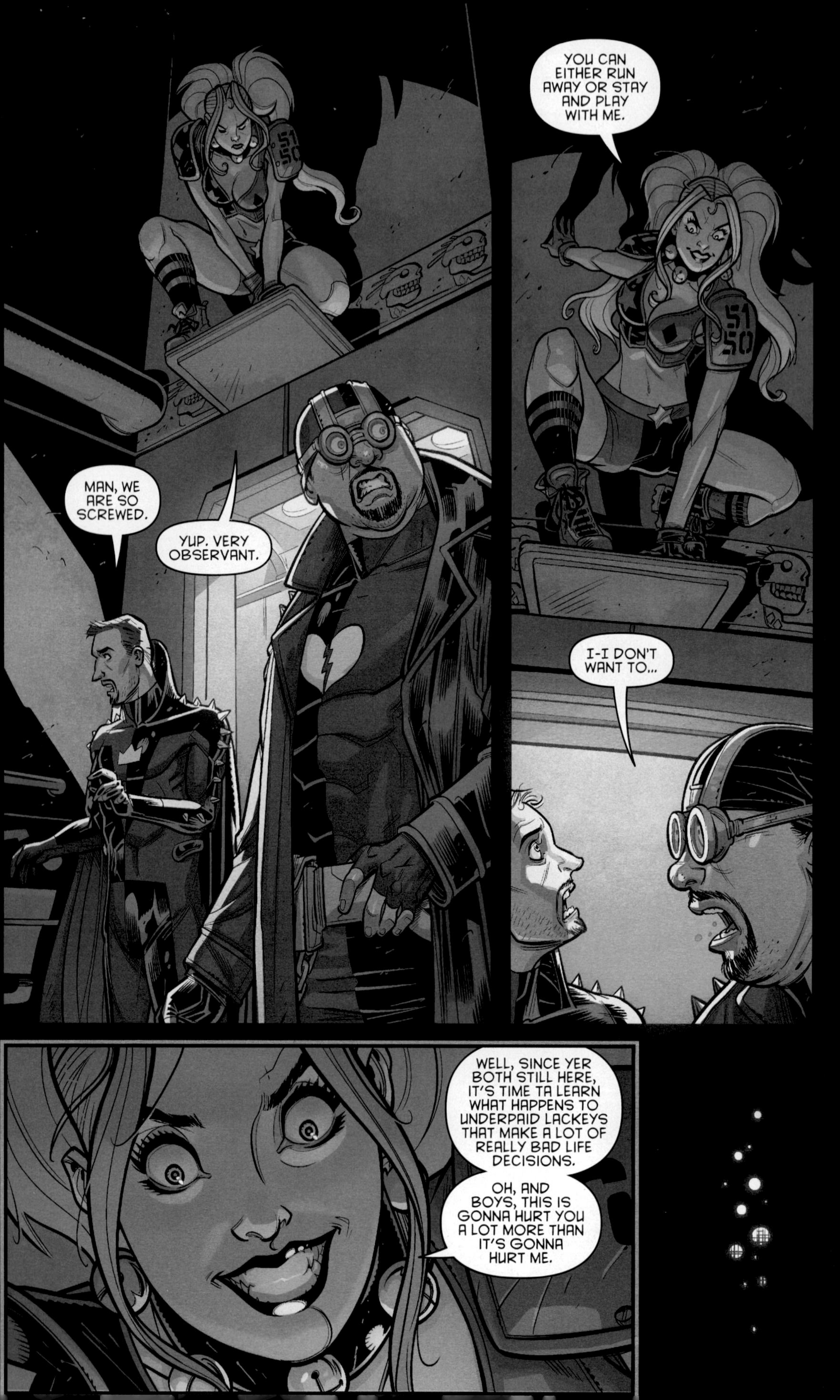
YOU CAN EITHER RUN AWAY OR STAY AND PLAY WITH ME.
MAN, WE ARE SO SCREWED.
YUP. VERY OBSERVANT.
I-I DON'T WANT TO...
WELL, SINCE YER BOTH STILL HERE, IT'S TIME TA LEARN WHAT HAPPENS TO UNDERPAID LACKEYS THAT MAKE A LOT OF REALLY BAD LIFE DECISIONS.
OH, AND BOYS, THIS IS GONNA HURT YOU A LOT MORE THAN IT'S GONNA HURT ME.

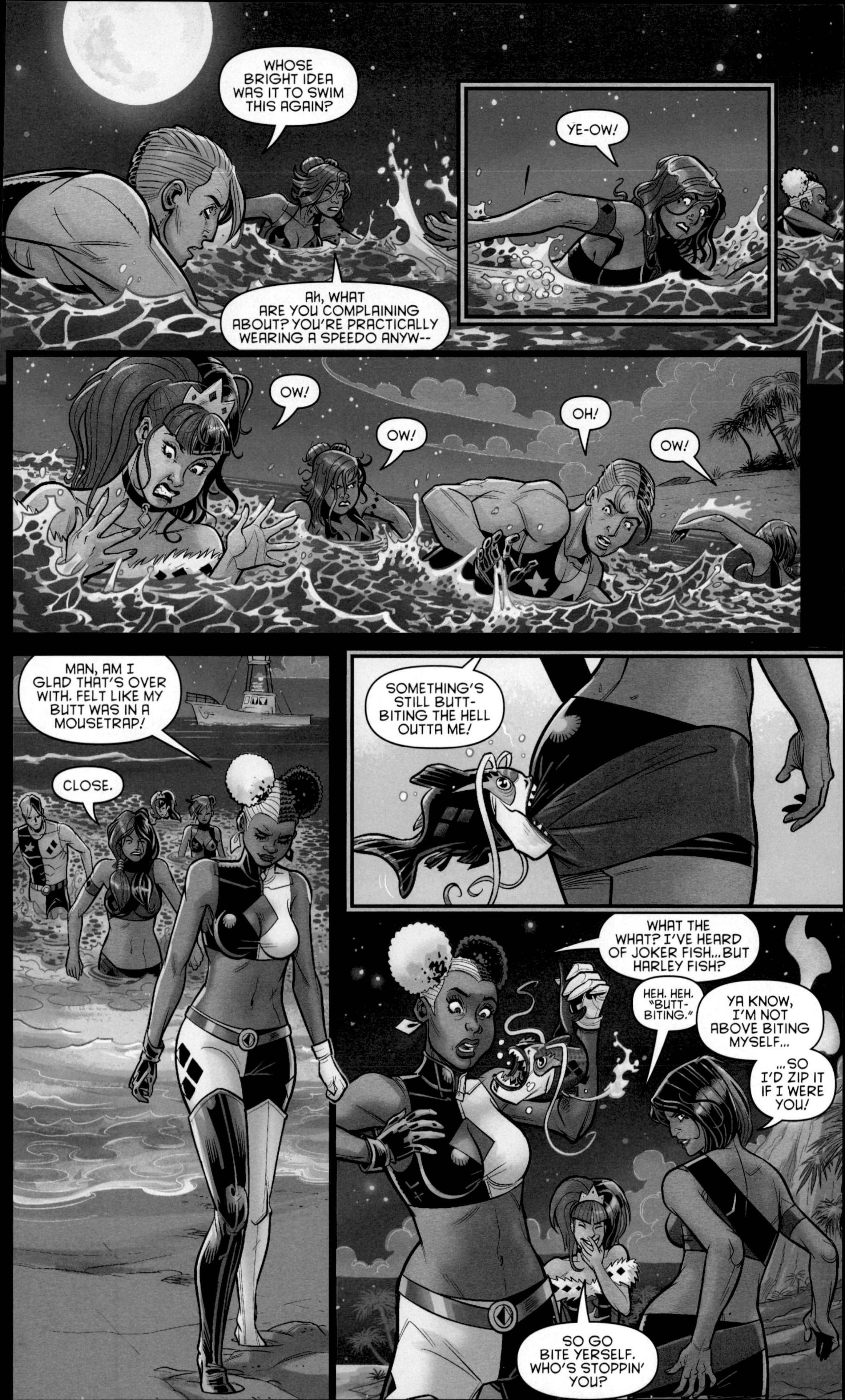
WHOSE BRIGHT IDEA WAS IT TO SWIM THIS AGAIN?
AH, WHAT ARE YOU COMPLAINING ABOUT? YOU'RE PRACTICALLY WEARING A SPEEDO ANYW--
YE-OW!
OW!
OW!
OH!
OW!
MAN, AM I GLAD THAT'S OVER WITH. FELT LIKE MY BUTT WAS IN A MOUSETRAP!
CLOSE.
SOMETHING'S STILL BUTT-BITING THE HELL OUTTA ME!
WHAT THE WHAT? I'VE HEARD OF JOKER FISH...BUT HARLEY FISH?
HEH. HEH. "BUTT-BITING."
YA KNOW, I'M NOT ABOVE BITING MYSELF...
...SO I'D ZIP IT IF I WERE YOU!
SO GO BITE YERSELF. WHO'S STOPPIN' YOU?

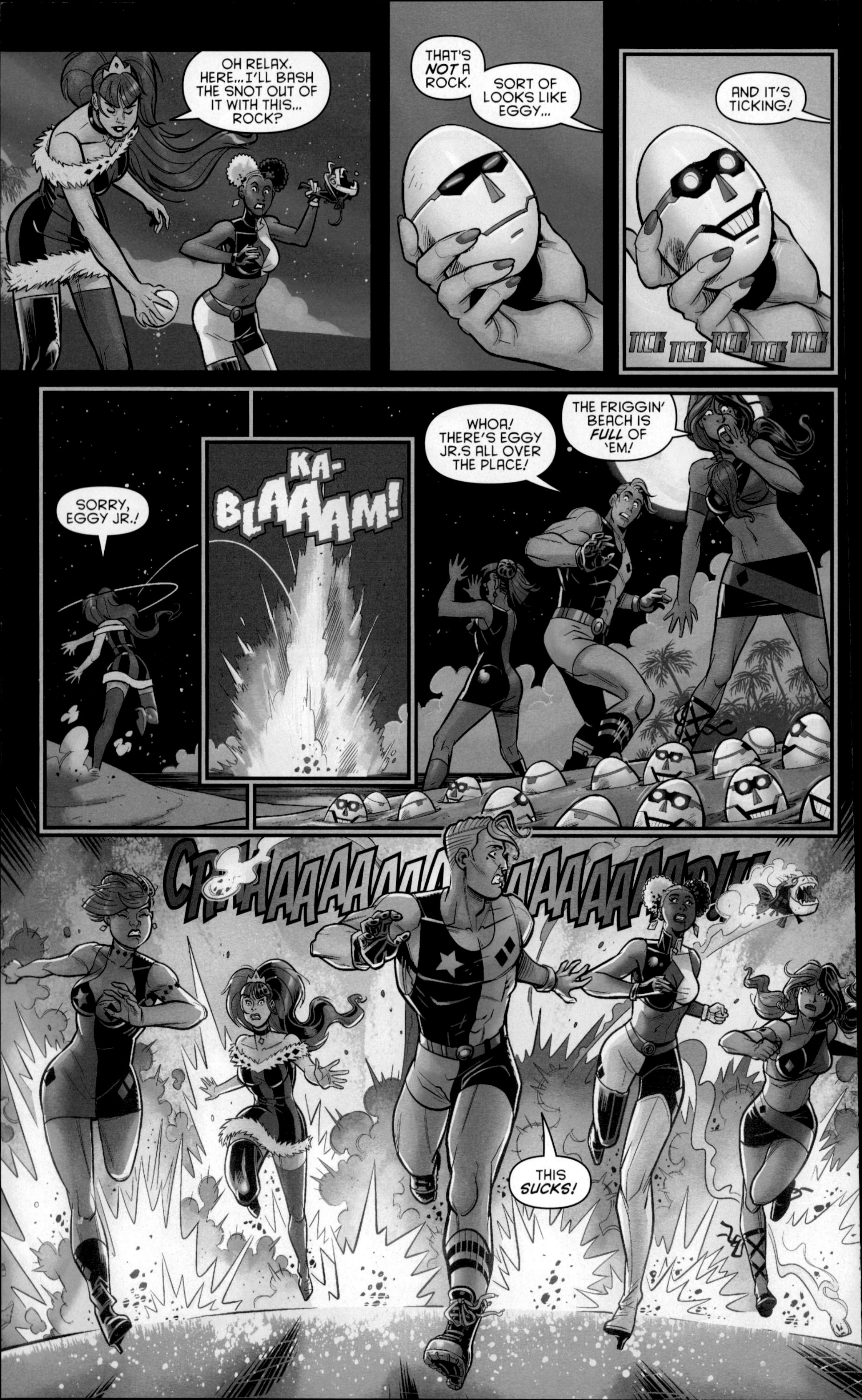
OH RELAX. HERE... I'LL BASH THE SNOT OUT OF IT WITH THIS... ROCK?
THAT'S NOT A ROCK.
SORT OF LOOKS LIKE EGGY...
AND IT'S TICKING!
TICK TICK TICK TICK TICK
SORRY, EGGY JR.!
KA-BLAAAAM!
WHOA! THERE'S EGGY JR.S ALL OVER THE PLACE!
THE FRIGGIN' BEACH IS FULL OF 'EM!
THIS SUCKS!

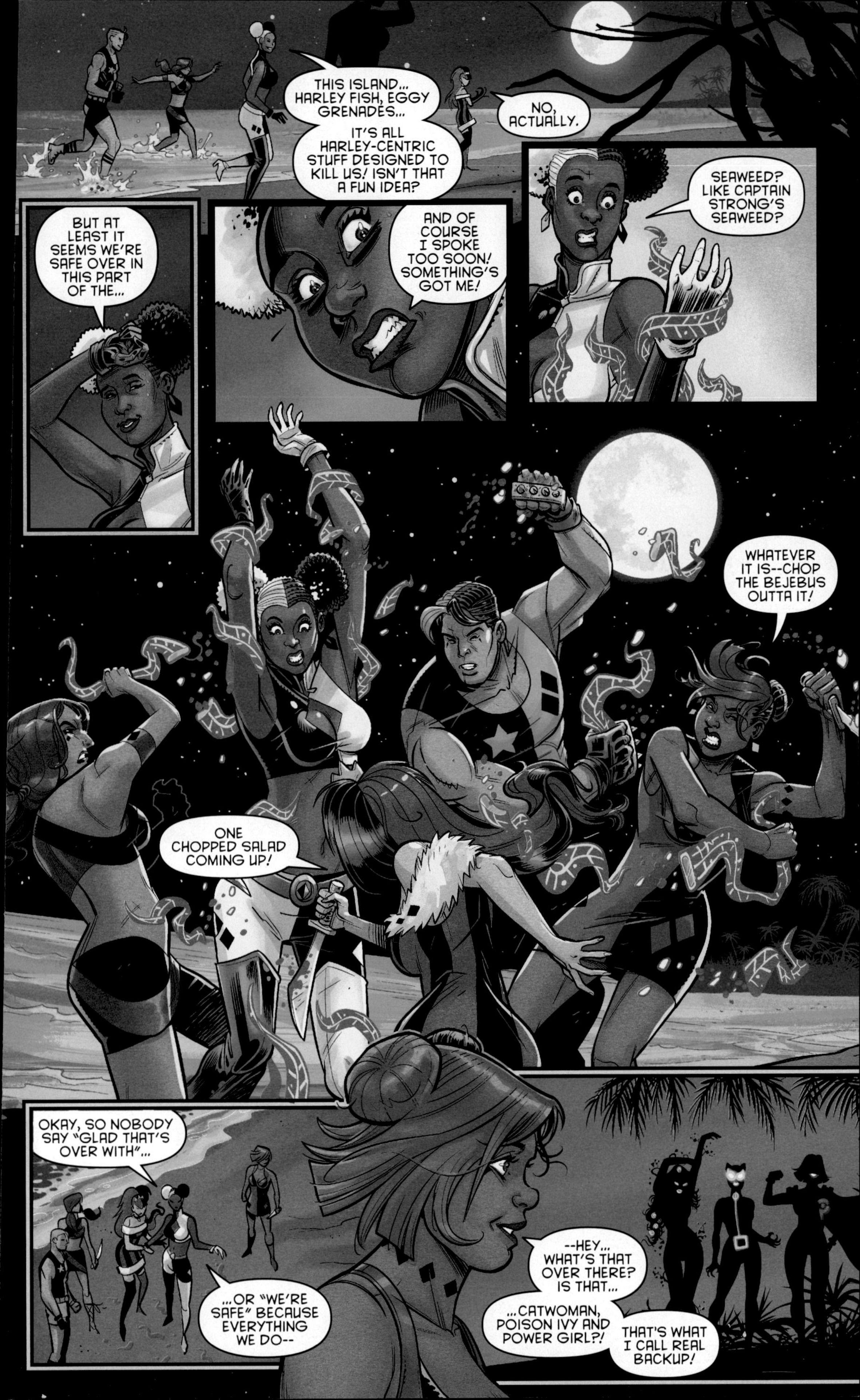
THIS ISLAND... HARLEY FISH, EGGY GRENADES...
IT'S ALL HARLEY-CENTRIC STUFF DESIGNED TO KILL US! ISN'T THAT A FUN IDEA?
NO, ACTUALLY.
BUT AT LEAST IT SEEMS WE'RE SAFE OVER IN THIS PART OF THE...
AND OF COURSE I SPOKE TOO SOON! SOMETHING'S GOT ME!
SEAWEED? LIKE CAPTAIN STRONG'S SEAWEED?
WHATEVER IT IS--CHOP THE BEJEBUS OUTTA IT!
ONE CHOPPED SALAD COMING UP!
OKAY, SO NOBODY SAY "GLAD THAT'S OVER WITH"...
...OR "WE'RE SAFE" BECAUSE EVERYTHING WE DO--
--HEY... WHAT'S THAT OVER THERE? IS THAT...
...CATWOMAN, POISON IVY AND POWER GIRL?!
THAT'S WHAT I CALL REAL BACKUP!

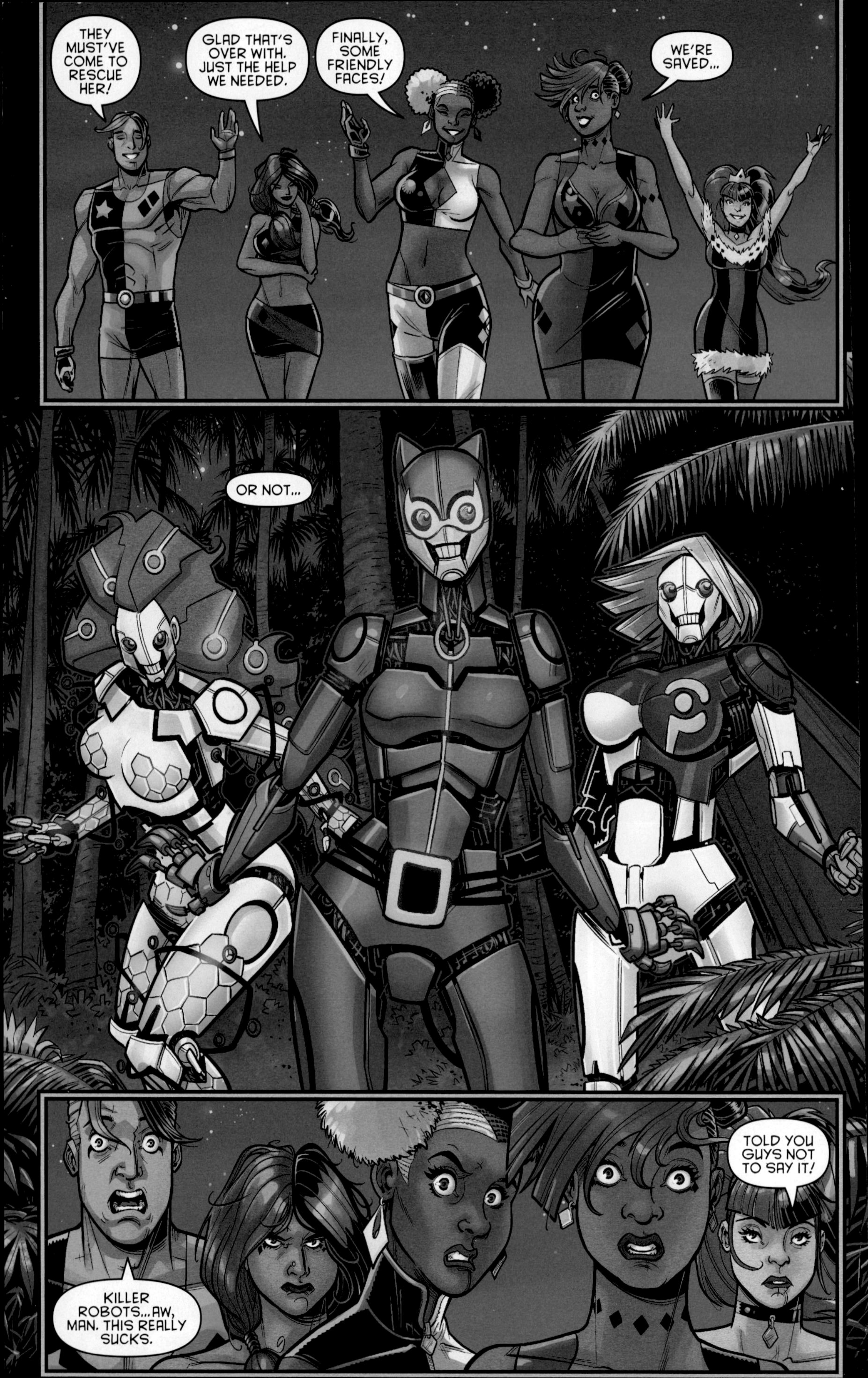
THEY MUST'VE COME TO RESCUE HER!
GLAD THAT'S OVER WITH. JUST THE HELP WE NEEDED.
FINALLY, SOME FRIENDLY FACES!
WE'RE SAVED...
OR NOT...
TOLD YOU GUYS NOT TO SAY IT!
KILLER ROBOTS...AW, MAN. THIS REALLY SUCKS.

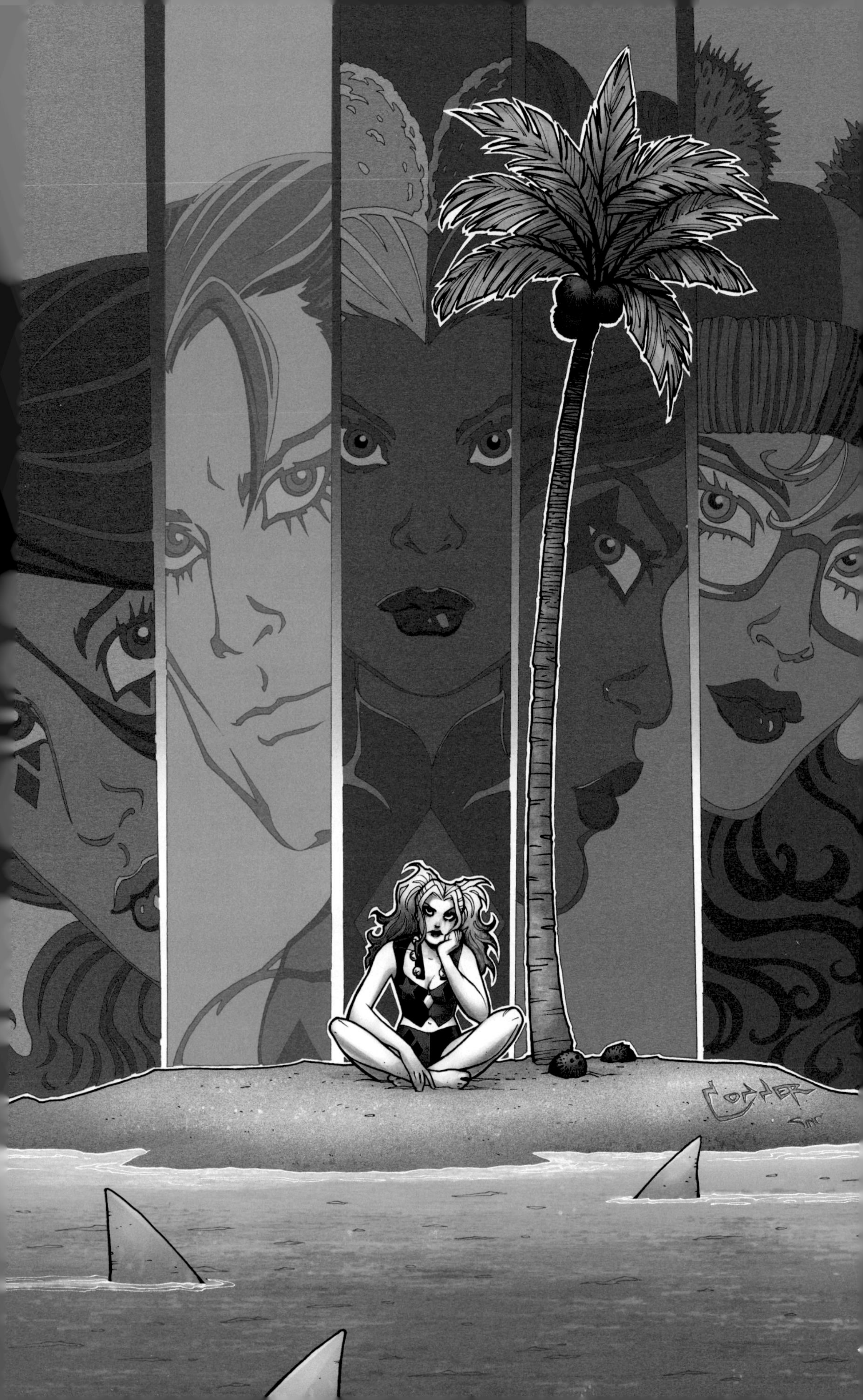

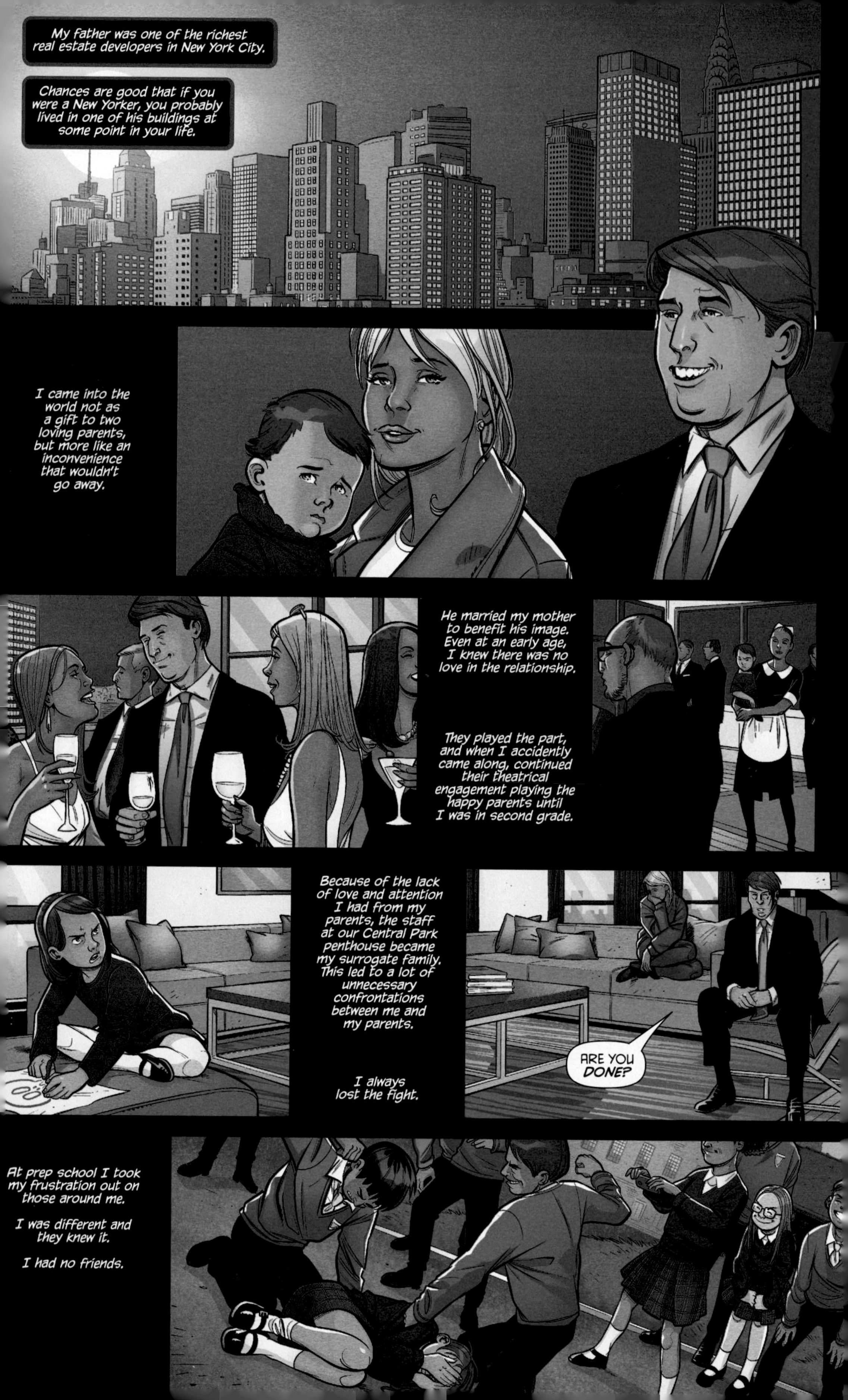

My father was one of the richest real estate developers in New York City.
Chances are good that if you were a New Yorker, you probably lived in one of his buildings at some point in your life.
I came into the world not as a gift to two loving parents, but more like an inconvenience that wouldn't go away.
He married my mother to benefit his image. Even at an early age, I knew there was no love in the relationship.
They played the part, and when I accidently came along, continued their theatrical engagement playing the happy parents until I was in second grade.
Because of the lack of love and attention I had from my parents, the staff at our Central Park penthouse became my surrogate family. This led to a lot of unnecessary confrontations between me and my parents.
ARE YOU DONE?
I always lost the fight.
At prep school I took my frustration out on those around me.
I was different and they knew it.
I had no friends.

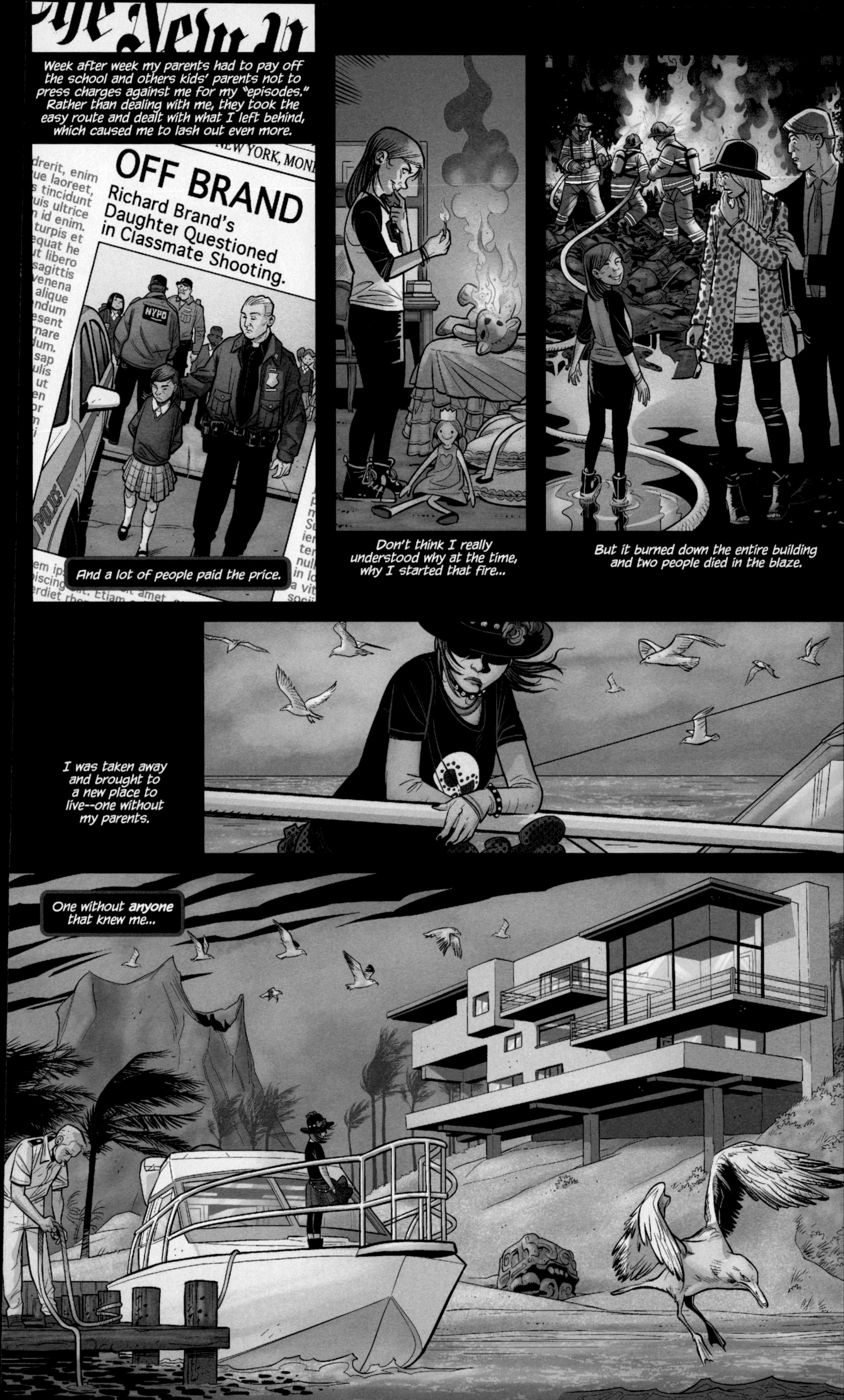
Week after week my parents had to pay off the school and others kids' parents not to press charges against me for my "episodes." Rather than dealing with me, they took the easy route and dealt with what I left behind, which caused me to lash out even more.
OFF BRAND
Richard Brand's Daughter Questioned in Classmate Shooting.
NYPD
POLICE
And a lot of people paid the price.
Don't think I really understood why at the time, why I started that fire...
But it burned down the entire building and two people died in the blaze.
I was taken away and brought to a new place to live--one without my parents.
One without anyone that knew me...

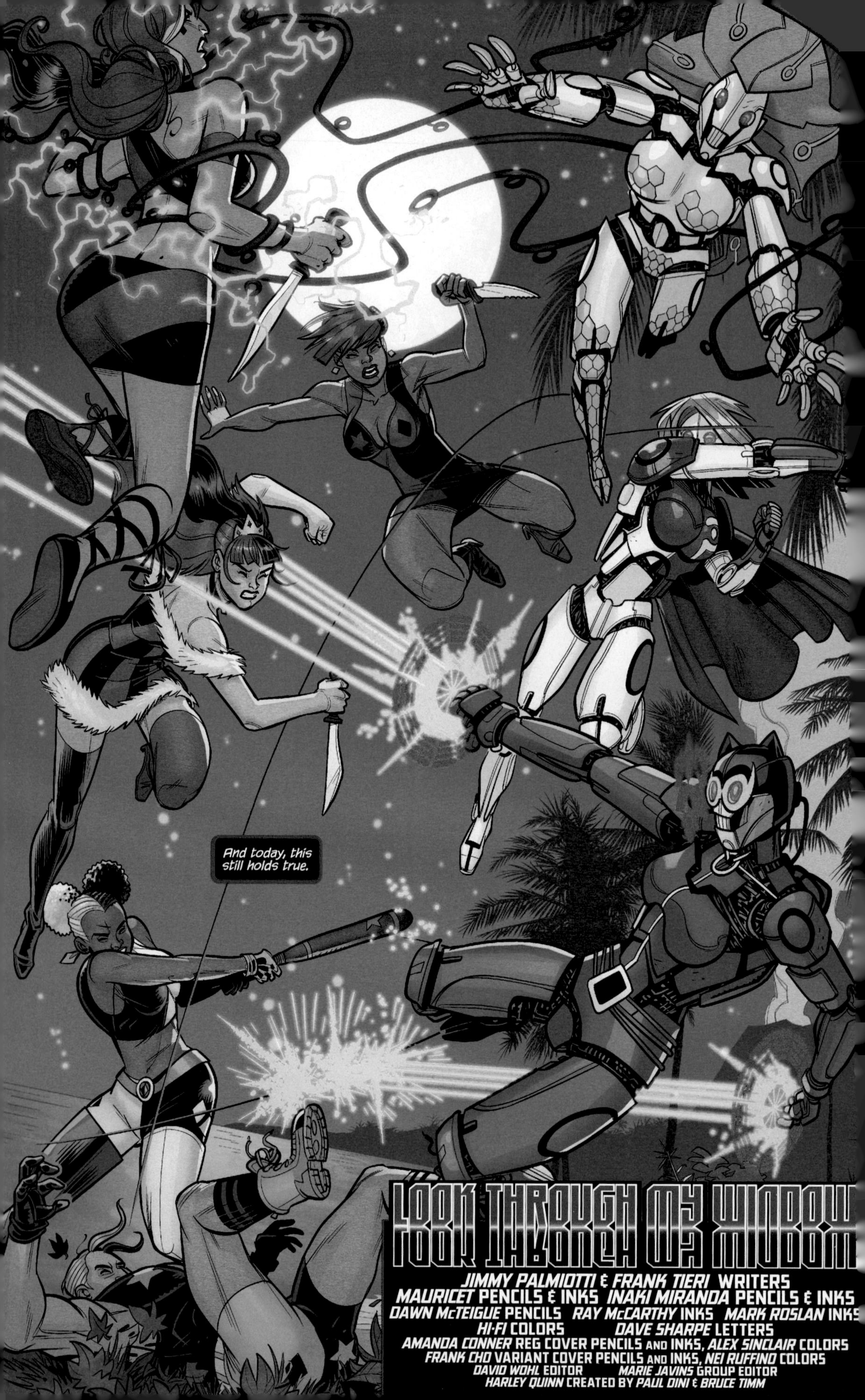

And today, this still holds true.
LOOK THROUGH MY WINDOW
JIMMY PALMIOTTI & FRANK TIERI WRITERS
MAURICET PENCILS & INKS INAKI MIRANDA PENCILS & INKS
DAWN McTEIGUE PENCILS RAY McCARTHY INKS MARK ROSLAN INKS
HI-FI COLORS DAVE SHARPE LETTERS
AMANDA CONNER REG COVER PENCILS AND INKS, ALEX SINCLAIR COLORS
FRANK CHO VARIANT COVER PENCILS AND INKS, NEI RUFFINO COLORS
DAVID WOHL EDITOR MARIE JAVINS GROUP EDITOR
HARLEY QUINN CREATED BY PAUL DINI & BRUCE TIMM

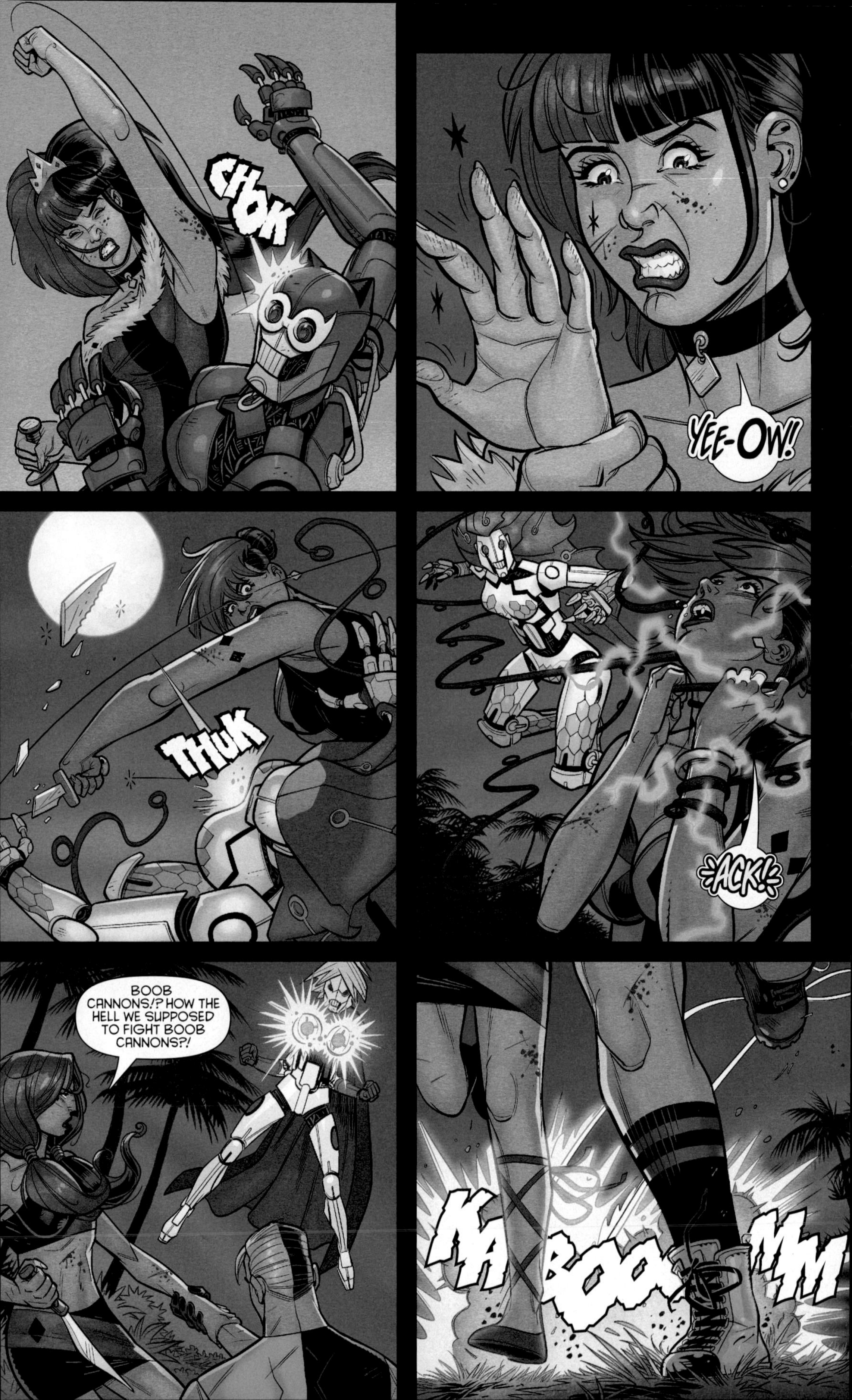
CHOK
YEE-OW!
THUK
ACK!
BOOB CANNONS!? HOW THE HELL WE SUPPOSED TO FIGHT BOOB CANNONS?!
KABOOMM

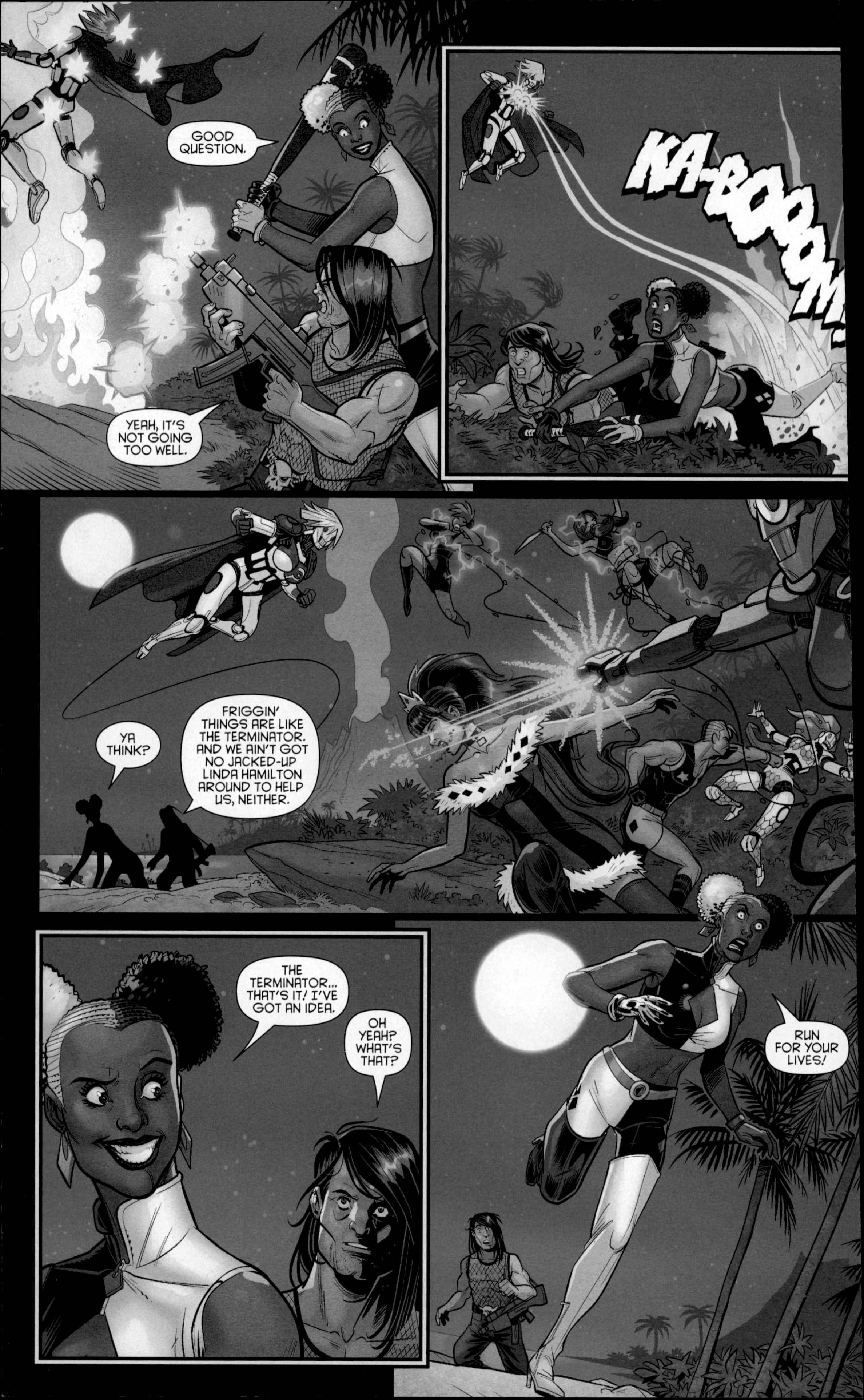
GOOD QUESTION.
YEAH, IT'S NOT GOING TOO WELL.
KA-BOOOM!
YA THINK?
FRIGGIN' THINGS ARE LIKE THE TERMINATOR. AND WE AIN'T GOT NO JACKED-UP LINDA HAMILTON AROUND TO HELP US, NEITHER.
THE TERMINATOR... THAT'S IT! I'VE GOT AN IDEA.
OH YEAH? WHAT'S THAT?
RUN FOR YOUR LIVES!

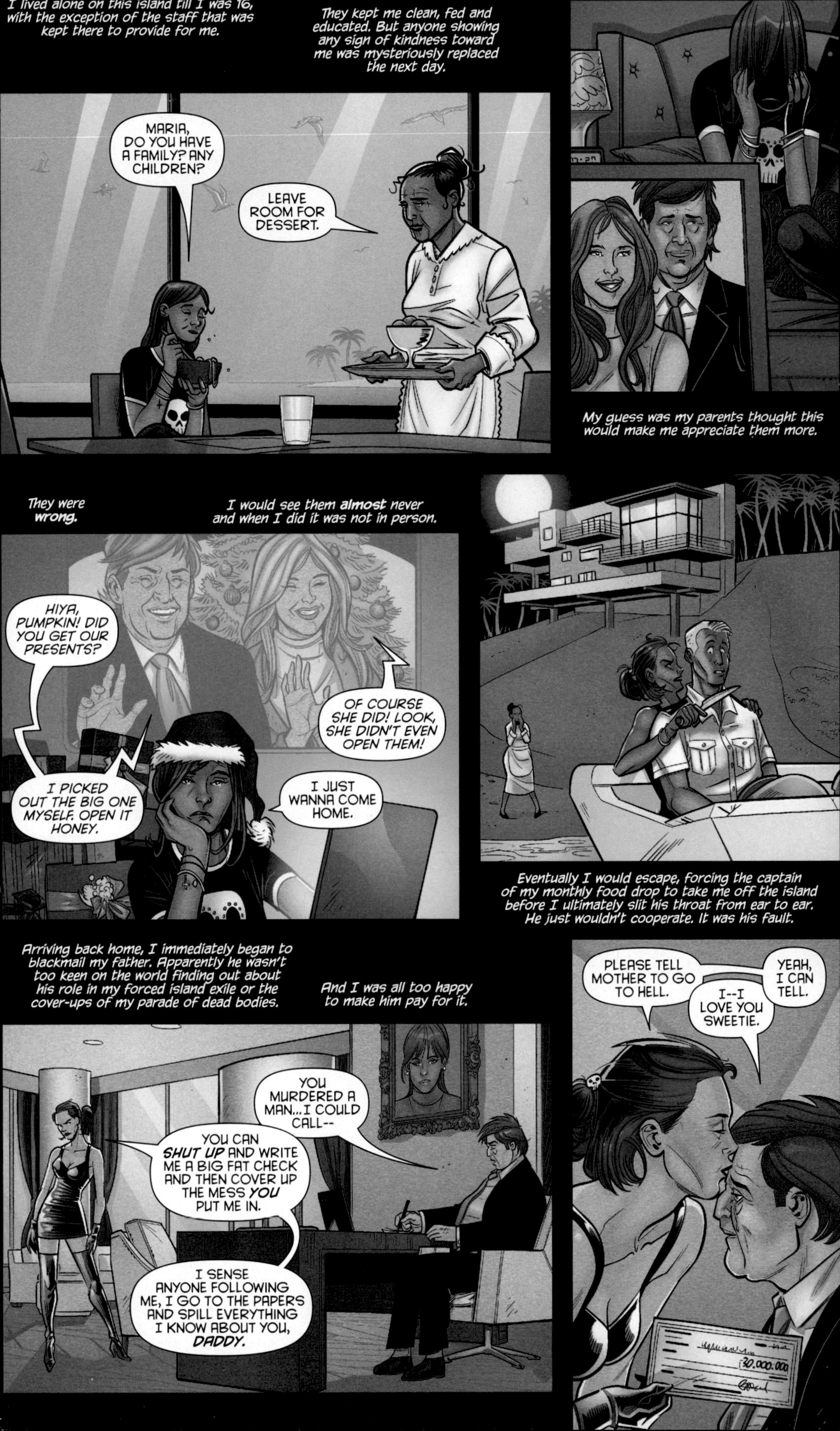
I lived alone on this island till I was 16, with the exception of the staff that was kept there to provide for me.
They kept me clean, fed and educated. But anyone showing any sign of kindness toward me was mysteriously replaced the next day.
MARIA, DO YOU HAVE A FAMILY? ANY CHILDREN?
LEAVE ROOM FOR DESSERT.
My guess was my parents thought this would make me appreciate them more.
They were **wrong.**
I would see them **almost** never and when I did it was not in person.
HIYA, PUMPKIN! DID YOU GET OUR PRESENTS?
OF COURSE SHE DID! LOOK, SHE DIDN'T EVEN OPEN THEM!
I PICKED OUT THE BIG ONE MYSELF. OPEN IT HONEY.
I JUST WANNA COME HOME.
Eventually I would escape, forcing the captain of my monthly food drop to take me off the island before I ultimately slit his throat from ear to ear. He just wouldn't cooperate. It was his fault.
Arriving back home, I immediately began to blackmail my father. Apparently he wasn't too keen on the world finding out about his role in my forced island exile or the cover-ups of my parade of dead bodies.
And I was all too happy to make him pay for it.
YOU MURDERED A MAN... I COULD CALL--
YOU CAN **SHUT UP** AND WRITE ME A BIG FAT CHECK AND THEN COVER UP THE MESS **YOU** PUT ME IN.
I SENSE ANYONE FOLLOWING ME, I GO TO THE PAPERS AND SPILL EVERYTHING I KNOW ABOUT YOU, **DADDY.**
PLEASE TELL MOTHER TO GO TO HELL.
YEAH, I CAN TELL.
I--I LOVE YOU SWEETIE.
30.000.000

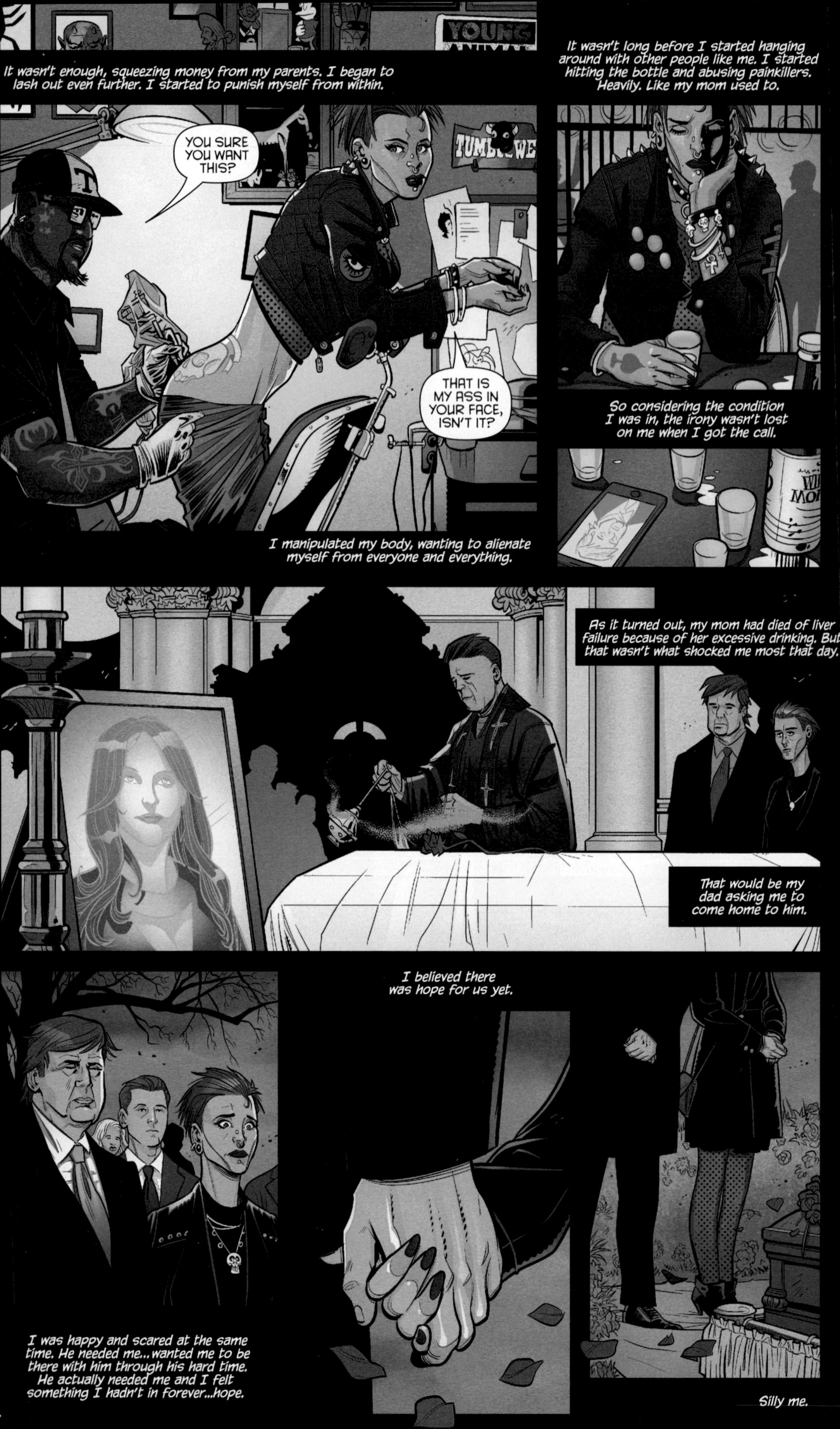

YOUNG
It wasn't enough, squeezing money from my parents. I began to lash out even further. I started to punish myself from within.
TUMBLEWE
YOU SURE YOU WANT THIS?
THAT IS MY ASS IN YOUR FACE, ISN'T IT?
I manipulated my body, wanting to alienate myself from everyone and everything.
It wasn't long before I started hanging around with other people like me. I started hitting the bottle and abusing painkillers. Heavily. Like my mom used to.
So considering the condition I was in, the irony wasn't lost on me when I got the call.
As it turned out, my mom had died of liver failure because of her excessive drinking. But that wasn't what shocked me most that day.
That would be my dad asking me to come home to him.
I was happy and scared at the same time. He needed me...wanted me to be there with him through his hard time. He actually needed me and I felt something I hadn't in forever...hope.
I believed there was hope for us yet.
Silly me.

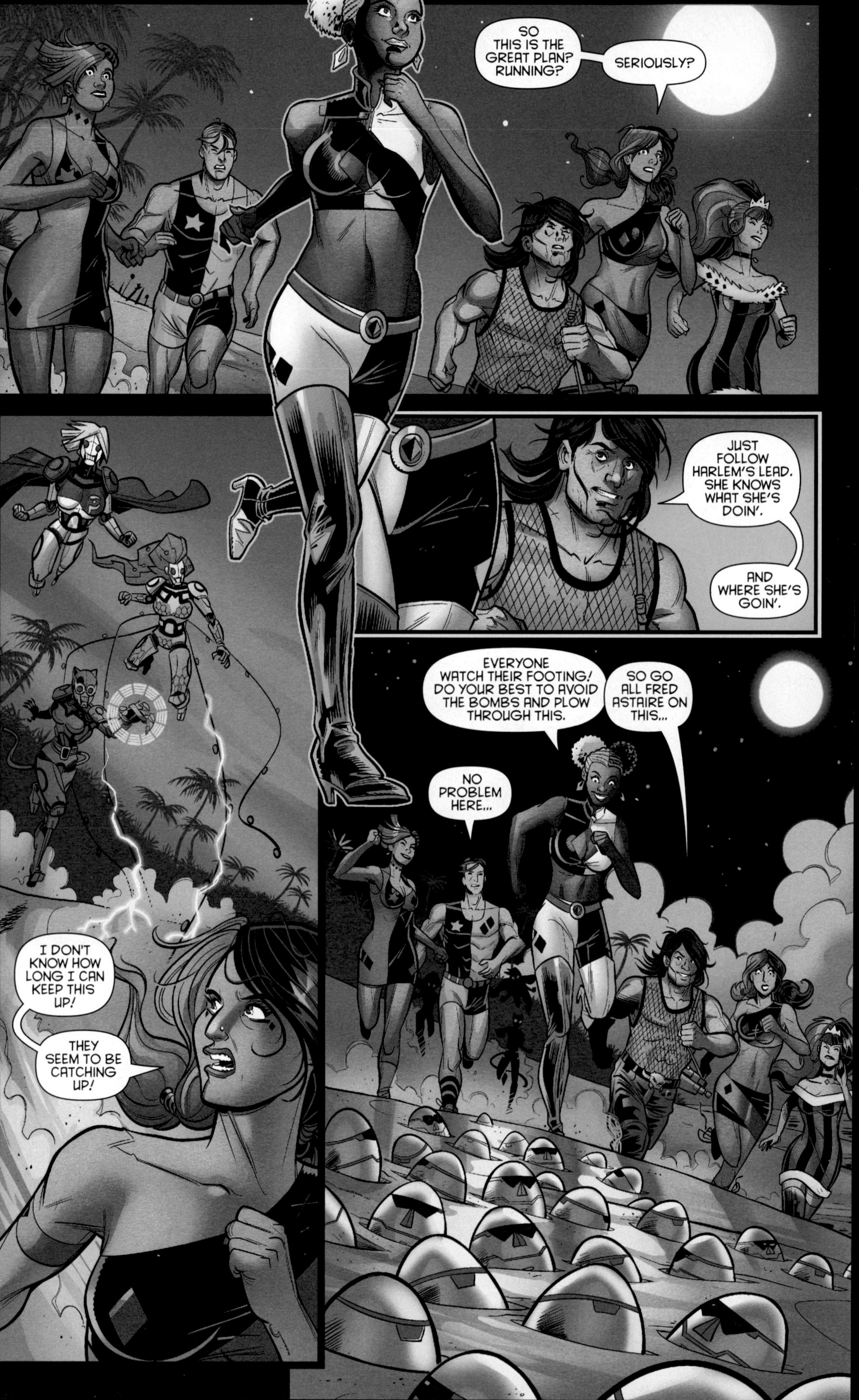
SO THIS IS THE GREAT PLAN? RUNNING?
SERIOUSLY?
JUST FOLLOW HARLEM'S LEAD. SHE KNOWS WHAT SHE'S DOIN'.
AND WHERE SHE'S GOIN'.
I DON'T KNOW HOW LONG I CAN KEEP THIS UP!
THEY SEEM TO BE CATCHING UP!
EVERYONE WATCH THEIR FOOTING! DO YOUR BEST TO AVOID THE BOMBS AND PLOW THROUGH THIS.
SO GO ALL FRED ASTAIRE ON THIS...
NO PROBLEM HERE...

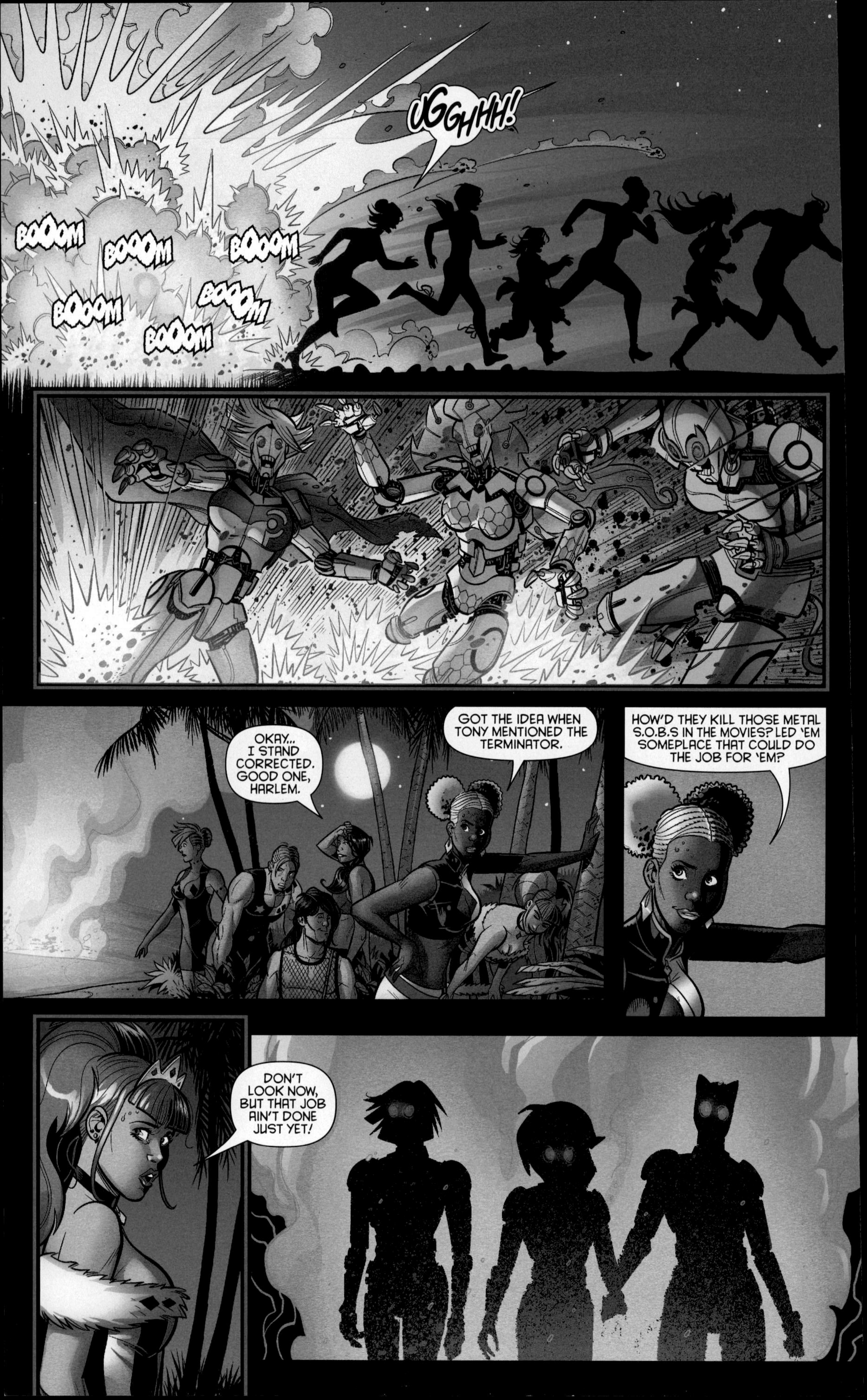
UGGHHH!
BOOOM
BOOOM
BOOOM
BOOOM
BOOOM
BOOOM
OKAY... I STAND CORRECTED. GOOD ONE, HARLEM.
GOT THE IDEA WHEN TONY MENTIONED THE TERMINATOR.
HOW'D THEY KILL THOSE METAL S.O.B.S IN THE MOVIES? LED 'EM SOMEPLACE THAT COULD DO THE JOB FOR 'EM?
DON'T LOOK NOW, BUT THAT JOB AIN'T DONE JUST YET!

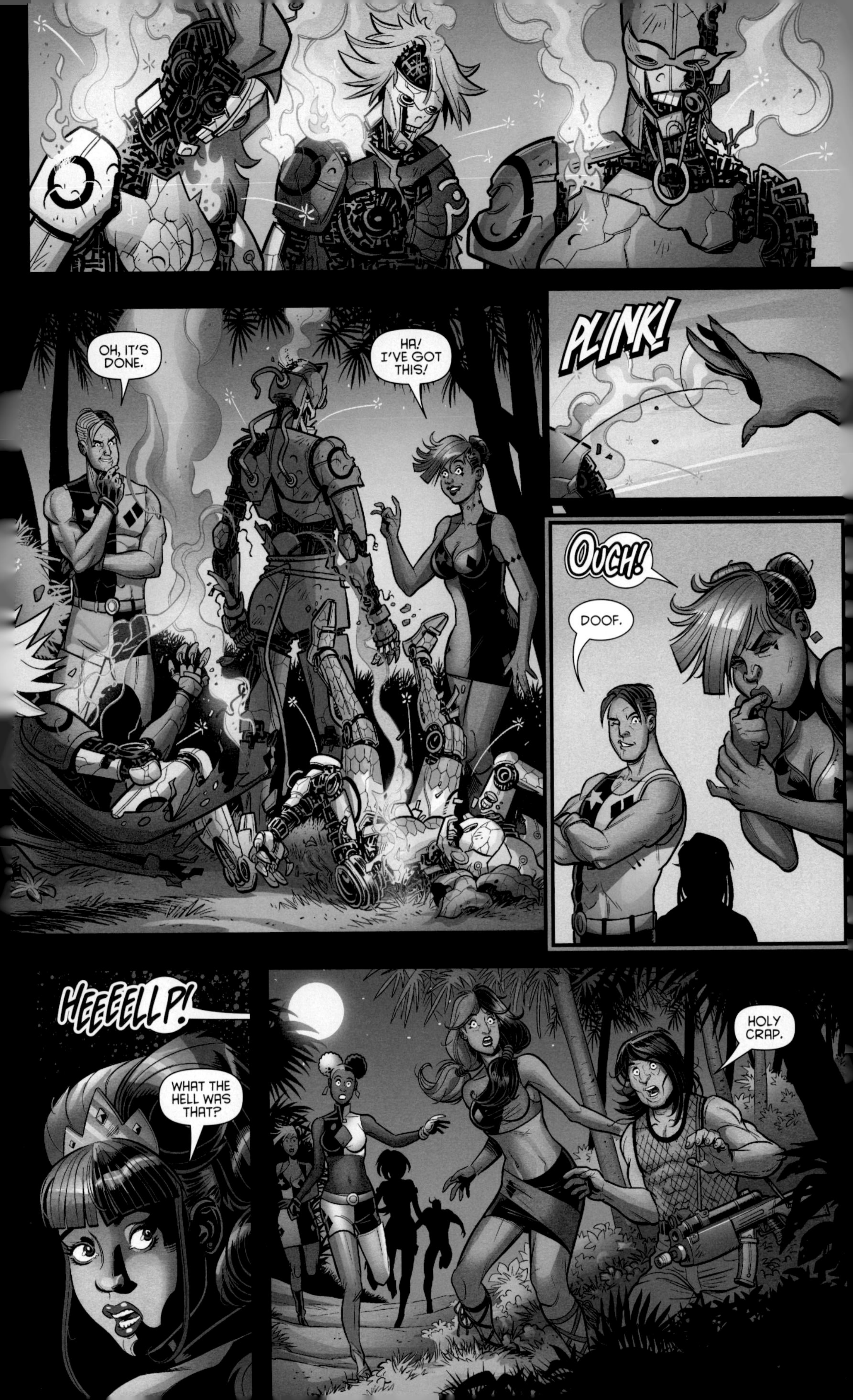
OH, IT'S DONE.
HA! I'VE GOT THIS!
PLINK!
OUCH!
DOOF.
HEEEEELLP!
WHAT THE HELL WAS THAT?
HOLY CRAP.

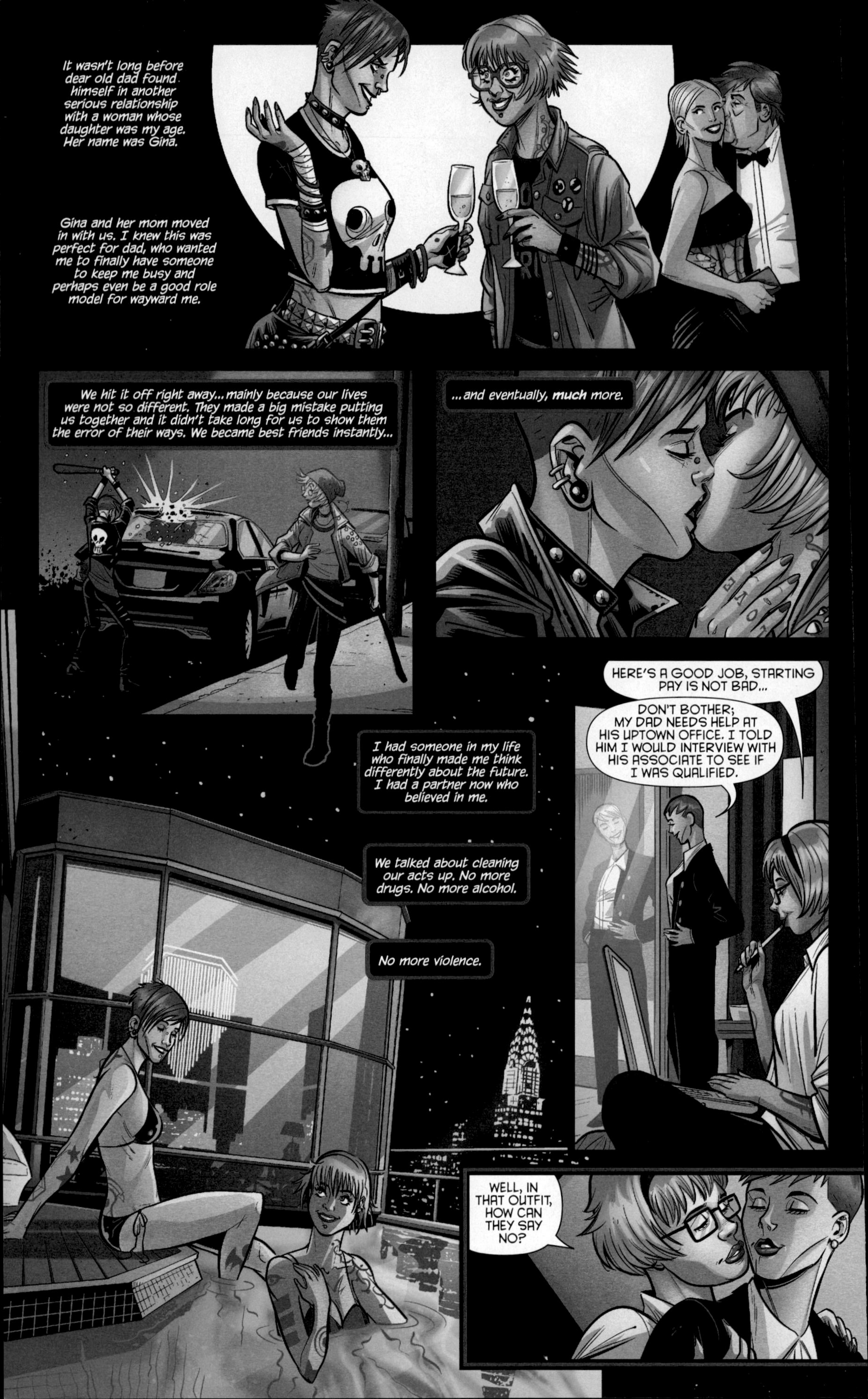
It wasn't long before dear old dad found himself in another serious relationship with a woman whose daughter was my age. Her name was Gina.
Gina and her mom moved in with us. I knew this was perfect for dad, who wanted me to finally have someone to keep me busy and perhaps even be a good role model for wayward me.
We hit it off right away... mainly because our lives were not so different. They made a big mistake putting us together and it didn't take long for us to show them the error of their ways. We became best friends instantly...
...and eventually, much more.
I had someone in my life who finally made me think differently about the future. I had a partner now who believed in me.
We talked about cleaning our acts up. No more drugs. No more alcohol.
No more violence.
HERE'S A GOOD JOB, STARTING PAY IS NOT BAD...
DON'T BOTHER; MY DAD NEEDS HELP AT HIS UPTOWN OFFICE. I TOLD HIM I WOULD INTERVIEW WITH HIS ASSOCIATE TO SEE IF I WAS QUALIFIED.
WELL, IN THAT OUTFIT, HOW CAN THEY SAY NO?

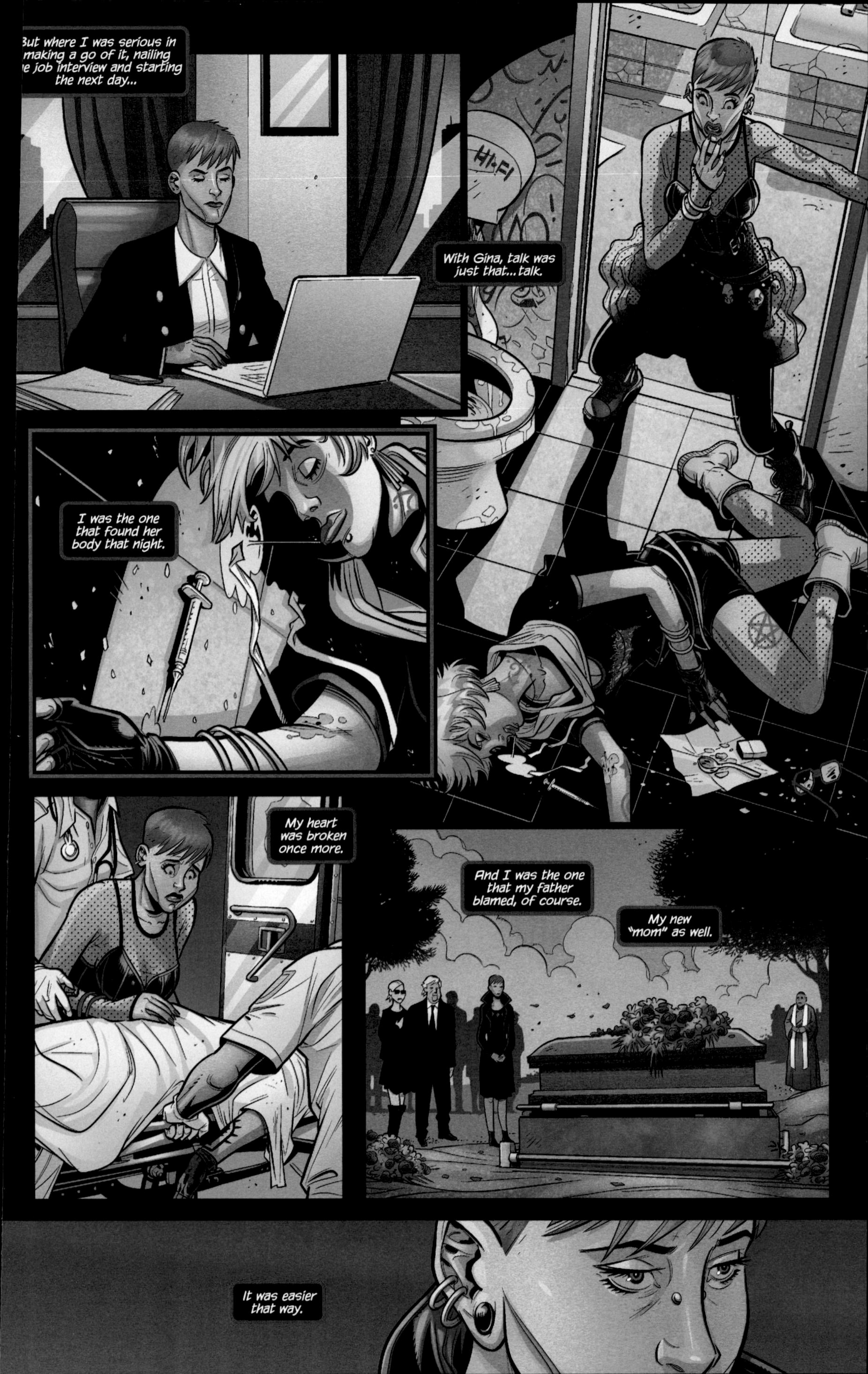
But where I was serious in making a go of it, nailing the job interview and starting the next day...
With Gina, talk was just that... talk.
HI-FI
I was the one that found her body that night.
My heart was broken once more.
And I was the one that my father blamed, of course.
My new "mom" as well.
It was easier that way.

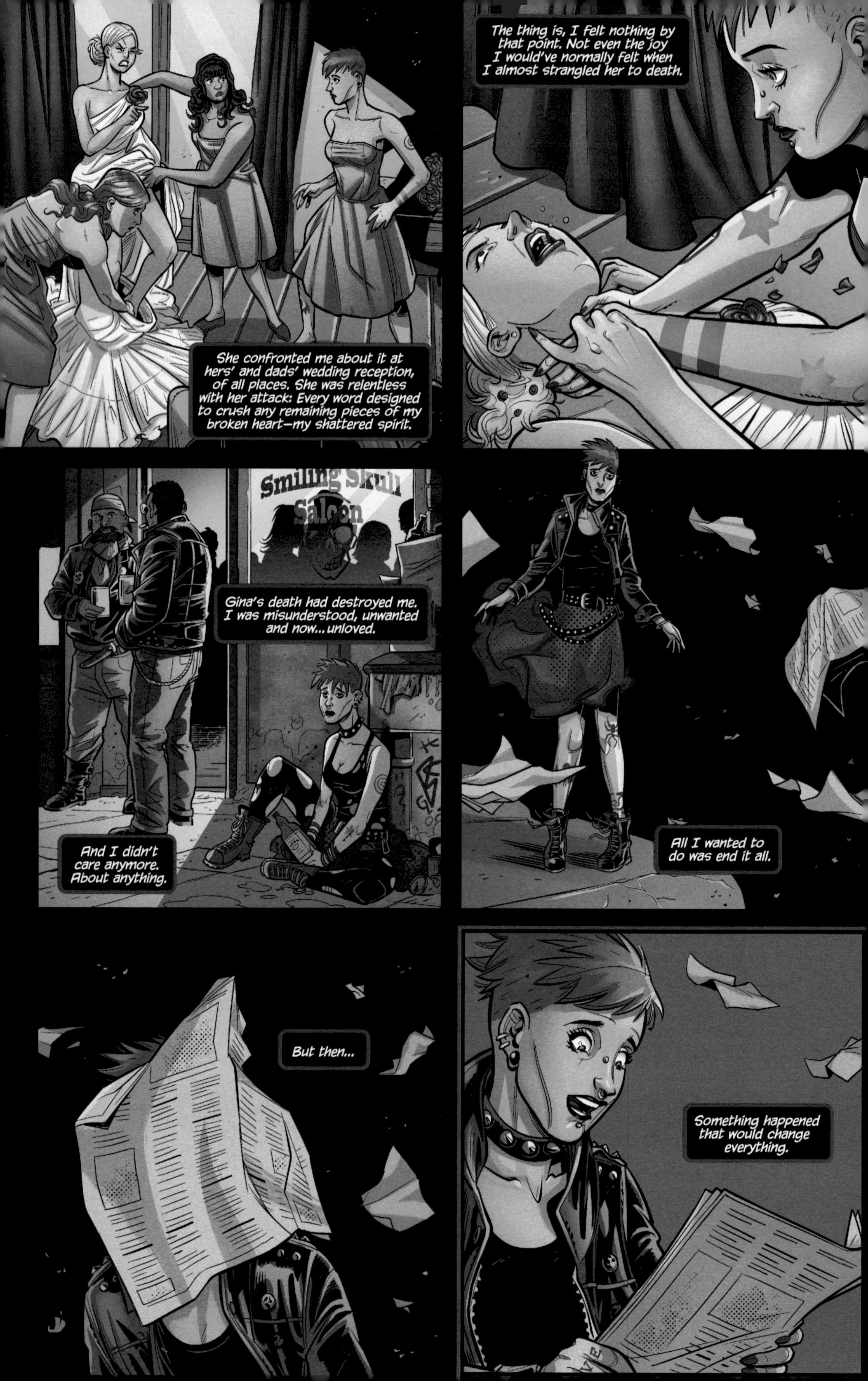
She confronted me about it at hers' and dads' wedding reception, of all places. She was relentless with her attack: Every word designed to crush any remaining pieces of my broken heart—my shattered spirit.
The thing is, I felt nothing by that point. Not even the joy I would've normally felt when I almost strangled her to death.
Smiling Skull Saloon
Gina's death had destroyed me. I was misunderstood, unwanted and now... unloved.
And I didn't care anymore. About anything.
All I wanted to do was end it all.
But then...
Something happened that would change everything.

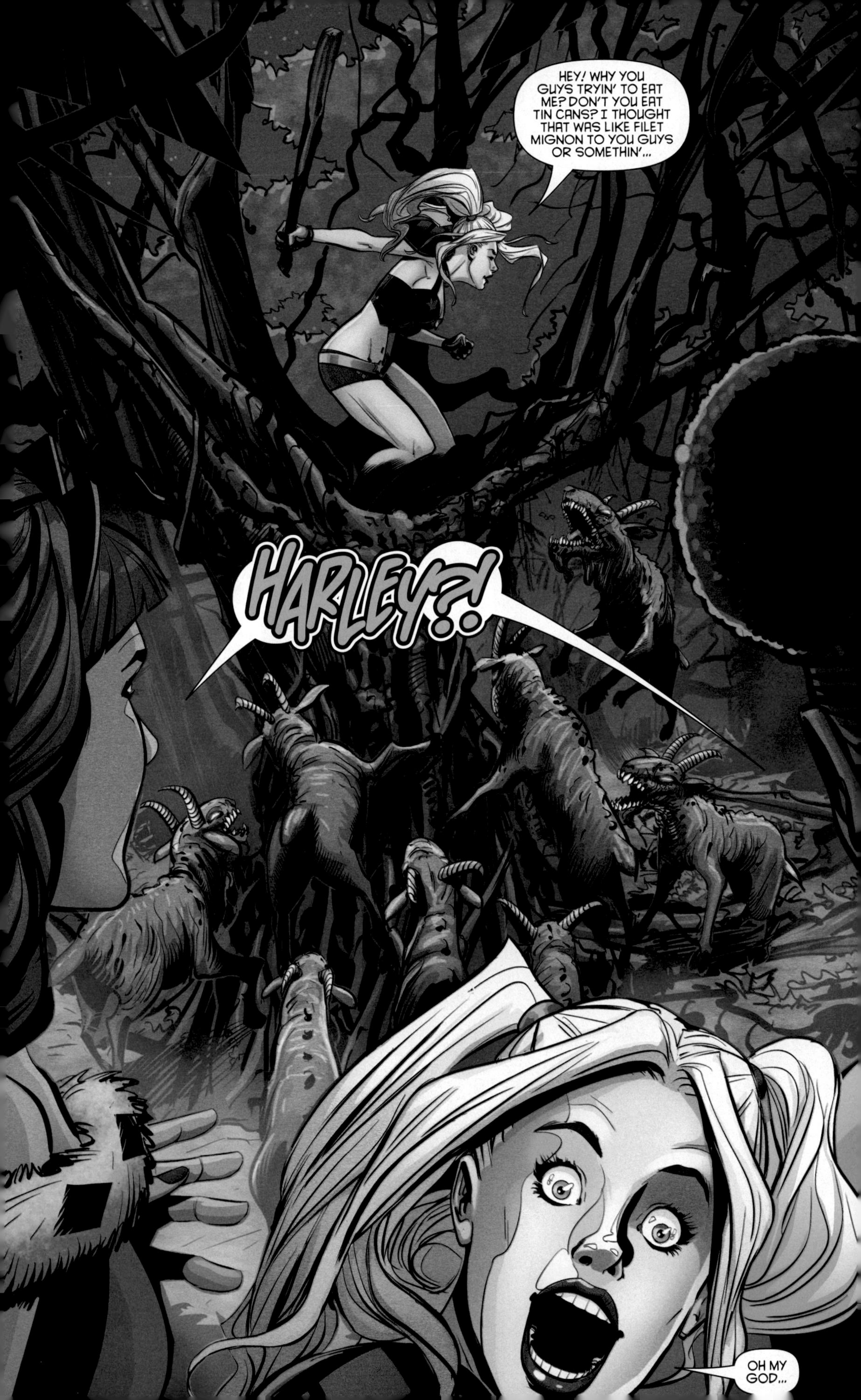
HEY! WHY YOU GUYS TRYIN' TO EAT ME? DON'T YOU EAT TIN CANS? I THOUGHT THAT WAS LIKE FILET MIGNON TO YOU GUYS OR SOMETHIN'...
HARLEY?!
OH MY GOD...

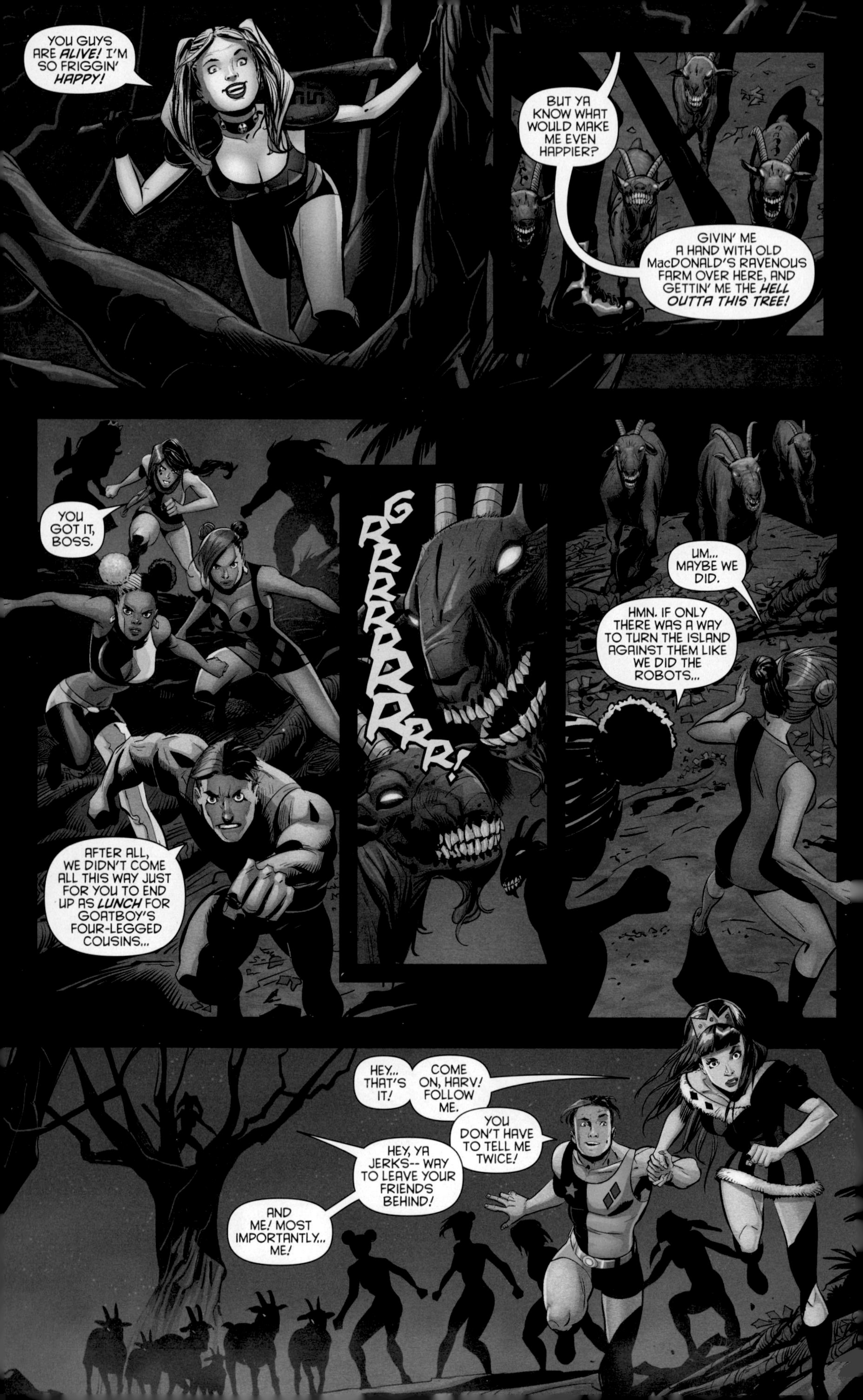
YOU GUYS ARE ALIVE! I'M SO FRIGGIN' HAPPY!
BUT YA KNOW WHAT WOULD MAKE ME EVEN HAPPIER?
GIVIN' ME A HAND WITH OLD MacDONALD'S RAVENOUS FARM OVER HERE, AND GETTIN' ME THE HELL OUTTA THIS TREE!
YOU GOT IT, BOSS.
AFTER ALL, WE DIDN'T COME ALL THIS WAY JUST FOR YOU TO END UP AS LUNCH FOR GOATBOY'S FOUR-LEGGED COUSINS...
GRRRRRRRRRR!
UM... MAYBE WE DID.
HMN. IF ONLY THERE WAS A WAY TO TURN THE ISLAND AGAINST THEM LIKE WE DID THE ROBOTS...
HEY... THAT'S IT!
COME ON, HARV! FOLLOW ME.
YOU DON'T HAVE TO TELL ME TWICE!
HEY, YA JERKS-- WAY TO LEAVE YOUR FRIENDS BEHIND!
AND ME! MOST IMPORTANTLY... ME!

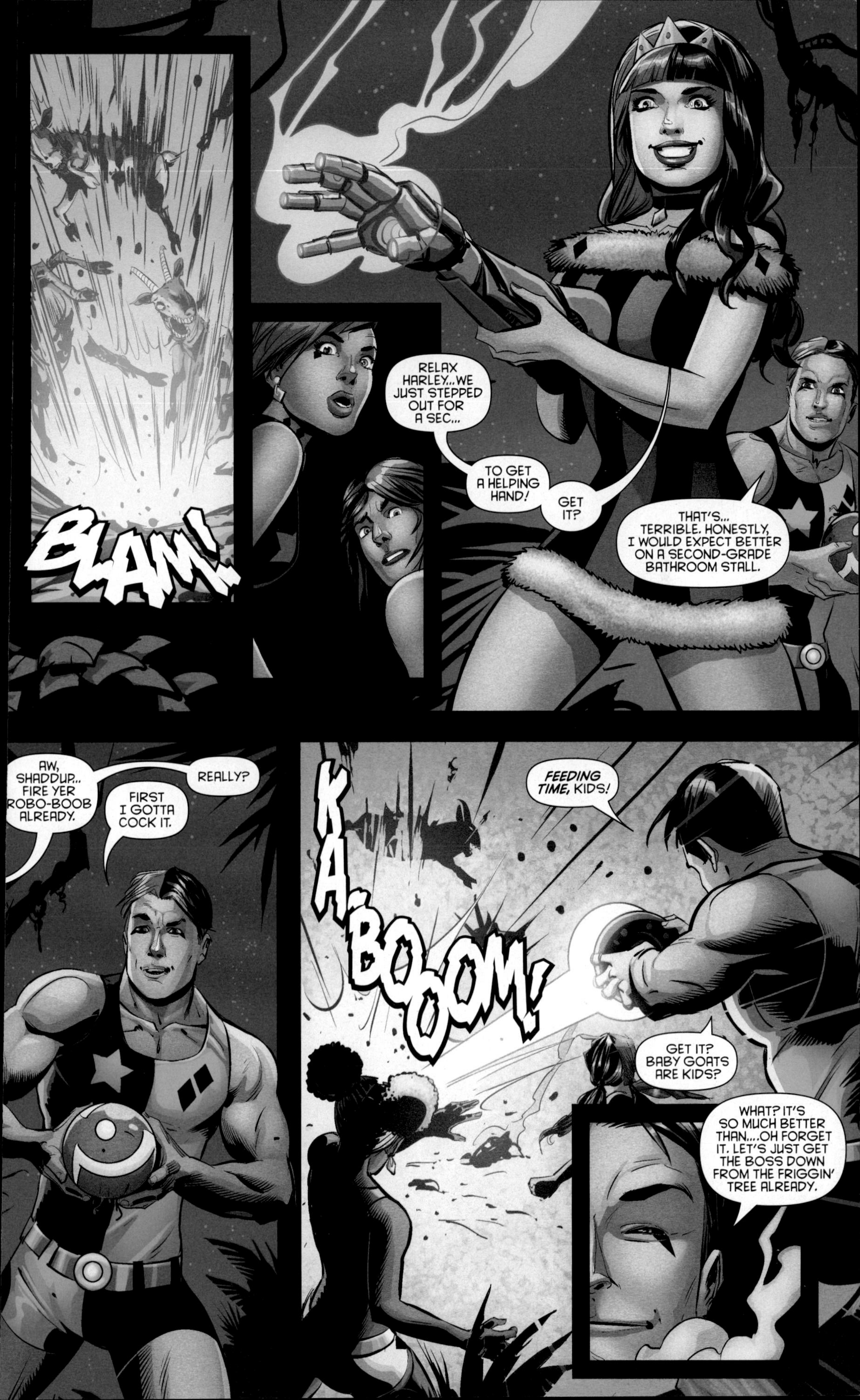
BLAM!
RELAX HARLEY...WE JUST STEPPED OUT FOR A SEC...
TO GET A HELPING HAND!
GET IT?
THAT'S... TERRIBLE. HONESTLY, I WOULD EXPECT BETTER ON A SECOND-GRADE BATHROOM STALL.
AW, SHADDUP... FIRE YER ROBO-BOOB ALREADY.
REALLY?
FIRST I GOTTA COCK IT.
KA-BOOOOM!
FEEDING TIME, KIDS!
GET IT? BABY GOATS ARE KIDS?
WHAT? IT'S SO MUCH BETTER THAN....OH FORGET IT. LET'S JUST GET THE BOSS DOWN FROM THE FRIGGIN' TREE ALREADY.

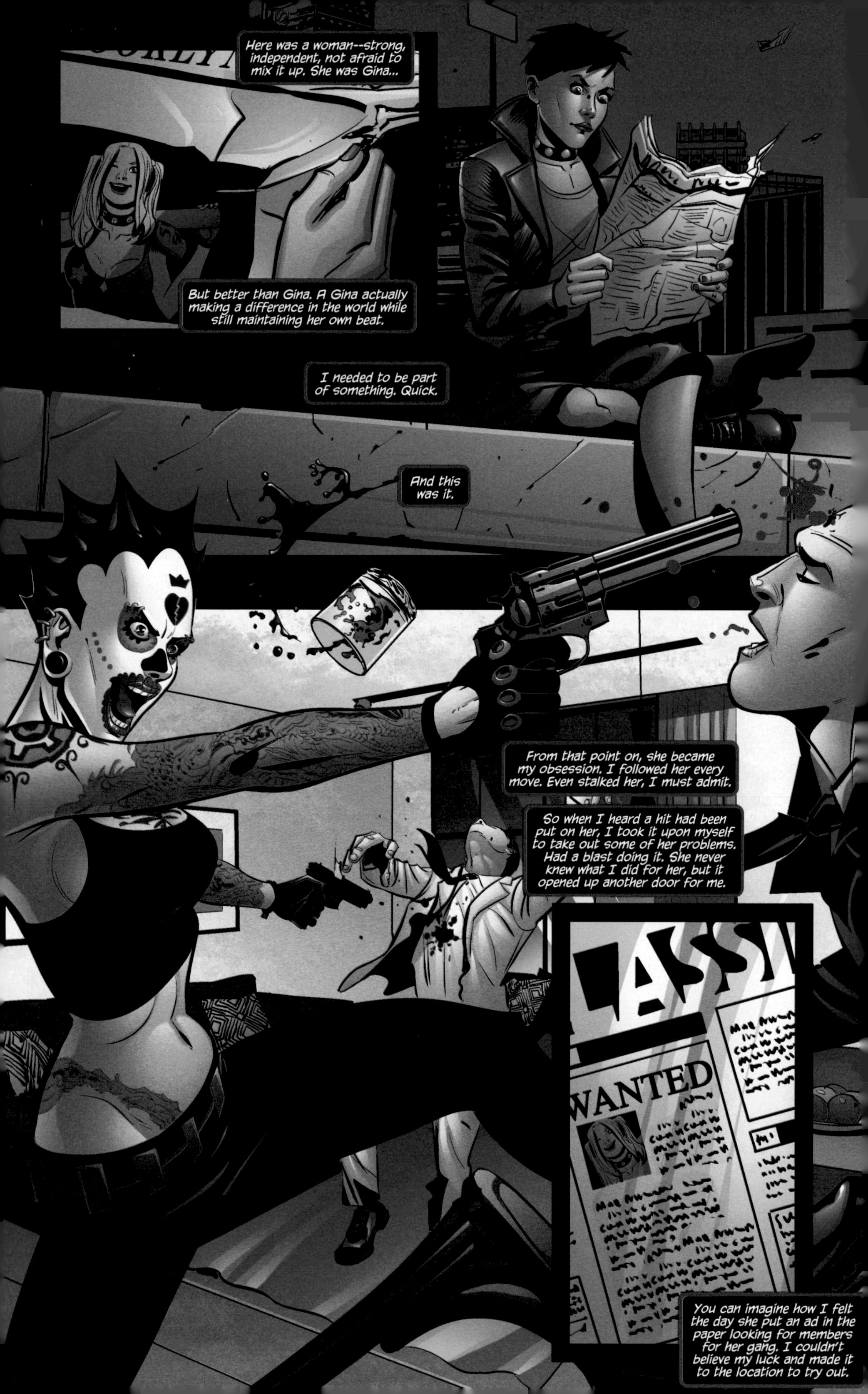
Here was a woman--strong, independent, not afraid to mix it up. She was Gina...
But better than Gina. A Gina actually making a difference in the world while still maintaining her own beat.
I needed to be part of something. Quick.
And this was it.
From that point on, she became my obsession. I followed her every move. Even stalked her, I must admit.
So when I heard a hit had been put on her, I took it upon myself to take out some of her problems. Had a blast doing it. She never knew what I did for her, but it opened up another door for me.
WANTED
You can imagine how I felt the day she put an ad in the paper looking for members for her gang. I couldn't believe my luck and made it to the location to try out.

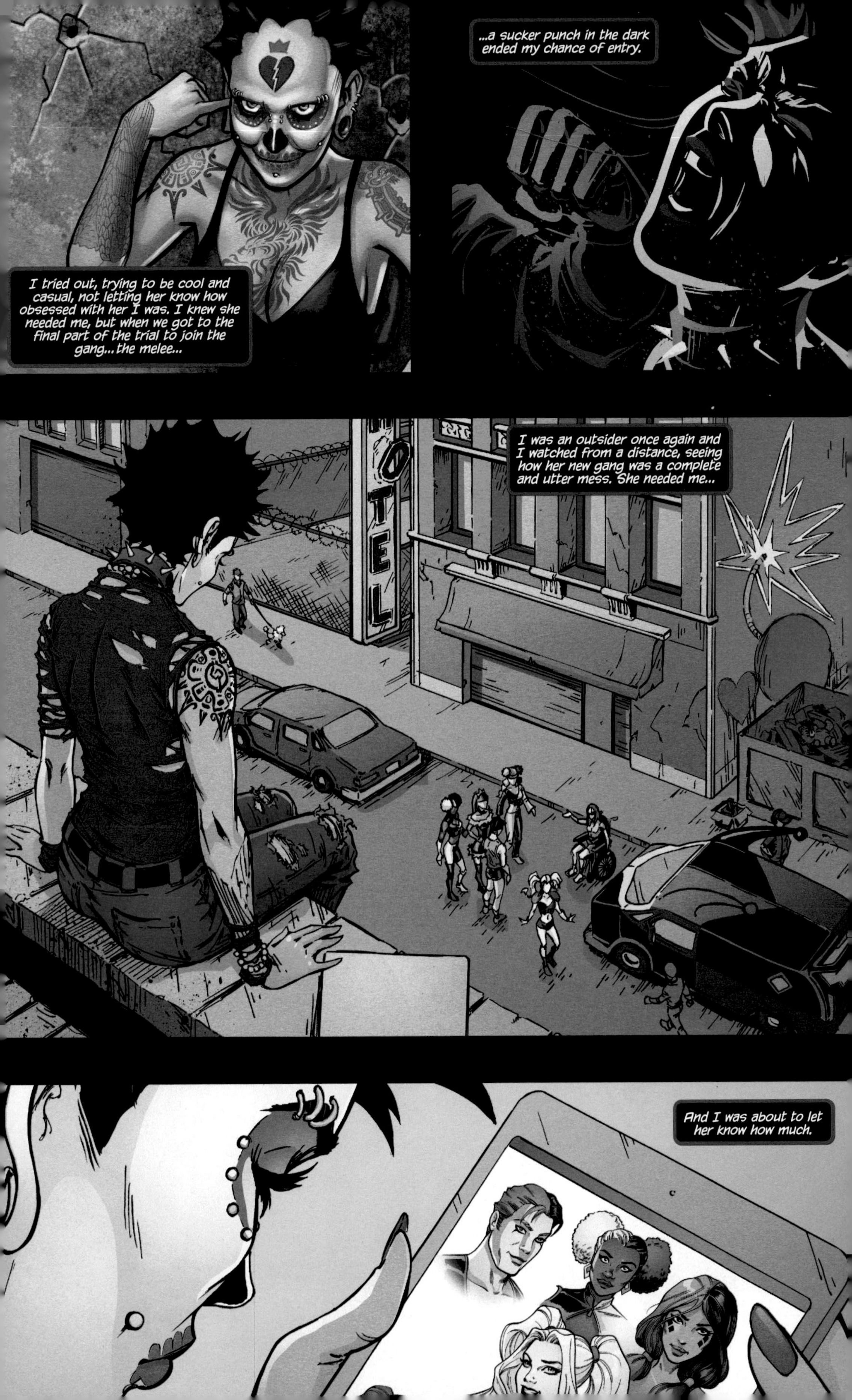
I tried out, trying to be cool and casual, not letting her know how obsessed with her I was. I knew she needed me, but when we got to the final part of the trial to join the gang...the melee...
...a sucker punch in the dark ended my chance of entry.
I was an outsider once again and I watched from a distance, seeing how her new gang was a complete and utter mess. She needed me...
And I was about to let her know how much.

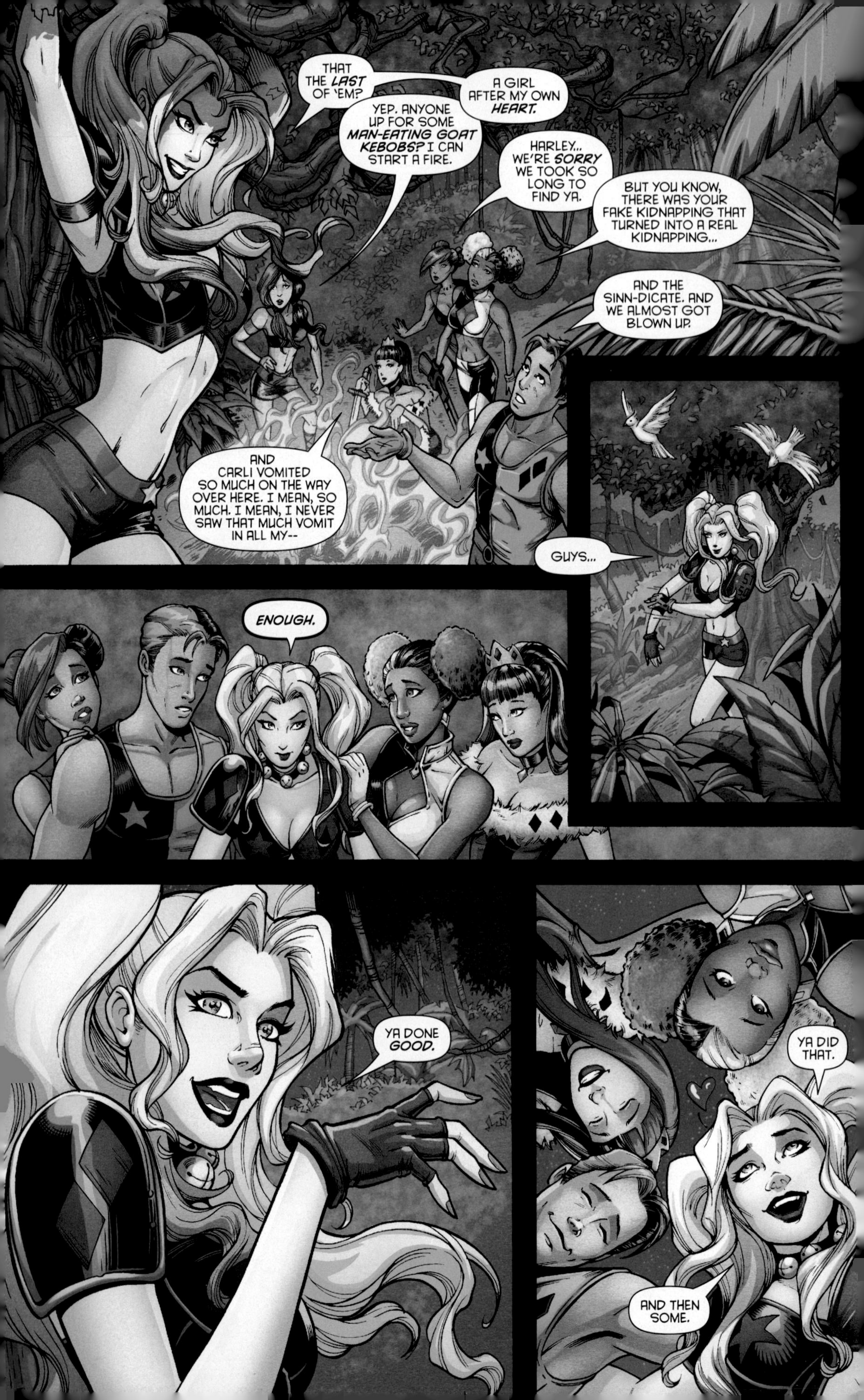
THAT THE LAST OF 'EM?
A GIRL AFTER MY OWN HEART.
YEP. ANYONE UP FOR SOME MAN-EATING GOAT KEBOBS? I CAN START A FIRE.
HARLEY... WE'RE SORRY WE TOOK SO LONG TO FIND YA.
BUT YOU KNOW, THERE WAS YOUR FAKE KIDNAPPING THAT TURNED INTO A REAL KIDNAPPING...
AND THE SINN-DICATE. AND WE ALMOST GOT BLOWN UP.
AND CARLI VOMITED SO MUCH ON THE WAY OVER HERE. I MEAN, SO MUCH. I MEAN, I NEVER SAW THAT MUCH VOMIT IN ALL MY--
GUYS...
ENOUGH.
YA DONE GOOD.
YA DID THAT.
AND THEN SOME.

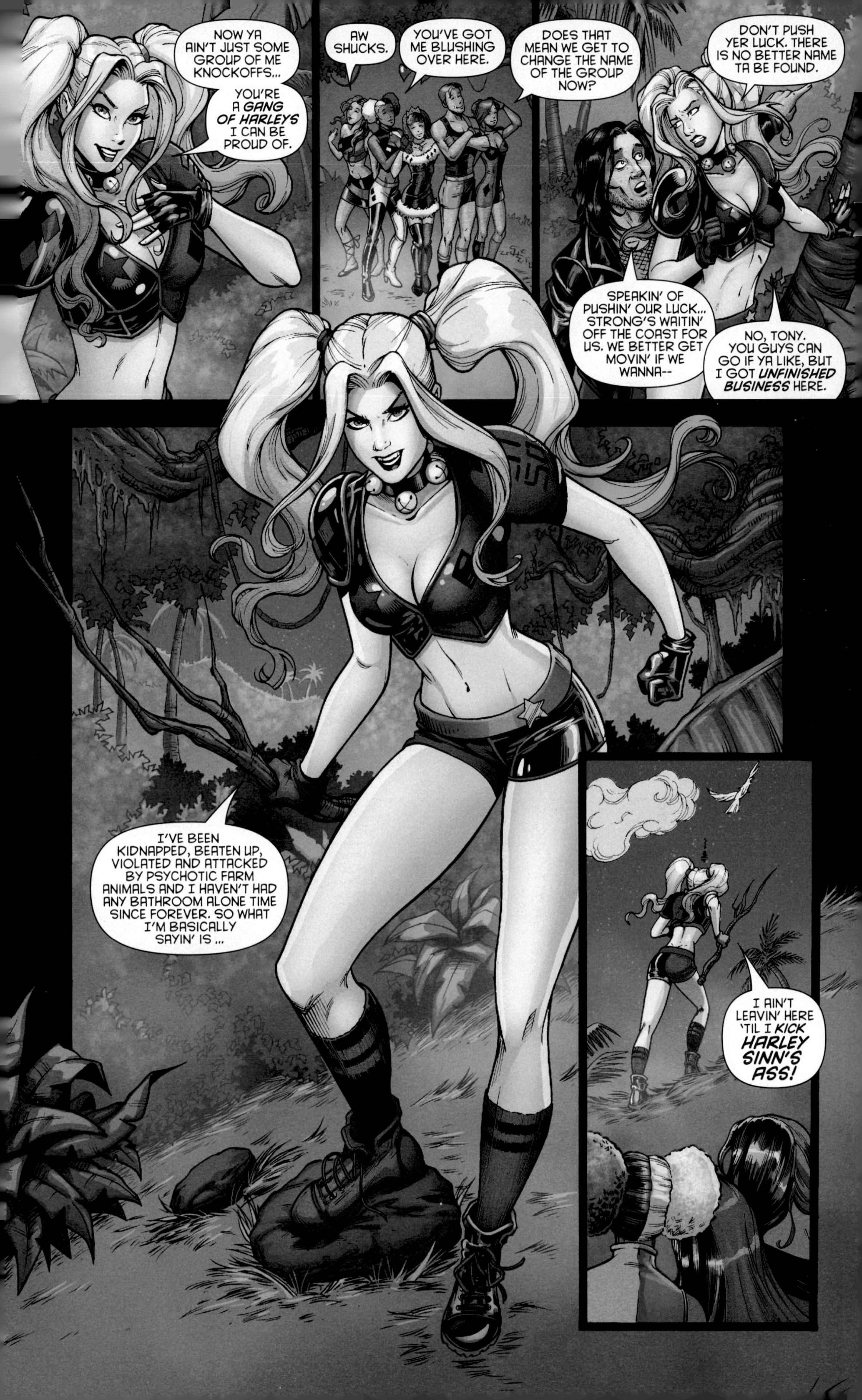
NOW YA AIN'T JUST SOME GROUP OF ME KNOCKOFFS...
YOU'RE A ***GANG OF HARLEYS*** I CAN BE PROUD OF.
AW SHUCKS.
YOU'VE GOT ME BLUSHING OVER HERE.
DOES THAT MEAN WE GET TO CHANGE THE NAME OF THE GROUP NOW?
DON'T PUSH YER LUCK. THERE IS NO BETTER NAME TA BE FOUND.
SPEAKIN' OF PUSHIN' OUR LUCK... STRONG'S WAITIN' OFF THE COAST FOR US. WE BETTER GET MOVIN' IF WE WANNA--
NO, TONY. YOU GUYS CAN GO IF YA LIKE, BUT I GOT ***UNFINISHED BUSINESS*** HERE.
I'VE BEEN KIDNAPPED, BEATEN UP, VIOLATED AND ATTACKED BY PSYCHOTIC FARM ANIMALS AND I HAVEN'T HAD ANY BATHROOM ALONE TIME SINCE FOREVER. SO WHAT I'M BASICALLY SAYIN' IS ...
I AIN'T LEAVIN' HERE 'TIL I ***KICK HARLEY SINN'S ASS!***

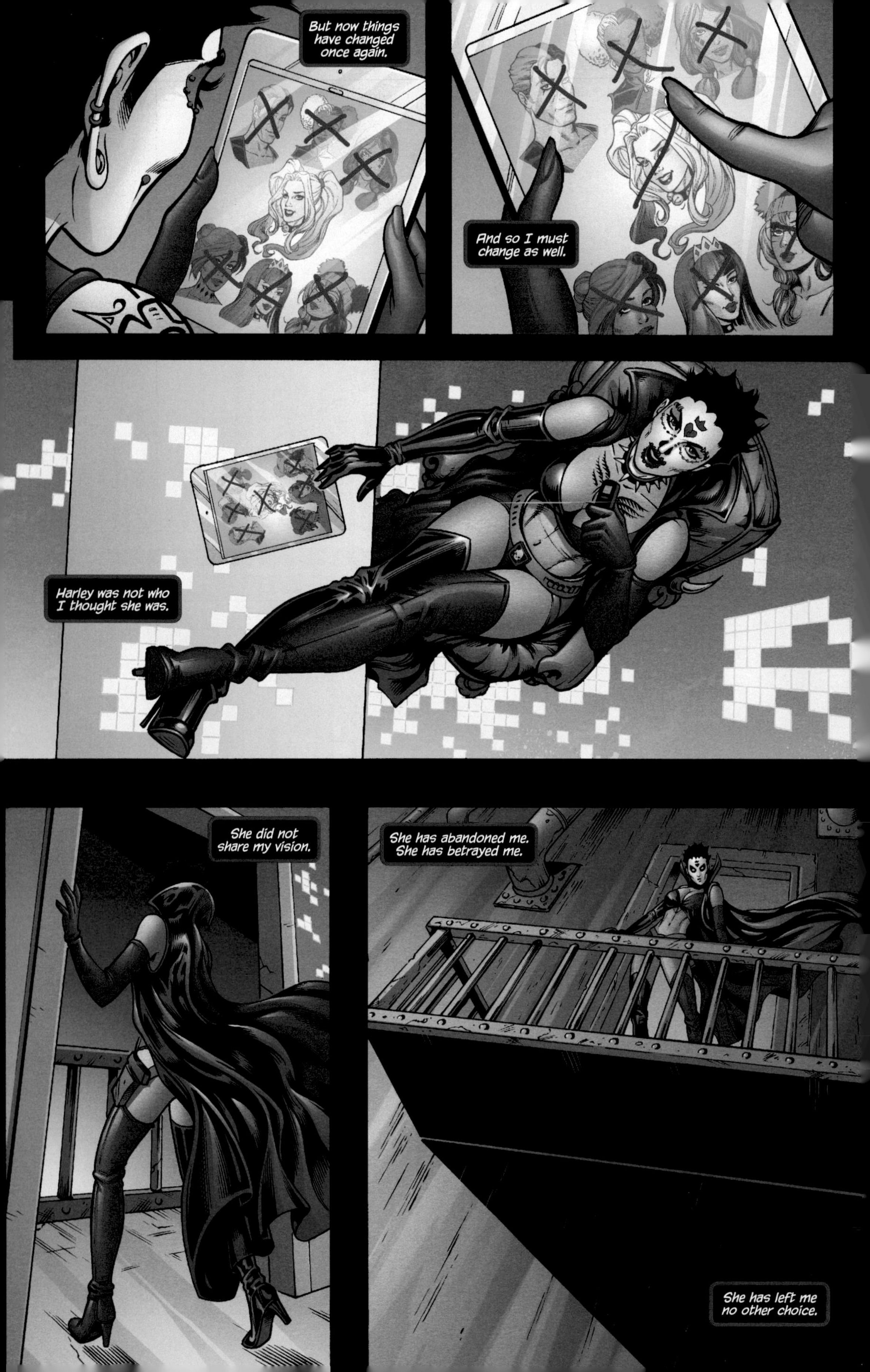
But now things have changed once again.
And so I must change as well.
Harley was not who I thought she was.
She did not share my vision.
She has abandoned me. She has betrayed me.
She has left me no other choice.

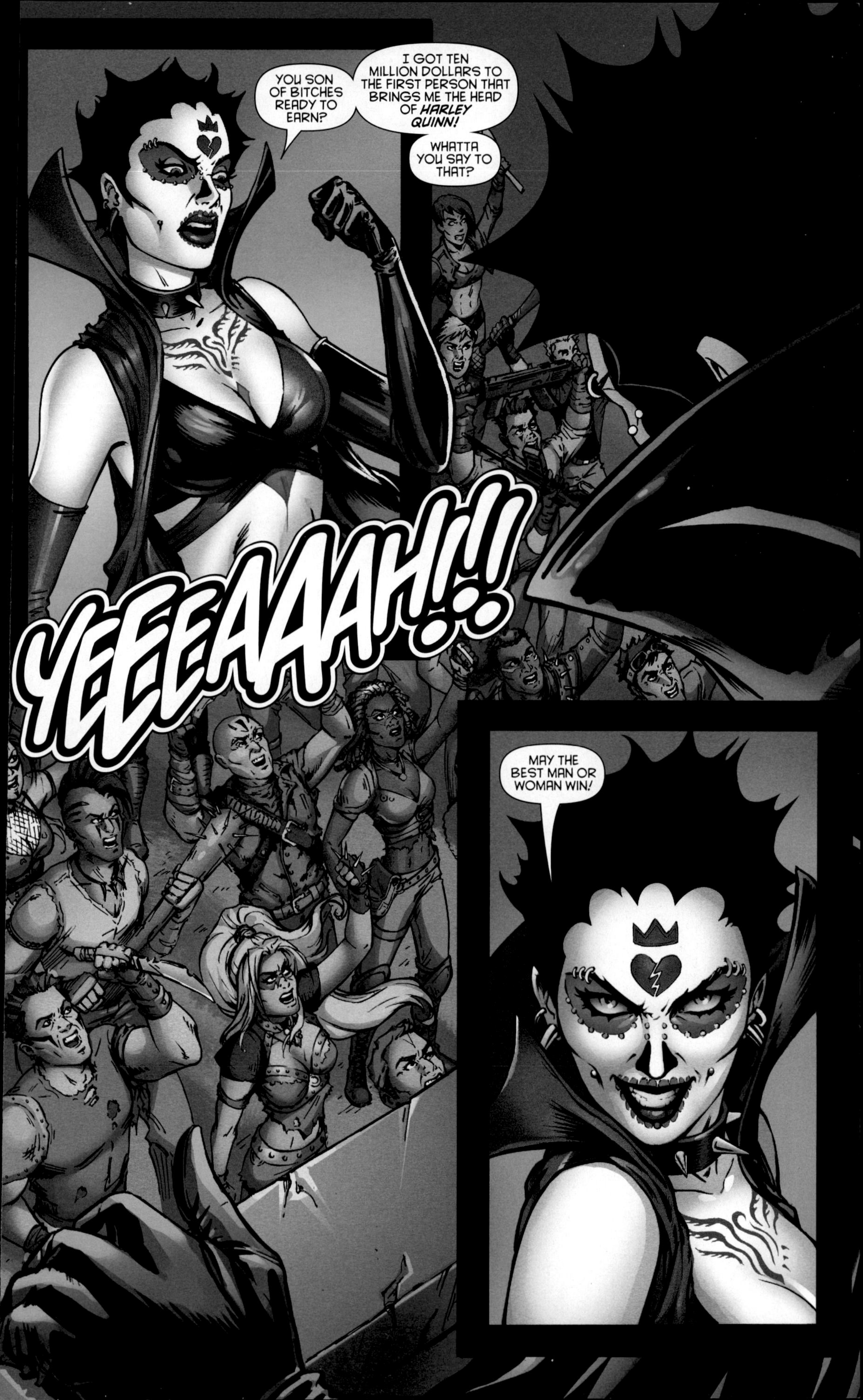
YOU SON OF BITCHES READY TO EARN?
I GOT TEN MILLION DOLLARS TO THE FIRST PERSON THAT BRINGS ME THE HEAD OF HARLEY QUINN!
WHATTA YOU SAY TO THAT?
YEEEAAAH!!!
MAY THE BEST MAN OR WOMAN WIN!

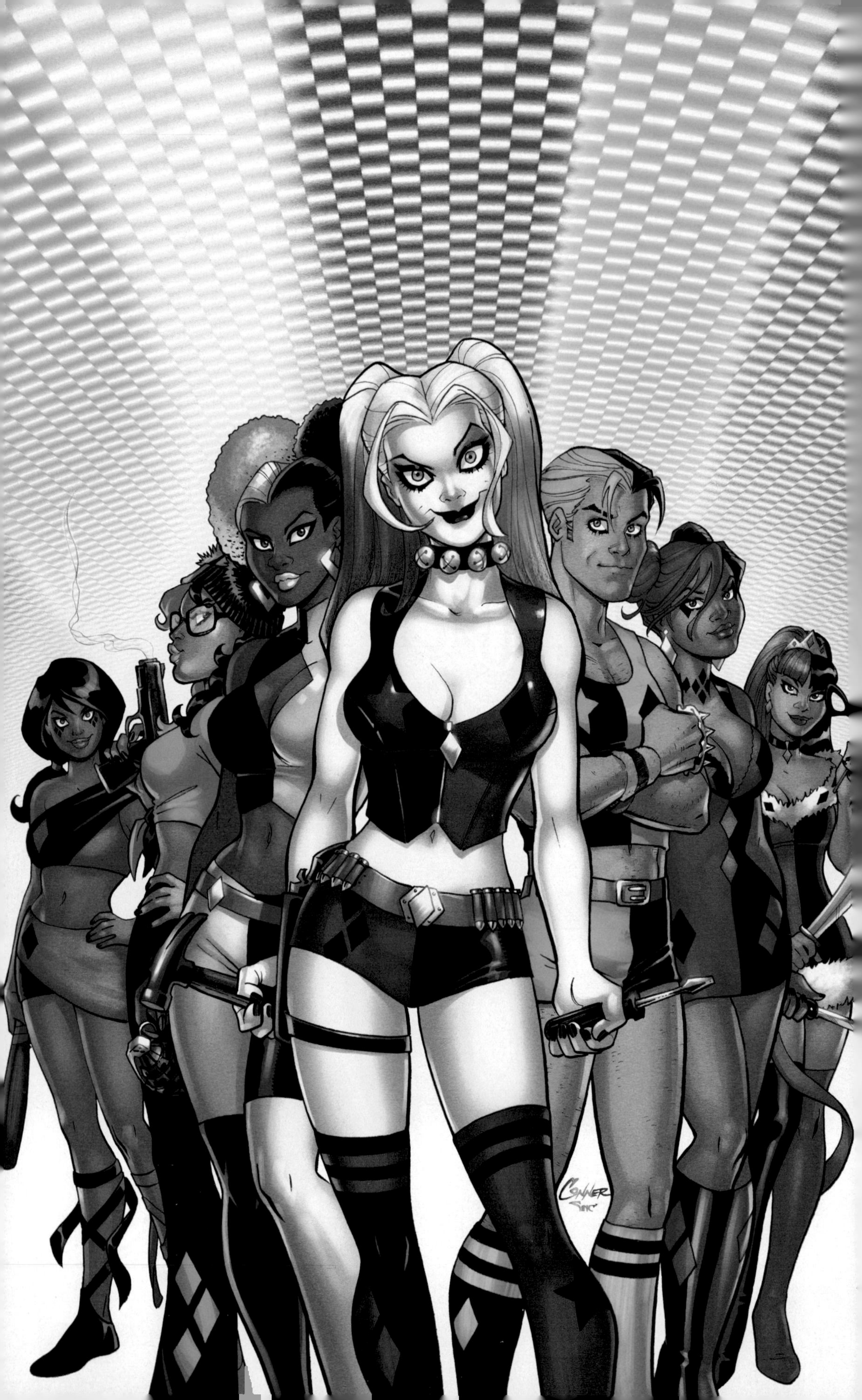

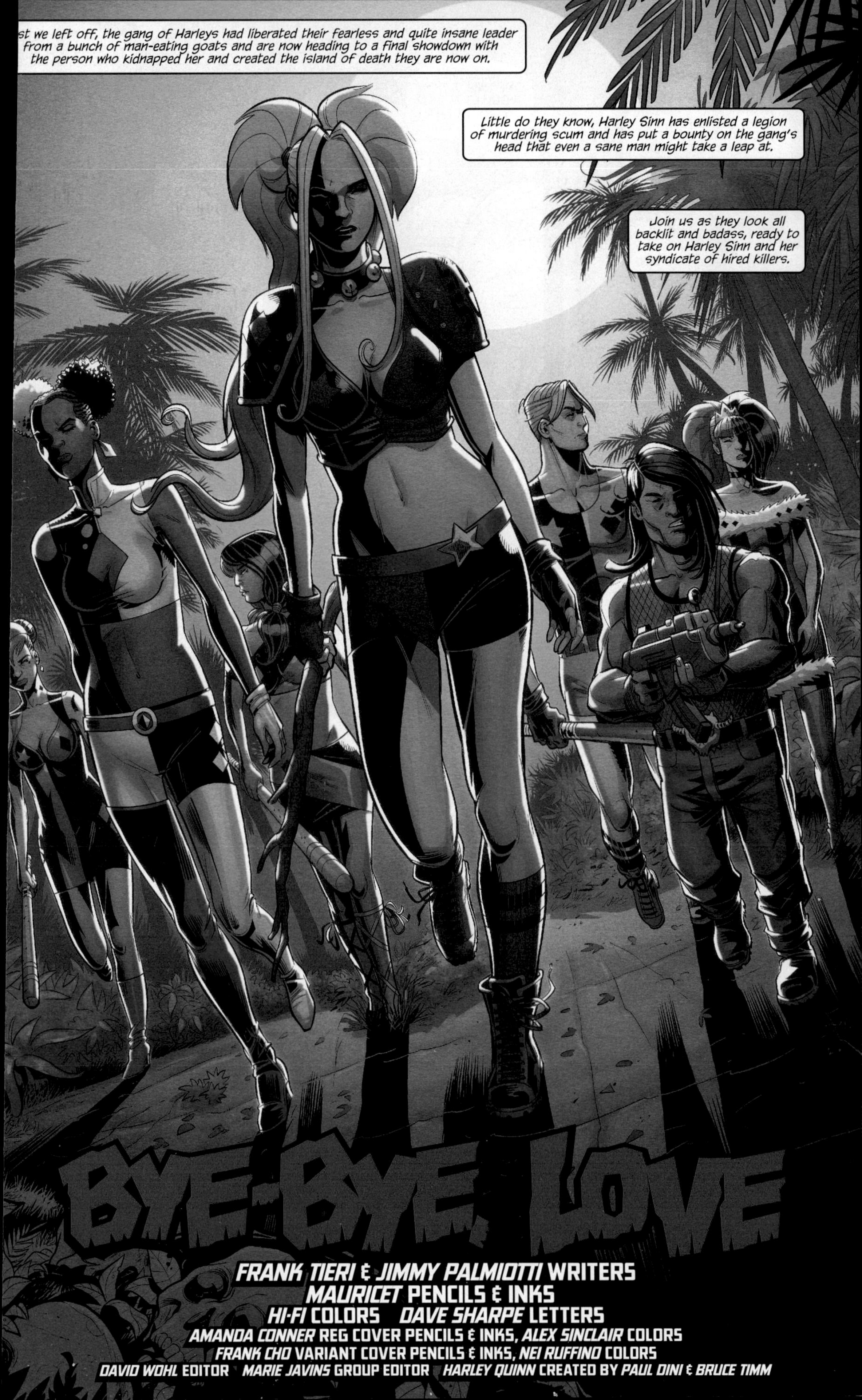
st we left off, the gang of Harleys had liberated their fearless and quite insane leader from a bunch of man-eating goats and are now heading to a final showdown with the person who kidnapped her and created the island of death they are now on.
Little do they know, Harley Sinn has enlisted a legion of murdering scum and has put a bounty on the gang's head that even a sane man might take a leap at.
Join us as they look all backlit and badass, ready to take on Harley Sinn and her syndicate of hired killers.
BYE-BYE, LOVE
FRANK TIERI & JIMMY PALMIOTTI WRITERS
MAURICET PENCILS & INKS
HI-FI COLORS DAVE SHARPE LETTERS
AMANDA CONNER REG COVER PENCILS & INKS, ALEX SINCLAIR COLORS
FRANK CHO VARIANT COVER PENCILS & INKS, NEI RUFFINO COLORS
DAVID WOHL EDITOR MARIE JAVINS GROUP EDITOR HARLEY QUINN CREATED BY PAUL DINI & BRUCE TIMM

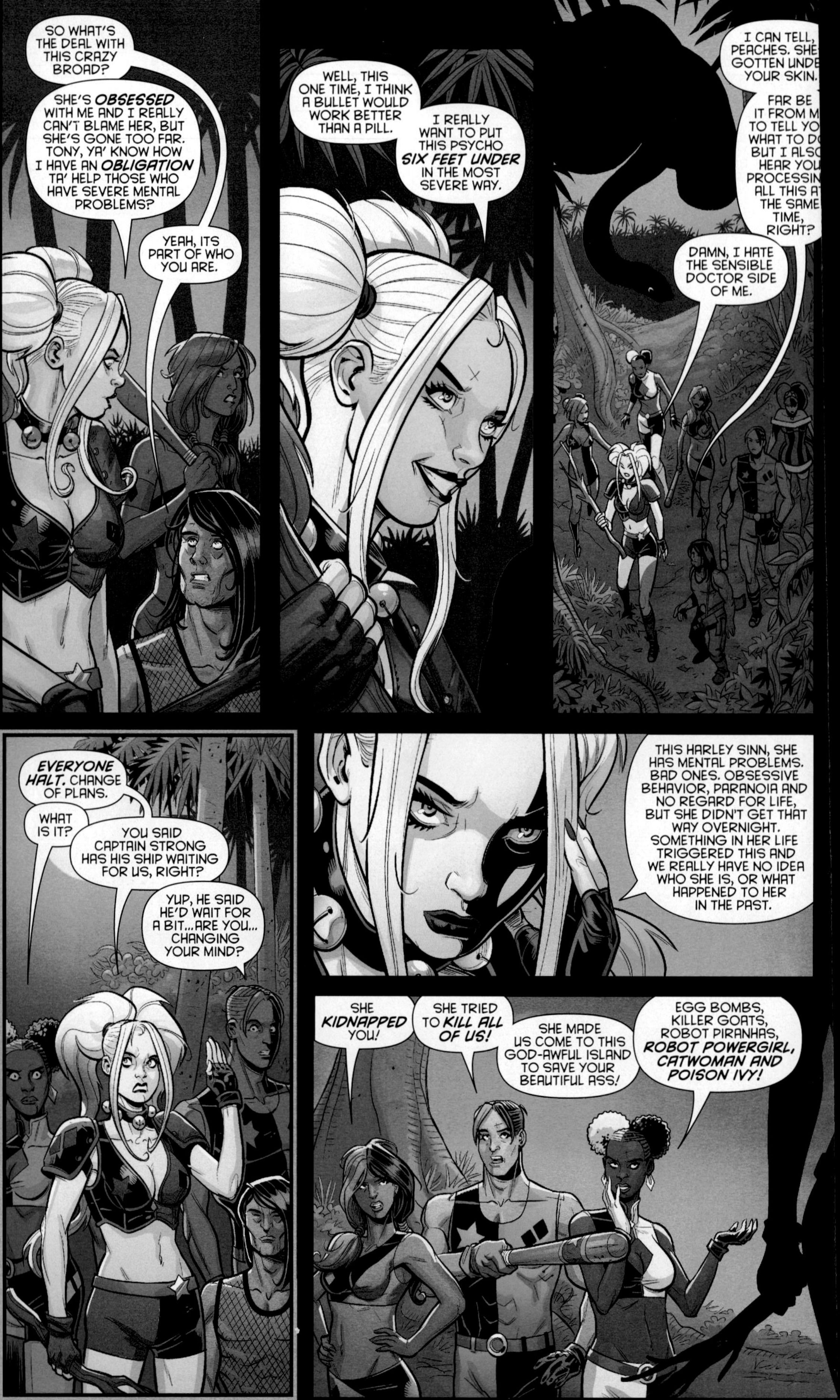
SO WHAT'S THE DEAL WITH THIS CRAZY BROAD?
SHE'S *OBSESSED* WITH ME AND I REALLY CAN'T BLAME HER, BUT SHE'S GONE TOO FAR. TONY, YA' KNOW HOW I HAVE AN *OBLIGATION* TA' HELP THOSE WHO HAVE SEVERE MENTAL PROBLEMS?
YEAH, ITS PART OF WHO YOU ARE.
WELL, THIS ONE TIME, I THINK A BULLET WOULD WORK BETTER THAN A PILL.
I REALLY WANT TO PUT THIS PSYCHO *SIX FEET UNDER* IN THE MOST SEVERE WAY.
DAMN, I HATE THE SENSIBLE DOCTOR SIDE OF ME.
EVERYONE HALT. CHANGE OF PLANS.
WHAT IS IT?
YOU SAID CAPTAIN STRONG HAS HIS SHIP WAITING FOR US, RIGHT?
YUP, HE SAID HE'D WAIT FOR A BIT...ARE YOU... CHANGING YOUR MIND?
THIS HARLEY SINN, SHE HAS MENTAL PROBLEMS. BAD ONES. OBSESSIVE BEHAVIOR, PARANOIA AND NO REGARD FOR LIFE, BUT SHE DIDN'T GET THAT WAY OVERNIGHT. SOMETHING IN HER LIFE TRIGGERED THIS AND WE REALLY HAVE NO IDEA WHO SHE IS, OR WHAT HAPPENED TO HER IN THE PAST.
SHE *KIDNAPPED* YOU!
SHE TRIED TO *KILL ALL OF US!*
SHE MADE US COME TO THIS GOD-AWFUL ISLAND TO SAVE YOUR BEAUTIFUL ASS!
EGG BOMBS, KILLER GOATS, ROBOT PIRANHAS, *ROBOT POWERGIRL, CATWOMAN AND POISON IVY!*

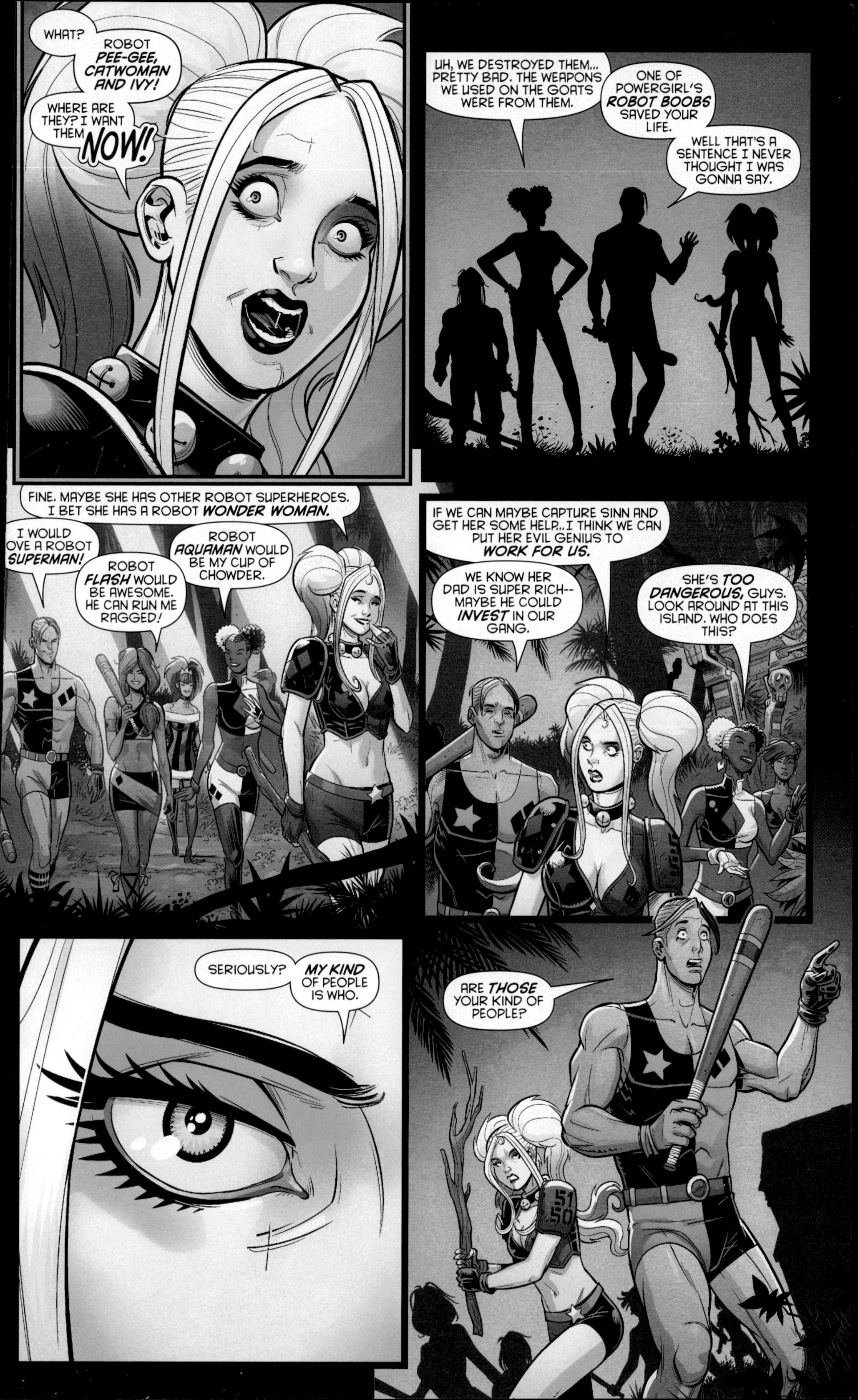
WHAT?
ROBOT PEE-GEE, CATWOMAN AND IVY!
WHERE ARE THEY? I WANT THEM NOW!
UH, WE DESTROYED THEM... PRETTY BAD. THE WEAPONS WE USED ON THE GOATS WERE FROM THEM.
ONE OF POWERGIRL'S ROBOT BOOBS SAVED YOUR LIFE.
WELL THAT'S A SENTENCE I NEVER THOUGHT I WAS GONNA SAY.
FINE. MAYBE SHE HAS OTHER ROBOT SUPERHEROES. I BET SHE HAS A ROBOT WONDER WOMAN.
I WOULD OVE A ROBOT SUPERMAN!
ROBOT FLASH WOULD BE AWESOME. HE CAN RUN ME RAGGED!
ROBOT AQUAMAN WOULD BE MY CUP OF CHOWDER.
IF WE CAN MAYBE CAPTURE SINN AND GET HER SOME HELP...I THINK WE CAN PUT HER EVIL GENIUS TO WORK FOR US.
WE KNOW HER DAD IS SUPER RICH-- MAYBE HE COULD INVEST IN OUR GANG.
SHE'S TOO DANGEROUS, GUYS. LOOK AROUND AT THIS ISLAND. WHO DOES THIS?
SERIOUSLY?
MY KIND OF PEOPLE IS WHO.
ARE THOSE YOUR KIND OF PEOPLE?

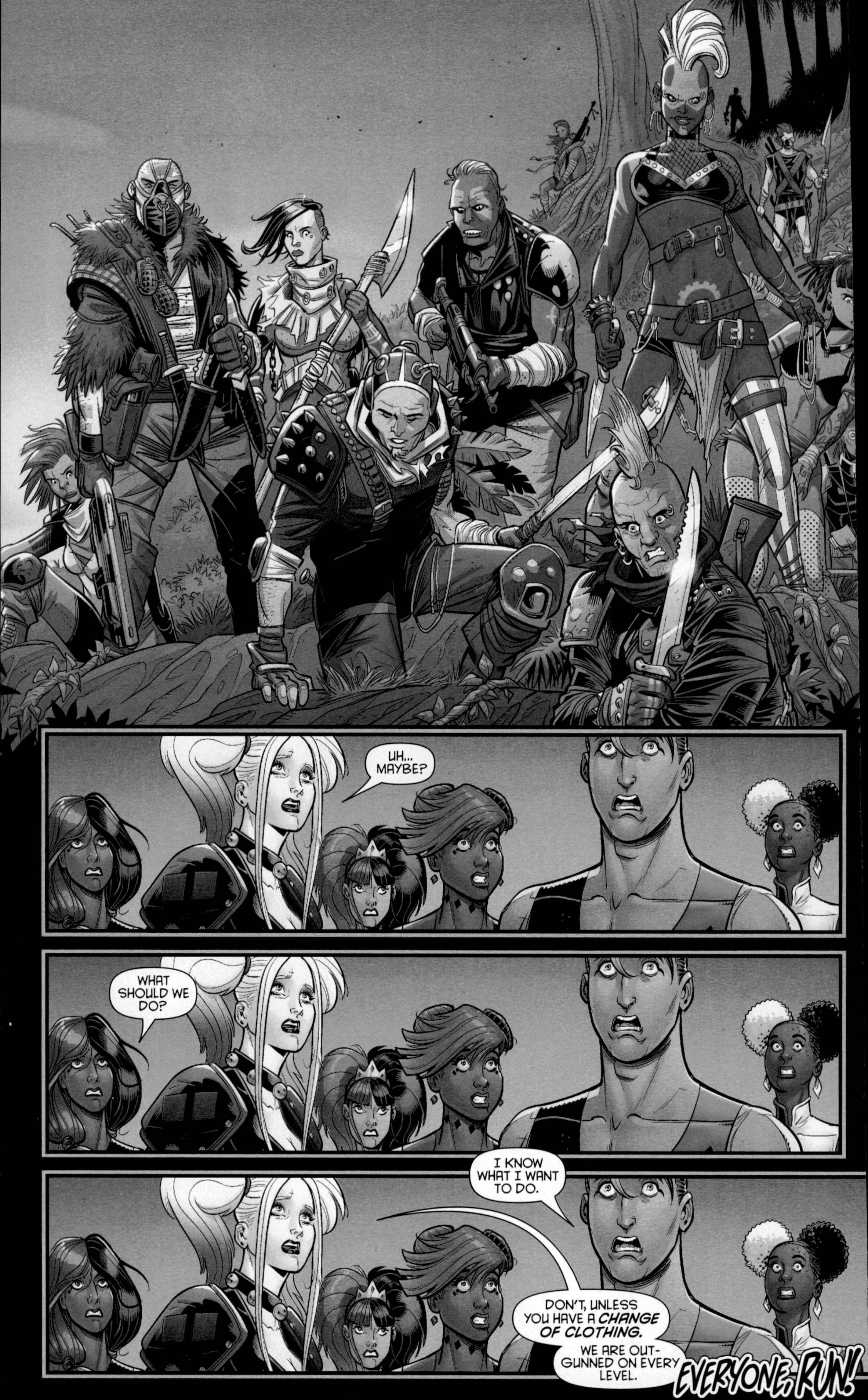
UH... MAYBE?
WHAT SHOULD WE DO?
I KNOW WHAT I WANT TO DO.
DON'T, UNLESS YOU HAVE A *CHANGE OF CLOTHING.*
WE ARE OUT-GUNNED ON EVERY LEVEL.
EVERYONE, RUN!

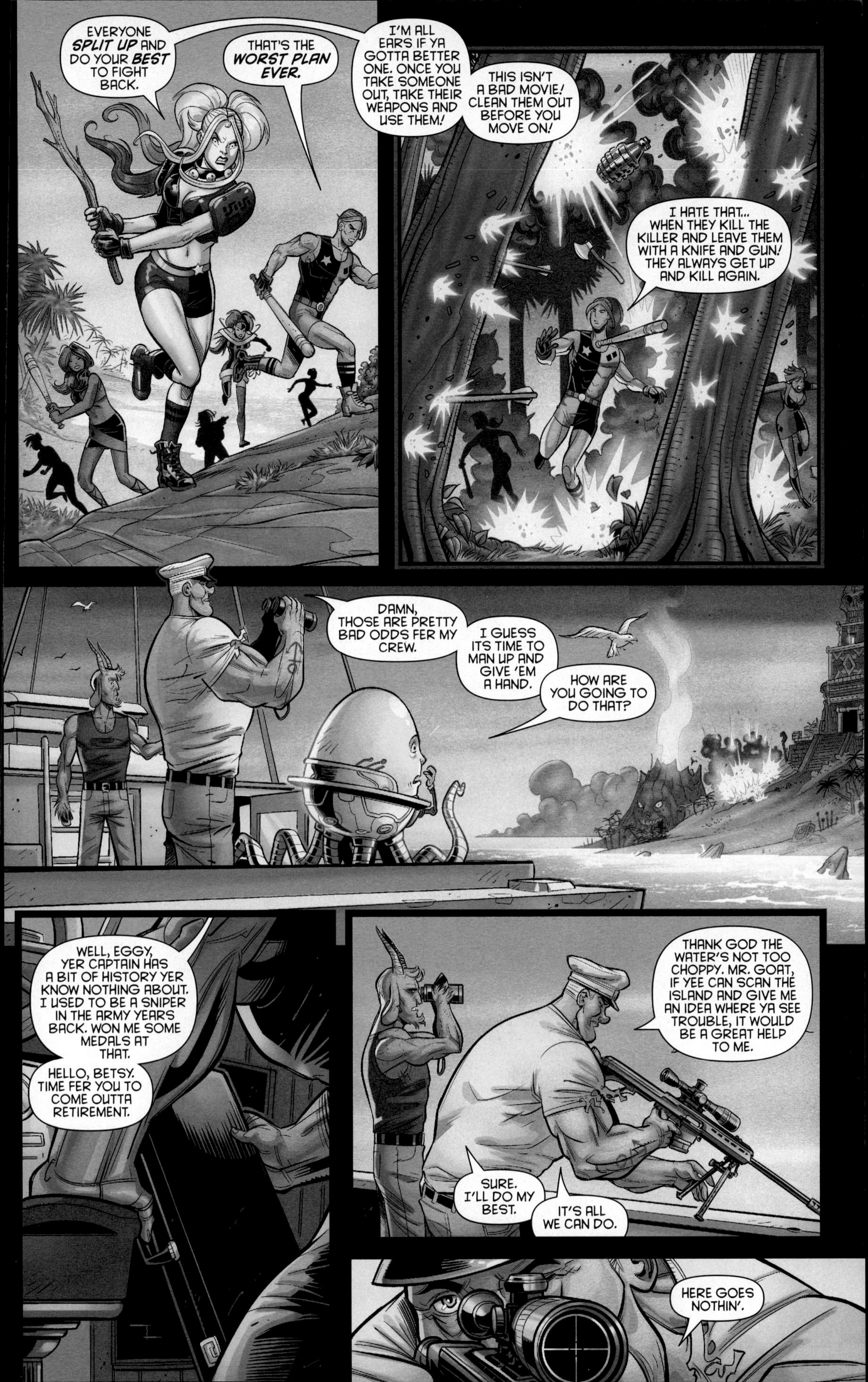
EVERYONE SPLIT UP AND DO YOUR BEST TO FIGHT BACK.
THAT'S THE WORST PLAN EVER.
I'M ALL EARS IF YA GOTTA BETTER ONE. ONCE YOU TAKE SOMEONE OUT, TAKE THEIR WEAPONS AND USE THEM!
THIS ISN'T A BAD MOVIE! CLEAN THEM OUT BEFORE YOU MOVE ON!
I HATE THAT... WHEN THEY KILL THE KILLER AND LEAVE THEM WITH A KNIFE AND GUN! THEY ALWAYS GET UP AND KILL AGAIN.
DAMN, THOSE ARE PRETTY BAD ODDS FER MY CREW.
I GUESS ITS TIME TO MAN UP AND GIVE 'EM A HAND.
HOW ARE YOU GOING TO DO THAT?
WELL, EGGY, YER CAPTAIN HAS A BIT OF HISTORY YER KNOW NOTHING ABOUT. I USED TO BE A SNIPER IN THE ARMY YEARS BACK. WON ME SOME MEDALS AT THAT.
HELLO, BETSY. TIME FER YOU TO COME OUTTA RETIREMENT.
THANK GOD THE WATER'S NOT TOO CHOPPY. MR. GOAT, IF YEE CAN SCAN THE ISLAND AND GIVE ME AN IDEA WHERE YA SEE TROUBLE, IT WOULD BE A GREAT HELP TO ME.
SURE. I'LL DO MY BEST.
IT'S ALL WE CAN DO.
HERE GOES NOTHIN'.

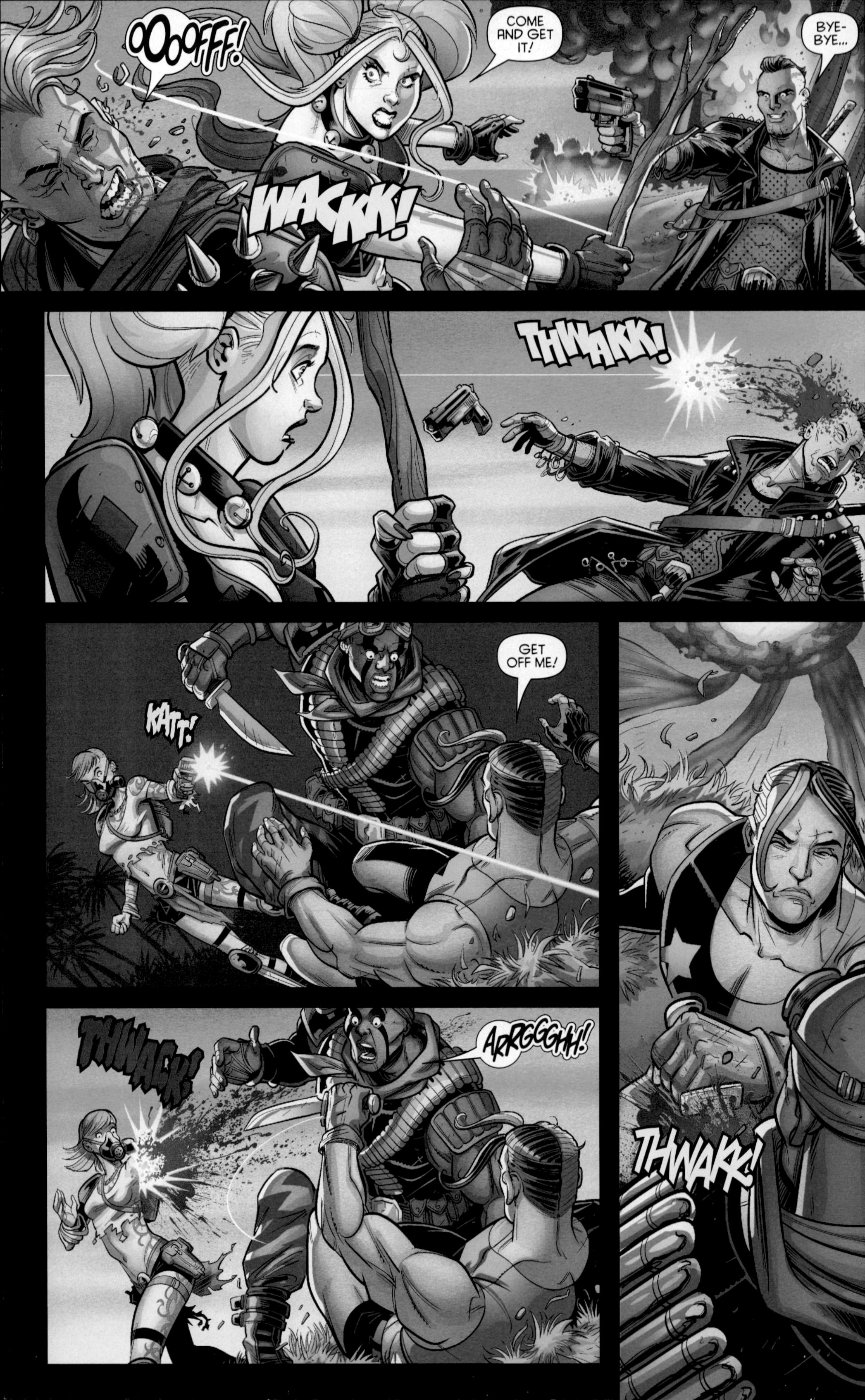
OOOOFFF!
COME AND GET IT!
BYE-BYE...
WACKK!
THWAKK!
KATT!
GET OFF ME!
THWACK!
ARRGGGHH!
THWAKK!

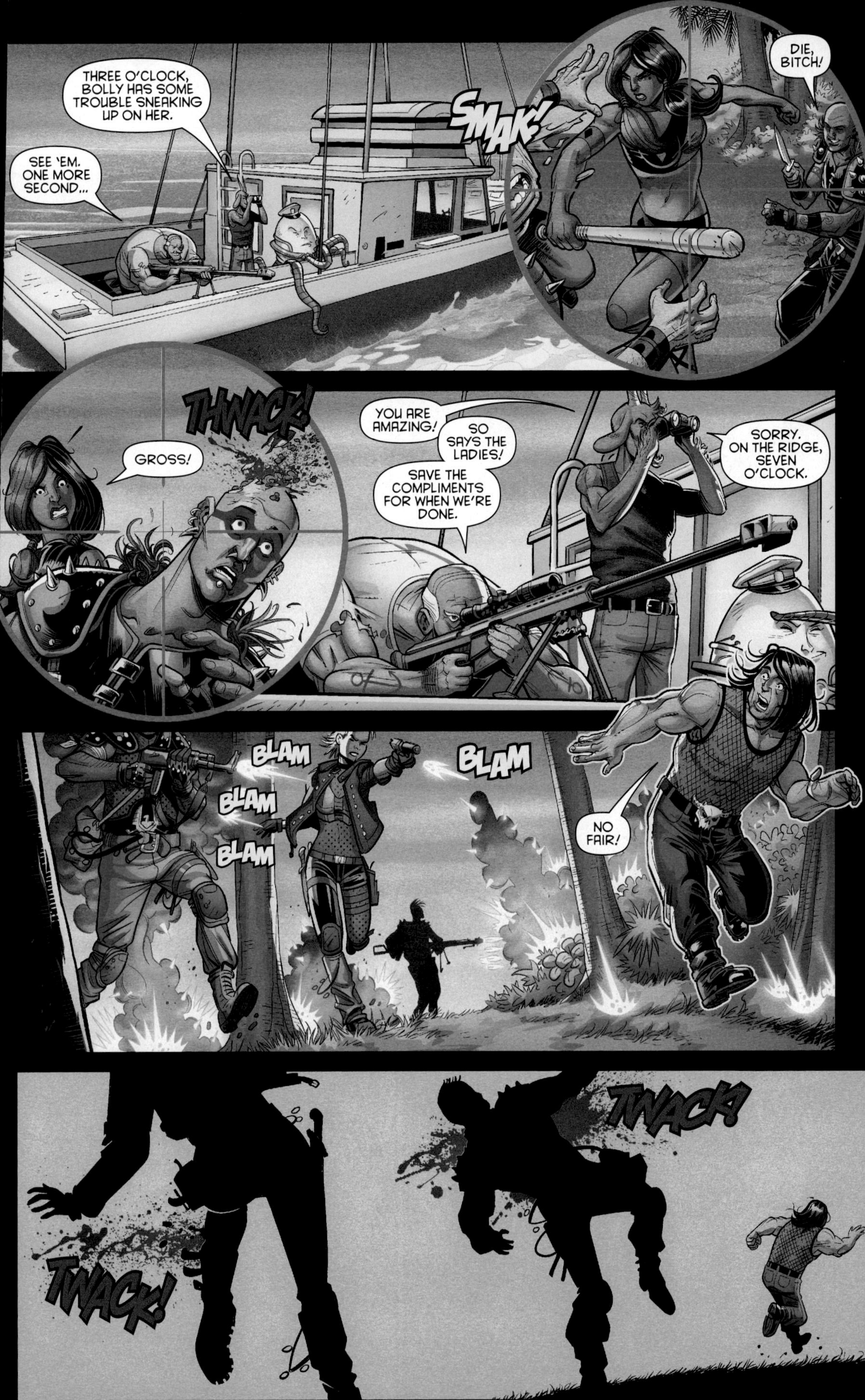
THREE O'CLOCK, BOLLY HAS SOME TROUBLE SNEAKING UP ON HER.
SEE 'EM. ONE MORE SECOND...
SMAK!
DIE, BITCH!
THWACK!
GROSS!
YOU ARE AMAZING!
SO SAYS THE LADIES!
SAVE THE COMPLIMENTS FOR WHEN WE'RE DONE.
SORRY. ON THE RIDGE, SEVEN O'CLOCK.
BLAM
BLAM
BLAM
BLAM
NO FAIR!
TWACK!
TWACK!

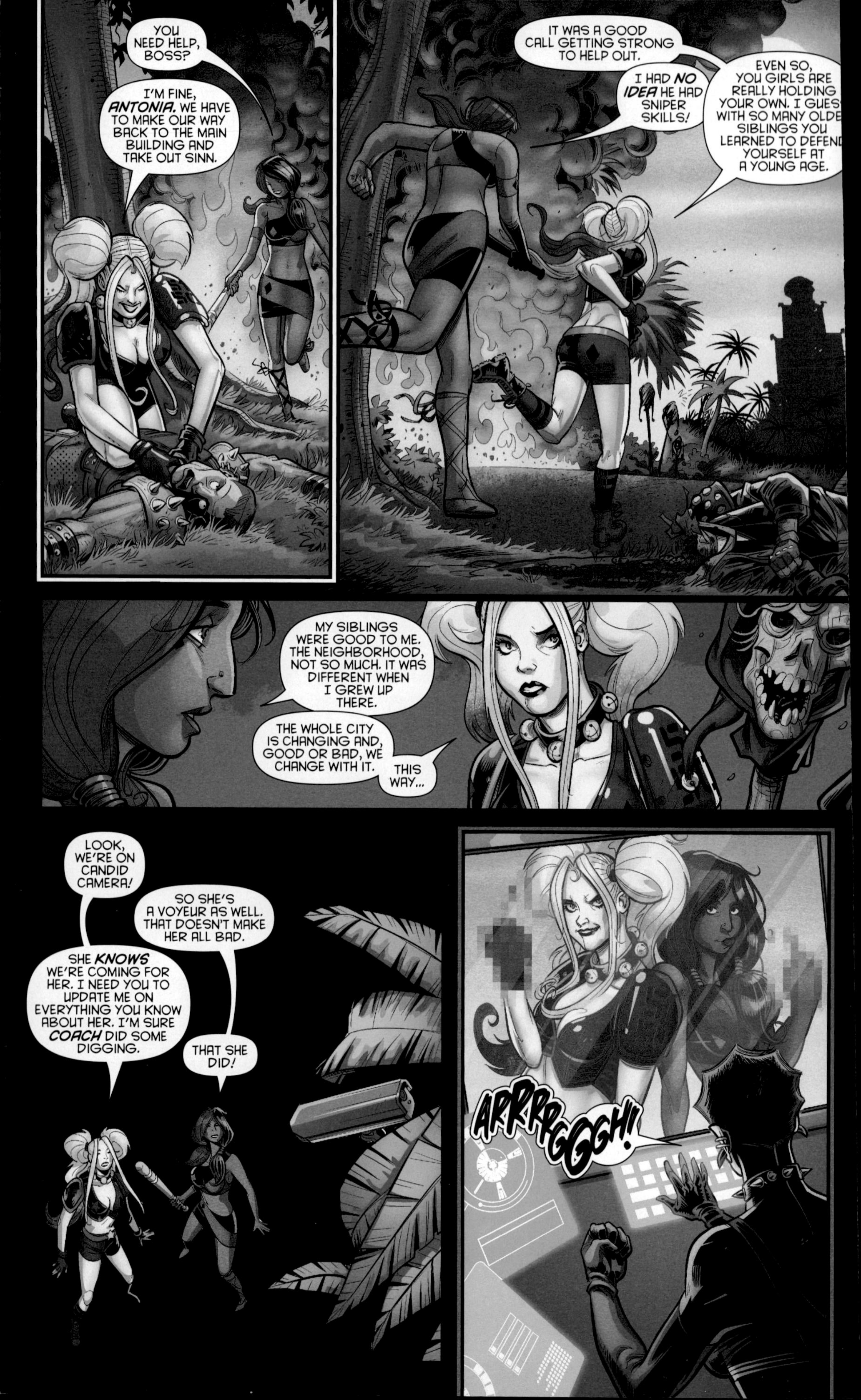
YOU NEED HELP, BOSS?
I'M FINE, ANTONIA. WE HAVE TO MAKE OUR WAY BACK TO THE MAIN BUILDING AND TAKE OUT SINN.
IT WAS A GOOD CALL GETTING STRONG TO HELP OUT.
I HAD NO IDEA HE HAD SNIPER SKILLS!
EVEN SO, YOU GIRLS ARE REALLY HOLDING YOUR OWN. I GUESS WITH SO MANY OLDER SIBLINGS YOU LEARNED TO DEFEND YOURSELF AT A YOUNG AGE.
MY SIBLINGS WERE GOOD TO ME. THE NEIGHBORHOOD, NOT SO MUCH. IT WAS DIFFERENT WHEN I GREW UP THERE.
THE WHOLE CITY IS CHANGING AND, GOOD OR BAD, WE CHANGE WITH IT.
THIS WAY...
LOOK, WE'RE ON CANDID CAMERA!
SO SHE'S A VOYEUR AS WELL. THAT DOESN'T MAKE HER ALL BAD.
SHE KNOWS WE'RE COMING FOR HER. I NEED YOU TO UPDATE ME ON EVERYTHING YOU KNOW ABOUT HER. I'M SURE COACH DID SOME DIGGING.
THAT SHE DID!
ARRRRGGGH!

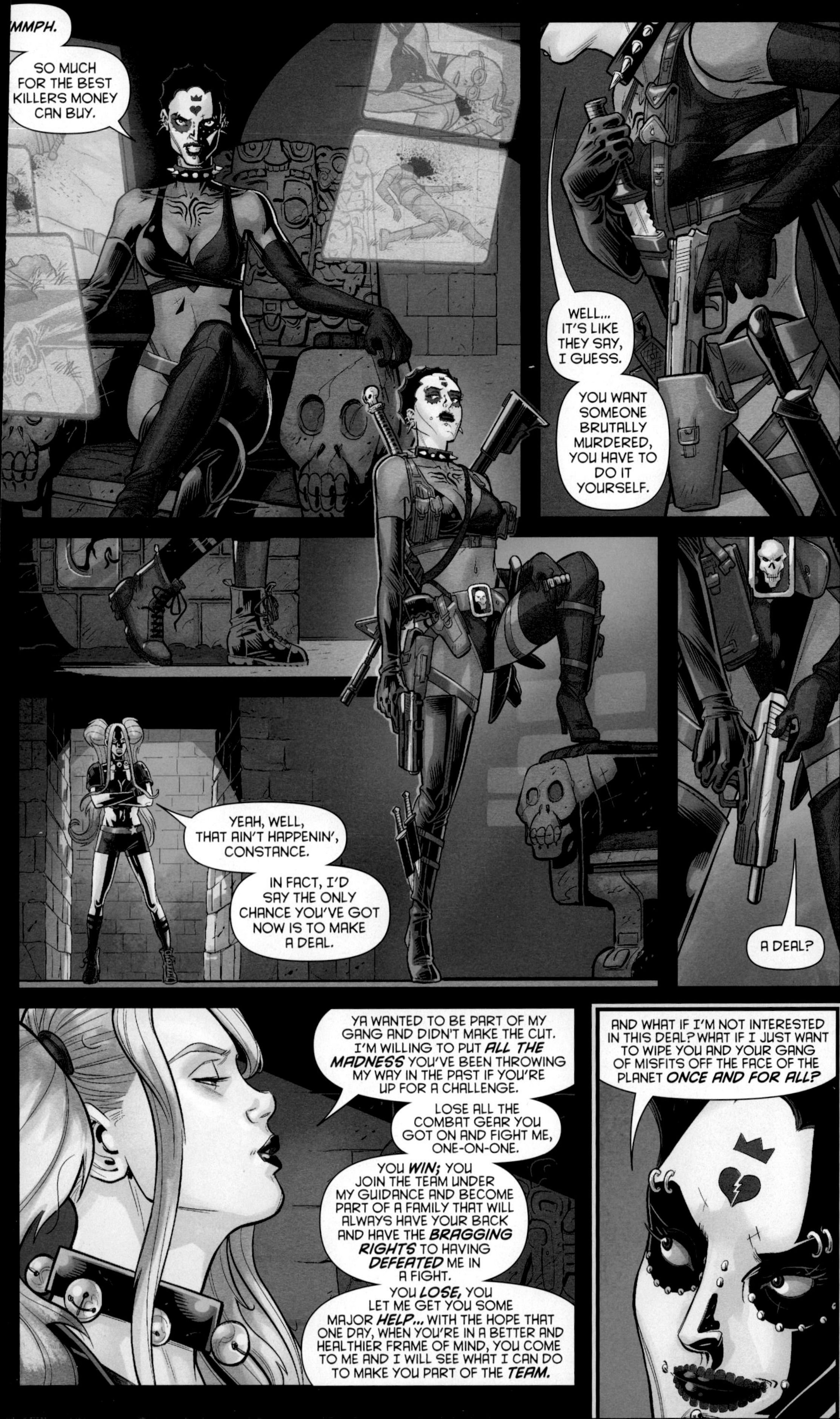
MMPH.
SO MUCH FOR THE BEST KILLERS MONEY CAN BUY.
WELL... IT'S LIKE THEY SAY, I GUESS.
YOU WANT SOMEONE BRUTALLY MURDERED, YOU HAVE TO DO IT YOURSELF.
YEAH, WELL, THAT AIN'T HAPPENIN', CONSTANCE.
IN FACT, I'D SAY THE ONLY CHANCE YOU'VE GOT NOW IS TO MAKE A DEAL.
A DEAL?
YA WANTED TO BE PART OF MY GANG AND DIDN'T MAKE THE CUT. I'M WILLING TO PUT ALL THE MADNESS YOU'VE BEEN THROWING MY WAY IN THE PAST IF YOU'RE UP FOR A CHALLENGE.
LOSE ALL THE COMBAT GEAR YOU GOT ON AND FIGHT ME, ONE-ON-ONE.
YOU WIN; YOU JOIN THE TEAM UNDER MY GUIDANCE AND BECOME PART OF A FAMILY THAT WILL ALWAYS HAVE YOUR BACK AND HAVE THE BRAGGING RIGHTS TO HAVING DEFEATED ME IN A FIGHT.
YOU LOSE, YOU LET ME GET YOU SOME MAJOR HELP... WITH THE HOPE THAT ONE DAY, WHEN YOU'RE IN A BETTER AND HEALTHIER FRAME OF MIND, YOU COME TO ME AND I WILL SEE WHAT I CAN DO TO MAKE YOU PART OF THE TEAM.
AND WHAT IF I'M NOT INTERESTED IN THIS DEAL? WHAT IF I JUST WANT TO WIPE YOU AND YOUR GANG OF MISFITS OFF THE FACE OF THE PLANET ONCE AND FOR ALL?

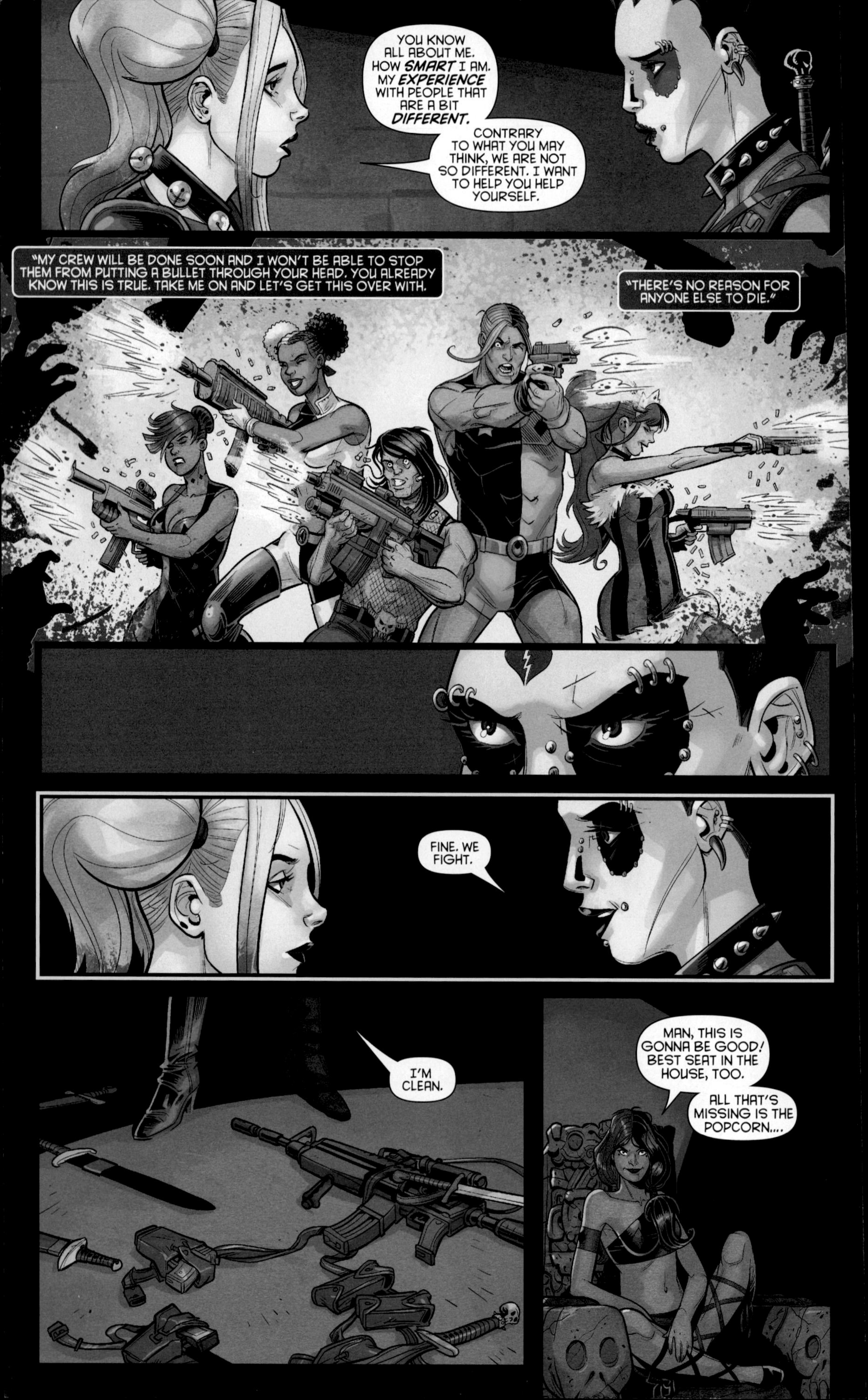
YOU KNOW ALL ABOUT ME. HOW SMART I AM. MY EXPERIENCE WITH PEOPLE THAT ARE A BIT DIFFERENT.
CONTRARY TO WHAT YOU MAY THINK, WE ARE NOT SO DIFFERENT. I WANT TO HELP YOU HELP YOURSELF.
"MY CREW WILL BE DONE SOON AND I WON'T BE ABLE TO STOP THEM FROM PUTTING A BULLET THROUGH YOUR HEAD. YOU ALREADY KNOW THIS IS TRUE. TAKE ME ON AND LET'S GET THIS OVER WITH.
"THERE'S NO REASON FOR ANYONE ELSE TO DIE."
FINE. WE FIGHT.
I'M CLEAN.
MAN, THIS IS GONNA BE GOOD! BEST SEAT IN THE HOUSE, TOO.
ALL THAT'S MISSING IS THE POPCORN....

TWACK!

NICE SHOT.

CRACK!

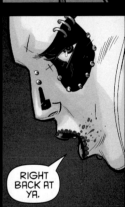

RIGHT BACK AT YA.

WHOOPSIE...

THUMP!

TWAKK!

HAD ENOUGH?

YOU KIDDING?

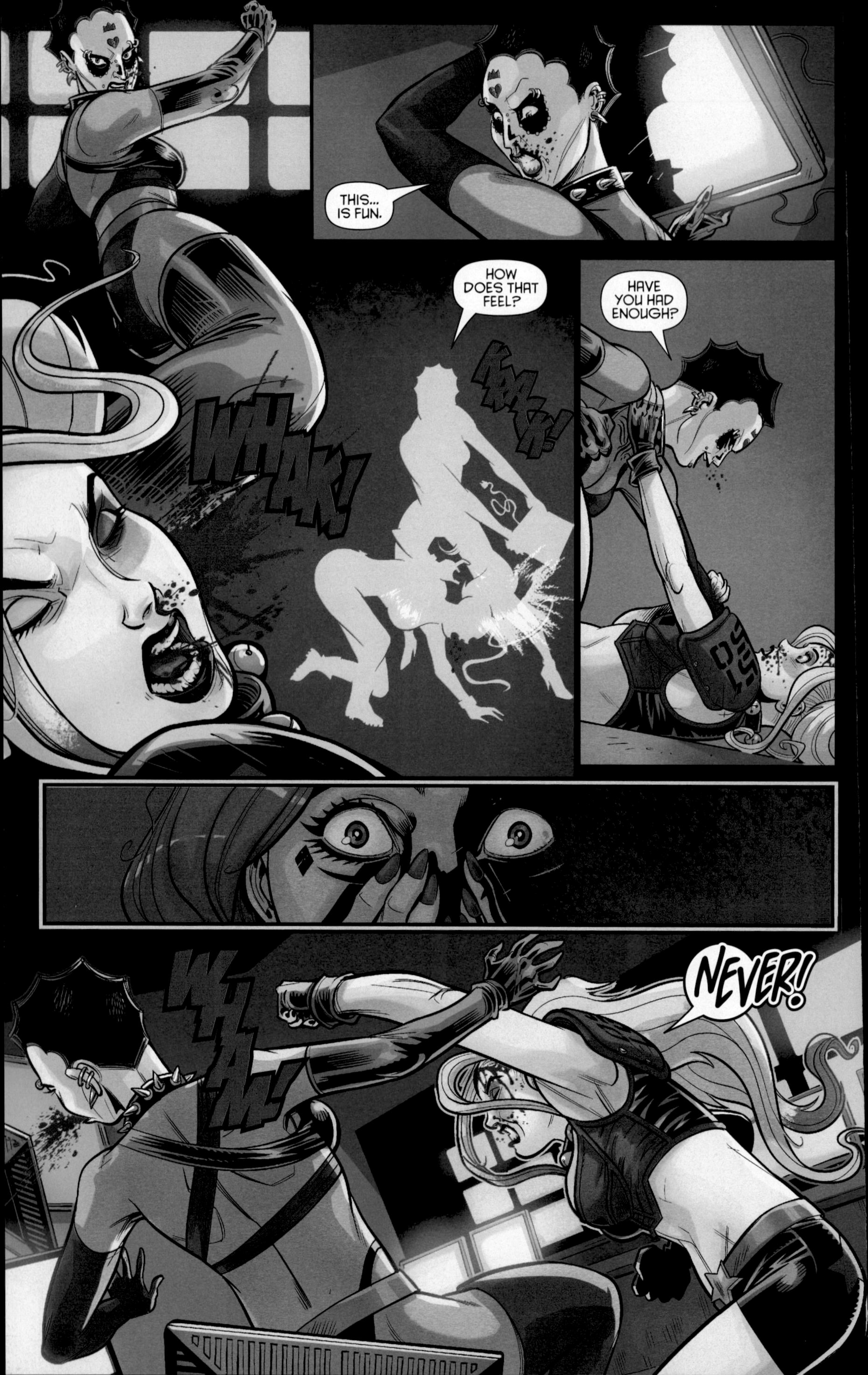
THIS... IS FUN.
WHAK!
HOW DOES THAT FEEL?
KRAKK!
HAVE YOU HAD ENOUGH?
NEVER!
WHAM!

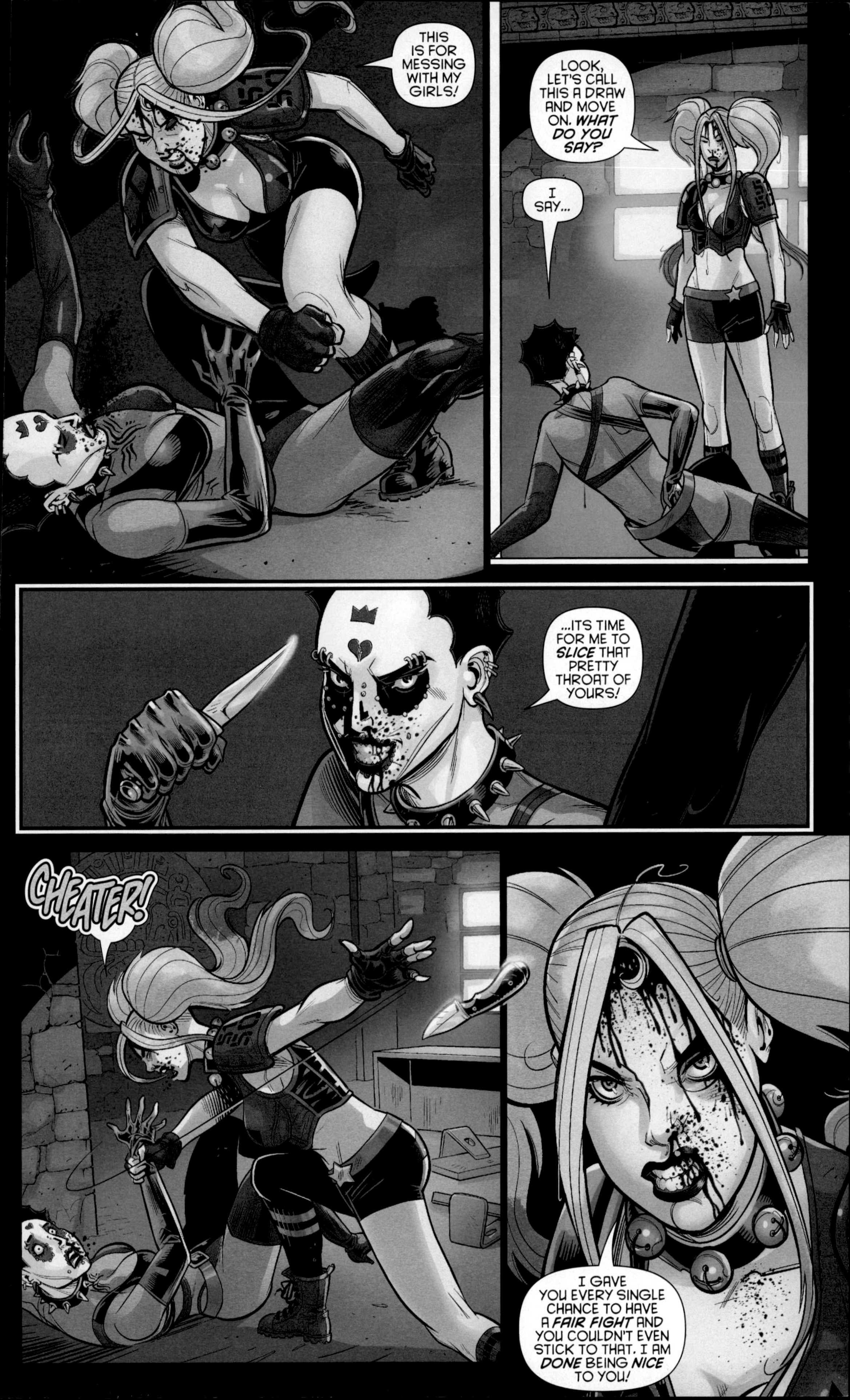
THIS IS FOR MESSING WITH MY GIRLS!
LOOK, LET'S CALL THIS A DRAW AND MOVE ON. *WHAT DO YOU SAY?*
I SAY...
...ITS TIME FOR ME TO *SLICE* THAT PRETTY THROAT OF YOURS!
CHEATER!
I GAVE YOU EVERY SINGLE CHANCE TO HAVE A *FAIR FIGHT* AND YOU COULDN'T EVEN STICK TO THAT. I AM *DONE* BEING *NICE* TO YOU!

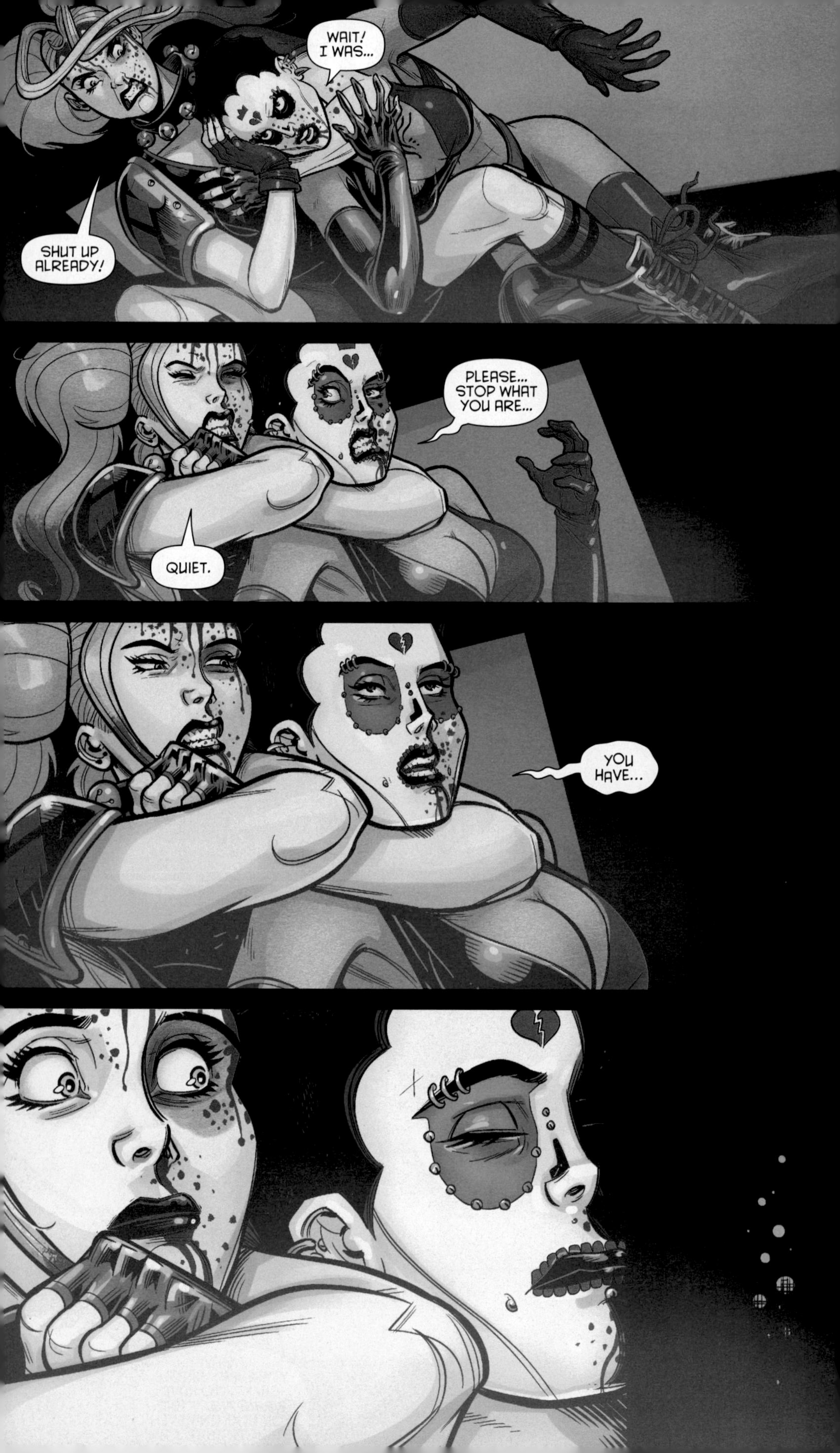
WAIT! I WAS...
SHUT UP ALREADY!
PLEASE... STOP WHAT YOU ARE...
QUIET.
YOU HAVE...

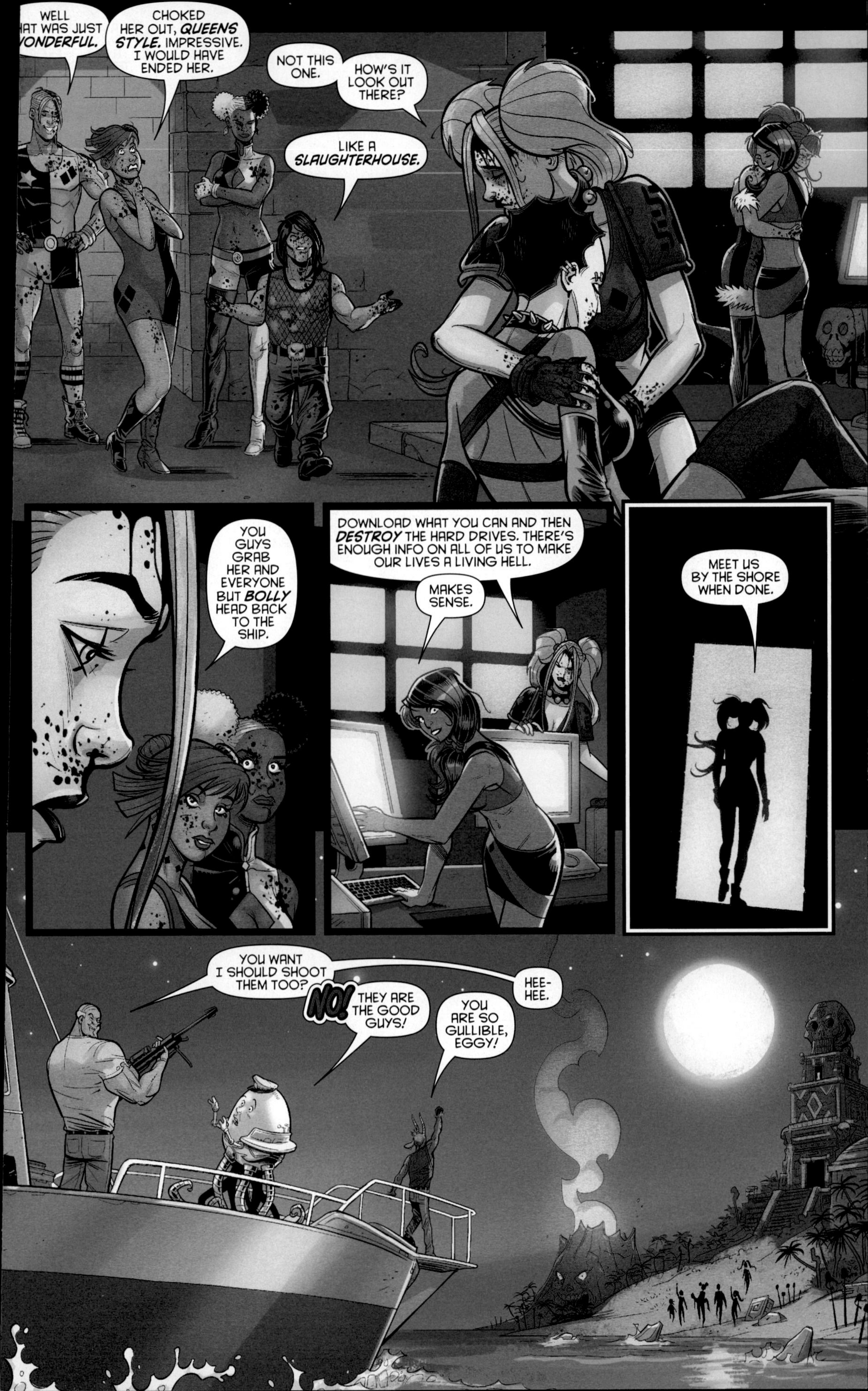
WELL THAT WAS JUST WONDERFUL.
CHOKED HER OUT, QUEENS STYLE. IMPRESSIVE. I WOULD HAVE ENDED HER.
NOT THIS ONE.
HOW'S IT LOOK OUT THERE?
LIKE A SLAUGHTERHOUSE.
YOU GUYS GRAB HER AND EVERYONE BUT BOLLY HEAD BACK TO THE SHIP.
DOWNLOAD WHAT YOU CAN AND THEN DESTROY THE HARD DRIVES. THERE'S ENOUGH INFO ON ALL OF US TO MAKE OUR LIVES A LIVING HELL.
MAKES SENSE.
MEET US BY THE SHORE WHEN DONE.
YOU WANT I SHOULD SHOOT THEM TOO?
NO!
THEY ARE THE GOOD GUYS!
HEE-HEE.
YOU ARE SO GULLIBLE, EGGY!

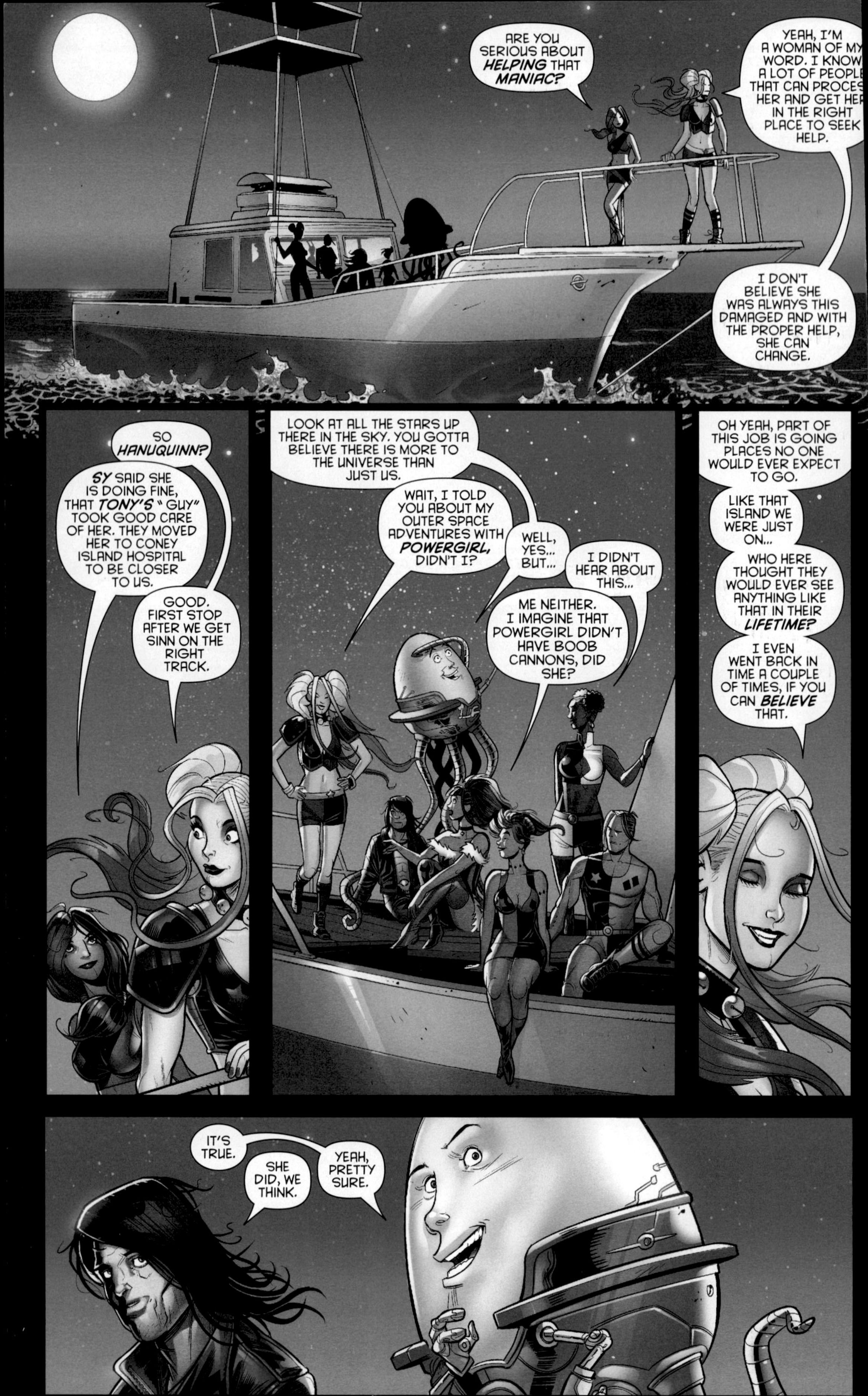
ARE YOU SERIOUS ABOUT HELPING THAT MANIAC?
YEAH, I'M A WOMAN OF MY WORD. I KNOW A LOT OF PEOPLE THAT CAN PROCESS HER AND GET HER IN THE RIGHT PLACE TO SEEK HELP.
I DON'T BELIEVE SHE WAS ALWAYS THIS DAMAGED AND WITH THE PROPER HELP, SHE CAN CHANGE.
SO HANUQUINN?
SY SAID SHE IS DOING FINE, THAT TONY'S "GUY" TOOK GOOD CARE OF HER. THEY MOVED HER TO CONEY ISLAND HOSPITAL TO BE CLOSER TO US.
GOOD. FIRST STOP AFTER WE GET SINN ON THE RIGHT TRACK.
LOOK AT ALL THE STARS UP THERE IN THE SKY. YOU GOTTA BELIEVE THERE IS MORE TO THE UNIVERSE THAN JUST US.
WAIT, I TOLD YOU ABOUT MY OUTER SPACE ADVENTURES WITH POWERGIRL, DIDN'T I?
WELL, YES... BUT...
I DIDN'T HEAR ABOUT THIS...
ME NEITHER. I IMAGINE THAT POWERGIRL DIDN'T HAVE BOOB CANNONS, DID SHE?
OH YEAH, PART OF THIS JOB IS GOING PLACES NO ONE WOULD EVER EXPECT TO GO.
LIKE THAT ISLAND WE WERE JUST ON...
WHO HERE THOUGHT THEY WOULD EVER SEE ANYTHING LIKE THAT IN THEIR LIFETIME?
I EVEN WENT BACK IN TIME A COUPLE OF TIMES, IF YOU CAN BELIEVE THAT.
IT'S TRUE.
SHE DID, WE THINK.
YEAH, PRETTY SURE.

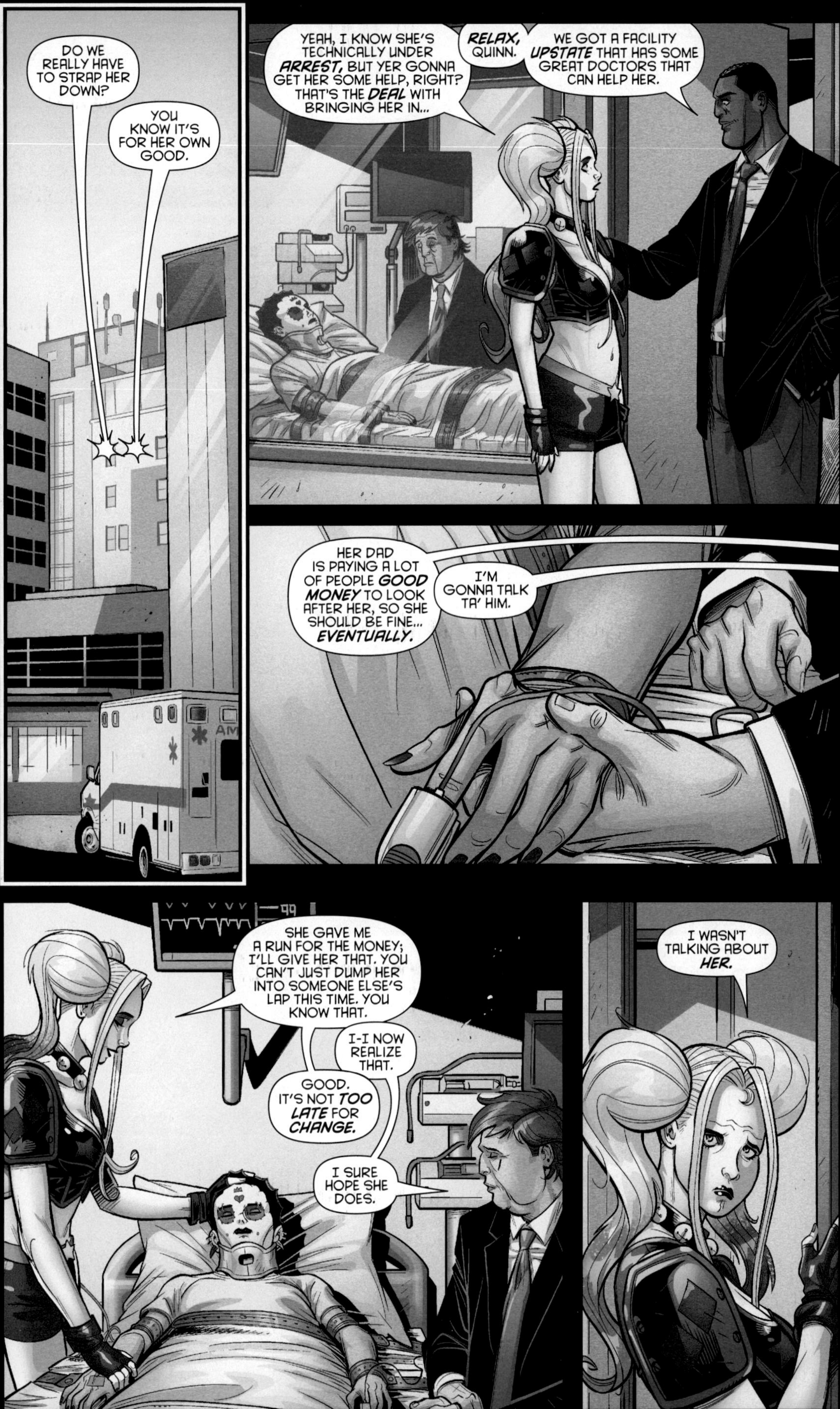
DO WE REALLY HAVE TO STRAP HER DOWN?
YOU KNOW IT'S FOR HER OWN GOOD.
YEAH, I KNOW SHE'S TECHNICALLY UNDER ARREST, BUT YER GONNA GET HER SOME HELP, RIGHT? THAT'S THE DEAL WITH BRINGING HER IN...
RELAX, QUINN.
WE GOT A FACILITY UPSTATE THAT HAS SOME GREAT DOCTORS THAT CAN HELP HER.
HER DAD IS PAYING A LOT OF PEOPLE GOOD MONEY TO LOOK AFTER HER, SO SHE SHOULD BE FINE... EVENTUALLY.
I'M GONNA TALK TA' HIM.
SHE GAVE ME A RUN FOR THE MONEY; I'LL GIVE HER THAT. YOU CAN'T JUST DUMP HER INTO SOMEONE ELSE'S LAP THIS TIME. YOU KNOW THAT.
I-I NOW REALIZE THAT.
GOOD. IT'S NOT TOO LATE FOR CHANGE.
I SURE HOPE SHE DOES.
I WASN'T TALKING ABOUT HER.

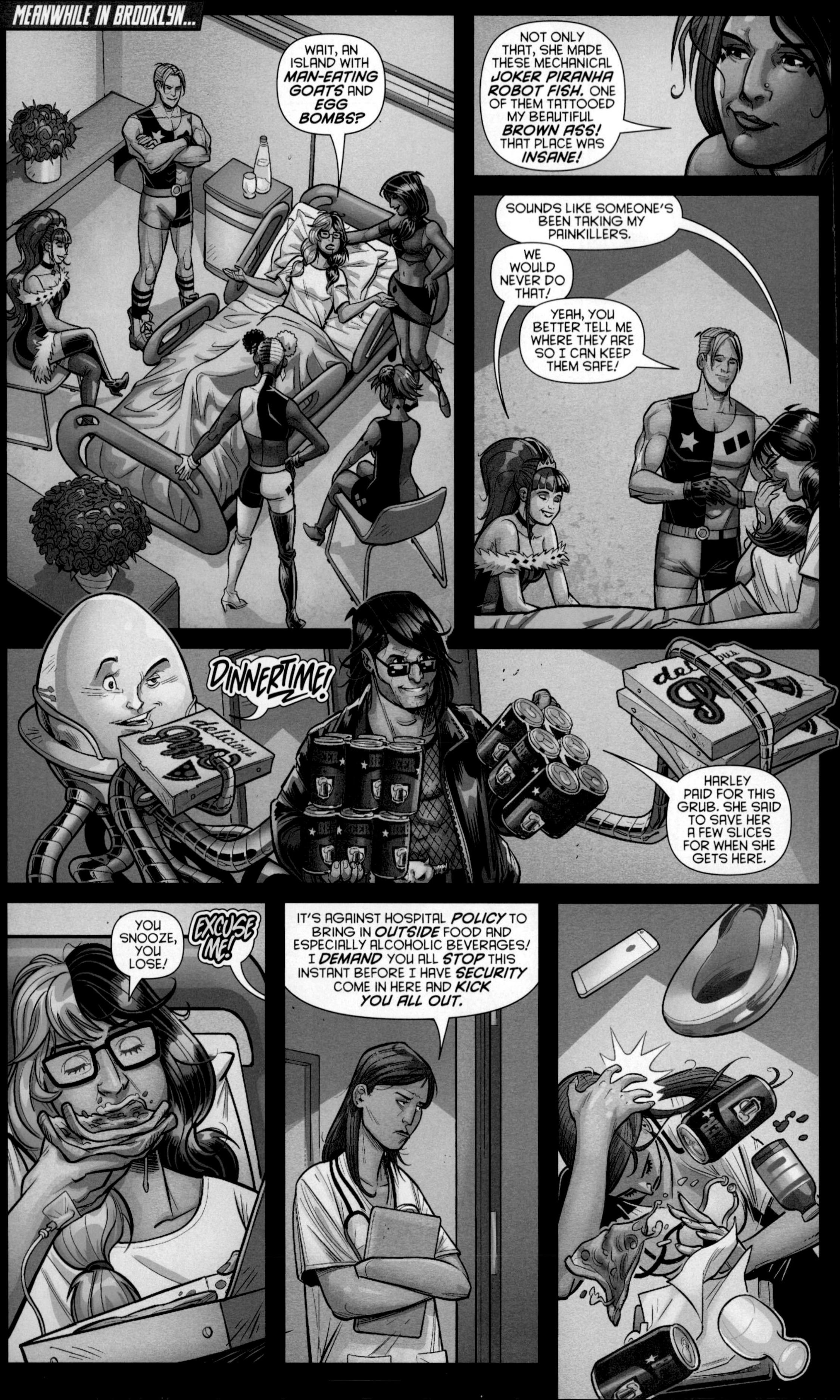
MEANWHILE IN BROOKLYN...
WAIT, AN ISLAND WITH MAN-EATING GOATS AND EGG BOMBS?
NOT ONLY THAT, SHE MADE THESE MECHANICAL JOKER PIRANHA ROBOT FISH. ONE OF THEM TATTOOED MY BEAUTIFUL BROWN ASS! THAT PLACE WAS INSANE!
SOUNDS LIKE SOMEONE'S BEEN TAKING MY PAINKILLERS.
WE WOULD NEVER DO THAT!
YEAH, YOU BETTER TELL ME WHERE THEY ARE SO I CAN KEEP THEM SAFE!
DINNERTIME!
delicious
HARLEY PAID FOR THIS GRUB. SHE SAID TO SAVE HER A FEW SLICES FOR WHEN SHE GETS HERE.
YOU SNOOZE, YOU LOSE!
EXCUSE ME!
IT'S AGAINST HOSPITAL POLICY TO BRING IN OUTSIDE FOOD AND ESPECIALLY ALCOHOLIC BEVERAGES! I DEMAND YOU ALL STOP THIS INSTANT BEFORE I HAVE SECURITY COME IN HERE AND KICK YOU ALL OUT.

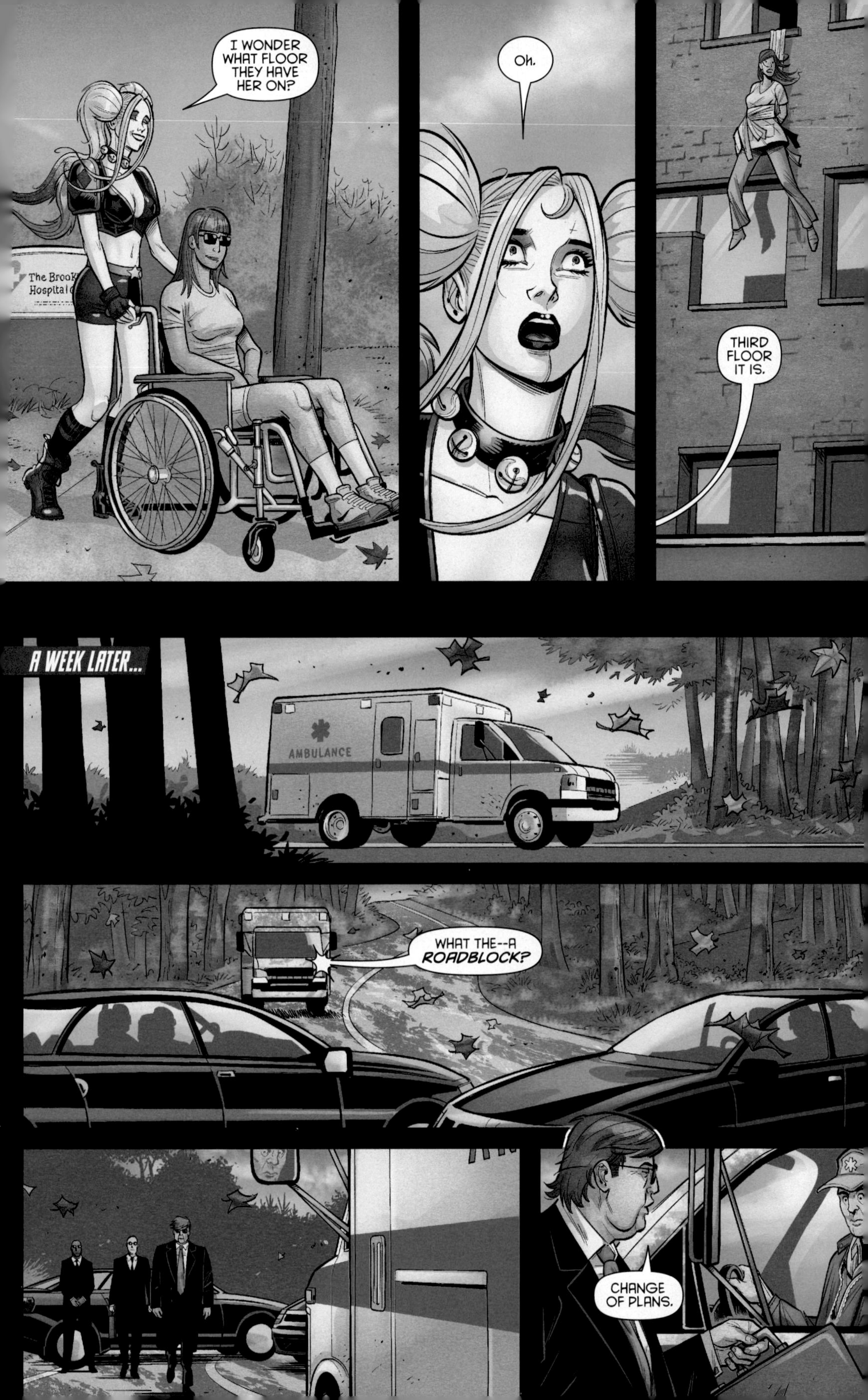
I WONDER WHAT FLOOR THEY HAVE HER ON?
The Brook
Hospital
Oh.
THIRD FLOOR IT IS.
A WEEK LATER...
AMBULANCE
WHAT THE--A ROADBLOCK?
CHANGE OF PLANS.

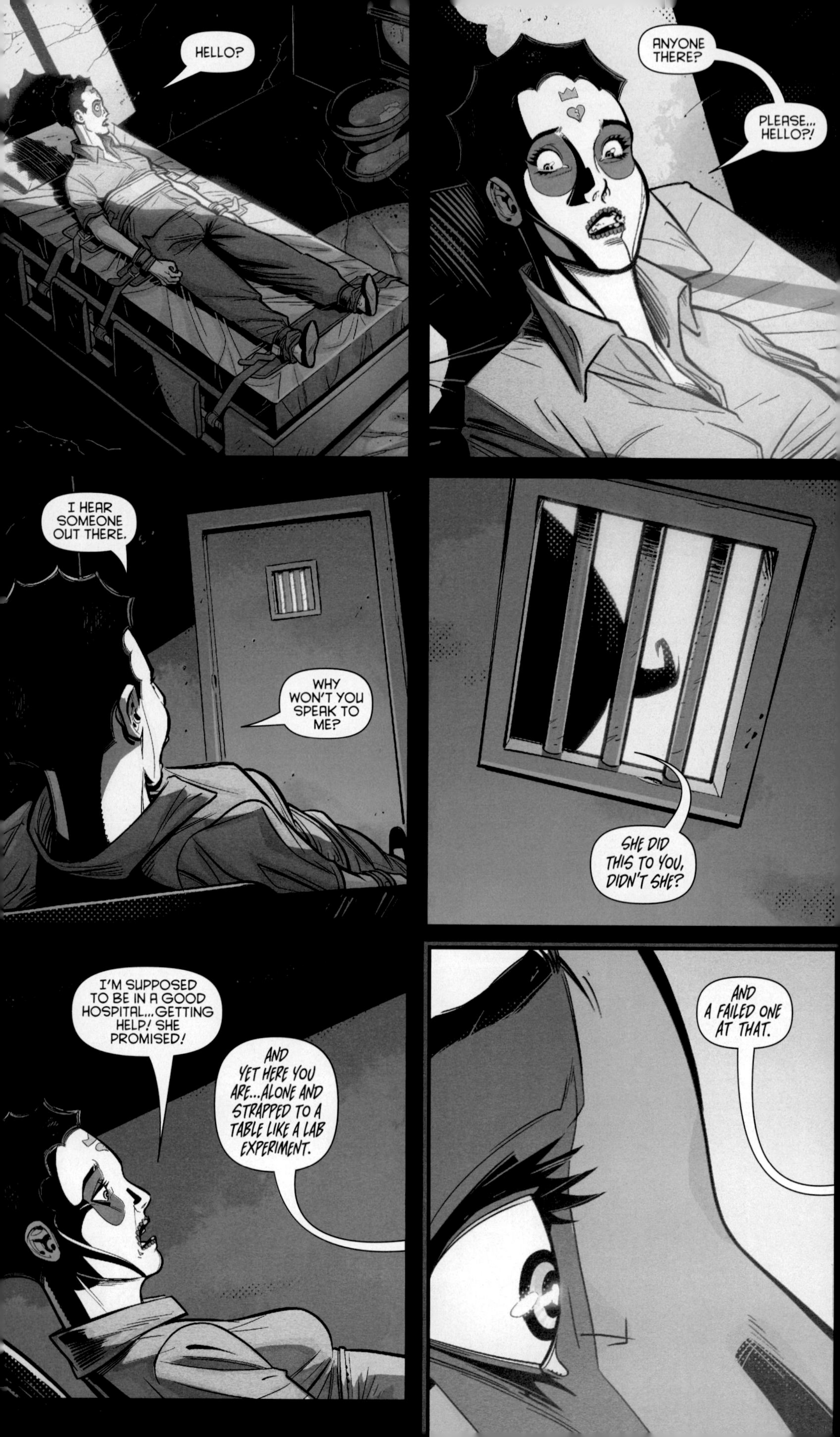

HELLO?
ANYONE THERE?
PLEASE... HELLO?!
I HEAR SOMEONE OUT THERE.
WHY WON'T YOU SPEAK TO ME?
SHE DID THIS TO YOU, DIDN'T SHE?
I'M SUPPOSED TO BE IN A GOOD HOSPITAL...GETTING HELP! SHE PROMISED!
AND YET HERE YOU ARE...ALONE AND STRAPPED TO A TABLE LIKE A LAB EXPERIMENT.
AND A FAILED ONE AT THAT.

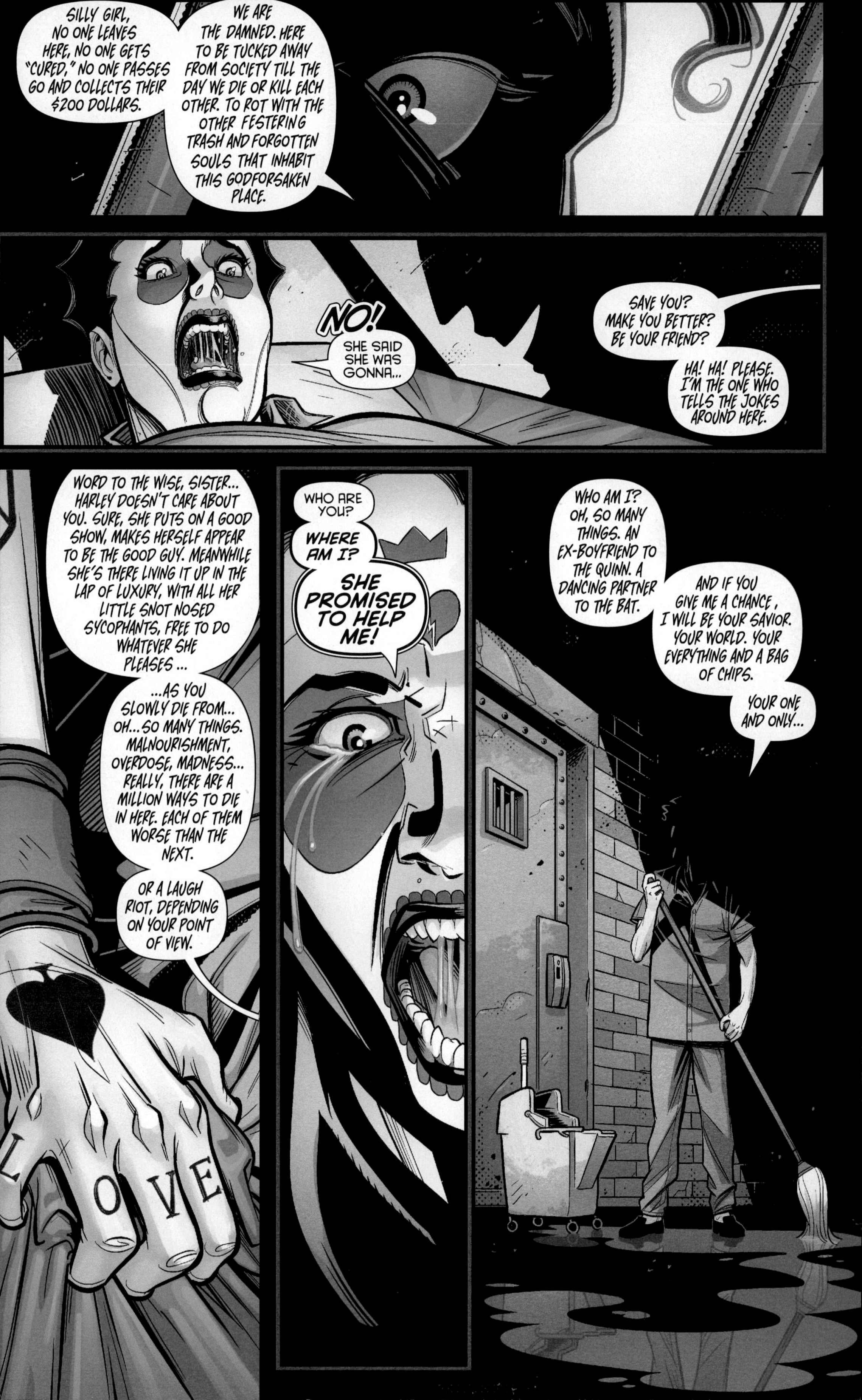
SILLY GIRL, NO ONE LEAVES HERE, NO ONE GETS "CURED," NO ONE PASSES GO AND COLLECTS THEIR $200 DOLLARS.
WE ARE THE DAMNED. HERE TO BE TUCKED AWAY FROM SOCIETY TILL THE DAY WE DIE OR KILL EACH OTHER. TO ROT WITH THE OTHER FESTERING TRASH AND FORGOTTEN SOULS THAT INHABIT THIS GODFORSAKEN PLACE.
NO!
SHE SAID SHE WAS GONNA...
SAVE YOU? MAKE YOU BETTER? BE YOUR FRIEND?
HA! HA! PLEASE. I'M THE ONE WHO TELLS THE JOKES AROUND HERE.
WORD TO THE WISE, SISTER... HARLEY DOESN'T CARE ABOUT YOU. SURE, SHE PUTS ON A GOOD SHOW, MAKES HERSELF APPEAR TO BE THE GOOD GUY. MEANWHILE SHE'S THERE LIVING IT UP IN THE LAP OF LUXURY, WITH ALL HER LITTLE SNOT NOSED SYCOPHANTS, FREE TO DO WHATEVER SHE PLEASES ...
...AS YOU SLOWLY DIE FROM... OH...SO MANY THINGS. MALNOURISHMENT, OVERDOSE, MADNESS... REALLY, THERE ARE A MILLION WAYS TO DIE IN HERE. EACH OF THEM WORSE THAN THE NEXT.
OR A LAUGH RIOT, DEPENDING ON YOUR POINT OF VIEW.
LOVE
WHO ARE YOU?
WHERE AM I?
SHE PROMISED TO HELP ME!
WHO AM I? OH, SO MANY THINGS. AN EX-BOYFRIEND TO THE QUINN. A DANCING PARTNER TO THE BAT.
AND IF YOU GIVE ME A CHANCE , I WILL BE YOUR SAVIOR. YOUR WORLD. YOUR EVERYTHING AND A BAG OF CHIPS.
YOUR ONE AND ONLY...

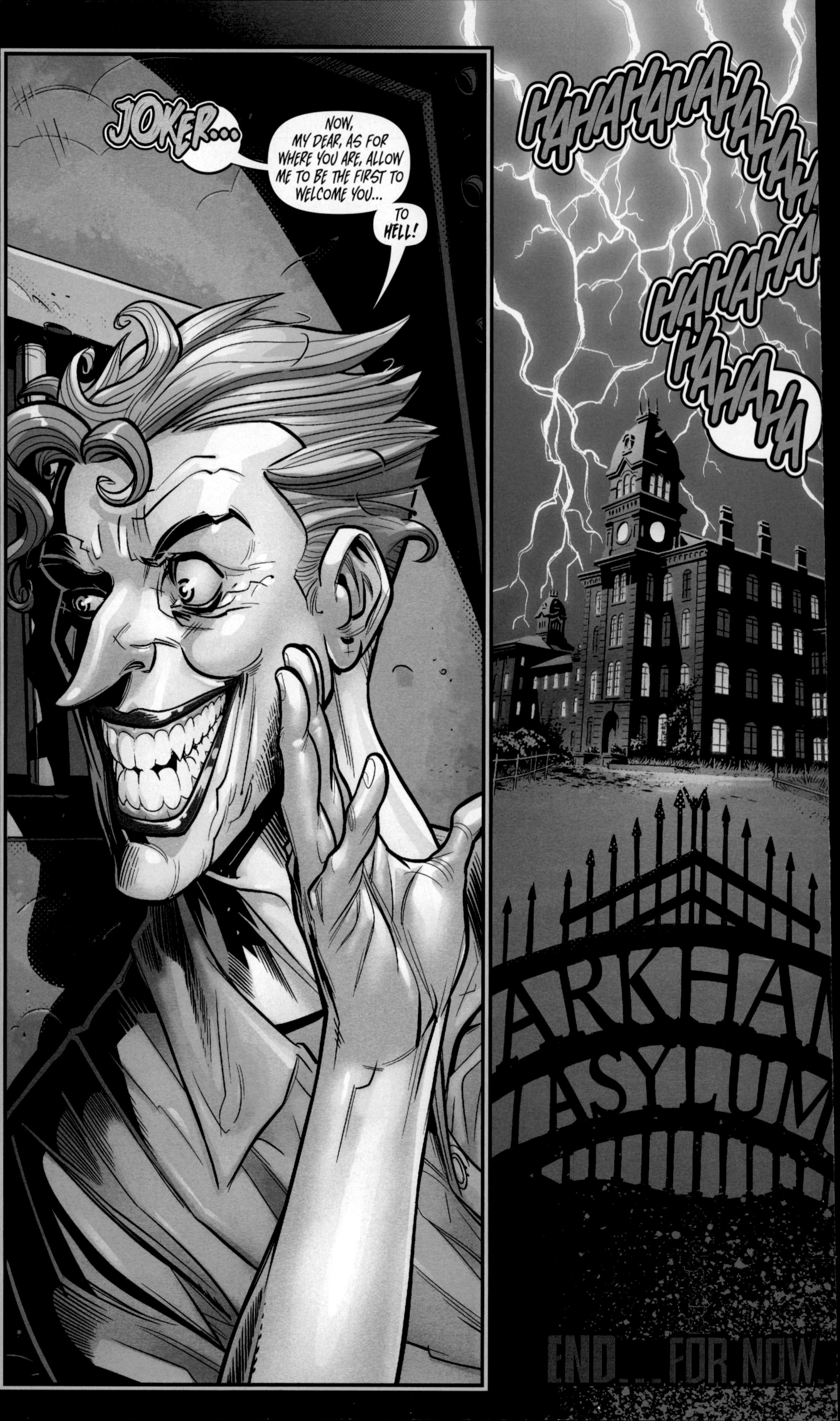
JOKER...
NOW, MY DEAR, AS FOR WHERE YOU ARE, ALLOW ME TO BE THE FIRST TO WELCOME YOU...
TO HELL!
HAHAHAHAHAHAHAHAHA
HAHAHA HAHAHAHA
ARKHAM ASYLUM
END... FOR NOW.

HARLEY QUINN AND HER GANG OF HARLEYS #1
Variant by Amanda Conner & Paul Mounts

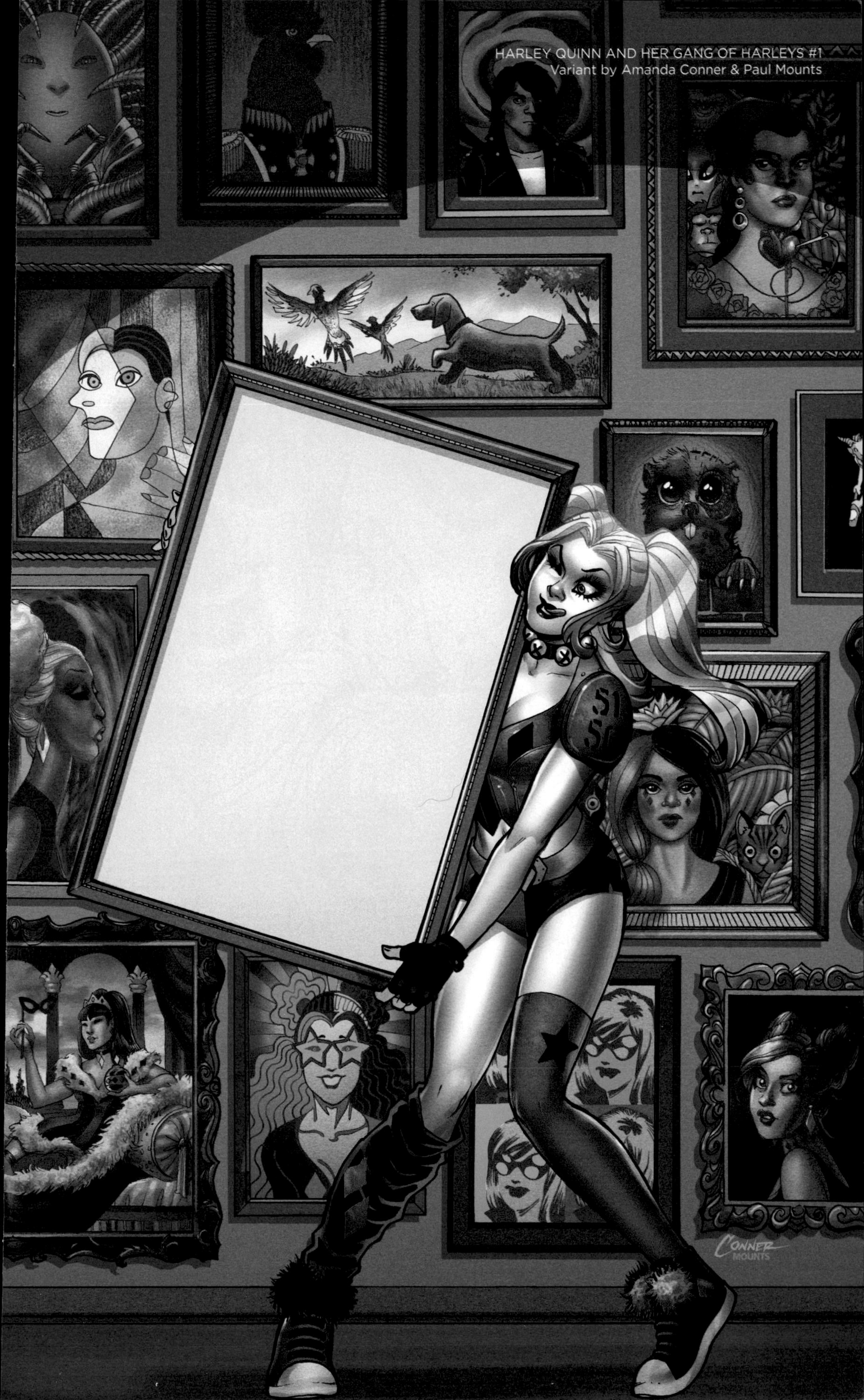

CONNER
MOUNTS

HARLEY QUINN AND HER GANG OF HARLEYS #2
Variant by Amanda Conner & Alex Sinclair

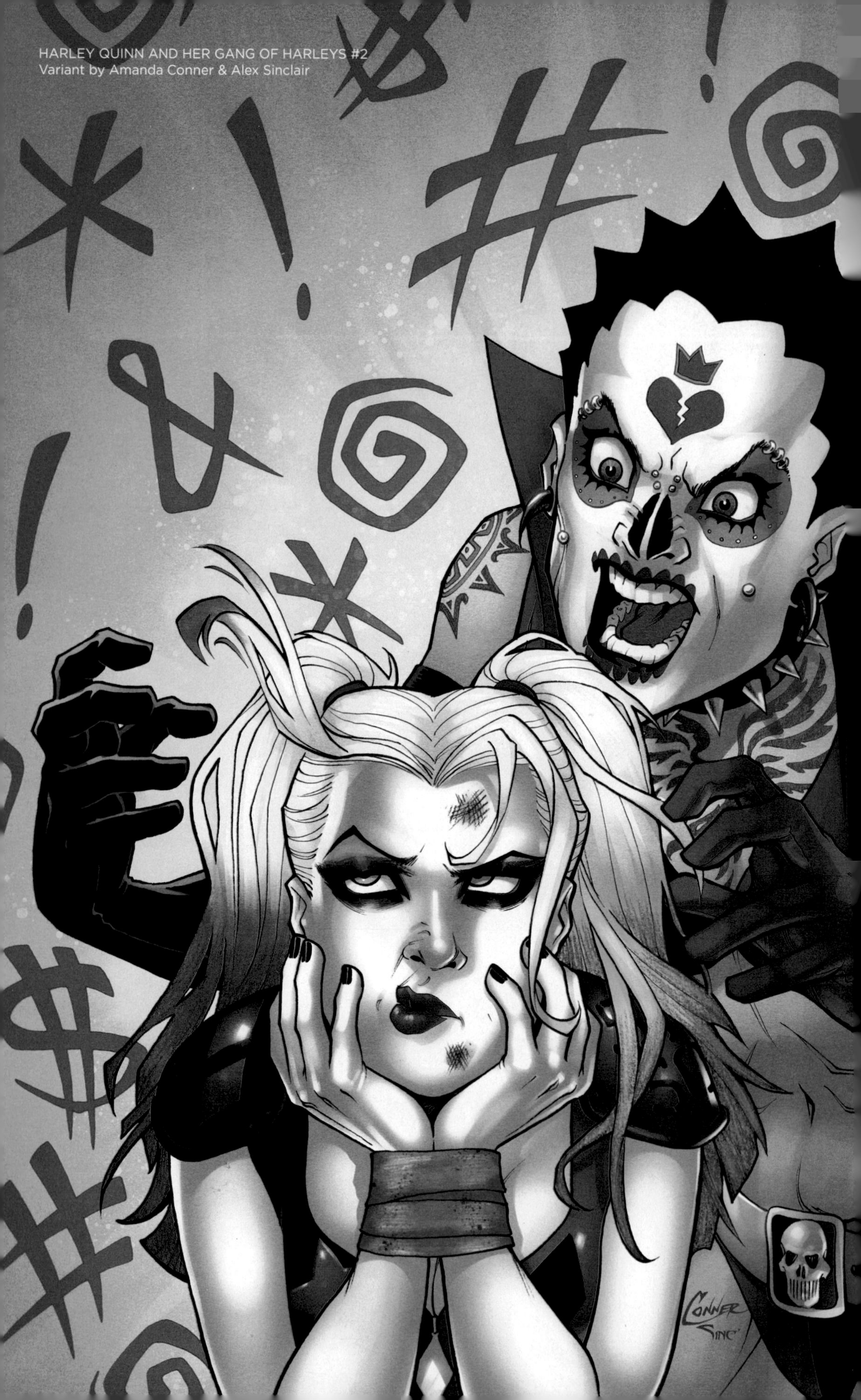
CONNER
SINC'

HARLEY QUINN AND HER GANG OF HARLEYS #3
Variant by Amanda Conner & Paul Mounts

HARLEY QUINN AND HER GANG OF HARLEYS #4
Variant by Frank Cho & Nei Ruffino

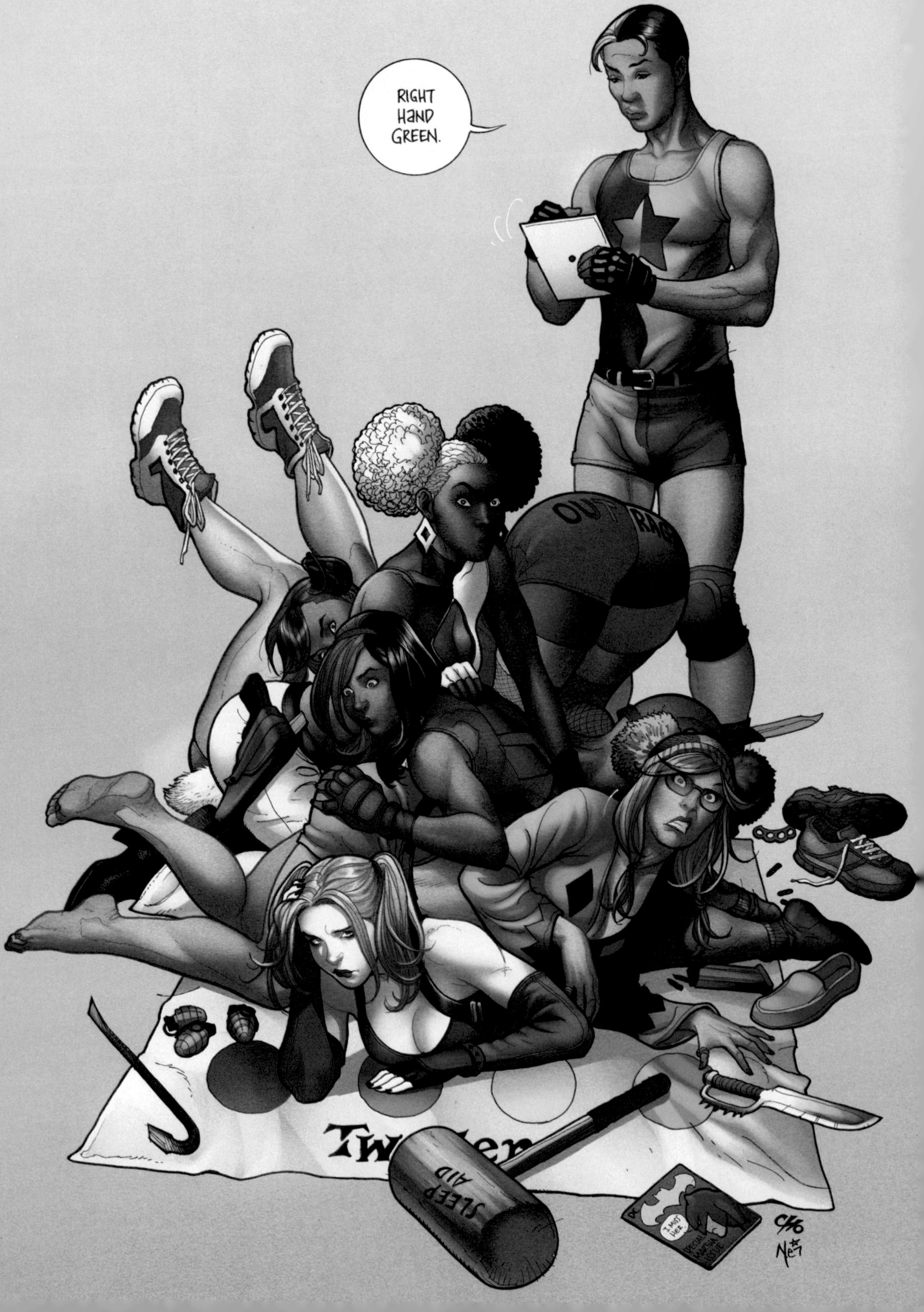
RIGHT HAND GREEN.
SLEEP AID

HARLEY QUINN AND HER GANG OF HARLEYS #5
Variant by Frank Cho & Nei Ruffino

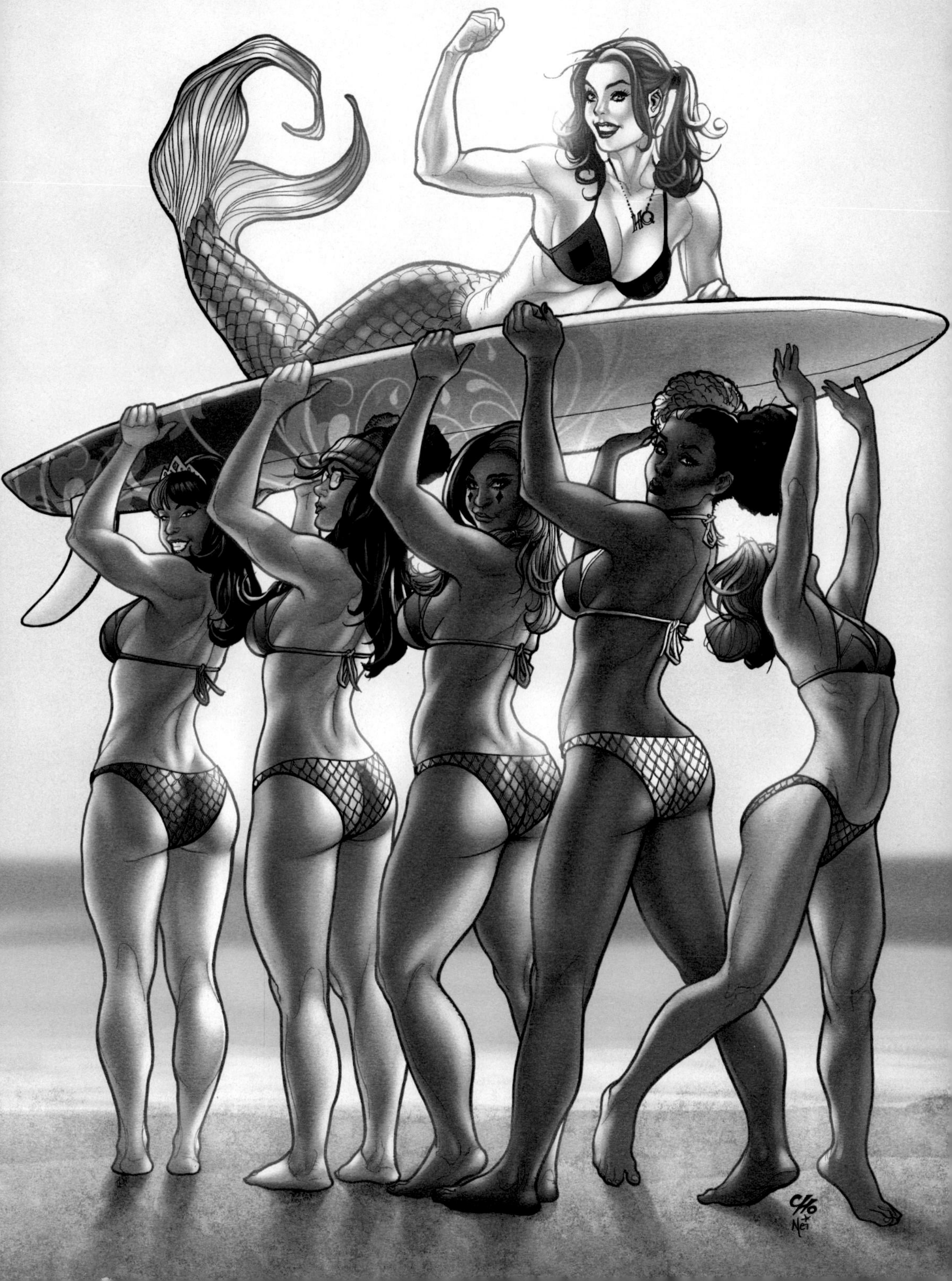

HARLEY QUINN AND HER GANG OF HARLEYS #6
Variant by Frank Cho & Nei Ruffino

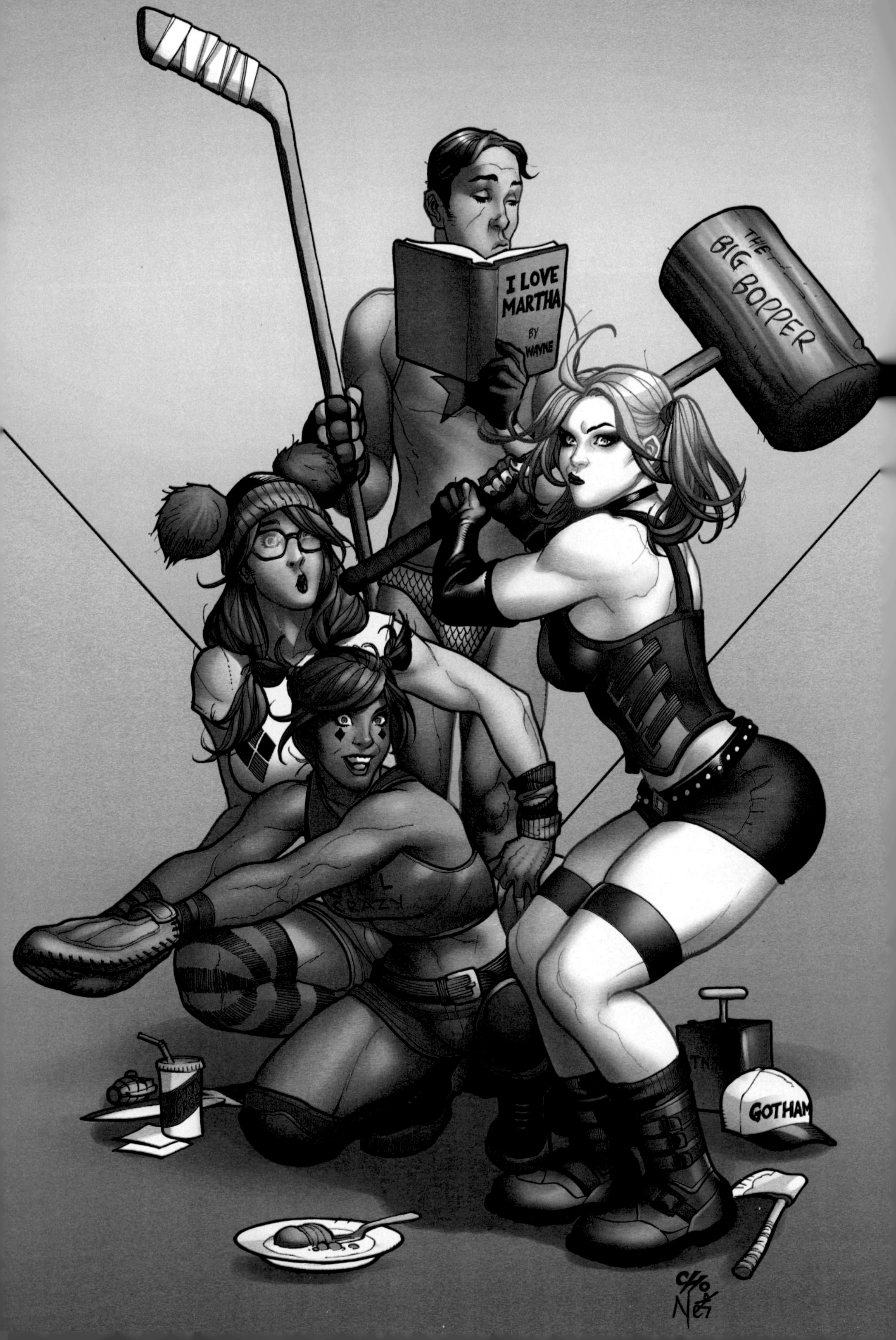
I LOVE MARTHA
BY
WAYNE
THE BIG BOPPER
GOTHAM

"Chaotic and unabashedly fun."—IGN

"I'm enjoying HARLEY QUINN a great deal;
it's silly, it's funny, it's irreverent."
—COMIC BOOK RESOURCES

HARLEY QUINN
VOLUME 1: HOT IN THE CITY

"Chaotic and unabashedly fun."—IGN

*"I'm enjoying HARLEY QUINN a great deal;
it's silly, it's funny, it's irreverent."*
—COMIC BOOK RESOURCES

HARLEY QUINN
VOLUME 1: PRELUDES AND KNOCK-KNOCK JOKES

**HARLEY QUINN VOL. 2:
NIGHT AND DAY**

with KARL KESEL,
TERRY DODSON,
and PETE WOODS

**HARLEY QUINN VOL. 3:
WELCOME TO METROPOLIS**

with KARL KESEL,
TERRY DODSON and
CRAIG ROUSSEAU

**HARLEY QUINN VOL. 4:
VENGEANCE UNLIMITED**

with A.J. LIEBERMAN
and MIKE HUDDLESTON

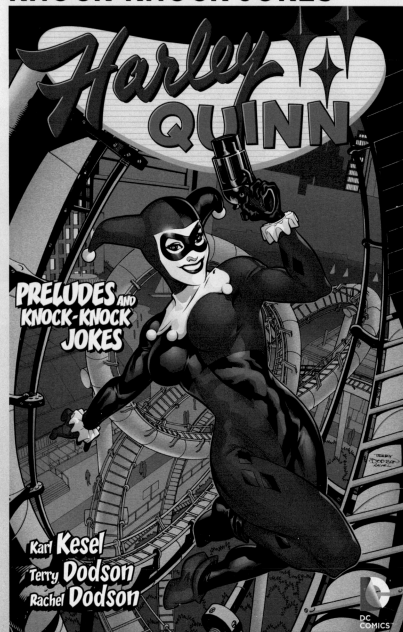

START AT THE BEGINNING!

SUICIDE SQUAD
VOLUME 1: KICKED IN THE TEETH

SUICIDE SQUAD
VOL. 2: BASILISK
RISING

SUICIDE SQUAD
VOL. 3: DEATH IS FOR
SUCKERS

DEATHSTROKE VOL. 1:
LEGACY

"A CLEVERLY WRITTEN, OUTSTANDING READ FROM BEGINNING TO END." — USA TODAY

THE NEW 52!

DC COMICS™

SUICIDE SQUAD

VOLUME 1
KICKED IN
THE TEETH

ADAM **GLASS** FEDERICO **DALLOCCHIO** CLAYTON **HENRY**

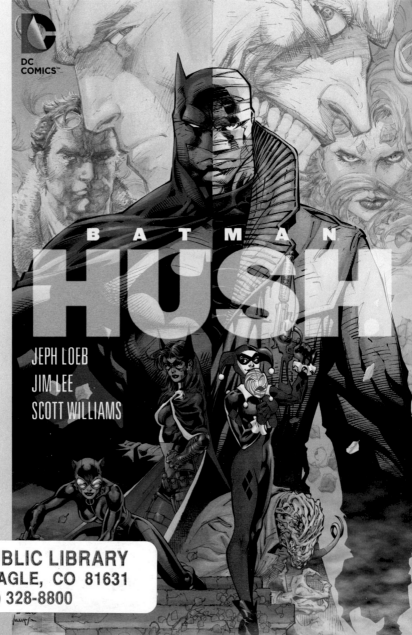